# THE HISTORY OF CIVILIZATION

# ANCIENT GREECE
# AT WORK

# THE HISTORY OF CIVILIZATION

## General Editor C. K. Ogden

The *History of Civilization* is a landmark in early twentieth Century publishing. The aim of the general editor, C. K. Ogden, was to "summarise in one comprehensive synthesis the most recent findings and theories of historians, anthropologists, archaeologists, sociologists and all conscientious students of civilization." The *History,* which includes titles in the French series *L'Evolution de l'Humanité*, was published at a formative time in the development of the social sciences, and during a period of significant historical discoveries.

A list of the titles in the series can be found at the end of this book.

# ANCIENT GREECE AT WORK

## An Economic History from the Homeric Period to the Roman Conquest

G. Glotz

Translated by
M. R. Dobie

LONDON AND NEW YORK

First published in 1926 by Routledge, Trench, Trubner
Reprinted in 1996 by Routledge

2 Park Square, Milton Park,
Abingdon, Oxon, OX14 4RN
&
711 Third Avenue, New York, NY 10017

*Routledge is an imprint of the Taylor & Francis Group, an informa business*

Transferred to Digital Printing 2008

© 1996 Routledge

First issued in paperback 2013

All rights reserved. No part of this book may be reprinted or utilized in any form or by any means electronic, mechanical, or other means, now known or hereafter invented, including photocopying and recording, in any information storage or retrieval system, without permission in writing from the publishers.

**British Cataloguing in Publication Data**

ISBN13: 978-0-415-15574-8 (hbk)
ISBN13: 978-0-415-84607-3 (pbk)

**Publisher's Note**
The publisher has gone to great lengths to ensure the quality of this reprint but points out that some imperfections in the original may be apparent.

# CONTENTS

INTRODUCTION . . . . . . 1

## PART ONE
## THE HOMERIC PERIOD

CHAPTER        PAGE
I: FROM FAMILY ECONOMY TO CITY ECONOMY.
Development at the time of the epics.—*Genos*, collective ownership, and family *autarkeia*.—Formation of private property.—Unequal distribution of landed property.—Movable property.—Wealth.—Beginnings of city economy.—The economic ideal in the epics . . . . 7

II: WORK IN THE FAMILY.
  1. THE MEMBERS OF THE FAMILY.—Work in common.—Work of the men.—Work of the women . . . 14
  2. THE SLAVES.—Small extent of slavery in Homeric times.—Sources of slavery.—Sale of slaves.—Household slaves.—Agricultural slaves.—Condition of the slaves . . 16

III: WORK OUTSIDE THE FAMILY
  1. THE PROFESSIONAL CRAFTSMEN (DEMIURGES).—Classes of Demiurges and division of labour.—" Liberal " professions: soothsayers, singers, doctors, heralds.—Manual professions: work in wood, metal, leather, clay.—Condition of the Demiurges . . . . . . . 24
  2. THE HIRED MEN (THETES).—Vagabonds.—Beggars.—Wage-workers.—Employments of the Thetes.—Their condition . . . . . . . . 29

IV: STOCK-BREEDING AND AGRICULTURE.
  1. STOCK-BREEDING.—Extension of pastures.—Appropriation of common pastures.—Odysseus' farm.—Life of the herdsmen.—Horse-breeding.—Polyphemos' dairy.—Hunting and fishing . . . . . . . 34
  2. AGRICULTURE.—Extension of agriculture.—The *temenos* as type of big property.—Methods.—Labour.—Progress of vegetable-growing and fruit-growing.—The small peasant . 38

V: INDUSTRY.
The forge.—Work at the customer's place.—No industrial employers.—Competition.—The *tekton* and work in wood.—The *chalkeus* (metal).—The *skytotomos* (leather).—The *kerameus* (pottery) . . . . . . . 42

v

## CONTENTS

CHAPTER | PAGE
### VI: PIRACY AND TRADE
1. PIRACY.—Insufficience of the home market.—Acquisition by piracy.—Foreign pirates in Greece.—The Phœnicians.—The Lemnians and Cretans.—The earliest Greek navigation.—Greek pirates . . . . . . . 48
2. TRADE.—Moral conditions of trade: hospitality.—Technical conditions: a system of weights and measures.—The ox as unit of value.—Metal units of exchange.—Trade by land.—Progress of trade by sea.—Scheria of the Phæacians.—Relations of Greece with Thrace, Egypt, the West, and the North . . . . . . . 54

## PART TWO
## THE ARCHAIC PERIOD

### I: ECONOMIC TRANSFORMATION. LAND AND MONEY.
Growing intensity of economic life.—Persistence of natural and family economy.—Progress of agriculture: reclamation and tree-growing.—Commercial and urban economy.—Weights and measures.—Beginnings of money.—Spread of money economy.—Expansion of trade: *chrematistike*.—Transformation of moral ideas.—Social and political development . . . . . . . 61

### II: SOCIAL TRANSFORMATION. THE CLASSES.
1. THE UPPER CLASSES.—The Eupatrids.—Their power on the land and military power.—The great commoners.—Fusion of the well-born and the rich: aristocracy and plutocracy.—Luxury . . . . . . . 73
2. THE LOWER CLASSES.—The middle class.—The lower class.—Impoverishment of the peasants.—Protests and conflicts.—Reforms in Attica . . . . . 79
3. SERFDOM AND SLAVERY.—Origins of serfdom.—Countries of serfs.—Development of slavery.—Industrial slavery.—Economic effects of slavery . . . . 82

### III: THE ECONOMIC AND SOCIAL LIFE OF SPARTA.
Unique nature of the Spartan system.—Its origins.—Its conservative and warlike character.—Land system: *civic land* and *Perioikis*.—The "Equals."—*Syssitiai*.—The Helots.—Their economic condition.—Their legal position.—The *Perioeci*.—Their monopoly of Industry and trade.—Sparta powerless to maintain an inhuman constitution . . 87

### IV: COLONIZATION.
Causes of colonization.—Agricultural colonization.—Commercial colonization.—Spontaneous colonization and organized colonization.—Colonists and natives.—Colonists and mother city.—Colonies in Thrace and on the Euxine.—Factories in Egypt and at Cyrene.—Colonies in Great Greece and Sicily.—Massalia.—Economic consequences of colonization . . . . . . . 98

## CONTENTS

CHAPTER
V: TRADE.
The Mediterranean market.—Security of the agora and conduct of fairs.—Trade by land.—Progress of navigation.—Money and writing.—Division of labour in marine trade.—Trade with Lydia, Egypt, and Cyrenaica.—The Milesians on the Euxine.—Corinth and trade in the West.—Sybaris.—Cumæ.—The Phocæans on the Adriatic and at Massalia.—Commercial prosperity of Greece.—Social and political consequences . . . . . . . . 112

VI: INDUSTRY.
Late development of industry.—Raw materials.—Technical education. — Inventions. — Industrial specialization. — The workshop of medium industry.—The textile industry.—Metalworking.—Pottery of Ionia, Corinth, and Athens.—Competition between craftsmen and between cities . . . 127

## PART THREE

## THE ATHENIAN PERIOD

I: DEMOCRACY AND PROPERTY.
Evolution of Greece towards democracy.—Progress of democracy in Athens . . . . . . . 145
1. THE STATE AND THE INDIVIDUAL.—Sovereignty of the people.—Misthophoria.—Radicalism, socialistic and conservative.—Advantages given to citizens by the State: Cleruchies, public works, assistance, *theorika.*—Social equilibrium.—State and individual in respect of property.—Rights of the " Crown."—Restrictions to the right of individual ownership.—Expropriation in the public interest.—No wholesale spoliation.—Financial policy of Athens . . . . 146
2. SOCIALISM. — Agrarian and aristocratic character of socialist doctrines in Greece.—The old systems: Pythagoras, etc.—Plato.—Popular socialism . . . . 154

II: IDEAS ON LABOUR.
Contempt of aristocratic cities for manual labour.—Prejudices of the oligarchy in democratic cities.—The ideas of Plato and Aristotle.—Athenian opinion on the whole favourable to labour.—Persistence of prejudices.—Distinction between professions.—Inclination towards liberal careers . . 160

III: THE CITIZENS.
The citizenship.—Disappearance of the census classes.—Persistence of social distinctions.—The nobles.—The peasants.—The working classes in the city.—Small participation of citizens in industry and trade.—The land and public offices . 168

IV: THE METICS.
Condition of the Metics.—Their origin and their grouping in Attica.—Economic rôle of the Metics.—Great part played by Metics in industry in the Vth century; further progress in

| CHAPTER | PAGE |
|---|---|
| the IVth.—Peculiar situation of the mining industry.—Preponderance of the Metics in trade in general, business on a big scale, shipping, banking.—Their wealth.—Metics in intellectual professions.—Stamp given by the Metics to sophistry, philosophy, eloquence, music, drama.—Service rendered to Athens by the Metics.—Formation of an international class in the days of the City State | 178 |

V: THE SLAVES.
1. THE RECRUITING AND CONDITION OF THE SLAVES.—Sources of slavery.—The slave-trade.—Prices.—Legal status of slaves in Greece in general.—The slave in Attic law.—Athenian "philanthropy" . . . . . . 192
2. SLAVE LABOUR. — Number of the slaves. — Relative number of male and female slaves.—Household work of slaves.—Agricultural slaves.—Industrial slaves . . 198
3. MILDER FORMS OF SLAVERY.—Hired slaves.—Slaves "living out."—Public slaves . . . . . 207
4. THE FREEDMEN.—Modes of manumission.—Condition of the freedmen.—Activities of the freedmen.—Rarity of manumission.—Slavery and the idea of the city . . . 214

VI: THE DIVISION OF LABOUR.
Division of political labour.—Division of economic labour.—Division of labour in Plato and Xenophon.—Specialization of trades in the production of food and clothing.—Division of labour in mining, pottery, building, etc.—True significance of the division of labour in ancient Greece . . . 220

VII: MONEY.
1. THE MONETARY SYSTEM.—Survivals of natural economy and triumph of monetary economy.—Disappearance of gold through hoarding in the Vth century.—Abundance of gold in the IVth century.—Political autonomy and monetary anarchy.—The "Laureiot owls."—Monetary hegemony of Athens.—Rise in prices . . . . . 230
2. INVESTMENTS AND INTEREST.—Circulation of wealth.—Return of investments in real property.—Return of slaves.—Loans at interest.—High rate of interest . . . 238

VIII: LANDED PROPERTY AND AGRICULTURE.
Importance of agriculture in Attica . . . . 245
1. THE DISTRIBUTION OF THE LAND.—Countries of large estates.—Property in Attica in the time of Solon.—Progressive splitting up of the soil.—Facilities for the reconstitution of the large property.—Buying up of small lots.—Speculation in land . . . . . . . . 246
2. THE RURAL POPULATION.—Large number of citizens owning land.—The great landlord.—The farm-manager.—The small farmer.—Prosperity of the peasant in the Vth century.—His growing difficulties in the IVth.—Tenant farmers.—Agricultural day-labourers . . . 250
3. RURAL ECONOMY.—Attic agricultural science.—Corn-growing: production, consumption, import.—Stock-breeding.—Tree-growing.—Market-gardening.—Social consequences of the agricultural transformation . . . . 255

# CONTENTS

**CHAPTER**

**IX: INDUSTRY.**
1. THE SITUATION OF INDUSTRY.—Growing importance of industry.—Small and medium industry.—Persistence of family labour.—Small number of workers in concerns.—Small amount of capital invested.—Absence of machinery.—Supply of raw materials.—Public works divided up.—Little over-production.—Returns of industry.—Industry and art . 263
2. WORKERS AND WAGES.—Skilled workers, labourers, and assistants.—Absence of legal measures in favour of workers. —Apprentices.—Engagement.—The worker's day.—Work in the workshop.—Work in the mine.—The foreman.—Return of labour.—Wages in kind.—Wages by the day.—Unemployment.—Pay by the piece.—Distribution of day-work and piece-work.—The standard of living . . . 275

**X: TRADE.**
Growing importance of trade . . . . 288
1. MATERIAL CONDITIONS OF TRADE.—*Kapeleia* and *emporia*. —Trade without a middleman.—Petty trade.—The Agora.— Traders at the festivals and with the armies.—Roads.— Means of transport.—Cost of transport by land.—Means of correspondence.—Progress of navigation.—Length of voyages. —Division of labour in *emporia*.—Cost of sea transport . 288
2. LEGAL CONDITIONS OF TRADE.—Commercial liberty.— State control: *Agoranomoi* and *Metronomoi*.—Supervision of the corn trade.—Customs.—The State as trader.—Commercial law . . . . . . . 296
3. COMMERCIAL COMPANIES AND BANKS.—Freedom of association.—Marine trading companies.—Temporary nature of commercial associations.—Mining and metal-working companies.—Banking.—Its origins.—Its principal operations.— The great bankers.—Speculation . . . . 301
4. THE COMMERCIAL HEGEMONY OF ATHENS.—The Peiræeus. —The sea-routes.—Relations with Thrace, the Euxine, the East, the West.—Barbarian custom.—Imports and exports.— Volume of business.—Athens the emporium of Greece.—The sea empire of Athens.—Tendencies towards the formation of a world market . . . . . . 307

## PART FOUR

## THE HELLENISTIC PERIOD

**I: POLITICAL AND SOCIAL ORGANIZATION.**
Small cities and large states.—Mixture of races and unity of civilization.—Monarchy.—The monarch divides and regulates social labour.—State interference.—Heredity of trades.— Progress of specialization.—Ideas on labour.—Associations and trade unions . . . . . . 317

**II: THE SPREAD OF THE MONETARY SYSTEM.**
Extent and intensity of the circulation of money.—Alexander's coinage.—Countries of natural economy.—Progress of money economy in Egypt in public and private life.—Prices . 325

# CONTENTS

CHAPTER

**III: THE TOWNS.**

Greek emigration.—Decay of the cities of Greece.—Displacement of the great centres towards the east.—The new towns. —Alexandria.—Rhodes.—Delos . . . . 332

**IV: LANDED PROPERTY AND AGRICULTURE.**

New distribution of the soil.—Land system in Macedonia.— Land system in Ptolemaic Egypt: Royal Land, Concession Land, Sacred Land, Gift Land, Cleruchic Land, Private Possession.—Agriculture in Egypt.—Land system in the Seleucid empire.—Landed property in Greece.—Decay of agriculture.—The food problem.—Tenant farmers.—Agrarian pauperism . . . . . . . 341

**V: INDUSTRY.**

1. THE SITUATION OF INDUSTRY.—Conditions favourable to industry.—Labour.—Slavery.—Technical education and apprenticeship.—Machines.—The State as manufacturer in Egypt.—Mines and quarries.—Monopolies.—Industry in the Asiatic kingdoms.—Private industry in Greece . . 349
2. WORKERS AND WAGES.—Convicts in the Egyptian mines.— Regulation of labour in Egypt.—Wages.—The value of wages. —Strikes.—Shortage of labour in Greece.—Fall in wages.— Influence of piece-work on pay by the day.—Strikes and State intervention.—Bad situation of the working classes . 356

**VI: TRADE.**

1. THE ORGANIZATION OF TRADE.—Conditions favourable to trade.—Markets and shops.—Commercial companies.—Speculation.—Diffusion of credit and fall in interest.—State banks. —Elaborate organization of credit in Egypt.—Development of means of communication.—Sea navigation.—River navigation.—Land transport.—The post . . . . 362
2. THE EXPANSION OF TRADE.—Importance of foreign trade. —Ethiopia and the Red Sea.—The Greeks in India.—Bactriana and China.—The voyage of Pytheas . . . 372

CONCLUSION . . . . . . . 377

BIBLIOGRAPHY . . . . . . 383

INDEX . . . . . . . . 387

# LIST OF ILLUSTRATIONS

| FIGURE | PAGE |
|---|---|
| 1. Gold disk from Mycenæ | 56 |
| 2. Women kneading bread to the sound of the flute | 62 |
| 3. Electron stater of Phocæa | 68 |
| 4. Silver stater of Ægina | 68 |
| 5. Male head, known as the Rampin head | 77 |
| 6. Maiden of Antenor | 78 |
| 7. A pirate ship | 100 |
| 8. Coins of Syracuse | 109 |
| 9. Warships and merchantmen | 115 |
| 10. Corinthian boat loaded with pottery | 118 |
| 11. Arcesilas vase | 120 |
| 12. Silver stater of Corinth | 122 |
| 13. Embroidery of a cloak, from the François vase | 131 |
| 14. Warrior wearing the Corinthian helmet | 133 |
| 15. Extraction of clay | 135 |
| 16. Potter at the kiln | 136 |
| 17. Potter at the kiln | 136 |
| 18. Demolition of a kiln | 137 |
| 19. Kiln full of pottery | 137 |
| 20. The suicide of Ajax, on a Corinthian crater | 138 |
| 21. The François vase | 139 |
| 22. Potter's workshop | 140 |
| 23. Amphora of Nicosthenes | 141 |
| 24. The Erechtheion | 173 |
| 25. Head of a Semite | 179 |
| 26. Slaves in a pottery works | 205 |
| 27. Woman preparing wool | 224 |
| 28. Work in the gynæceum | 224 |
| 29. Cyzicene of electron | 232 |
| 30. Gold stater of Lampsacos | 234 |
| 31. Attic tetradrachm (archaic style) | 235 |
| 32. Attic tetradrachm (late style) | 235 |
| 33. Ploughing and sowing | 256 |
| 34. Peasants taking pigs to market | 258 |
| 35. Satyrs gathering grapes | 259 |

xi

# LIST OF ILLUSTRATIONS

| FIGURE | | PAGE |
|---|---|---|
| 36. OLIVE-GATHERING | | 260 |
| 37. SALE OF OIL | | 261 |
| 38. SPINNING-WOMAN DRAWING OUT HER YARN | | 264 |
| 39. THE WEAVING-LOOM | | 265 |
| 40. THE WEB OF PENELOPE | | 265 |
| 41. HOIST | | 269 |
| 42. THE VASE-PAINTER | | 275 |
| 43. COMPETITION OF APPRENTICE VASE-PAINTERS | | 277 |
| 44. BRONZE-WORKER'S STUDIO: CASTING AND PUTTING TOGETHER | | 278 |
| 45. BRONZE-WORKER'S STUDIO: FINISHING | | 279 |
| 46. SHOE-MAKER AT WORK | | 279 |
| 47. ASS CARRYING A PACKAGE | | 289 |
| 48. GOLD STATER OF ALEXANDER | | 326 |
| 49. DIDRACHM OF RHODES | | 326 |

For the illustrations of this volume I have borrowed largely from the publications of the firm of Hachette, and especially from the *Dictionnaire des Antiquités* of MM. Saglio and Pottier. I take this opportunity of thanking the publishers for their permission to do so. I also owe a debt of thanks to MM. Crès and Burthe d'Annelet, who were good enough to lend me their blocks.

(In the references given under the illustrations "Perrot" refers to Perrot and Chipiez's *Histoire de l'art*, *D.A.* to the *Dictionnaire des Antiquités* of Saglio and Pottier, and *B.C.H.* to the *Bulletin de Correspondance Hellénique*.)

# INTRODUCTION

THE economic history of ancient Greece must manifestly be of interest not only to those who study antiquity for its own sake but to those also who wish to see the material development of human societies in one typical and complete example. For Greece presents the unique spectacle of a race passing in a few centuries from family institutions to a system of individualism in the sovereign city, and extending its horizon rapidly beyond the small districts in which it was once contained to the whole basin of the Mediterranean. For political changes there are, necessarily, corresponding economic transformations. Evolution appears in a simplicity which is instructive; the big periods are clearly defined one from another, and we may hope to discover general laws.

But it must be said in advance that economic facts do not appear in the ancient city with the same characteristics as in the modern state, and above all they are not so clearly marked. Many questions remain unanswered, and many answers remain vague and obscure, and sometimes seem contradictory. These difficulties are serious, and often insurmountable, either when one undertakes the necessary research or when one ventures to set forth a conclusion even of a partial kind.

First of all, what gaps there are in our documentary evidence ! No doubt the most eminent of the Greek historians and philosophers perceived the importance of material interests both in public life and in international relations. Thucydides connects the migrations and revolutions of past times with the conditions of agriculture, trade, and navigation as well as with the conflicts of social classes. The political doctrines of the Vth century explain the triumph of democracy and imperialism in Athens by the desire to make the lot of the greatest number secure. Plato zealously studies the problems arising from the distribution of the land and movable wealth; Aristotle seeks for the economic causes of external wars, civil struggles, and constitutional changes; the moral theory of the Cynics and Stoics leads in the end to a communistic ideal. But it is very rarely that the ancient authors give us precise information on the phenomena which they record.

Numbers interest them less than anything else. Statistics, that precious instrument for investigation and for government, were totally unknown both to the cities themselves and to students. This is no reason, it is true, for giving up this kind of information in despair and not obtaining from certain data, by deductions which may be more or less direct, approximate results. There is no objection, for example, to computing the number of citizens from the military recruiting-lists. But the method requires delicate treatment; the processes of calculation are often deceptive and the conclusions are generally doubtful. For agricultural or industrial production, for commercial exchanges, for the population of free men or slaves, use must be made of this method; but one hardly ever gets mathematical certainty. In ancient history there is no quantitative truth, or very little.

Fortunately means are not lacking to make up in part for these regrettable silences. They even become more numerous as time goes on. For the beginnings the only data which we possess are supplied by archæology and epic poetry. We are obliged to interrogate ruins, broken vases, jewels, and swords—mute witnesses which, however, reveal the centres of manufacture, commercial relations, sea routes, and spheres of influence. And then we hear the voices which sing the deeds of Achilles and Odysseus; among the fictions of the poet we find exact details about the men who work beside the men who fight, the wealth of the nobles in land and slaves, the humble pride of craftsmen, and the daring of captains who go to seek their fortune in fabulous countries. Later the poets, instead of recounting legends, speak in their own name and of their own time. Hesiod gives advice to farmers and sailors, and Solon and Theognis turn the elegiac into a fighting weapon and rush into the strife of parties. At the same time the narrations which treat of peoples or cities are written in prose, and simply relate what happened; these are the first stammerings of history. Coins circulate, and the study of numismatics, which tells us whence they come and how they go about, shows us the main currents of commercial dealings. A time comes when, especially in Athens, history attains its full maturity. It presents to us rather the political aspect of events, but it allows us to sketch their economic background, and often, by mere allusions, reveals to us the changes which took place in the course of the centuries. Then, too, philosophy comes, and on facts observed more or less faithfully founds ideal or practical constitutions. A novelty of capital importance appears in the Vth century, when the inscriptions begin to supply us with first-class information. The registers of sales of real estates and of marriage settlements, the mortgage notices, the contracts of hire and loan, the wills and the deeds of gift tell us exactly what were the land system, the value of land, the composition of patrimonies, and the procedure of private transactions; the deeds of manumission throw a little light on the question of slavery; and the works-contracts, and especially the accounts for public works, give us detailed information—statistics this time—on the distribution of free and slave labour, the price of commodities and transport, the scale of salaries, and the division and intensity of labour in industry. One inventory, carved by order of the administration of a temple, even tells us the amount of cereals produced in Attica. Finally, when Greek civilization has extended all over the East, the traditional sources are supplemented by the papyri, which bring abundant information about the material life of Hellenized Egypt. Thus, if we are careful not to consider economic questions in ancient Greece as we should in the case of a contemporary nation, we shall not find it too difficult to obtain some light upon them.

It is also wise to let the documents speak for themselves and not to impose upon them *a priori* conceptions of our own. There is a great danger of taking hold of isolated facts, exaggerating their value, and finding in them the confirmation of some vast theory. This danger has not been escaped, in general, either by the economists when they have sought in antiquity for the origins of their theories or by the historians of the ancient world when they have stood at the economic point of view. The former, accustomed to define and describe the complicated elements of an industrial and banking system, fail to recognize it anywhere in past centuries, and, since they do not find in the Greek cities a class which monopolizes means of production and surplus-values, they infer from obvious differences a radical disparity. The latter, who almost seem to have taken up their quarters in a vanished world, nevertheless try, in order to make it better understood, to set it continually in comparison with the world of to-day; in spite of professional prudence they often let themselves be led to infer from superficial resemblances a fundamental identity; they do not hesitate, whenever they find themselves in the presence of rich and poor, to speak of capitalists and proletariate. Without seeking to maintain one or the other of these two theories or to reconcile them, and without thinking (so far as we can avoid it) whether such-and-such facts or laws which we shall note might be twisted to suit some system or other, we shall endeavour to satisfy the demands of the historic method, which rejects venturesome hypotheses, and at the same time not to disappoint too cruelly the economist, who wants definite answers to technical questions.

Against hasty and rash generalizations we shall observe one essential precaution: in the development which we are studying we shall distinguish different epochs. It is neglect of this necessary distinction and the practice of taking examples haphazard from every century which have led opposite schools to accuse each other of being wrong, through being themselves too easily right. The dialectical method proper to the philosophy of history is always wrong if it is not based on chronology. Therefore, while we shall not hesitate to return to the same series of facts on different occasions, at the risk of apparent repetition, we shall present complete pictures, period by period. By a coincidence which is not at all fortuitous, but is due to the close connection of social phenomena, the stages of Greek economy correspond to successive increases of the documentary evidence which enables us to study them. We thus have four stages to traverse:

I. The Hellenes, having brought to the shores of the Ægean patriarchal and pastoral institutions, pass during the centuries described in the Homeric poems to household and agricultural economy, and then to city and commercial economy, and begin to visit distant lands.

# INTRODUCTION

II. The predominance of money economy in archaic Greece leads to the triumph of individualism in the most various forms. While poetry becomes personal, the class of craftsmen and traders sets itself against the landed aristocracy, the great ports vie for supremacy, and colonization distributes the Greek race all round the Mediterranean.

III. In the great years of the Vth and IVth centuries, when perfected institutions appear in the works of the great historians and in innumerable inscriptions, Athens places herself at the head of Greece. Since she needs a sea-empire to maintain her democracy, she makes the Peiræeus the centre which receives the natural products of the whole world and sends out manufactured goods in every direction. The economic system is that of the city in one sense and that of the whole Mediterranean in another.

IV. When the framework of the city breaks down, when the whole East is opened to Hellenism and Egypt records the effects of this revolution on the papyri, the monetary system penetrates into new regions, the division of labour develops unceasingly, and a network of interests is created between country and country. It is the first rough outline of a world market.

# PART ONE
# THE HOMERIC PERIOD

## CHAPTER I

## FROM FAMILY ECONOMY TO CITY ECONOMY

IF the Greeks were able in a few centuries to achieve unequalled progress in every branch of human activity, it was because they settled in lands which had long been under the influence of an advanced civilization. From Crete to Mycenæ the Bronze age had shone with a brilliant lustre and had sent abroad masterpieces made by the artists and craftsmen of a pre-Hellenic people.

In the four hundred years which pass before our eyes in the *Iliad* and the *Odyssey* memories of Mycenæan glory still abound, and yet all is beneath the sway of the warriors of the Northern hordes. The Achæans of the poet wield swords and spears of bronze, but they know iron and forge it into pointed tools and even weapons. So at the beginning of the Homeric period two civilizations exist side by side, and among the last manifestations of a highly developed culture all kinds of primitive manners reveal themselves. But that happened which always happens when a rude society establishes itself by force in the midst of a higher society: we can say for the first time, in speaking of Greece, that the vanquished race conquered its savage conqueror. The invaders adapted themselves to new conditions of life. The pastoral folk, once settled, appreciated the advantages of agriculture. The families, hitherto grouped in tribes, took their place in cities, and without abandoning their old organization they had to modify it. From the XIIth century to the end of the VIIIth the Homeric poems show this transformation enacted before us. They show us the Greeks passing from an economic system, which was essentially that of the family, to that of the city.

The family (*genos*), as the Greeks first knew it, is an extensive group. All who own the same hero for ancestor remain united round the same hearth. Although they are married, the fifty sons and the twelve daughters of Priam dwell together under the paternal roof. While the family group has obligations towards the city, the individuals composing it depend on it alone. It keeps its autonomy, and has its own chief, its own worship, its own administration, and its own justice.

This political independence was only possible with economic independence. At first economy is, by the very etymology of the word, the management of the house. The family tries to be self-sufficient, to make its autonomy complete by *autarkeia*.[1] Forests and pastures are open to all, but the family must have lands of its very own. Those who dwell under the same roof and eat at the same board possess a collective patrimony. The property of all belongs to each, and therefore to no one. For this very reason it is inalienable and indivisible, and the question of the succession does not arise. Whoever lives on the common property is strictly bound to contribute to the common work; if he refuses he is banned by the community. Since every piece of work is of general use, none is degrading. If the family takes on a few slaves, or occasionally engages outside labourers or craftsmen, the reason is that its members are not sufficiently numerous, or that certain tasks require a special capacity; but no occupation is despised as servile or mercenary.

Family economy is almost exclusively pastoral and agricultural. Where the land is good the family is rich; it harvests enough corn and owns enough live-stock to obtain the slaves which it needs and to induce craftsmen or traders to make or bring it valuable articles. Rich or poor, it can always add to the resources of its domain the profits of war, piracy and brigandage.

But the system of family economy cannot exist in all its purity; it is always contaminated by the need for seeking from elsewhere, in addition to supplementary labour, materials which the sub-soil does not yield everywhere. In Greece the system was destined to rapid transformation through the existence of the city. From Homeric times the *genos* begins to disintegrate and tends to split up into small families. On

---

[1] The Greek αὐτάρκεια is best translated by the English " self-sufficiency." It is what the economists call " close household economy."

all sides ties are loosened. Younger sons and bastards protest against a vexatious inequality; young men of adventurous spirit cannot resign themselves to dull work; criminals are driven out. All these are individuals who come out of the traditional framework. Even when the breach has not yet taken place it is preparing; all have less inclination for the work and want a greater share of the returns, and all acquire a taste for comfort and luxury. So individualism is born, while the power of the city increases. Then it is inevitable that the economic system should be altered.

In the very bosom of collective property private property is formed. At first it is confined to acquests—movables, beasts, slaves, ships, ingots of metal, precious vases, arms, and clothing. But the man who means to live apart needs a house, and house property becomes individual. Finally appropriation is extended to the essential property, the soil. The city sets the example. In new settlements the allotment of lands takes no account of the family groups. When Nausithoos led the Phæacians to the isle of Scheria, " he built the houses of the citizens and shared out the fields." The peoples reward the chiefs by giving them a highly productive estate (a *temenos*). The public powers authorize or tolerate the clearings made by individuals on the waste land of the collective reservation (*eschatie*). The collective ownership of the family is also affected. The typical case in which a family dares for the first time to cut a part out of its undivided land is that in which the family of a guilty man gives him a portion, and thus clears itself from the responsibility for his acts which would otherwise fall on them all. But distribution is too much in conformity with the new ideas to be thus exceptional for long. In many families the collective system is abandoned joyfully, each receiving his portion or *kleros* by lot. A share can be split up again on every new succession. The heirs maintain their rights fiercely. " With measure in hand they contest the place of the landmarks which shall divide a common field, and dispute over the smallest plots of land, that the shares may be equal." Everywhere the land becomes covered with signs of seizure by individuals—landmarks, ditches, fences, and hedges.

But appropriation is not yet complete or permanent. In the *eschatie* individuals have taken possession only of the most fertile portions. Most of the great *gene* obstinately maintain the rule of substitution. In certain countries public law extends to the property of the small family the prohibitions which custom formerly imposed upon the domain of the *genos ;* the *kleros,* though transmissible on death, is indivisible and inalienable. Elsewhere the *genos* maintains an eminent domain over the lands of its members; each part may be split up indefinitely but must never leave the *genos.* Thus the system of collective family ownership persists to a great extent, whether it maintains its rigid principles within reduced limits or is reconciled with the system of individual property.

In any case the appropriation of the soil results in unequal distribution of landed property. Certain heads of families take advantage of the situation to declare themselves owners of the estates which their ancestors merely administered. The kings even come to regard themselves as absolute lords of the territory which they govern. At the head of the agrarian aristocracy the " kings of tribes " place themselves. We see the " king of a field " as he stands on a furrow and looks on at the harvest, leaning on his sceptre and surrounded by his heralds. By the side of these great lords the proprietors of a simple *kleros* are very small folk. When an estate has been too much split up by a division on death the peasant painfully works a minute plot of land. And already there is a herd of unfortunates who no longer have a right to any portion of ground; they lead a wretched existence on the wages which they earn on the land of others or on the alms which they beg from door to door.

The growing importance of movable property at least gave these landless men a prospect of compensation. The craftsmen, the *Demiourgoi,* place their services at the disposal of the public and make an honest living. But these professionals are not very numerous. Furthermore certain adventurers go as pirates and bring home rich spoils. But there are not many of these forerunners of overseas trade, and they hasten to enter the landed aristocracy by marrying some " daughter of wealthy men." In a society in which natural economy prevails movable property automatically goes to the families who own the land.

Wealth is already for the heroes of Homer a great power and a matter of pride. No doubt the chief pride of their

# FROM FAMILY TO CITY ECONOMY

heart is that they are sons of gods; but fortune also constitutes a social qualification. To assert his importance a man displays his family tree and the list of his goods. Diomede, after enumerating his ancestors to the fourth generation, declares that his father " owned a broad house, rich in treasures, and round about it fertile fields of wheat, orchards planted with trees, and countless herds."

Livestock above all is desired, The rich man has numbers of oxen, horses, and sheep; a fertile land is the mother of many ewes. The herdsman Eumæos wishes to give an idea of the boundless resources of his master Odysseus, so he enumerates his flocks and herds and byres. As in all pastoral societies, war becomes reiving, and cattle form the usual means of exchange. Yet movable property already appears in the shape of treasure. In the great houses a large part of the ground-floor is arranged as a walled magazine, the *thalamos*. The palace of Odysseus contains one, which is high and broad. " There stand in rows against the wall the jars of old sweet wine," and the vases which contain " much scented oil "; there too are heaps of gold, bronze, and iron, rich stuffs crammed in coffers, rare arms, and fine chased cups. But such stores are not formed by trade or for trade. They show that the owner has brought from distant lands large shares of booty and splendid gifts from hospitable friends. Wealth is hoarded but not capitalized, for it sleeps and does not breed of itself.

We are therefore in a time when groups of the patriarchal type, smaller families, and isolated individuals all exist together, when collective ownership continues to exist by the side of personal ownership, when vast estates are surrounded by medium-sized fields and small plots, and when movable wealth allows industry to put in a timid appearance. What social and economic unity can exist then ? Since the *gene* no longer comprise all the interests present, there is only one framework which suits all equally—the city. Formerly it was only a political association of tribes and *gene;* henceforward it will possess a centre where all can meet for the mutual satisfaction of their needs. City economy is commencing.

An acropolis rises to ensure defence; it is situated a little way from the shore, so as to be in touch with a port but out of reach of the sea-rovers. Below lies the agora, which is thronged on certain days by all who wish to exchange produce or services. These are the essential elements of the city. At an early date the institution is greatly extended. Crete is still the isle " of the hundred cities." Agamemnon reserves for his daughter seven towns, all in the neighbourhood of Pylos. Menelaos owns enough cities in Argolis to think of offering one to Odysseus, exclusive of the transport elsewhere of the evicted inhabitants. The very fact that cities are so numerous, and can be given away or moved about so easily, proves that they are not as a rule agglomerations of any size. We must imagine them chiefly as small country towns. Farmers and herdsmen come to market to exchange their surplus for what they need.

Towards the end of the Homeric period the development of the towns already takes on very different dimensions at certain places. Great crowds seethe on the market-place of Ithaca. New classes come into being. Domestic industry now hardly suffices for any but the simplest operations; for more finished work more perfect tools and more constant practice are necessary, and so the craftsmen earn their living by working for others. At the same time the Greeks are visited with increasing frequency by foreign traders, always ready to transform themselves into pirates, while they themselves go to foreign lands to win by piracy the fortune which they will one day win by trade. Such is the progress of an urban economic system which is still impregnated with the family system but already shows the signs which forebode an international system.

Such is the reality which the poet adorns with magical colours when he depicts the life led by the Phæacians in Scheria. The city rises in the midst of fields, orchards, meadows, and copses crossed by a carriage road. The harbour is surrounded by slips. On a market-place hard by there are stores of rigging, masts, and oars. The palace has a marvellous appearance with its high porticoes and majestic halls; everywhere there are walls plated with brass and adorned with lapis lazuli, doors encrusted with gold and silver, statues of natural size, chased candelabras, and seats covered with purple. Beside the palace the garden yields vegetables and fruit in profusion. With the king Alcinoos

# FROM FAMILY TO CITY ECONOMY 13

dwell his wife Arete, his daughter Nausicaa, and his five sons, of whom two are married. Fifty captives do the work of the house. But the king's family work too: Arete spends the whole day beside the hearth, turning the spindle with her women, Nausicaa goes to the washing-place with the servant-women, and her brothers load the waggon. As for the king, he gives orders, and goes and sits on his throne " to drink wine like an immortal." For his palace serves both for the meetings of the Council and for the reception of strangers; every sitting is accompanied by a feast at which the " wine of honour " flows, and every ceremony is the occasion of a gorgeous banquet which ends with songs, gymnastic contests, and dances. A refined aristocracy seeks out delicate pleasures and savours the joy of living. This *élite*, whom the gods cherish, require that slaves should ensure leisure for them, that craftsmen should surround them with conveniences and luxuries which must always be new, and that bold free-lances should " furrow the broad sea " in quest of riches. The " self-sufficiency " of the city, supplementing that of the family and supplemented by certain products from outside—that was the economic ideal of the Greeks in the VIIIth century.

CHAPTER II

WORK IN THE FAMILY

1. THE MEMBERS OF THE FAMILY

WHETHER large or small, rich or poor, the family of the Homeric period tried to be self-sufficient with the help of a household staff of varying size. Each owed his share of the work to all. In these communities of kinsfolk and servants, continually brought together by their common labour, no occupation is degrading. None is so low as to detract from the dignity of the noblest men and women, or even of the gods.

Kings and princes do agricultural and pastoral work. They are proud of excelling in it. Listen to the challenge cast by Odysseus at a suitor: "If we should vie, which of us could do the more work in the meadows in spring, in the long days, I should have my well-curved sickle and you would have yours, and we should mow without eating till the dusk, so long as there was any grass. If we had to drive a good pair of oxen . . . to plough a field of four acres, you would see how straight I drive a furrow." The sons of kings are shepherds of their free will; so was Apollo. But only the men are employed in agriculture and stock-breeding; the women do not even milk the ewes or make cheese. There is only one rustic occupation in which we see the girls working with the young men—the vintage.

The men still ply all kinds of crafts at home. The nobles do not disdain the craftsman's tool any more than the plough. Every task is fit for them. They are saddlers and shoe-makers; Odysseus cuts straps from a cow's hide, just as the herd Eumæos makes himself sandals. They are masons; Odysseus builds himself a house all alone, just as Eumæos builds a pigsty. They are cart-wrights, carpenters, cabinet-makers, boat-builders, and, to begin with, they are woodmen. Eumæos surrounds his sties with a stout fence of heart of

## WORK IN THE FAMILY

oak. As for Odysseus, when he has built his house he makes doors for it and then he furnishes it, taking a great olive-tree and constructing a bed from it, which he plates with gold, silver, and ivory. If he needs a boat he fells, squares, fits, and nails until the mast and yards are up with the rigging and sails. If the king of Ithaca shows pre-eminence it is only by his technical skill; all work with their hands like him. Every farmer knows the length and the species of the wood which he should choose for his grinder and mortar, the wheels of his waggon, and the mould-board, pole, and stock of his plough. The apparatus of a farm even includes a block of iron, for the ordinary staff are able to make the simpler tools and implements.

The women work as hard as the men. They go for water, sometimes a long distance. They prepare the food. Baking is their duty, and even grinding. Among smaller folk the grain is simply pounded, but in the big houses mills are used to produce fine flour. The size of the quern-stones makes this labour very hard, so it is left to the servant-women, especially to the slaves. In days when food is extremely simple the time of the women is chiefly taken up with clothing. The whole process of manufacture of a garment is done at home. The wife hands out the wool to the servants to card or comb, arranges the hanks which have been prepared in baskets, and spins and weaves with all her women. In the palace of Alcinoos the dawn overtakes Arete " seated at the hearth with her women, turning the spindle laden with purple wool," and the evening finds her there still, leaning against a column rather wearily. The loom was fatiguing, for the warp hung vertically from a beam, and to pass the woof through on the shuttle you had to stand close to the warp. To pass the time they sang. But embroidery is the art over which the great ladies, Helen as well as Andromache, spend their days for choice. They have a heavenly patroness; Athene weaves and figures the wonderful *peploi* which are the pride of the coquettes and bucks of Olympos. Washing too is done by the women, even in the palaces. Near Troy "there were fair broad washing-places of stone where the wives and daughters of the Trojans washed their rich clothing." Nausicaa knows that her brothers want clean clothes for the dance, so she gets into a carriage with her maidservants, whips up the mules, and drives to the washing-place. However proud her lineage, woman must be ever at work. The ideal wife is she who combines beauty, fortune, and intelligence with clever hands. The distaff is her sceptre. To remind her of it is no insult. When Telemachos sends Penelope back to her web and her distaff his mother marvels at the wisdom of her son.

Thus the palaces of kings and the humblest huts presented the same spectacle; in every family men and women alike were accustomed to hard work. The *genos* which owned large herds and broad lands could exist on its estate and hardly ever needed to call upon resources from outside. Even when the patriarchal system had lost the rigidity of its first constitution these old manners did not disappear. For many centuries there was family autonomy in Greece.

2. THE SLAVES

One condition of such a system was slavery. But this institution was not yet largely developed. Trade and industry hardly required slave labour, and the domestic, agricultural, and pastoral occupations needed but little. It is true that Odysseus owns a fair number of slaves. His palace contains fifty women, his flocks and herds are guarded by thirty herdsmen, and his father Laertes, who has retired to the country, keeps by him an old Sicel woman to look after him, and Dolios, who works the farm with six of his sons and some other labourers. Altogether there are about a hundred slaves, and the men in the fields are not so many as the women in the house. But the fortune of Odysseus is represented as quite exceptional, and belongs almost to the realm of fairy-tales. As a general rule one had to be rich to own slaves, and one had to be a prince to own a few dozen.

In the Homeric period the slaves are seldom children of slaves. Certainly there are in the epics captured or purchased women who share the bed of their master, but the son of the free man is free. We find almost only one instance of a slave with children. Dolios has a daughter, whom the queen Penelope has taken with her for the house-work, and seven sons, of whom one is a goatherd and the six others work in the orchards with their father.

## WORK IN THE FAMILY

The most usual source of slavery is war. Prisoners are taken on the battle-field and still more in captured cities. Some of these captives are able to obtain their repurchase, but a large ransom is necessary, " unbounded gifts." The rest are sold by their master, unless he keeps them in his own service, as he usually does with skilful and beautiful women. The tents of Achilles contain many servant-women " conquered by the arm." Hector knows what fate is in store for Andromache if he falls. " You will go to Argos to weave cloth for another and to draw water at the well, with bitterness in your heart, under the burden of hard necessity." And when Andromache hears of the death of her husband she is quite clear about the future of her son. " You will follow me; over there you will do base tasks, toiling beneath the eye of a cruel master." Enslavement by the spear is the normal origin of slavery.

But the laws of war allowed piracy, and, from barbarians to Greeks and from Greeks to barbarians, the rovers of the seas were constantly at work. The Phœnicians and Taphians were especially feared. Eumæos tells us how he became a slave. His father had bought a girl of Sidon from Taphian pirates. This girl escaped on a Phœnician ship, carrying off the son of her master, a child " good to sell among far-away peoples and already of great value." Some days later the young Eumæos was landed in Ithaca and became the property of Laertes. In those days of violence no one was ever sure that he would not see " the day of slavery." The adventure was almost commonplace. One easy method by which sailors could procure slaves was to lay hands on their passengers. Odysseus tells how he left Egypt on the ship of a Phœnician, who wished to sell him in Libya, and how immediately afterwards the Thesprotians who should have set him down in Ithaca prepared to rob him of his liberty. But the Achæans, too, practised piracy and kidnapping. The Greek epic when speaking of the Phœnicians and Taphians never utters such doleful plaints as the Egyptian stele which mentions the Akaiwasha who penetrated into every arm of the river, " numerous as reptiles which one cannot drive away." On two occasions Odysseus has been to the banks of the river Ægyptos " to pillage the splendid fields, to carry off the women and little children, and to kill the men." Another time it is on the coast of Asia that he gathers " women and wealth." There was nothing discreditable about these adventures—quite the contrary, since they were profitable. Certain rules of customary law, the same for piracy as for war, laid down the manner in which the booty was shared.

Violence in every form is the means by which slaves are recruited. When a slave is asked how he came down to that condition there are only two possible suppositions—war and piracy. But, since everything is permitted in respect of strangers, they are not only seized in their own land. In the towns there is growing up a mob of poor men whose origin is not known. Since they have no rights the liberty which they enjoy is a precarious blessing. If a hired man asks for the pay which has been promised him he is told that he will be sold in a distant island. Whoever is unable to defend himself is liable to be carried off by the slave-trade.

In whatever way a man or a woman may have been reduced to slavery, his first master generally gets rid of him as soon as possible. The warrior keeps some servant-women and a concubine, and trades in the rest. Transactions are sometimes effected at great distances. Naturally no one goes and looks for a purchaser in the slave's own homeland. But those who have made a slave never sell him in their own country either. What was the reason for all this transport to distant markets, when the pirates, once they had secured their prize, needed only to return to their own port? This apparent anomaly is explained by the economic situation of the period. A man who wishes to exchange a movable commodity would get in his own country only goods of which he already has a sufficiency; barter is only profitable abroad.

So a " good profit " is always expected from the slave whom " one sends among men who speak another tongue." A human body is an article of value. It may reach an " infinite " value in the case of a prisoner who boasts membership of a great family, a woman " of fair form " or " skilful at the works of her sex," a Lydian or Carian woman who can paint on ivory or one of Sidon accomplished in embroidery. Prices therefore vary. An average slave-woman can be had for four oxen, and as many as twenty are paid in exceptional cases.

The slave is an article which can be transferred, not only

by sale and purchase but by any other transaction. A woman may be offered as a prize at the games. The father who gives his daughter in marriage sends with her a slave who forms part of the dowry. Captives commonly appear among the gifts of hospitality or reconciliation.

Most of the slaves are employed on domestic work. The word generally used for them (*dmos, dmoe*) means "houseling," like *oikeus* and *famulus* later. Already the practice of having a personal servant is so habitual that a slave spends his first savings on the purchase of another slave.

The work of the house itself is chiefly done by women. In the humble house from which Laertes supervises his orchards an old woman prepares the food of the labourers and looks after the master. The palaces contain as many as fifty girls. The hardest of their tasks is the grinding of the corn; they start at night, and sometimes the dawn finds them still at work, " their knees broken with weariness." But the greater part of their time is given to the multifarious work connected with clothing. From morning to night they comb, spin, weave, sew, and embroider. Their room is a workshop which is never idle. House-work therefore does not as a rule entail a true division of labour; the fifty women can all work wool, but as need arises twelve are called to the mill and twenty to the spring. When Helen appears before Telemachos she is surrounded by three women. One brings a chair, the second a cushion and the third her work-basket. But we must not infer from this little ceremony that the domestic staff is generally used in a wasteful way and that the organization of the royal household is on a sumptuous scale; as soon as the reception is over the attendants and their mistress resume their interrupted work. It is only exceptionally that certain slave-women, like the Sidonian embroiderers offered to Hecuba, confine themselves to their special art, or that an old nurse, treated with particular respect, is attached as personal maid to the daughter of her masters. However, in the palaces the queen hands over a certain amount of supervision to a trustworthy person, and she may choose a slave-woman for this. She who is thus raised to the position of housekeeper or manageress teaches the novices their duty and commands the free and slave staff; she has the keys of the stores and knows their most secret hiding-places.

We find also male slaves employed inside the house. Alcinoos orders menservants to harness the waggon for Nausicaa. In the palace of Ithaca the maidservants are assisted by a bath-boy. When a feast is preparing the men chop the wood and serve and cut up the meat. But we must not imagine that there was a large staff of grooms and carvers. Slaves from the land have just brought in beasts for slaughter; they are asked to lend a hand. One day the swineherd Eumæos distributes the cups, a cowherd takes round the bread, and a goatherd acts as cup-bearer. It is the same for the slaves employed as rowers—the master takes his crew from among the men on his land.

Guarding the cattle and agriculture are the usual occupations of the male slaves. Moreover it does not seem that the family has many workers in addition to its own members for these tasks. Let us look at the estate of Odysseus, which is a typical large property. Thirty men are enough to look after the beasts, and a dozen, or a score at the most, are employed on the corn, vines, and fruit-trees. If only about fifty men were needed for an estate of this size, rural slavery cannot have been very much developed. We see why in war the conqueror spared so few men in comparison with the women.

The position of the slave was not bad. The savage manners which so often shock us in the *Iliad* and the *Odyssey* exist almost entirely as between individuals of different families. Now the slave is part of a family. Once he has been taken into a house by a kind of inferior adoption, there is established between him and his masters a reciprocity of obligations which, reinforced by common labour, easily leads to reciprocal affection. So the slave is not considered as a beast of burden. He has his own personality. No doubt the master has the right of life and death over his slave, but no more so than the husband over his wife or the father over his children, as head of the family. The legal position of the slave, under the law of the family, raises his moral condition considerably. The little Eumæos is treated as a son by his mistress Anticleia, and is brought up with the daughter of the house. When he grows up he continues to feel " a mother's affection " watching over him from afar. Anticleia dies, and her daughter-in-law Penelope takes on this duty of protection as an inheritance. She also takes the daughter of the slave Dolios to be with her, " tends and cherishes her like her own child, and puts joy in her heart by her indulgence." What Eumæos deplores most of all in the misfortunes which the usurpation of the suitors brings upon him is the rupture of relations which are like blood-ties. " Now," he groans, " I lose all that. The gods have given increase to the work I do, and I have enough to eat and drink and can even entertain guests, but it is no longer given to me to hear the sweet words of my mistress or to receive marks of friendship from her. Yet slaves sorely need to see their mistress, to speak to her, to ask her advice on everything, to eat and drink in her house, and then to bring back to the fields one of the gifts which ever delight the heart of slaves."

Benevolent authority is met by devoted obedience, kindness by respect. Grateful for the security which he enjoys, and sensitive to consideration, the slave forgets his birth little by little and tries to deserve an improvement of his lot and an old age free from care. In a house which has lost its master discipline is necessarily relaxed, " for, in casting a man into slavery, Zeus takes from him half his virtue." Yet the long absence of Odysseus has not weakened the sense of duty of the country slaves. His flocks and herds and his vineyard are still well tended. When he comes back and makes himself known to the swineherd Eumæos and the cowherd Philœtios, and later to Dolios and his six sons, they give vent to touching expressions of feeling and declare themselves ready to support the good cause. The women, it is true, have more easily allowed themselves to become demoralized by the state of anarchy. But only twelve out of fifty, the light-headed ones, have failed after ten long years. The other women remain firmly attached to the family which has become their own, and they take part in its sorrows and its joys. When they see their master once more " they surround him, greet him, embrace him, cover his head and shoulders with kisses, seize his hands. And he feels a sweet desire to weep, for in his heart he recognizes them all."

By being given a position in the family the slave found that his material condition was tolerable. Patriarchal slavery does not appear in such very dark colours. No doubt Eumæos, the " godlike swineherd," is a particularly successful slave;

he lives in a retired corner of the estate in complete independence. But many other slaves were employed thus in distant fields and pastures, and the house-slaves were no worse off than those of the country. It is so easy to make life endurable in days when wants are so limited!

The slave gives his whole time and his whole labour to the master; the master therefore must ensure his living. In the good houses he is well fed. Eumæos has barley-meal, bread, and wine *ad lib.*, and he is not forbidden to kill now and again one of the beasts under his care. When the subordinate swineherds return from the pasture they expect a " plentiful meal." The masters do not look too closely into these things; the labourers must be kept in good condition.

Dress was not at all an expensive matter. Before he is sent to the fields Eumæos is given a cloak of a she-goat's skin, a fine chiton, and good shoes. Later he owns a great cloak of wild-goat's skin for going out at night and another, longer and thicker, against the rain. He cuts himself sandals, from a cow's hide. He has even enough goats' and sheep's skins to cover an extra bed when a guest comes. But it costs an owner of live-stock hardly anything to allow a few skins in this way to his herdsmen. As a rule there is nothing brilliant about the dress of the slaves. " We have," Eumæos says himself, " neither many cloaks nor a spare tunic; only one for each of us." Homer also describes for us the rags of the country slave—a dirty patched tunic, leggings and gloves of cow-hide to protect him from scratches, and a goat-skin cap.

The quarters vary according to the place. Laertes' men shelter in a shed, lying in all their clothes on the ashes of the hearth. But the palaces are provided with servants' quarters for the female staff. The slaves who are scattered about the land can build themselves comfortable cabins. Eumæos has built himself on high ground a big stone house with a forehall and a gallery. The furniture, even in the house of Eumæos, is primitive in its simplicity—a trough, a table, and a bed consisting of a board covered with skins. There is no chair; to give a seat to a guest he gets a faggot and spreads a skin from the bed over it. There are a few utensils— dishes, baskets, pots, a little urn of ivy-wood, and a goblet—and a few tools—an axe and a club for killing the pigs. There is as much wood as could be wanted, for the forest is close by.

How does a slave come to make any savings ? The generosity of the master is his usual resource, but he may collect a little property by his own efforts. Eumæos has acquired a slave " alone, without the help of anyone," paying for him " out of his own possessions."

But how much happier he would have been if Odysseus had been there! " He would have given me a house, land, and a comely wife, all the good things which a kind master gives to the slave who has toiled hard for him and whose work has been made fruitful by a god." All these wishes are fulfilled by Odysseus on his return, and he promises to treat his faithful herdsmen " as comrades and brothers of Telemachos." The right to form a family of his own, with the use, if not the ownership, of a bit of landed property—that is the supreme reward to which the slave with a good record aspires. The position which he can obtain in this way remains fairly obscure. Is it a very easy form of serfdom, or is it gratuitous manumission, including settlement on land which the freedman retains near the patron ? It seems that it is both at the same time, or rather that it is neither, since it does not include the cessation of slavery by a formal deed. We are going ahead of the time if we see in the *Odyssey* those two intermediate conditions between slavery and liberty—serfdom and freedman-ship—but if we deny that they existed in embryo we are refusing to perceive institutions before their full development.

CHAPTER III

# WORK OUTSIDE THE FAMILY

### 1 THE PROFESSIONAL CRAFTSMEN (DEMIURGES)

THOSE who work for the public and not only for their family are called *demiourgoi*, Demiurges, in Homeric society. The word is extended to anyone who places his activity at the service of the public (*demos*) and even, in certain countries, to the magistrates. It therefore applies to all professional workers.

If we knew all the categories included under such a general term we should thereby know to what extent there was division of labour in the VIIIth century. It is not enough to observe that it did not go very far in the villages. In Hesiod's time the Bœotian farmer still weaves his own chiton and *chlaina*, makes his own shoes, and manufactures his own utensils, waggon, and ploughing implements; but this might be the case in the rustic parts of countries where the industrial towns already have a fairly developed division of labour. Let us therefore examine more closely the employment of the Demiurges.

We must exclude certain occupations which retain their purely domestic character. Such are the preparation of food (including grinding and baking), the manufacture of clothes, and wood-cutting. Of true professions four are mentioned in a passage in the *Odyssey*—the soothsayer, the doctor, the singer, and the carpenter. But this list, which includes the "liberal" professions side by side with the manual, is certainly incomplete.

In the former class, which comprises all the disciples of Apollo, another passage in the *Odyssey* definitely includes the *protégés* of Hermes, the heralds. Thus we see four liberal professions in the formation or already formed.

First there is soothsaying, the mantic art. That men have declared themselves able to disclose the secrets of the past, the present, and the future is a fact common to every country. The peculiarity of Greece is that it never reserved relations with the gods to one priestly caste. The gift of prophecy may be revealed within the family, but more often intuition settles into a kind of science and the soothsayers exercise a profession, which is sometimes hereditary.

The same distinction is to be seen still more clearly in the singers. The *Iliad* depicts the period in which the members of the family in their house and the warriors in their tent indulge in free improvisations. But in the *Odyssey* we see professional bards. This calling is especially adopted by the blind; shut up within themselves, they sometimes attain the internal clairvoyance which makes the soothsayer, but usually they devote their long hours of isolation to music, and these self-taught men (so they describe themselves) acquire a superiority which ensures them a means of livelihood. They go from town to town, welcomed with joy in the banqueting-halls, and sometimes they are kept permanently in the palaces. Some enjoy a great reputation, like Phemios of Ithaca and Demodocos whom the Phæacians love.

Medicine has already made a considerable advance, and the doctor is held in great esteem. Not that the art of healing is the exclusive privilege of the professionals; a woman has the reputation of knowing the virtues of all the plants, and warriors who are renowned for their skill in tending the wounded are none the less combatants. But certain doctors are professionals.

The heralds hold an important position in society. They are attached to the person of the chiefs, and are the sacrosanct representatives of their authority as well as the obedient executors of their orders. Thus they have a political and religious function and at the same time act as pages. Whether officials or servitors, they are honoured by all and inviolable. Their material position is often equal to their moral position.

After enumerating the liberal professions, the list in the *Odyssey* seems to reduce all the manual occupations to that of the *tekton* or carpenter. In reality it does no more than mention the best known and most versatile type of craftsman. But the word which we translate " carpenter " for want of a better term implies many various occupations, all placed under the patronage of Pallas Athene, from the felling of trees to ship-building and artistic cabinet-making. Moreover the Homeric period knows many other classes of craftsmen.

There is one kind of work which can only be done by a professional, and that is smith's work. It requires a relatively complicated outfit, and the man who possesses it can let others profit by it only in exchange for remuneration. Moreover metal-working needs a special skill which can only be acquired by a period of training. So the smith's profession has a place even in the most rudimentary division of labour. It is therefore impossible that metal-working did not constitute a profession where wood-working did. And indeed Homeric Greece knows the *chalkeus*. In the patriarchal society of Olympos the smith Hephæstos does not work for his family alone; Thetis comes to him and orders a suit of armour for Achilles.

Leather was chiefly worked at home. The owner has the hides of his beasts tanned and stretched in his courtyard. The herdsman makes his own sandals. Yet for more finished articles, greaves, bowstrings, weasel-skin caps, and wolf-skin cloaks, a specialist is already necessary, the leather-worker (*skytotomos*). A town in Bœotia possesses a true artist, who makes the celebrated shield of Ajax, and at Scheria a house is famed for its speciality in red balls.

Besides the carpenter, smith, and leather-worker the towns of the epic poems have a potter (*kerameus*) working for them. Altogether the Homeric city knows four classes of craftsmen following a skilled profession, those who produce and work in wood, metal, leather, and clay.[1]

[1] These include only the crafts (*technai*) which required technical skill and afforded exclusive and permanent work. The principal craft was fairly frequent, and the accessory craft still more so. To distinguish the former type from the latter we may perhaps attach some importance to the terminations of the words which indicate craftsmen in the epics, *eus* and *os*. The former seems to indicate the occupations which at an early date were carried on as a permanent profession, and the second (except *tekton*) those which were accidental and temporary at first but later became, some of them, regular professions. Thus the smith (*chalkeus*) and the potter (*kerameus*) seem to have carried on a true profession, like the herdsman (*nomeus*) and fisherman (*halieus*), long before the leather-worker (*skytotomos*). Moreover, when a man calls himself a woodman (*hylotomos, drytomos*), cart-wright (*harmatopegos*), gold-beater (*chrysochoos*), or horn-turner (*keraoxoos*), this is no reason for regarding him as the representative of a specialized profession. Hector is not a coachman by trade because he appears on his chariot as *heniochos* (mule-driver).

## WORK OUTSIDE THE FAMILY

So the division of labour is not yet definite. The epics never lose the memory of the time when the swineherd Eumæos built his own sties and made his own shoes, and his master was ploughman, mason, roof-maker, woodman, carpenter, cabinet-maker, ivory-worker, goldsmith, saddler, and boat-builder. The lines between the different trades are not clearly marked. The shield of Ajax with its seven ox-hides covered with brass is the work of Tychios, " best of curriers "; the shield of Sarpedon with its stout leather casing, plates of bronze, and border of gold comes from the hands of a smith. Even when it remains in its own proper domain every profession embraces a multitude of future trades. Hephæstos, the patron of smiths, is at the same time locksmith, armourer, goldsmith, and engraver, and the *chrysochoos* or gold-beater is not distinguished from the *chalkeus*. When we see a *drytomos* wielding the axe we might suppose that the woodman supplied the wood industries with their raw material; but the name of *hylotomos* is given to the warrior who is sent on wood-fatigue. The fact is that the professional craftsman acts as the private individual who cuts the branches and trunks which he needs. The cart-wright fells a poplar and dries it before cutting a felloe from it, and the carpenter who wants to build a boat goes to the forest for his materials. The *tekton*, at once woodman, cart-wright, and builder, also does everything connected with building—masonry, cabinet-making, turning, and decoration. It is he who best shows how rudimentary the division of labour is in Homeric times. The smith, potter, and leather-worker at least have each his own raw material; the carpenter works not only in wood but also in horn, ivory, and even stone.

All these professions are open to all. But, since they require knowledge and experience which are most easily transmitted within one family, the son prefers to follow the same trade as his father. This is frequent in the liberal professions; the Melampidæ appropriate divination and the Asclepiadæ medicine, just as the Homeridæ supply the most celebrated bards; often, too, the herald's office becomes a family monopoly, so that in historical times Eleusis still had its Ceryces and Sparta its Talthybiadæ. But among the craftsmen also talent is hereditary; Phereclos, the skilful boat-builder, is son of the carpenter Harmonides.

The craftsmen are all free men. There is not one example in the *Iliad* or the *Odyssey* of a slave following a skilled trade. There is therefore nothing humiliating about the work of the professional craftsmen. At a day when nobility and wealth are bound up with landed property the craftsmen are relegated to an inferior class, that of the "poor men," but they are none the less surrounded with consideration. As soon as movable property begins to be of consequence their position improves. They can grow rich and rise accordingly in public opinion. The soothsayers accumulate wealth and often earn the title of "hero." The bards are welcomed wherever they go; " among all the men of the earth they have a right to their share of honour and respect." The heralds enjoy not only fortune but a certain glory; we find that the renown of such men as Talthybios and Stentor survives them.

Even in the manual crafts it is possible to make a name. Among the "carpenters" there is mention of Epeios, the constructor of machines in the Greek camp, Phereclos, the boat-builder in Troy, and Icmalios, the cabinet-maker in Ithaca, among the "smiths" there is Laerces, the goldsmith at Pylos, and among the "leather-workers" there are Tychios, the maker of shields at Hyle, and Polybos, who makes balls at Scheria. The fame of craftsmen goes beyond the bounds of their city. They are summoned from one town to another to do a single job or to settle permanently. But the craftsmen do not work for glory alone. A soothsayer or a herald can make a fortune; why not a craftsman? When he accepts an order he works in the house of his patron. He is supplied with raw material, kept generously, and covered with attentions and honours; he is treated as a distinguished guest, and, like a guest, he is given presents proportionate to the wealth of the donor and to the service done.

Nevertheless, if we attempt to form a general notion about the craftsmen of Homeric times, we must not let ourselves be deceived by details which give the impression of a favoured position. The professional does not hold an important place in society. The demand, kept down by domestic industry, was not sufficient to keep a large number employed and to confine them to narrowly specialized lines. One smith or one potter was enough for the work of a big township. Carpenters and leather-workers were known far and wide because such craftsmen were not to be found everywhere, and they were summoned to perform tasks of exceptional importance. But it was just the rarity of the occasions on which their talents were required that raised them to the level of the soothsayers, bards, doctors, and heralds. To live by their trade they had to travel about, and they were all the more honoured because they had so few competitors. The personal reputation of the Demiurges does not prove that their class was important.

### 2. THE HIRED MEN (THETES)

Beneath the class of the craftsmen there gradually formed a humble class of workers.

From one end of the Hellenic world to the other roamed a mass of vagabonds, tossed hither and thither by their distress or by their love of change. Besides a few runaway slaves they were chiefly banished men and adventurers, some cast out by their family and others fleeing from a blood-feud. All these men were free, but they had hard work to defend their existence. Without a hearth one did not count as a citizen, and one had no rights. The stranger above all was destitute of any recourse against the gravest offences or the cruellest treatment, for he had not the value of a man.

How were they to live, then? " Your cursed belly gives you sore trouble when you roam, a prey to hardship and suffering." For many the ordinary resource was mendicancy. How many of these vagrants we see passing through the *Odyssey*, wan, lean, famished, and dirty! They wander over the country, bent on their staff, with a patched wallet over their shoulder. In the city they go from house to house, and wear out their backbones against the door-posts as they wait for the fragments of the meal to be thrown to them, or for leave to be given to walk round the table. When night falls they retire to the public gallery, the *lesche*, or, in winter, to the forge, which is always warm. As a rule these unfortunates are not treated hardly; they are the envoys and *protégés* of Zeus. But the pity of others affords no security. In the Homeric period beggars are exposed to insults and violence, and they may even be thrown into the hold of a ship and sold abroad.

There were some to whom this condition was not uncongenial. These so detested every kind of work that they preferred even this life of ravenous privation, with its happy moments of guzzling. For them mendicancy was a profession. They possessed all its subtleties and devices. They knew the favourable moments, and they had their repertory of piteous tales. When one of them had secured a good post he claimed the exclusive enjoyment of it and defended it with his fists. Thus the great houses had their recognized parasite; to the palace of Odysseus Iros is attached, the typical beggar by profession.

But most of the poor people were only too glad to earn their living with their hands. It was a disgrace to pass as " a being incapable of any work and any effort, a mere burden upon the earth." It was in this mob of unemployed that the land-owners and heads of houses sought the workers whom they needed in addition to their usual staff, and these workers were called *Thetes*.

The Thetes, then, are free men who let themselves out for a wage. In some cases the reason for the engagement is a crime. In days when property was not yet generally personal an offender often could not compensate the person offended except by a certain amount of work. But usually the Thetes are poor wretches who go into service because they do not possess a bit of land or a skilled trade. Whatever the reason for the engagement may be, the result of it is the same: the employer and the employee are bound by a true contract of hire of service.

Far the most of the hired men were required for stockbreeding. In the sheep-folds of Ithaca there are hired " strangers " among the slaves. When Odysseus appears disguised as a beggar the herdsman Eumæos would be glad to keep him as an additional worker, and the goatherd Melantheus proposes that he should act " as stall-keeper, to sweep the yard or to carry fodder to the kids."

The working of the big estates afforded also a variety of other employments to men from outside. The suitor Eurymachos makes this proposal to Odysseus: " Stranger, if you would work as hired man I should employ you on the far part of my land to build stone dikes and to plant trees." In a harvest scene it is hired men who wield the sickle and bind the corn. Even small farms needed wage-workers. The *Odyssey* speaks of the agricultural labourer who is obliged to work for others and goes into the service of a poor crofter who is clearing a little plot of ground.

Industry had far less need of hired hands. Yet we see Poseidon building the walls of Troy in the service of Laomedon, and free men tanning a hide for a master.

Lastly, there were Thetes attached to the great families for service of every kind. When Telemachos has left for Pylos they ask whether he has taken for his rowers " Thetes and slaves of his own." At one moment Odysseus pretends that he is ready to place himself at the disposal of the suitors: "I shall do quickly and well all that they wish . . . light the fire, split the dry wood, cut up the meat, roast it, pour the wine, and do all the services which small men do for great men."

The women hardly went into service with others except for household work. If they go to the fields it is only to prepare the dinner of the harvesters. The palaces contain as many free servant-women as slaves. Sometimes they are wet-nurses; usually they wait at table, make the beds, prepare the baths, do the washing, and spend the rest of the time spinning and weaving. But sometimes the usual household staff is not enough for the work, and a poor woman is brought in from outside to spin the wool.

The conditions of engagement varied at the will of the parties. Certain work was done by the job: Augeias makes Heracles clean his stables, and workmen are retained to bring in the harvest or to tan a hide. Generally labour was hired for a definite period. Poseidon and Apollo serve Laomedon one year, Heracles remains with Omphale three years, and Cadmos has to engage himself to Ares for the period described as " eternal," which in reality ceases at the end of eight years. But there is no evidence which suggests that there was a fixed term for domestic service. In any case the term was renewable indefinitely. So the great houses had a permanent staff of Thetes and female servants as well as slaves. From the way in which the word *Thes* is used in Homeric language it would seem that the length of the engagement already limits the liberty of the hired man and binds him to his employer.

The remuneration for labour was always specified as clearly as possible; the employee had a right to a salary, " to a wage fixed beforehand." Like all payments at the time, this could only be effected in kind. Augeias promises Heracles a tithe of the cattle. Thus we have the practice, which exists in all societies whose economy is still simple, of allowing the hired man a share of the fruits of the ground or of the increase of the beasts. The same is probably done with the materials on which they work and the articles which they manufacture. This share is never very large. A spinning-woman in the *Iliad* has great difficulty in feeding her children from her " meagre wage." And the hired man cannot always count on the word given by his employer ! The only remuneration of which he is sure is his keep. As a rule it is the only remuneration due to him. " Will you be a hired man with me ?" a land-owner says to a beggar. " I offer good terms. I shall give you as much to eat as you can, I shall dress you and give you shoes." When Odysseus pretends to want to enter the service of the suitors he asks for nothing but " his meals." Moreover the hired man cannot be too sure of a substantial and varied diet. A man who is taking on a boy as goatherd promises him, with malicious irony, that he " will grow fat drinking whey." Even the day-labourers get no more than good keep for a few days. When the harvesters have work a great ox is killed for them; this feast is their whole salary. Telemachos when setting out for Pylos takes on the flour and bread needed for his crew; when they come home he gives them all a banquet, and all scores are settled.

So the position of the hired man is very precarious and very humble in the Homeric period. There is only one class of hired people who can attain a condition which, though still humble, is tolerable—the female servants in a great house. It is true that they are not distinguished from the slaves. But they are spared the most fatiguing tasks. They regard themselves as members of the family. Those who are called by their own name and their father's are women of honourable birth who deserve consideration. Nausicaa sings and plays with her women. In the palaces a female housekeeper is placed at the head of the other servant-women in a position of trust; but such situations are rare.

While domestic service gave a living to a fairly large

number of women, and a decent living to some, as a rule the rudimentary wage-system of Homeric times afforded the poor quite insufficient resources. The Thetes are mentioned with the slaves. And indeed they do the same work, and their material condition is the same, minus security for the morrow but plus the ownership of their own body. They come out of the mass of beggars, and when their engagement expires they return into it; all that they have done in the meantime has been to work at a more arduous and sometimes less lucrative occupation. Their only advantage lies in a precarious liberty. The most grievous thing in their existence is that they are never sure of anything. The contract which binds them does not bind their employer, for there is no right against might. What can they do if the master does not keep his word? When Apollo and Poseidon have completed their year of service Laomedon refuses them any salary and threatens, if they do not clear off as fast as they can, to cut their ears off; the two unfortunates go away with bitter hearts and empty hands. What precaution can they take? Heracles, it is true, secures his three years' wages in advance from Omphale by the device of a fictitious sale, but his case is exceptional. The Thetes have to trust to a good faith which frequently fails. Even their liberty, their sole pride, is not guaranteed. Just like the beggars, they are in danger of being put into chains and sold as slaves in a distant island.

We can understand the utter distress which lay behind such an existence. When Achilles in hell expresses his despair that he is no longer among the living, he wants to contrast with the most illustrious shade the most miserable of human creatures, and this is what he says: " Sooner would I work as a hired man on fields not my own, for a man without inheritance or resources." To resign himself to such a wretched condition a man must be hard driven by need. He who accepted it could just keep off starvation so long as he worked. The spinning-woman of the *Iliad* can still just earn bread for her children, but the time is near when the farmers will have no more married men or women working for them. Down to the VIIIth century those who had neither land nor skilled trade formed the waste matter of society, and nothing could reduce their numbers or better their lot.

CHAPTER IV

## STOCK-BREEDING AND AGRICULTURE

### 1. STOCK-BREEDING

DURING the period of the migrations Greece was continually traversed by peoples who brought their flocks and herds trailing along with them and could not have a taste for agriculture. Thucydides describes in sober, brief terms these distant centuries in which "each worked the ground only enough to live, without possessing a surplus or even planting," and "the best land changed masters most often." It was still more natural that the contemporaries of Homer should retain definite memories of a time when the only wealth known was cattle. The Cyclopes are for them the type of the men who do not eat wheat. Although in epic times the fields and plantations are beginning to spread, pastures still take up the greater part of the land. The grass-land does not even tend to diminish, for, though agriculture encroaches on it at certain points, it gains elsewhere at the expense of the forest and the brush, which are destroyed by woodmen, beasts, and huge fires.

The rural economy of the Homeric period distinguishes between two kinds of pastures, those of the plain and those of the mountain. Beyond the ploughed and planted land about the towns, villages, and isolated houses lies the distant waste, the reservation, the *eschatie*. The estates are thus surrounded by uncultivated land, and the territory of a village or city always has its fringe of forest or bare pasture. In Ithaca the traveller as he lands sees before him vast spaces where cattle are browsing, with a few huts adjoining byres. The herdsman often sleeps out of doors, and if he goes at night to a cabin sheltered in a valley he has no neighbours. Still more than the plains, the mountains have great stretches of grass-land, surrounded by forest. The shepherd of the epics hears the torrents roaring in the valley and dreads the

## STOCK-BREEDING AND AGRICULTURE 35

mists " favourable to theft " in which the north wind wraps the heights.

In the *Iliad* the shepherds, be they kings or peasants, lead their flocks where they will, in full liberty, for the pastures, especially in the mountains, are usually collective properties. When the poet enumerates the possessions of an individual he never includes pasture-land, although he is most careful to count all the cattle. Nor are there any grass meadows in the enclosures granted as public rewards. In the Vth century there were still mountain pastures which had not been appropriated by individuals, and they were numerous in the remote past of Greece.

Nevertheless we see in the *Odyssey* a large part of the common pasture being transformed into private property. The king of Ithaca has forty-eight herds on the mainland. Does he own the land itself or merely the right to pasture ? In any case here are pastures of which at least the use has ceased to be common. On the island itself the royal *eschatie* is so vast that a stranger cannot cross it without a guide; over all this area the crofts and the herdsmen belong to the king, and everything indicates a permanent establishment. Already the owner of these pastures has even made his men put the more fertile parts under corn, so true is it that his right appears to be incontestable. This progressive appropriation of pasture-land takes place everywhere. Every suitor has his *eschatie*, and one of them has made an enclosed orchard in it. Thus large properties are formed with a view to live-stock, at the expense of the common properties and to the profit of a few families.

The most remarkable of these ranches is that which belongs to Odysseus. " No chief," says Eumæos, " owns such wealth, not on the mainland nor in Ithaca, and twenty men together would not own so much." We have the inventory of it: " On the mainland, twelve herds of cattle, as many sheep-folds, as many pigsties, as many big pens for goats, all guarded by strangers or slaves; in Ithaca, on the pastures of the reservation, eleven great herds of goats and twelve of pigs "—altogether seventy-two flocks and herds. Although decimated by the suitors, the pigs still number fifty sows in farrow and thirty boars in every herd; the normal herd therefore contains a hundred pigs, and we can reckon the live-stock of Odysseus at seven or eight thousand head. The twelve pigsties on Ithaca cover a whole rising ground with their stone walls, fences, and hedges. Hard by stand the cabins of the swineherds and the comfortable house of their chief. The staff is thoroughly organized. It comprises six gangs, one for every twelve herds. Each gang consists of four men under an overseer. Altogether these make twenty-four herdsmen and six chiefs. Each herdsman looks after between 240 and 300 beasts. Five shepherds are sufficient to-day for a flock of 1,800 sheep, and they were not so very far from these figures in the Homeric period. But in addition to the herdsmen a certain number of hands are needed to look after the folds, and each group of folds has its guardian and sweeper. Thus on the estate of Odysseus about forty men are employed on the live-stock.

The life of the herdsmen is hard enough. So long as the season allows, the herd remains out of doors. In summer the smaller beasts go out at dawn and come in at dusk, whereas the oxen spend the night outside and return to the byres in the early morning. The herdsman has to be continually on the watch, for fear of robbers and birds of prey. In the evening, to keep off marauders and wild beasts, great fires are lit. While the young swineherds go to sleep Eumæos wraps himself in a big cloak, takes his arms, and goes his rounds in the darkness. The herdsman must also, like the byre-boy, cut the grass and green-stuff for the winter, he chooses the beasts for slaughter and kills them, and he does the preliminary work of preparing the hides.

For the cattle intended for ploughing, slaughter, and dairy production the great land-owners after a certain date confine their own share in the work to general supervision. Not so with horses. Horse-breeding is not only a source of wealth but a luxury, a sport and a guarantee of military superiority. The nobles look after their stables with care. The horses are given barley or wheat; Andromache herself takes wheat and wine to her husband's chargers. Whenever possible the horses are put out to grass in chosen meadows. From Ithaca one of the suitors sends his mares as far as Elis, and in the flooded meadows beneath Mount Ida countless herds of horses run loose. The owners break in their horses themselves, and are proud to bear names which recall this

## STOCK-BREEDING AND AGRICULTURE

favourite pursuit. They improve the breed by skilful crosses. We have a figure which shows the economic value of horse-breeding: Erichthonios of Dardania, "the wealthiest of mortals," was believed to keep three thousand brood-mares with their foals. We have a fact which proves its social importance: in most of the cities, from Ionia to Sicily and from Thessaly to Cyrene, the landed aristocracy came later to be formed of the "Horsemen" (*Hippeis*) or "Horse-Breeders" (*Hippobotœ*).

By the side of the concerns in which breeding is done on a large scale the cave of Polyphemos presents the simpler spectacle of a model dairy. "We went in, and we wondered at all that we saw. The wicker crates sank beneath the weight of the cheeses, and the pens were crowded with lambs and kids, arranged in lots—here the oldest, there the middling, and further away the newly born. And the pans were brimming with whey, near the milking bowls." The master of the house arrives. At once he sets to work. "He sat down and milked the sheep and the bleating goats, all in turn and by each he placed her young. Then he curdled half of the shining white milk and put it in plaited baskets. The other half he stood in the pots, to drink for his supper."

To the resources of stock-breeding the Greeks of the Homeric age add those of the chase and fishing. Hunting was for long a necessity in a land covered with forest and infested with wild beasts. Legend preserves the memory of the drives carried out by the heroes. Later they hunt for pleasure and also for profit, to procure venison, wild-goats' horns, boars' tusks, and wolf-skins. The hunters often share the bag like the warriors and pirates; the chief takes first choice and the rest is divided equally.

The nobles do not go fishing; that is a sport for men without means. Fish is a despised food. The comrades of Odysseus or Menelaos must feel " hunger griping their inwards " before they decide to take birds and fish, " all that falls to their hand." Yet the waters of the Ægean, which were full of fish, must have exercised a strong attraction on the population of the coast. Among all the blessings shed on a people by the virtue of a good king the *Odyssey* mentions, after fat harvests and trees bending beneath the fruit and the fertility of ewes, this consolation of small men, "the sea abounding in fish."

Hunting and fishing hold a limited place in Homeric society; stock-breeding, with agriculture, comes before all other economic factors. Its products form the basis of the food supply. The heroes of the *Iliad* and the *Odyssey* are great eaters of meat. Agamemnon at a ceremony kills a fat ox five years old, cuts it up, and puts it on the spit. To do honour to his guests Achilles cuts up joints of mutton, goat, and pork on a block and makes Patroclos roast them. Every morning the herdsmen of Odysseus bring the fat beasts to the palace and keep the young pigs for themselves. A good roast generally appears on every table. Dairy-produce is equally popular; the milk of goats and sheep is drunk and cheese is eaten in quantities, fresh or hard. Stock-breeding is even more important for clothing than for food; the chitons are of wool, caps, cloaks, and bedding are of goat's or sheep's skin, and shoes, leggings, and gloves are of cow-hide. Then there is the service rendered by bulls and oxen, horses and mules as draught animals. We can understand why wealth was reckoned in head of cattle and the ox was the unit of value, and we can see how the stock-breeder was more than anyone else able to maintain a great number of people and held the highest rank.

2. AGRICULTURE

Although pasture holds its own in the Homeric countryside it is only by encroachment on the forest that it makes good the losses which it suffers from the extension of cultivated land. The Hellenic race, once settled on the soil of Greece, adopts a sedentary life and takes to agriculture. By epic times the Greeks have long counted among the men " who eat barley." For them agriculture is at the source of all civilization. They despise as savages the wretched beings who do not till the ground. If the Cyclopes are " proud and lawless men " it is because, " trusting in the gods, they do not till the fields nor sow any plant with their hands." Later the Greeks made Demeter the Thesmophoros, the protectress of the principles which govern the family and the city.

In the time of the *Iliad*, although the pasture-land has hardly yet become the object of private appropriation, the large property prevails everywhere. The typical estate is the

# STOCK-BREEDING AND AGRICULTURE 39

*temenos*, the enclosure with which public gratitude rewards heroes, " the proud domain of fifty measures, half vineyard and half plough-land." To the poet's mind this enclosure is enormous. But the idea of a large property varies according to country and time. We may reckon that the " proud domain " of fifty *gyai* is not as much as fifty acres.[1]

Whatever the extent of an estate may be, it is always worked direct. The kings themselves live as much as possible in the neighbourhood of their lands. The eye of the master exercises constant supervision. When Telemachos unexpectedly leaves for Pylos, they think that he is " somewhere in the fields," and indeed, on his return, he has hardly landed but he goes to see how the crops are doing. On the great day of the harvest the owner presides over the work; in the midst of his servants " he looks on in silence and rejoices in his heart." Moreover, however great a man he be, he does not think it below his dignity to lend a hand to the work. Old Laertes has only one passion left—his orchard. Odysseus can mow and drive a furrow, none like him.

This persistence of old ways does not impede the development of agricultural enterprises. The separation of the building in which the master dwells from the premises devoted to the work of the estate is significant; the proprietor gives up living on his domain because he erects on it all kinds of constructions for the material, the beasts, and the men. Laertes, loyal to the habits of the good old days, instals himself in his beloved orchard, but even his house is surrounded by the sheds in which the servants live. Thus the extension of property and the intensification of farming both lead to an increase in the agricultural staff. Laertes is assisted by the steward Dolios with his six sons and some other slaves. But cereals require many more workers. Two armies meeting are compared in the *Iliad* to two bands of harvesters who start from the two ends of a field and meet

[1] There are different opinions about the value of the *gyes*. But we know that it represents the area which a man can plough in a day, that it has as a submultiple the " furrow " or *plethron*, and that later, in the Æginetan system, the *plethron* measures about 980 square yards. Now we may consider it probable that the unit is to its submultiple as 4 to 1. Therefore it is very likely that the *gyes* measures nearly 4,000 square yards. And indeed our French agricultural treatises allow a two-horse plough to do about 4,000 square yards to a depth of about six inches in a day. So the normal *temenos* of 50 *gyai* contains about 49 acres.

in the middle across the mown sheaves. In a harvest scene the men who cut the sheaves and the children who pick them up keep three binders busy the whole time, and the meal given to all these people requires the sacrifice of a great ox. When we have made allowance for poetic exaggeration we still have the impression that some estates needed a very large staff.

But the constitution of the big estate and the ease with which workers were recruited produced very different effects in the case of arable land and in that of plantations.

The production of cereals had made some progress only because the large estate had developed. Waste land is taken into cultivation; but methods do not change. Fallow in alternate years is the rule. The plough is still the primitive swing-plough. But we can distinguish between a simple type cut from a single piece of wood and a composite type in which the pole, stock, mould-board, and tail are fixed together with stout pins. To this implement oxen or preferably mules are harnessed. The ploughman works hard and drinks hard without succeeding in driving the stock deep into the ground. But he does not spare his labour; good land receives three ploughings. Thus the sods are broken up sufficiently and there is no need to harrow after sowing. In spite of all this labour barley is, more than wheat, "the marrow of men." The harvesters use sickles and cast the sheaves in a long line to their left, while the children behind gather them up in armfuls for the binders. The ears are trodden by oxen on a good flat threshing-floor. For the winnowing there is a shovel shaped like an oar.

Whereas the corn-fields still have a primitive appearance the cultivation of vegetables and trees is improved by the use of intensive methods. The big land-owners, who leave the horned cattle to their men and devote themselves to the horse, are also content with a vague supervision of the corn-land, and give all their care to the kitchen-garden, orchard, and vineyard. The manure heaped at the farm gates is laid on the orchards. Irrigation is practised, and specialists, the "fountain-makers," lead the water from the springs by channels and runnels into trenches dug under the trees. By means of skilfully exposed terraces and espaliers early and late fruit are obtained at will, and the same vineyard supplies grapes for eating, for wine, and for drying into raisins. The

## STOCK-BREEDING AND AGRICULTURE 41

cultivation of these luxuries is the chief occupation and the chief source of pride. Among the marvels of the palace of Alcinoos nothing comes up to his gardens. Thus towards the end of the Homeric period Greece becomes covered with vineyards and lays the foundation of the olive-groves which will one day be its adornment and its fortune. It has no oil for eating or burning, and it gets its perfumed ointments from the East; but already it makes stout handles and valuable furniture from olive-wood. For a long time it had obtained its wine from abroad; Thrace supplied the delicious Maroneian, and Pramnian came from Asia. But now it makes its own wine and knows how to keep it in goatskins. Nestor offers his guests a vintage eleven years old. Everywhere the vintage is the occasion of a festival.

While the epics delight in describing the life of the landed aristocracy, they leave the small holder in the shade. But they introduce the typical peasant to us in the person of Laertes. He appears in his orchard, uncovering a tree. " He is clad in a dirty, mended chiton; about his legs he has tied patched leggings to keep him from scratches; gloves protect his hands against thorns, and his head is covered with a goatskin cap, which completes the wretchedness of his appearance." To fill in this portrait we must turn to Hesiod. The small farmer desires " first a house, and then a wife and a plough-ox." He is as hard on others as on himself. At the hearth his wife spins, weaves, and sews. With his beasts, he has a few slaves, whom he wakes before dawn at harvest-time and allows to rest after the hay-making. He engages day-labourers, a man and a woman, but he will only take unmarried people, that he may not have to feed useless mouths. He helps his neighbours in return for like services, but mistrusts them. If he succeeds by hard work and thought in making his land thrive, he is afraid of it being split up some day, and wants only one son. Already towards the end of Homeric times the small peasant inspires some contempt in the great ones of the earth, and especially in the townsfolk. His horizon is limited and his thoughts narrow. Sometimes one cannot help calling him a " silly yokel who has no mind but for to-day." As for the poor man whose only possession is a corner of ground which he clears in the sweat of his brow, only one lot is known worse than his—that of his hired servant.

## CHAPTER V
## INDUSTRY

WE have already noted that a large part of industry, all that was connected with food and clothing, was a domestic occupation in Homer's time. We also know that in professional industry the trades which were truly separated were as yet only distinguished by their raw material, and numbered only four, the *tekton* (wood and stone), the *chalkeus* (metal), the *skytotomos* (leather), and the *kerameus* (clay). Clearly industry is not highly developed, Let us try to see more closely the point at which it had arrived.

There was only one kind of workshop—the forge. A special plant was absolutely necessary to manufacture a strong or delicate article of metal. The poet takes his inspiration from reality when he describes Hephæstos at work. The divine blacksmith moves about his bellows and his fires, naked and running with sweat. He distributes the fire among all his braziers, fixes his anvil securely, and beats the iron indefatigably, hammer in one hand and tongs in the other. Every village has its forge; the beggars come and spend the night there in the warmth, and the neighbours come there to gossip in winter.

But the case of the smith is exceptional. The other craftsmen always go to their customer's house, and even the *chalkeus*, when the job does not need a big fire, does the same. The craftsmen are "invited" to the house. They all have very simple tools and they are all provided by the customer with the raw materials required for the task. Pandaros needs a bow, so he stalks a wild goat, kills it, and, "master of its horns six palms long, hands them to a skilful turner, who polishes them, fits them, and adorns them with gold tips." When the king of Pylos wishes to offer up a sacrifice he sends for Laerces to gild the horns of the victim; "the smith arrives, with the tools of his trade in his hands, the anvil, the hammer, and the well-shaped pincers, with which he

# INDUSTRY

beats the gold; old Neleus gives the gold and the craftsman lays it about the horns of the ox." This system of working by the job in the employer's house is not only adopted in cases where the raw material is precious. The prudent landowner has in his treasury not only ingots of gold but lumps of bronze and of iron. The use to which he puts them is clearly indicated in the words in which Achilles proposes as the prize of a contest the same disk as serves for the test: "However broad his fertile fields may be, he who wins it will not need for five years to send to the town for iron for his herdsmen and ploughmen." So the farmer or cattle-raiser needs raw metal for his implements and utensils. His own people make simple, ordinary articles, but for the rest he must procure a professional craftsman, and, whether he sends the work out to him or "invites" him to his own house, he buys nothing but work from him. An arrangement like this well suits a method of remuneration which obliges the employer to provide only the keep of the employee.

As there are no workshops, so there are no workshop-owners. The craftsman places himself directly at the service of the public. He is both master, since he deals with the customer without any middleman, and workman, since he lives on wages. Occasionally several workers may combine for a task, but they never form a permanent gang under the orders of a head who pays them; their employer is the consumer of their collective production. There is not even a contractor who undertakes to recruit labour. To build his house Paris collects the *tektones* whom he considers the best. One does the same if one needs a boat, if one does not build it all alone. We hear of a gang of men dressing a skin on order, but these are working for a land-owner and not for a manufacturer.

Between these isolated craftsmen competition was not severe. The self-sufficiency of the family hardly left enough work to the craftsmen of the little town to employ more than one man for each trade. So competition could only arise between one place and another, or even between two countries. To make his famous shield Ajax the Locrian sends for Tychios from Hyle in Bœotia. This example is typical; the customer readily sets aside the nearest professional for the most renowned. "Men summon a stranger from far countries if he is of the order of the Demiurges, a soothsayer, an experienced doctor, a carpenter skilled at fashioning wood, or a divine singer who charms us. These are the mortals whom, all over the earth, men love to invite." Thus there is no idea of protectionism, and competition is carried on at distances, freely. Only in the big towns, where several craftsmen exercise the same calling, can competition become local. Paris chooses the best masons in Troy. Increase in population had to stimulate movement everywhere before the people of Hesiod's time could make a proverb of the rivalry of potter with potter, of carpenter with carpenter.

The essential features of industry in the Homeric age give the impression that it was not yet much developed. At the most a more intense life appears in the latest portions of the epics. If we examine the trades which existed, one by one, we still have the same impression.

The *tekton* has for tools the axe, the saw, the adze, the chisel, the drill, the lathe, the compass, and the plumb-line. His main work is in wood, and because wood is chiefly used in building he has annexed work in stone. What he can do as a mason we gather to-day from the Sixth City of Troy, the city of the *Iliad*. He is capable of building a house large enough to hold Priam and all his family, but the gigantic structures of past times astound him and he ascribes them to the gods or the Cyclopes. As carpenter and joiner he does fine work, thresholds of oak or door-posts of cypress. As cart-wright he makes the war chariot, the travelling carriage, and the transport waggon; his wheels are no longer solid, but have naves and spokes protected by felloes of aspen or black poplar, and the seat is hung on straps. As cabinet-maker he manufactures luxurious furniture; Icmalios delivers to Penelope an arm-chair set with ivory and precious metals. As turner of wood, horn, and ivory he makes handles and oars, fits bows, and carves key-handles, sword-sheaths, and horses' frontlets. As sculptor he carves holy images. But the *tekton* is most highly esteemed for ship-building. This is regarded as an art which requires quite a special science, a *sophia*, and it is placed under the protection of Athene. Favourites of the goddess are mentioned, such as Harmonides and his son Phereclos of Troy.

The trade of *chalkeus* comprises all metal-work. But the

# INDUSTRY 45

production of raw metals is not included; there are no mines in Homeric Greece and the ingots come from abroad. Menelaos brings a whole cargo of gold from Egypt. "The land where the silver grows," Alybe, is inhabited by a mysterious people, and the white metal reaches Greece after long voyages. Copper comes from Cyprus. As for iron, tin, and lead, no one knows whence they come. The importation of metal is for a long time done by middlemen. The Taphians, the " bold sailors," play an important part in these transactions. Their ships go to Cyprus with iron and bring back copper.

The smith, accustomed to bronze, is slow in taking to iron, which is hard to work.[1] In any case the substitution of the one metal for the other does not lead to any revolution in apparatus and technique; the bronze-worker, the *chalkeus*, only needs a pair of skin bellows to be able to make iron red or white. The craft remains what it was. It is specially suited to lame men, who make up for their infirmity by exceptional development of the trunk and arms; Hephæstos is a patron worthy of them. The raw metal is melted in a furnace; the bloom is held on the anvil with the tongs and beaten with the hammer. The most delicate operation is tempering, without which the edge and point are useless. But it is just here that the armourer fails; he cannot give his products a temper which is proof against everything. From the faults revealed by bronze weapons in the Homeric battles we can judge what iron weapons would have been like. The javelin of Paris is blunted on the shield of Menelaos, and the latter's rapier breaks on his opponent's helmet. The pike of Iphidamas cannot pierce Agamemnon's baldric, " and the bronze point, striking a silver plate, is turned like lead." The *Odyssey*, which describes the tempering of iron admirably, at the same time tells us that it was still only used for the manufacture of tools which were easy to repair. " When a

---

[1] Statistics have been drawn up on this subject. In the first books of the *Iliad* 309 cases of the use of bronze are mentioned as against 16 of iron, whereas in the latter part of the *Iliad* and the whole of the *Odyssey* the corresponding figures are 109 and 32. But we must not draw from this the mathematical deduction that at the beginning of the Homeric age bronze was used 19 times more than iron and at the end of the period 3 or 4 times; for poetic tradition always favoured bronze. But we see in what direction and to what extent the relative position of the two metals altered.

smith tempers in cold water a great axe or an adze it gives off a hissing; this is what gives iron its strength." When Achilles proposes a disk of raw iron as a prize he tells some warriors that it will supply enough metal to make agricultural implements for a long time; he says nothing of weapons.

It would be natural to suppose that Homeric goldsmith's work reached a considerable level. The "melter of gold," although he is a " smith " by trade, does work which already requires a special designation (*chrysochoos*). The epic poet revels in descriptions of gems and masterpieces of jewellery. Gold, silver, electron or white gold, and *kyanos* or lapis lazuli gleam on weapons and clothing, on the ears and arms of the women, and on the furniture and even the walls of the palaces. It was impossible to display any other luxury or to make any other use of the surplus of natural resources; this is a guarantee that though the fancy of the bards may exaggerate it does not invent. The question remains whether the goldsmiths who enjoyed renown in Greece were the authors of the works which were prized the most. The poet tells us whence the celebrated objects came; they were all imported from the East. The silver mixing-bowl which Achilles offers as a prize, " the fairest of all which are on the earth," was chased by " cunning Sidonians." Another mixing-bowl of silver overlaid with gold, " the most precious of the jewels which the palace of Menelaos holds," was given to him by the king of Sidon. Helen shows with pride a work-basket of silver encircled with gold and a golden distaff, gifts brought home from Egypt. Agamemnon's cuirass, ribbed with enamel, was sent to him by the king of Cyprus. Diomede owns a gold cup which his grandfather got from Lycia. It is true that artistic jewellery might have come from abroad without the ordinary jewel of trade being imported. But we see Phœnicians landing a quantity of gew-gaws, including a gold necklace with electron pendants.

So only second-class work is left to the native goldsmith. Laerces performs a child's task: he beats a leaf of gold and rolls it round the horns of an ox. " The skilful craftsman, he to whom Hephæstos and Pallas Athene have taught all their art," knows how to dip a silver plate into a bath of gold and to weave filigree. But it is not absolutely impossible that some few secrets of an advanced technique survived from

# INDUSTRY

the Mycenæan goldsmiths. The shield made by Hephæstos for Achilles is assuredly a masterpiece. It is formed of five plates of gold one on the other, it is covered all over with fine chasing, and happy use of incrustation and colour-effects obtained by subtle alloys increase the illusion and the beauty. But it is not at all likely that such effects were produced by a humble *confrère* of Laerces; we must rather suppose it an imaginary combination of Cretan or Mycenæan works.

From the instances of Eumæos and Odysseus cutting sandals and straps from dyed cow-hides we see that in leather-work family industry did not leave much to the professional. Tanning was done on the estate, and if the owner did not employ his ordinary staff he called in a few workmen. " The men who have been given the skin of a great ox, soaked in grease, to stretch, take it, stand in a wide circle, and stretch it; soon the water runs out and the grease goes in as they pull, and at last the leather is stretched every way." Recourse is had to the *skytotomos* for tasks which require special training or an artistic gift. Ajax sends for Tychios because he wants a shield "like a tower, with brass covering seven ox-hides." But the leather articles which form part of the usual clothing and armour are seldom made by craftsmen.

Pottery, on the other hand, was in Homeric times a thriving industry. In countries with good beds of potter's clay each family no doubt made its own everyday utensils. But by working for populations who did not possess this clay one could gain a living which was not to be despised. It is certainly a craftsman who "turns the potter's wheel, to see if it answers well to the drive of his hands." All the same, the clumsiness of the sub-Mycenæan vases was such that anyone could supply local requirements, and the differences which constantly appear under general similarities of style do not justify us in supposing that there were factories working for a large sale.

The presence of craftsmen in the epics might easily deceive us regarding the degree of development attained by industry. In reality social life imposed on work, and on each craft in particular, conditions which made production on a large scale quite impossible.

CHAPTER VI

PIRACY AND TRADE

1. PIRACY

IT was impossible, as we have seen, for the *genos* to be self-sufficient. To exchange his surplus for what he lacks the head of the family goes to the market of the town. This is where internal traffic centres. Transactions of a simple kind bring the producer and consumer together. The herdsman, cultivator, and craftsman sell their products and dispense with middlemen. Each does business only so far as he actually needs. No one makes a living by selling the products of others; the profession of merchant appears nowhere in the class of the Demiurges. Thus the Homeric age realizes, for a moment, the commercial system which consists in selling one's own products, which Plato calls *autopolike*.

But at a very early date the home market ceased to be such that all families could dispose of their surplus and obtain what they lacked. The extension of city economy was connected with a set of social causes which increased wants much more than the means of satisfying them locally. Men wanted more refined food. Even Laertes in his rustic cabin had a bath-tub and scented oils. The formation of a treasury became for the nobles not only a method of amassing articles of consumption and instruments of exchange but a necessary condition of political influence. A great house could not be without fine coffers, embroidered stuffs, purple carpets, bronze and iron in ingots, plaques of gold, jewels, chased vases, and rare weapons. Now Homeric Greece had neither the materials nor the men to make these articles. They had to be brought from outside.

This was not easy at the beginning. Every stranger was an enemy. There was only one known method of obtaining what he possessed—to take it. War, brigandage, and piracy

## PIRACY AND TRADE 49

were for a long time modes of acquisition no less indispensable and no less legitimate than hunting and fishing. The Homeric poems are full of tales of raids and reprisals in which Greek is against Greek. In this way flocks and herds are increased and slaves recruited. But metal and precious articles were only found in distant countries, especially in the East. To win these, vast seas full of monsters must be crossed and countless warriors must be braved. On rare occasions a chieftain with heart of brass essayed the adventure. As a rule it was the strangers who came to Greece. There the pirates found a tempting prey and the merchants an excellent market.

Since the fleet of Minos had disappeared, from every side there arose the " peoples of the sea " who infested the Ægean, unpacking merchandise when they did not feel themselves strong, and looting at the first opportunity. The Taphians, for example, go to Cyprus to exchange iron for copper, sell slaves in Ithaca and the neighbouring islands, and make raids on the Thesprotians and into the heart of Phœnicia.

Nevertheless it was the Phœnicians who gained the upper hand and exercised a thalassocracy of a kind. They saw that it was to their interest not to frighten people, and preferred to draw the natives with bargains (incidentally cheating them), reserving violence for the moment when nothing more was to be gained by amiability. In the far west, with the savage peoples whose language they did not understand, they practised the " silent trade." In the east they picked an island or promontory opposite the market to be exploited, using it as an observation post and a fortress. There they set up their tents and passed their goods on to the mainland in small boats. In places where the public authority was strong they bought the right to trade by a rich gift to the king, the ancient way of paying customs duty and obtaining a trade licence. In this way Sidon became the warehouse for goods exported from Cyprus, Egypt, Libya, and Ethiopia. With slave labour this city manufactured embroidered cloth, carpets, bronze, artistic jewellery, and trinkets for export. So the Phœnicians had all they needed, including a spirit of enterprise, to make profitable voyages in the Ægean. The Cyclades were rich in food-stuffs and convenient for raiding. To the north Lemnos received all the products of Thrace and the Troad. The kingdoms of the Peloponnese offered abundant resources. The Phœnicians conquered all these markets.

A scene in the *Odyssey* shows them at work, the " skilful sailors, deceitful traders." They land in Syria, an island rich in wine and corn, sheep and oxen. They come to sell trash, " gew-gaws without number," and a few good jewels. They remain a whole year displaying and hawking their stuff. The more pushing of them go into the wealthy houses and dangle the finest articles before the eyes of the women. Meanwhile one of them meets and seduces a fellow-countrywoman, a rich Sidonian's daughter who had been sold as a slave by pirates. He offers to take her back to her own country, he swears he will. But she insists on paying her passage, in order that her freedom may not be the price. When the ship has her full return cargo, just as she is getting under sail, the woman comes running up, hiding vases in the folds of her dress and holding her master's child by the hand. In this way the Phœnicians come to Greece with luxury articles and return with natural products, and on both voyages they are quite pleased to make up the freight with slaves and, on occasion, to carry passengers.

So long as Greece lent itself passively to piratical and commercial enterprise only two islands were in a position to take active part in it. These were, at the ends of the Ægean, the two lands in which the pre-Hellenic population had survived; the Pelasgians of Lemnos and the Eteocretans continued to rove the seas. The Lemnians carried on exchanges between Thrace and the Asiatic Hellespont. We find them in the siege of Troy, supplying the Achæan army with wine, which they fetch from the region of Maroneia in " many ships "; they give a thousand measures of it to the kings and barter the rest for bronze, iron, oxen, hides, and prisoners. War, which is permanent in these parts, makes their island a slave-market. As for the Cretans, they lived on exchange and rapine. Reviving the relations established by their ancestors, they frequented the Attic coast, the market of Pylos, and the great gatherings of Delphi. They were well known in Ithaca; Odysseus, to conceal his identity, gives himself out for a shipwrecked Cretan. But the mariners of Crete were especially attracted by the countries of the south. The fictitious adventures which Odysseus relates have a historical foundation. He starts for Egypt with a band of bold fellows. At first they try to win fortune with a high hand, but the Pharaoh's army soon brings them to their senses. Their leader then amasses great wealth by peaceful methods. Seven years go by, and he meets a Phœnician; he is to find his master. The artful one takes him in hand—they must form a partnership, go together to Phœnicia—that's the place to do business! The unwary dupe yields to the charmer. At the end of a year the partnership no longer prospers. However, there is still a cargo to be taken to Libya. On the way our hero is added as a slave to the goods to be sold. He is saved by a shipwreck. He is taken on to a Thesprotian ship, is nearly reduced to slavery a second time, and escapes by swimming. A Cretan can always get out of a hole.

In their turn the Greeks, the true Greeks, perceived the facilities which their country afforded for navigation. Everywhere there were sheltered harbours or beaches on which you could draw up your boat in case of alarm; and the sea was so dotted with islands that you could cover great distances without any long crossing. They set themselves to build ships. These were of two kinds. The war or pirate ship was long and narrow; she must hold a little merchandise on the outward voyage and as much loot as possible on the return; but above all she must make her goal with sails and oars, with her crew ready to lay down their oar for a spear. The cargo boat was the "hollow" ship; her bulk made her more stable and she was broader, with a round bottom and roomy sides, sacrificing speed to burden.

But these landsmen did not become sea-wolves in a night. Nautical science was for long in its infancy. To steer a course the Greek sailor has no other guide than the sun, moon, and stars. He rarely ventures forth at night. Once Odysseus suggests it to his men, and "their hearts break" and they mutiny. If a voyage is at all prolonged no one knows if he is "on the side of the darkness where the sun goes down beneath the earth, or on the side of the dawn where he rises." In these circumstances distances appear enormous. The voyage from Troy to Lacedæmon and home again by Phœnicia is regarded as a marvellous adventure.

They let land out of sight only when it cannot be helped. As soon as the sea is bad they take refuge in a cove. Against a contrary wind they do not attempt to tack, but wait till it has fallen; the southeaster keeps Odysseus in Trinacria three months. To double a promontory is a great undertaking. Cape Malea is dreaded by the boldest. In short, the Greek mariner sails only in the good season, by day, and in sight of the shore, and is ready to take refuge anywhere at the least gust of wind.

It is a hard trade. " It is distress of the hungry belly that makes men fit ships and plough the waves." Whether citizen, hired freeman, or slave, the rower has no pay but his keep, or at the very most some meagre gift in addition. For a long time the typical sailor will be the peasant whom his land does not feed, who goes to seek a living afar.

For these ragamuffins who were obliged to rove the seas comfortable people for a long time had nothing but contempt and pity, the contempt of the landsman for the " fish-eater " and of the son of a good family for the man who works for lucre, and the pity of the land-owner, sitting in peace by his fire, for the unhappy wretch " who is sad that he is kept on board a whole month, far from his wife, by the storms and the angry waves." Hesiod does allow this means of gaining a livelihood, by the side of agriculture, but he does not disguise the dislike he feels " for the men who risk their lives at it in their madness." The son of Alcinoos jeers at Odysseus, saying that he is like " the captain of a merchant ship who has nothing in his head but goods and profit," and the hero feels " bitten in his heart " at such disparagement.

Nevertheless the aristocracy was soon converted to the type of sea ventures which suited its warlike qualities. Trade is vulgar, but piracy is noble. You are proud if you bring off a foray on land; why not be proud if you carry off herds and herdsmen after crossing an arm of the sea, or if you bring home ships laden with spoil from distant expeditions? The spear never disgraces a man. When an unknown guest is received, he is asked with deference whether he is a pirate. The same man who grows indignant if he is called a merchant captain relates that he has led pirate gangs nine times, and concludes with pride " Thus all goods fell to me abundantly;

my house grew quickly greater; I became mighty in my country and worthy of honour."

The example was set by the younger sons and bastards, who found their scope limited by the rigid system of the family. A pirate relates how he chose that calling. The son of a rich man and a female slave, he received, on the death of his father, a house and part of the inheritance. "But," he says, "I had no liking for peaceful work and the home cares which make a good family; boats and oars, fights, spears, and arrows were my only joy." Once the road had been opened the chiefs of the nobility took it; glory and gain—what could one want more ? Kings were no longer content with the gifts which they took from foreign traders; they competed with them. When Menelaos shows in his palace "the splendour of the brass, the gold, the electron, the silver and the ivory," he indicates the source of all this wealth with the conceited modesty of the merchant who has grown rich: " Is there one mortal man who could vie with me in riches, or is there not ? For indeed it cost me many hardships and many wanderings to bring these goods on the ships which I led home after seven years. I have been over Cyprus, Phœnicia, and Egypt; I have visited the Ethiopians, the Sidonians, the Erembi, and Libya." Odysseus is the true type of the captain who is greedy for lucrative adventures. "I could," he says, "have returned to my country long ago; but it seemed to me better to amass more treasure, roaming over a great part of the earth." Wherever he goes he manages to obtain "precious gifts." He hides them in a coffer closed with a knot of which he alone has the secret. While his cargo is being unloaded he takes the inventory and hastens to place it in security. Amid the emotion of the first embraces he reassures each of his folk as to his financial position, and declares that he has brought back " enough to feed the family to the tenth generation." These, surely, are sufficiently typical merchants, except that they carry cargo only when homeward bound. There is not much exchange, but pillaging. The Greek needs metals for ornament and use, both raw and manufactured, and luxurious textiles; he has nothing to offer but farm produce, cattle, and a few slaves. To make the balance he throws his sword into the scale.

## 2. TRADE

All the same, in these international activities trade, as we understand the term, has its share.

Once people realize the advantages of peaceful exchanges merchants are gradually admitted to trade freely between city and city. The privilege which was thus enjoyed by the stranger who had no rights was due to the ever growing practice of hospitality. To understand the influence which hospitality exercised upon social relations we must see more in it than a religious duty enjoined by Zeus Xenios, the god of guests. It is a legal institution; a solemn contract creates between two individuals an artificial kinship and consequently an imprescriptible obligation of mutual protection, hereditary for ever. The passing stranger is asked in without question; he is made inviolable by communion, cup in hand, before he is asked his name and the object of his journey. Henceforward he has a right to bed and board so long as he stays and the means to continue his journey or to return to his home, and he is given all kinds of presents according to the wealth of his host. The more generous the host shows himself, the more claim he has on the generosity of his guest. No doubt the epics introduce us almost entirely to the entertainments of princes. Nevertheless certain details are significant: Telemachos obtains hospitality at Pylos, Pheræ, and Sparta in succession, and Œneus when he receives Bellerophon exchanges a purple baldric with him for a vase of gold. Let us substitute for these heroes an ordinary man looking for articles to take home, a merchant on a business tour. The stranger, enjoying protection for his person and his goods, can compensate his host for the gifts received or, if he cannot settle the account at once, the creditor has only to present himself at the house of the debtor any day he likes. Thus transactions in which payment is made at once or on a fixed date are encouraged. The pact of hospitality, a primitive formality of international law, is like an exchange of passport and safe-conduct bringing with it an exchange or an advance of goods. It enables the trader to go into distant countries without fear, and it starts connexions which are handed down for ever. Thereby the chief obstacle to exchanges between peoples is abolished. It is true that in itself the

## PIRACY AND TRADE

institution only grants its benefits to isolated individuals and their families; but it soon shows a remarkable tendency to develop. The *Iliad* mentions a rich man who lived in a house by the roadside and welcomed all travellers. This is striking evidence of the way in which hostility towards the stranger changed to kindly welcome, or, as the Greeks said, *axenia* changed to *euxenia*.

In addition to the moral conditions which commerce necessitates there are certain technical conditions. However primitive a system of exchanges may be, it requires weights and measures. Homeric Greece has for measures of length the palm, the cubit, and the *plethron*, and for measures of area the square *plethron* and the *gyes*. The most usual measure of capacity is the choenix, which holds enough grain for a man for one day. Since the balance is only used for precious materials, the word " talent " designates at once the scale of the balance and the unit of weight in gold.

But how were values to be fixed and compared ? As unit the most easily estimated commodity was taken, the ox. A beautiful, capable, or well-born girl is worth many oxen, a female slave is worth from four to twenty, a tripod twelve, and a piece of armour nine or a hundred. The ox does not actually appear in the exchange; it is a standard with reference to which prices are indicated. There is a kind of scale of values, a prototype of the monetary system, in this practice of comparing all articles with a single one.

Once commercial relations became extended the drawbacks of a system like this were felt. The advantages of payment in metal were recognized; convenience of transport and preservation were imperative. The Lemnians receive copper and iron for their wine; the Taphians exchange iron for copper; the warrior who has been struck down offers bronze, iron, and gold as ransom. But advantage is not taken of the divisibility of metal to give a fixed value to a determined quantity. For this it would have been necessary that almost all families should have a reserve of metals, that the scales should have been in general use, and that a single system of weights should have been generally adopted. Greece had not reached that point. It had only kept the gold standard used in the Mycenæan period, the talent. Its weight is not great, nor, in consequence is its value; a bronze caldron is worth more than two talents. But, since gold is rare in Homeric society, the talent is not used as current coin, nor even as a theoretical standard. There could be no question of silver—there is too little of it. Bronze and iron, on the other hand, are very widespread. For want of a large enough balance they are not weighed but measured. They are shaped into utensils of constant types, in graduated sizes or capacities. Thus there is a utensil-currency. The iron disk which Achilles proposes as a prize is the maximum of the regulation weights; the axes and double axes of iron are units and multiples analogous to the normal axes of copper which had come from Cyprus from the most remote times.

FIG. 1. GOLD DISK FROM MYCENÆ. (Perrot, Vol. VI, Fig. 540.)

Other objects were better suited to exchange because they were used in all houses—caldrons and tripods. People acquired them for domestic use, but also as a form of investment. They varied in size or capacity, weight, and value; for example a caldron of four measures is worth over two gold talents. But these utensils were, like the talents, instruments of exchange and not units of value. In the Homeric poems an object is never assessed at so many tripods or caldrons, whereas we hear mention of a tripod worth twelve oxen and a caldron worth one.

Trade, which began on the sea, found no facilities on the land of Greece. High mountains, swampy valleys, and raging torrents or their dry beds opposed continual obstacles to communications. Goods were generally carried on the backs of men or mules. Carts with two or four wheels were also used, but these vehicles were fragile, and if there was an accident no cart-wright was to be found in the neighbourhood. "If the axle breaks," says Hesiod later, "the load is lost." The roads were those which the Mycenæans had made, with ruts cut in the rock and doubled in places for vehicles to pass. If any new roads existed they were equally narrow and broken by short steep gradients. They were however improved and widened as they approached the big towns, fortresses, and ports. For all their shortcomings these roads made communication possible at long distances. From Pylos to Sparta a vehicle takes two days, with a few hours' rest at night.

It is navigation which keeps foreign relations active. We see remarkable progress taking place in the division of marine labour. The transport of passengers and goods is organized. Once it had been a serious matter to embark in a boat which you did not own yourself. There was a great temptation for the sailors to sell you and seize your luggage, and you had to buy your liberty in advance. The Sidonian woman who obtained her return home from sailors of her own country gave them for the fare (*epibathron*) three gold vases and a little slave. A Cretan who wanted to go to Pylos appealed to Phœnicians and handed over to them "a fair portion of his treasure." But now traders are no longer obliged to have a ship of their own or to hire one. Transport is ensured, often by public services. Between Ithaca and the mainland ferries take men and beasts over the straits. Among the Thesprotians the king's ships carry passengers to Dulichion and Ithaca. The Phæacians are "excellent sailors who are accustomed to convey strangers." This practice has become so regular that in the *Odyssey* a special word, *emporos*, designates "the passenger who pays a fee, having neither ship nor rowers," "the passenger brought by a ship which continues on her way after putting him down"; and the passenger is so commonly a merchant that it was not long before this word was applied to the wholesale importer.

Thus towards the end of the Homeric period the language of business begins to develop. Capital and brains combine in business partnership; a Cretan and a Phœnician found a house for export to Libya. The usages of war are passed on to peaceful transactions through piracy, and tend to create an embryo of commercial law. Profits are shared according to the same rules as booty—the captain has first pick out of the whole, in return for the cost of the ship and the conduct of the expedition, and the rest is equally divided among all partners, including the captain. Already, too, in a maritime town, the leaders have other things to do than to go on board themselves; they form a veritable Admiralty, or, in the Athenian phrase, they are the " Prytaneis of the Naucraries." They leave the command of the ships to subordinates. Ship-owners are no longer skippers, and they grow rich from shipping without going to sea.

The Scheria of the Phæacians shows the highest development of a commercial town in the Homeric age. The whole of its life centres on the harbour, with its slips and its stores. New requirements create in marine matters a separation of functions which were formerly merged. A city appears in which agricultural interests do not predominate. Therefore in certain places the landed and military aristocracy is succeeded by an aristocracy of wealthy ship-owners. The epic, which was born in Æolian country on the acropoles of rural townships, is transported to the palaces of Ionia built beside the sea; and it abandons great sword-blows to sing the subtle daring of heroes who bring " boundless riches " from far away. Poetry, anticipating history, heralds the greatness of Miletos.

Homeric Greece could not therefore confine its activities to the limits of the Ægean. Its horizon becomes wider. All these sailors, burning " to visit many cities and to know the manners of divers peoples," amass a wealth of geographical information and open many lasting connexions.

From Thrace came wines, fine swords, and precious vases. Lydia and Caria were renowned for their carved and painted ivories. Cyprus exported copper, and to maintain good relations with the Peloponnese its king sent Agamemnon a magnificent cuirass. But trade looked especially to Phœnicia and Egypt, without neglecting the neighbouring countries as far as Ethiopia and the obscure people of the Erembi. The Phœnicians went themselves to Greece to exchange silver vases, trinkets, carpets, and glass-ware for corn, cattle, wine, and slaves; but the more enterprising of the Greeks competed with them in their own country. Egypt, that rich and inoffensive land, attracted adventurers from everywhere. Formerly it had appeared so remote that, it was said, no one ever hoped to come back from there. Men came back, and the fable was shattered. "The favourable breath of Boreas," says Odysseus, "bore us away from long Crete as swiftly as a river; in five days we came to the mouth of the fair Ægyptos." The Greek traveller now knows that behind the isle of Pharos he will find a safe anchorage and that if you go up the river long enough you come to the city with a hundred gates, Thebes where the gold abounds. From there you can bring back precious metals in the shape of bars or of works of art, linen cloth, ivory, papyrus fibre for ropes, ointments, perfumes, and medicines. Many Greeks go to seek their fortune in Egypt. In Ithaca there was a very rich old man who was called "the Egyptian," whose youngest son followed his example in running after adventures. Lastly, the Peloponnesians and above all the Cretans visited the regions of Libya. A Phœnician merchant who wants to do business there takes a Cretan for guide, as the men of Thera did later. Here we have, in the history of trade and colonization in Africa, a valuable landmark between the visits of the Minoans, followed by the Akaiwasha, and the foundation of Cyrene.

On the side of the western seas the Greeks of the Homeric period seldom went beyond the line of islands which fringed their country. Pylos stood at the end of the great route which ran from Lesbos and Chios to Eubœa by sea and avoided the storms of Cape Malea by crossing Bœotia, the Isthmus of Corinth, Mycenæ, and Sparta. Pylos thus became an important market and a unique centre of information. The island of Cephallenia marked the limit of the accessible world. Beyond, towards the north, were unbounded sea, winds ever hostile, and awful lands of fable. Yet some fearless sailors made their way as far as Corcyra and even to the tip of Italy. Slaves were exchanged in Sicily. To go further was an enterprise beyond the power of men. To escape the whirlpools of Charybdis the sailor must go close under the enormous rock from which Scylla used to spring, and he must battle with awful gales and still more deadly magic. Nevertheless it was by this route that the Greeks procured silver. The precious metal came from Alybe, the land where dwelt " men surrounded by the sea," which can only be the Iberian peninsula. Odysseus is well received there in the palace of Aphidas the Wealthy; the Samian who discovered Tartessos at the end of the VIIth century had his predecessors.

In spite of the dread with which the mists of the north inspired the Greeks brave explorers ventured among them. From the Hellespont they attempted expeditions into the Euxine. They crossed, in the bad season, a sea on which " the shadows darkened every road "; they came to " peoples for ever wrapped in clouds and mist." They saw the terrible winter in which " awful night ever hangs over unhappy mortals." Thus they reached the lands of the Læstrygons and the Cimmerians. But how far did these heroic pioneers go ? Far enough, in any case, to bring back definite ideas of the long days and light nights of the northern summer. The stories of these journeys were not forgotten by the navigators.


This first survey of the commercial relations of the Greeks allows us to obtain a glimpse of the future in the epics. Household economy still predominates. But city economy has already made such progress that enterprising men leave their city to seek foreign commodities at great distances, and they are beginning to create some kind of Mediterranean economic system. The time will come when the Greeks will be able to defend themselves against the invasion of foreign merchants and to compete with them on distant markets. They, who formerly spoke with admiration of Sidonian goods, now have nothing but contempt and hate for the deceitful Phœnicians. But they still lack something to triumph completely over these tenacious rivals—their industry is still in its childhood. Let them increase their cargoes of natural products and supplement them with manufactured goods, and they will conquer the world.

# PART TWO
# THE ARCHAIC PERIOD

## CHAPTER I

### ECONOMIC TRANSFORMATION. LAND AND MONEY

THE social phenomena which before the end of the VIIIth century had brought about remarkable changes in the economic life of Greece were to act with increasing intensity during the two and a half centuries of the following period, the archaic. More and more the *genos* breaks up and within the narrow family the power of the father becomes weaker; the growing freedom of the individual keeps pace with the growing strength of the State. The survivals of collective ownership vanish in favour of personal ownership. There are awakenings of initiative and releasings of energy.

At all costs other resources must be found than those of the land. The total of wants grows to dimensions which the total of agricultural output cannot attain. The population increases so fast that war which "relieves the earth, nurse of men" comes to be regarded as a blessing from Zeus. The problem of material existence becomes acute in the tangible shape of the progressive diminution of patrimonies by division among successors. Peoples and individuals are driven by vital necessity to seek outside not only superfluities but their daily bread, and not only the raw materials which their own country does not yield but the foodstuffs which it does not yield in sufficient quantity. Greece must make up for the insufficiency of agriculture by trade and industry.

Nevertheless the change was neither general nor complete. Family industry everywhere continued to play its part in economic life. The terra-cottas of the period frequently represent woman at her work, washing clothes and making bread. In the country especially home work retained much of its importance. In Bœotia the farmer still made his own plough and waggon.

The family organization, holding its own in the agricultural towns, gave them a conservative and often aristocratic character. The territorial divisions of Teos were the domains formed by the noble families around a stronghold or *pyrgos*. In Sparta, Crete, and Thessaly the old system of ownership was maintained, the sale and division of certain lots were forbidden, and the owners of the ground made considerable use of serfs. Elis was ruled by kings, like the Homeric Scheria, and contained only villages. It was not till the VIIth century that it limited the collective responsibility of the *gene*, and it first had a town in 472. Even then the country people adhered obstinately to the " sacred life " of their ancestors, and there were families in which for two or

Fig. 2. Women kneading bread to the sound of the flute. Terracotta from Bœotia, in the Louvre. (*B.C.H.*, Vol. XXIV, Pl. ix.)

three generations no one had ever gone to the town. Mountainous and poor districts remained faithful to the pastoral system and the old ways. In Phocis and Locris slavery was almost unknown. Acarnania and Ætolia presented even to Thucydides a picture of Homeric society, with brigandage and piracy.

Elsewhere the family system collapsed in favour of individualism. Certain cities thus came to obtain democratic institutions and to find the main source of their power in trade and industry. But even these long gave the farmers an important place both in politics and in economic life. In Attica most of the demes had a *genos* for nucleus, and the customs which governed them were made for peasants. When Athens was the economic capital of the Greek world

## LAND AND MONEY

the great majority of her citizens were still tilling the soil and living in the country.

Where agricultural life predominated the old methods of assessment persisted and payments were ordinarily made in kind. Under the Roman domination certain lease-contracts still provided for payment of rent in corn, oil, and wood; in the archaic period clauses of this kind were the common rule. In Sparta towards the end of the VIIIth century the State gave cattle in exchange for a house. Nothing could be more natural in a country in which the Helot paid his dues in barley, wine, and oil, and the citizen must contribute for the public meals barley-meal, wine, cheese, figs, and only ten obols in coin. A similar state of things prevailed in Attica until the time of its great prosperity. Dracon assessed certain fines in oxen; Solon was the first to convert the bounties granted by the treasury into coin. The citizens were classed by their production of dry and liquid goods. Peisistratos demanded of the peasants the tithe of their harvest. So, when Athens began to coin money, specie had an enormous purchasing power there; a sheep or a medimnus of barley ($1\frac{2}{8}$ bushel) cost one drachma ($9\frac{1}{4}d$.). In Sicily, long after the wealthy cities had struck beautiful coins, the country people weighed copper to pay for their minor purchases, and paid their tax in corn.

This vitality of natural economy was bound up with the very progress made by agriculture. The reclamation of waste land which had begun in the time of the epics went on apace. The *eschatie* disappeared. Woods were cut down ruthlessly. Zacynthos, covered with forests in the *Odyssey*, was stripped bare in historical times. Cyprus saw the adornment of its mountains diminish, and Attica soon had nothing but underwood. But agriculture chiefly attacked the pasture-land. It annexed the best, and then the less good. Stock-breeding lost land, and, with it, importance. For want of grazings cattle became rare. A significant change in the public diet took place. The heroes of Homer ate meat in quantities; their descendants consumed little, and the common people only had it on holy festivals. So fish, so long despised, came into demand; the rich ate it fresh and the poor pickled. The shortage of meat food was chiefly made up by cereals. Henceforward a complete meal consisted of the *sitos*, in the shape

of bread or porridge, and the *opsonion*, which was a mere
" extra " of fish, fruit, or vegetables.

The results of the reclamation of waste land at once
appeared in social and political life. The heads of the powerful
families had set the example of cultivating new ground and
had taken their choice of the suitable land. The barren
portions were left to the poorer peasants. When Hesiod's
father came and settled "near Helicon, in the wretched
valley of Ascra, bad in winter, unpleasant in summer, and
good never," he had to put a piece of waste under cultivation
to obtain a little corn, a little wine, and a few beets. In
Attica the nobles owned the whole plain and sent their flocks
and herds into the mountains. Eventually small agriculturists replaced the herdsmen on the stony hill-sides, and
the Eupatrids were confronted with the party of the Diacrians.

In spite of the extension of land under cultivation the
production of cereals did not increase greatly. The methods
and implements did not change: fallow in alternate years;
three ploughings a year with the swing-plough and mellowing
of the sod with the hoe; the short-handled sickle for the
harvest; treading of the ears by the beasts. It is true that
reclamation entailed certain improvements; to deal with
slopes terraces were cut, to dry marshy bottoms large drainage
operations were effected, and for purposes of irrigation many
wells were dug and the use of the water was controlled in
great detail. But all this progress did not improve the sowing
of corn. The shortage of home-grown corn obliged the State
to pay attention to the food-supply. Even before she had
attained industrial and commercial power, Athens forbade
the export of agricultural produce in order to save her bread.

The newly conquered ground, being almost always dry
and stony, was best suited to tree-growing. Homer's Laertes
was a forerunner. The vine spread over considerable areas.
A whole swarm of places took their name (Œnoe) from it.
Dionysos was Hellenized and his feast became a national
holiday. As for the olive, the glory of ancient Crete, it now
grew everywhere, and its oil was used for food and lighting.
In Attica, where the noble tree was protected by the Goddess,
it was developed to such an extent that Solon authorized the
export of its oil. The island of Thera afforded a remarkable
instance of prosperity due to the new forms of cultivation.

## LAND AND MONEY

That mass of lava and pumice suddenly appeared adorned with vine and olive, and sending its overflow population abroad.

Henceforward agriculture in Greece had the characteristics which it would always preserve—shortage of grain and excess of wine and oil. Thus it caused a double current of exchange, guaranteed freights both ways to the merchant fleet, and contributed to the international division of labour. Commercial economy was inaugurated, to be encouraged subsequently in every possible way. Following the example of the Phœnicians, the Greeks renounced violent methods and did regular trade with the barbarian peoples. Little by little they established themselves on every shore of the Mediterranean. By colonization they continued beyond the seas the progressive occupation of arable land, extended their country immensely, and, in every new Greece, monopolized the profits of trade. The simultaneous development of agriculture and colonization gave a fruitful impulse to industry. To store great quantities and good qualities of liquid products the potteries were constantly at work, and applied themselves to artistic experiments. The demands of the colonists, who were accustomed to the metal and textile goods of their mother city, encouraged the manufacturers to more intense production. Industry in its turn stimulated trade. As a result of all these causes together, the time was gone when exchanges were made directly between producer and consumer; between one country and another, and within the same city, they had a middleman in the trader. Direct exchange, *autopolike*, gave place to indirect exchange, *metabletike*.

At the same time as the commercial system, city economy assumed dimensions hitherto unknown. For a long time the city had comprised, with a certain number of villages on which it lived, a centre provided with a market-place and often with a port. Even in the epics some of these centres had grown large. From the VIIIth century onwards the phenomenon became general. The progress made by agriculture increased the number of exchanges, and the local market became sufficiently important to transform a village into a town. When this town was situated by the sea it might even extend its relations and attract the produce of the interior without changing in its essential character. Cyme in

Æolis, for all its wealth, maintained the manners of old times and brought ridicule upon its head for waiting over three hundred years before it levied harbour dues. At Locri the law compelled the peasant to sell his produce direct to the consumer. But the towns which rose to the first rank were those which combined the advantages of a fertile territory and a good harbour with the resources given by industry or by an exceptionally good situation.

At first it was the centres on the coast of Asia Minor which took the lead. The neighbouring valleys, which sent them foodstuffs and precious metals, obtained from them receptacles for wine and oil, the inland plateau supplied their textile works with wool, the great overland trade-routes brought them the models which they had long needed, and the great sea trade-routes started from them in every direction, especially towards the Euxine. All this was what made the greatness of Miletos. In Europe Chalcis obtained from her copper mines and forges a speciality which she exploited largely, thanks to intelligent colonization. When Greece came to expand over the whole circuit of the Mediterranean, business would concentrate near the isthmus where the Hellenic East and West met, in Corinth, Ægina, and Athens.

The international division of labour, which the supply and demand of agricultural produce were sufficient to determine, was greatly advanced by colonizing, commercial, and industrial activity. In Greece the progress of city economy and that of international economy can hardly be distinguished, so constantly was the development of its towns bound up with external trade, and so rapidly were its markets brought into touch by shipping.

Such active movement as this could not put up with any uncertainty in weights and measures, and still less in means of exchange. In this respect the Homeric age left much to be done. How was definite progress realized ?

One result of the numerous political divisions of ancient Greece was that there was always a great variety in the metrical systems. Uniformity would have seemed a violation of autonomy. But, although the standards were very varied, they were always borrowed from one of the great

## LAND AND MONEY

systems which had prevailed in the East from time immemorial; they were based on identical principles. Moreover a large number of towns which came late into commercial life adopted, under the force of circumstances, the weights and measures of the port which had won economic preponderance. Two systems thus came to prevail, the *Æginetan* and the *Euboic*.

These systems had already become greatly extended when ingots, bars, and utensils of metal were still being used as means of exchange. Since the use of the balance had become general this mode of payment had not been as inconvenient as before, at least for small sums paid in common metals. Caldrons and tripods remained in circulation in the towns of Crete, iron was used in the exchanges of the Spartans until the IIIrd century, and in Sicily and Italy the practice of reckoning in pounds of copper continued for a long time. For greater convenience the Greeks had conceived the idea of issuing iron in little thin rods, called *obols*, and of combining six obols in a " handful " or *drachma*. But it was no use; objects of base metal could only suffice for local and unimportant transactions. The precious metals, cast in ingots or cut into disks, gave rise to all kinds of complications and frauds; at each payment the metal had to be weighed and its standard of purity determined. When commercial operations had become wider and the public power had become stronger the State guaranteed the weight and the fineness of each piece by affixing its name and emblem.

This need first made itself felt on the confines of the Greek world and the Eastern world; and there, at the beginning of the VIIIth century, money was invented. Lydia, the land of the Pactolos, lay on the great road from Asia to the Ægean Sea. The capital, Sardis, was the caravanserai whence goods from every source were sent forth in every direction. Its rulers, the Mermnadæ, worked with great energy to encourage relations with the Greeks of the seaboard. They guaranteed honest dealings by giving an authentic value to the precious metal in which payment for them was made. The earliest coins were intended to facilitate the relations of Lydia with the Greek ports.

For a long time only the precious metals were coined. The oldest pieces are of electron, a pale gold which was yielded in abundance by the Lydian washings and contained an average of 30% of silver. Of these coins the most popular were the staters of Lydia and Phocæa. The kings of Sardis were also the first to coin pure gold and silver. The gold stater weighed half the electron stater, while the silver stater weighed two-thirds of the gold. When they adopted this scale of weights the Persians fixed the value of the silver

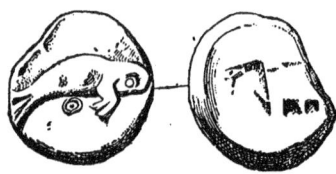

FIG. 3. ELECTRON STATER OF PHOCÆA. (*D.A.*, Fig. 6984.)

standard at a twentieth of the gold standard. They thus established between the two metals a relation of $1 : 13\frac{1}{3}$. The good alloy of the Persian coinage and its conformity to the Phocæan standard brought the gold daric on to the Greek market. Greece in its turn accepted the ratio of $1 : 13\frac{1}{3}$. Thus the monetary system of Persia had considerable effects on the monetary system of the whole ancient world. It was a fruitful experiment in bi-metallism.

From Asia the practice of striking coins was quickly communicated to Europe. In less than a century it was adopted in the greater part of the Greek world. But the

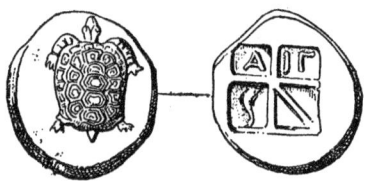

FIG. 4. SILVER STATER OF ÆGINA. (*D.A.*, Fig. 6567.)

countries to the west of the Ægean did not produce gold, except the small island of Siphnos, and the little which they possessed was immobilized in the temples. In exceptional cases they struck electron, but never gold. The predominant system was silver monometallism. Each of the two prevailing systems of weights and measures was supplemented by a monetary system. The Æginetan standard imposed itself

## LAND AND MONEY 69

for a long time on Greece proper, and many towns even confined themselves to giving free circulation to the "tortoises" of Ægina. The Euboic standard had modest beginnings, in Chalcis and Eretria, but later it expanded to a remarkable extent. It was adopted in Corinth and Athens, out of rivalry with Ægina, and Chalcidian colonization and Corinthian trade opened to it Chalcidice in Thrace, Cyrenaica, and almost the whole of Greater Greece and Sicily.

In spite of its rapid development money economy did not kill natural economy. In the middle of the VIth century hardly any town except the big cities of Asia Minor and the Saronic Gulf had a mint. The two systems existed side by side, and the advance of the one or the persistence of the other is a certain indication by which we may estimate the economic situation of a city. There is a great difference between rural or closed-in countries and those enriched by a port, and even between the countryside and the town in a commercial state. But, in spite of these distinctions, in Greece as a whole there prevails, from the VIIth century onwards, an economic system which is commercial, urban, and, consequently, monetary. The effects of this transformation were to be immense from every point of view.

The very conditions of commercial life were bound to alter rapidly. In such a matter all is action and reaction. The development of trade has made a practical and certain instrument of exchange necessary, and the invention of money contributes mightily to the expansion of trade. Without ceasing, new wants give rise to new means for satisfying them. Merchants, ship-owners, and private individuals plan operations and contracts of infinite variety. Credit gives transactions an amplitude hitherto unknown. Cash dealings are extended into credit dealings. The money of others is usefully employed through extensive borrowing at interest, especially bottomry loans. In next to no time the commercial genius of the Greek rises to the notion of speculation and forestalling. All means are fair to acquire movable fortune, and capital accumulated is only an investment with a view to accumulating more. Thus there grows up a system which is already capitalist, in opposition to the primitive "economy," and it is called *chrematistike*. Of the two systems Aristotle has made an analysis which is as penetrating as it is biassed. " Economy " had for its object the satisfaction of natural wants by the acquisition of such natural goods as were strictly necessary for life in common, and it legalized the use of natural means, agriculture, stockbreeding, fishing, hunting, war, and piracy. The "chrematistic" system set out to satisfy artificial wants and to accumulate wealth in the form of money, which is useless in itself, by means of trade, which creates no value and has no other object than gain. After making the reservation that Aristotle is the first of the Physiocrats, we may accept this as a true picture of the order of things which begins in Greece in the VIIth century.

One consequence of this new situation was a complete change in moral ideas. What they became in these strongly individualistic and commercial societies we can easily guess when we observe the outburst of energy in every direction, the sudden rise of cities to prosperity and power, and the growth of a civilization which heralds all the glories of future centuries. But it is natural that the poets of the day should have bitterly compared the new notions with the old ideal, and should have prepared arguments for the philosophers who sided with the agrarian and conservative aristocracy. Whereas Homer described in brilliant colours the life of heroes with a well-balanced conscience, Hesiod finds nothing all round him but toil and misery, and he sadly takes refuge in past ages. The downfall of the family—that is the worst he sees in the Iron Age, his own time. The breaking of sacred ties has driven away all notions of justice and hard work. Selfishness seeks to triumph by bad faith and violence, and turns aside from fruitful labour. It is here that Hesiod, all unconsciously, shows himself the child of his time. Formerly ideas about work were all based on the "self-sufficiency" of the family;[1] each did his task and took it as a matter of course. To-day idleness is a more frequent fault, and consequently the necessity for work is better understood. " The idle man is a greedy hornet which grows fat, without doing anything, on the labour of the bees. . . . He who works sees his herds increase and his fortune swell. . . . If your heart is possessed with the desire for riches, you have only to work, and to go on working." There is nothing

[1] See p. 8.

humiliating in this obligation; it is the law of Zeus. Work is thus sanctified; it redeems man and ennobles him. " By work you will become dearer to gods and men. To work is never a shame; there is no shame but for idleness." Emulation therefore is mutual encouragement to fulfil the common duty. " It drives the laziest man to work. . . . · If he sees another growing rich he comes out of his laziness and hastens in his turn to plough, to plant, to manage his house. Neighbour eggs on neighbour by his keen desire for gain." From agriculture competition extends to industry—" Carpenter is jealous of carpenter, and potter of potter." And society as a whole profits by this struggle for betterment—" This rivalry is good for mortals."

Such profound changes in material and moral life must bring with them a social and political development. The possibility of increasing wealth and luxury without end, the insatiable greed which Solon denounced, all the unchaining of individualism inevitably led to inequality. The agrarian aristocracy, which took the initiative in the great colonizing and business enterprises, for some time enjoyed the profits of them exclusively, but in general it owed its strength to its possession of the land. Movable fortune, money, belonged to a class which was new or at least had hitherto been unformed, the Demiurges of the epics, now become the masters of trade and industry. Whether they held the land or the cash, the rich more and more needed plentiful workers. They found them chiefly among the Thetes, whom they reduced to serfdom in countries of large properties and to destitution in countries of the commercial system. The rest they obtained through the extension of slavery. Thus the individuals who were once united in the same group and dedicated to a common task were separated from one another by an increasing divergence of interests, and on the other hand they felt that they were at one with individuals who once belonged to other groups and had left them for the same reasons. Everything was ready for a class struggle. The landed nobility defended its privileges and its revenues either against the newly enriched merchants, who demanded a better distribution of justice and a fairer division of political rights, or against its tenants, who were crushed down by rent and wished to shake off their burden. Everywhere there were dissensions, disorders, revolutions. Finally the conflicts of interests, which set the citizens of one town against each other, let loose the great wars of rival cities, and in the VIth century we see all the commercial states of Greece crashing together in a furious confusion of struggles, pending the day when the whole of Greece, from the Ægean to the Tyrrhenian Sea, will have to form up against the barbarians.

CHAPTER II

SOCIAL TRANSFORMATION. THE CLASSES

WE have obtained a glimpse of the way in which the development of colonization, trade, and industry, the active circulation of money, and the growth of movable wealth determined, towards the VIIth century, a profound transformation in social and political organization. But we must, if we would understand the economic history of Greece down to the Persian Wars, lay stress upon the new relations which grew up between different classes, and consider the human element more closely.

1. THE UPPER CLASSES

From the end of the Homeric period and long afterwards the aristocracy is everywhere predominant. The heads of the great families take the style of kings. They are all " sons of Zeus," they all have right to the sceptre, they meet in council to pass resolutions which they announce to the people, and they form the court of arbiters which sits in the agora, in the " sacred circle." They hold the government in their hands.

Their power is based on possession of the soil and cattle. Whether they boast the name of Eupatrids, of Geomori, or of Hippobotæ, they monopolize the plough-land and pasture. A pious and interested tradition keeps patriarchal customs alive on their domains. When property has ceased to belong to the whole *genos* collectively it still remains subject to the right of the *genos* to repurchase it. Every estate must enable the master, his family, and a large staff to live. But production is no longer limited, as formerly, by the consumption of the family. Land is reclaimed and vine and olive are planted as extensively as possible. For it is possible to dispose of the surplus profitably, however large it may be. Part of it is lent to the needy peasant. For one medimnus of corn he will pay back one and a half at the next harvest;

for security the proprietor has not only the man's ground but his person and those of his wife and children. In every way the transaction is good; it increases the lender's revenue, his real estate, his circle of dependants, and, in addition, his political influence. Any of the surplus which is not employed in loans may be converted into cash. Money procures all the precious objects which are hoarded, and is itself the most precious of them all; but it is still better to use it for placing people in your debt, for extending your property, and for filling it with slaves. The days are gone when the great landowner worked with his own hands, aided by his sons and a few servants. In countries which belong to a conquering race the lords of the land, taken up with military exercises and public affairs, turn the conquered race into serfs attached to the soil. In countries where the land-owners have time to manage their estates they endeavour to reduce insolvent debtors to a condition bordering on serfdom, but have recourse chiefly to slaves and hired men. Manual labour now inspires only the contempt of those who profit by it.

The occupation suited to nobles is that of arms. Their fathers gave to reiving all the time which their work in the fields left them. The sons have inherited their warlike instinct and their spirit of domination, but they have nothing in common with those who cultivate their land. For the noble alone has the complete armour which makes the warrior like a man of bronze, the chariot, the footmen, and above all the horse, which ensures superiority on the battle-field. " It is in the countries suited to horse-breeding," says Aristotle, " that the establishment of the oligarchic system is most natural." This nobility of horsemen has for its privilege the right to wear a sword, *siderophoria*. They were proud of it, and when a haughty Eupatrid was laid in his tomb his arms were buried with him. They abused the privilege, carrying on terrible blood-feuds. So, whenever a lawgiver or a tyrant means to stand up to the aristocracy, his first care is to forbid *siderophoria*. The disappearance of weapons from the graves of Athens marks the triumph of democracy.

Despite its preference of rural and military life the nobility eagerly sought after the luxury which movable wealth can

## THE CLASSES 75

give. The transformation of rapine into peaceful trade had not caught it napping. Although capital was so small, yet to set an enterprise afoot a certain outlay was necessary. Advances could only come from those who had enough land to increase their production beyond their needs; the fine ships " with hollow sides " which brought home so much wealth could only be built for men who were already wealthy. The big merchants and the big ship-owners therefore often belonged to the landed aristocracy. At Miletos the same class drew large revenues from stock-breeding and sat in the council of the *Aeinautai*. In Chalcis the Hippobotæ who watched their colts galloping over the plain supervised the working of their copper-mines and sent their transports to the colonies. In Corinth the Bacchiadæ made business genius a family tradition, and absorbed the government of the city into the firm. Even in countries where agriculture was done on a large scale sons of good families did export business; the Lesbian Charaxos, Sappho's brother, used to go to Egypt with cargoes of wine. Thus in many big towns no distinction appears between the landed aristocracy and the merchant aristocracy.

But where the nobility did not rejuvenate its economic ideas in time it was the most active and intelligent of the Demiurges who took the first place in commerce and industry. Thus there were cities in which those with movable wealth for some time formed a class apart. This does not mean that in these cities a few individuals did not detach themselves from the nobility to try their luck in business; but they had to brave the prejudices of their class and they sank socially. Such was the case, in Athens, with Solon, an outcast Eupatrid among the tradesmen. Such was the case, in Megara, with certain nobles who were despoiled by the democrats and were defended by Theognis for seeking resources in commerce. But these very instances show to what an extent men whose fortune was not rooted in the soil were kept at arm's length by men of birth who owned land. None the less they came to exercise great influence. In Ægina, a barren islet where the land-owners led a mean existence, the merchants who succeeded in establishing relations with the Peloponnese suddenly became masters. The power which lay with the business men of Ionia may be compared to that of the Lombard and Florentine bankers of the Middle Ages.[1]

Between the nobles and the rich commoners relations varied. At the beginning there were violent collisions. In Athens political rights went only with landed property, even after the reforms of Solon. This bar gave formidable leaders to the mass of discontented. The Demiurges combined with the peasants against the Eupatrids and secured equal rights for agricultural wealth and movable wealth. The constitution no longer made any difference between the rich.

But custom still made such a difference. Then the princes of trade and industry tried to obtain landed property; the parvenus passionately coveted the goods the possession of which was a mark of nobility. All means were fair to them. Revolutions led to the confiscation of estates; here excellent purchases were to be made cheaply. But the commoner desired above all to find a noble who, to dung his fields, was resigned to a misalliance. " Well-born men," Theognis exclaims, " do not scorn to marry a base woman, a base man's daughter, provided she bring them plenty of money. Money, that is what they appreciate." But the poet's indignation is in vain; he was born too late.

Thus, while the noble makes money in business, the moneyed man invades landed property. They meet half-way and treat each other as equals. " Money mixes the classes," Theognis grumbles once more, " and it is not without reason that men honour you above all, O Plutos; for through you the base man becomes noble." And indeed the merging of the two aristocracies creates a kind of plutocracy. Even in the countries which are destined to a democratic future the citizens are classed according to their income, and rights and honours are made proportionate to fortune. Already the

---

[1] The heads of the State applied to these bankers for loans. Here is a characteristic anecdote. Crœsus has to raise an army in his father's name. He has no money. He seeks out the wealthiest merchant in Lydia. The latter sends word that he is in his bath, and the royal petitioner is left to dance attendance at the door. At last the merchant consents to receive him, but answers him with a callous refusal. " If I had to lend money to all the sons of Alyattes," he says, " I should not have enough." After this rebuff Crœsus goes to Ephesos. There Pamphaes, whom he does not scorn to call " my dear friend," gets a loan for him out of his father, 1,000 gold staters. In all times millionaires have been courted by princes.

# THE CLASSES 77

pirate in the *Odyssey*, "as his house grew, became mighty in his country and worthy of honour." A little later Hesiod said: "Virtue and glory follow riches." And now Alcæos utters this profound observation: "Money makes the man." History supplies a commentary on it in the interminable tale of furious struggles between the "good" and the "bad," the rich and the poor.

Wealth, thus formed into a class, requires industry and trade to procure new delights for it and to seek precious commodities for it in every country. As there are no bounds to the acquisition of wealth, there are none to the display of wealth acquired. In princely dwellings Eastern carpets and hangings show off the beauty of marquetery beds, finely carved

FIG. 5. MALE HEAD, KNOWN AS THE RAMPIN HEAD, IN THE LOUVRE. (*D.A.*, Fig. 1803.)

tables, and chairs plated with bronze, silver, and gold. Zealous slaves hand round plate and chased cups containing rare foods, exotic fruit, and old vintages, sweet or dry. In the temple or on the market-place the rich display the most gorgeous apparel. Purple cloaks show up vividly on snowy chitons which sweep the ground, golden grass-hoppers glitter about corkscrew curls, plaited or curly periwigs are twined with filigree, and wrists are clasped in bangles of exquisite workmanship. They go by, and leave a trail of scent behind them. As for the ladies, sculpture presents them adorned for some festival, and from their load of embroidered chitons we recognize those daughters of ancient lines whom Solon would have seen dowered with good land, while their fathers preferred to give them a trousseau worth a fortune. No ceremony gave occasion for such expensive ostentation as an interment. A whole family was on show, and the dead man at its head. He was buried in a profusion of magnificent winding-sheets, with bottles of scent, jewels, and, that he might still be served in his tomb, statuettes of hair-dressers, bakeresses, cooks, and confectioners. Whole hecatombs were sacrificed to him, and on the sepulchral sod his favourite wine

FIG. 6. MAIDEN OF ANTENOR, IN THE ACROPOLIS MUSEUM, ATHENS.
(*D.A.*, Fig. 6596.)

was poured from a bottomless vase. This prodigality was not all sheer vanity. When the individual is reckoned according to his wealth luxury becomes a political institution. As Aristotle observes, it is bound up with oligarchy as effect with cause. It makes manifest the distance separating the rich from the less rich, and fills up by an infinity of gradations the crude scale drawn up by constitutions.

## THE CLASSES

### 2. THE LOWER CLASSES

Below the rich the middle class was composed of citizens who earned their livelihood. First it comprised the country people. These were the owners of *kleroi*, in countries in which the law declared these patrimonies indivisible; where equal division was the rule, they were the land-owners to whom forbears not too prolific had handed down land of adequate size. In Attica they were called *Zeugitœ*, because they owned the pair of oxen necessary to produce two hundred measures of grain. In the towns this class absorbed the majority of the craftsmen. The number of these Demiurges had grown much greater since the Homeric period. The increase of demands and the improvement of tools had brought about in industry and commerce a division of labour hitherto unknown. The professions had grown numerous and enlarged their scope. Out of this mass certain persons were enabled by their wealth to detach themselves and to join the aristocracy, while others, who never succeeded in rising above the humble condition of hired men and small retailers, remained relegated to the proletariat of the Thetes. But those whose movable fortune was equal to a medium-sized landed property strove to obtain constitutional recognition of this equality. The middle class, carried along by the craftsmen who filled up its ranks, for a long time combated the political privileges of the nobility. Generally it took for its leader a tyrant and combined with all parties which had economic claims to press.

The lower class comprised the unhappy herd of Thetes. This name had at first designated the hired men, but now, the law consecrating the fact, it designated all who, for want of the legal minimum income, were not entitled to full citizen rights. For the mass of small craftsmen and labourers, seamen and retailers, industry and commerce may perhaps have provided a tolerable existence. But then what a difference there is between them and the peasants and agricultural workers! Seldom has a rural proletariat presented such a melancholy spectacle.

Already in the *Odyssey* the peasant who toils over a scrap

of reclaimed land is an object of great pity, and it is the last stage of degradation to be in the service of such a poor wretch. But the new times will be terrible for these unfortunates. The land is split up, and the prudent father wants only one son. The use of money produces disastrous effects in the country. Since all values are assessed in money, the scale of prices is set up to the disadvantage of the countryman, in consequence of his ignorance on the subject and of the extension of the market to new lands. Natural products are assessed very low—you can buy a medimnus of grain (1⅞ bushel) or a sheep for one drachma (9¼$d$.) and an ox for five. So the peasant needs money, and he cannot get it. Suppose he thinks of increasing his returns by improving his land. Then he must have a large sum. How is he to borrow it? Interest is enormous, because it is reckoned on the profits of overseas trade. For the same reason loans are short-date transactions. It is impossible to make up by intensive cultivation for the constant diminution of property and the low price of farm produce. There is no remedy; the peasant is condemned to drag out a mean existence on a piece of land which is too small and gives an indifferent yield.

What became of the sons of the man who had just enough to keep himself? What happened in bad years to the man who could hardly get along in the good years? The farmer in difficulties could only apply to the lord of the neighbourhood. Once it had been the glory of the great man to be for small men " an acropolis and a tower "; in the days when the only wealth known was that which was consumed, the rich man was glad to employ his surplus in extending his circle of dependants. But now that everything is bought and sold the big land-owner converts the surplus of his harvest into money. As luxury increases, he needs ever greater revenues and more land. He used to give; now he lends, and we know at what interest. Once in the toils of usury, the peasant is lost. The best that can befall him is that his creditor should be content with his land as security. He sells it with a right of redemption. The day of payment arrives, and he has not the sum due; the stone set in his field in sign of mortgage becomes the sign of permanent alienation. But as a rule the debtor is compelled to pledge not only his property but his person and those of his wife and children.

## THE CLASSES

If he is insolvent he is not only evicted from his property; he falls, with all his family, into the power of a master who can do with them what he will. Many unfortunates are sold abroad. More often the new owner leaves the old on the land which was once his; he will be one tenant the more. In this way small ownership is gradually replaced by the system of *colonatus*.

In Attica at the beginning of the VIth century the condition of the tenant appears in the darkest colours. He is called the Hectemor, the *hektemoros* or "sixth-parter." The sixth part of the returns, from which he takes his name, is not what he owes to the landlord, but what he keeps. We have here not a mere *méayage* on fairly easy conditions but exploitation to the last ounce, which gave rise to terrible hatreds. This abomination actually existed in Attica—of the grain which he produced in the sweat of his brow the farmer had a right to one sixth only. Two classes stand face to face: the great landlords own almost all the ground and the greater part of its returns, and the tenants, attached to the soil, work and die of hunger.

For a long time this excess of misery seemed to be beyond remedy. The great held in their hands the wealth, the military power, and all other powers, including justice. There was no resort against the worst cruelties; the Eupatrids handed down the customs in their own families and interpreted them as they fancied. In the lines of Hesiod we hear the cry of despairing generations. The law of the stronger reigns in the whole of nature. A series of falls has lowered man to the rank of the wild beasts; the Iron Age has inaugurated the struggle of all against all. Woe to the weak! The only attitude which becomes them is that of the nightingale in the talons of the hawk, resignation. Yet one hope remains: from a moral and religious reformation social rebirth may come. Some must submit cheerfully to the divine obligation to work; let the others remember that Zeus sends thirty thousand messengers to watch mortals, and his daughter, infallible Dice, reports all iniquities to him.

The mystics were followed by the politicians, the resigned by the violent. From individual sentiments there is born soon or late a collective conscience. All who suffered from arrogant pride or pitiless rapacity wrested a first concession from the nobles. The chief prayer of Hesiod was granted and Dice received satisfaction of a precious kind: the laws were published. But the aristocracy held and reinforced its other positions. Then the class struggle broke out everywhere. In most cities it went on for ever, in a succession of savage revolutions and reactions in turn. To what a pitch of frenzy hatred rose we know from the aristocrat Theognis. He burns "to drink the black blood of his adversaries." He bitterly regrets the time when the " stupid " rabble were in their proper place, and the base, " with a goatskin about their sides, browsed outside the walls like deer," where the brutes " knew neither law nor right." For him there is only one good rule—" It is right that all the good people should own the wealth and that the base should toil in misery."

One city, however, was able to make an equitable solution of the agrarian question, the city in which the contrast between the big landlord and the tenants was perhaps the most flagrant —Athens. When Solon was given the mission of putting an end to the crisis the evil seemed desperate. He was able to remedy it. By suppressing every form of slavery that burdened the land of the *genos* he encouraged the transfer of the soil. Moreover he declared the person of the humblest citizen inviolable, forbidding " loans on the person." By simply giving *Habeas Corpus* a retroactive validity he restored thousands of Hectemors to freedom; this was the *seisachtheia*, the " shaking-off of the burden." Nevertheless Solon did not abolish the division into classes based on landed property, and he refused to allow the land to be distributed. By a new reform the Demiurges were granted equal rights for landed and movable property. Then the peasants of the mountains, the sons of the Hectemors, obtained from the tyrant Peisistratos the ownership of the land which they occupied. Athens was ripe for democracy.

### 3. SERFDOM AND SLAVERY

Although serfdom never became established in Attica it was fairly widespread in Greece.

Like all social phenomena, it is of mixed origin. We first see it appear at the end of the Homeric period, from two sides

# THE CLASSES

at once. The slaves who are employed in the country far away from their master are already remarkably like serfs. Eumæos, who has a few savings and buys a slave, looks forward to the reward of good servants, a house, a wife, and a field. His dream is of a position intermediate between those of the freedman and the serf. Another example, that of Dolios working an orchard with his sons, shows us how the development of fruit-growing, and especially of vine-growing, contributes, as in our own Middle Ages, to the development of servile tenure. But, while a certain class of slaves rises to the limited freedom of serfdom, a certain class of free men sinks into it. A number of Thetes make engagements of fixed duration, and the "perpetual" period, at first susceptible of cancellation, becomes a reality. It is to the advantage of both parties to make the bond uniting them permanent and hereditary; the noble makes himself sure of certain returns, while the hired man obtains security for the morrow, an inferior kind of ownership—for no one can take him from the land which he makes fruitful by his toil—, and the hope of bettering his lot by increasing the returns. Thus free men were transformed into serfs by a kind of personal emphyteusis. Law, which relegated the Thetes in general to a class intermediate between full citizens and non-citizens, cast a fraction of the Thetes into a class intermediate between free men and slaves.

It was not possible for this development to become complete in all parts of Greece. The ancients were struck by the fact that wherever serfs existed a victorious race had reduced a conquered population to subjection; the Spartiates had their Helots, the Cretans their Mnoitæ and their Clarotæ, and the Thessalians their Penestæ. But serfdom is not based solely on the law of the spear. If it developed chiefly in countries where the land system was created by conquest, it was because in these countries, as a result of the conquest itself, the aristocratic system was particularly long-lived and could produce all its effects. Serfdom necessarily belongs to a time when a ruling class maintains an exclusive right over landed property and refuses to work for itself. In Greece, as elsewhere, the nobility was led by this twofold principle to settle on its lands workers whom it compelled to work them, in return for a portion of the produce, and forbade to leave them. Thus each was sure that his fields, being provided with the requisite labour, would bring him the revenue which he needed. And the material bond which attached the man to the soil was at the same time a personal bond which kept him under a master and prevented him from ever aspiring to the dignity of a citizen. The Dorian of Crete could sing, as he pointed to his great spear and his fine shield, " With these I reap, with these I harvest the sweet wine of the grape, and I make my serfs call me lord."

Where, on the other hand, land was alienable and divisible and was continually being split up, the proprietor had few labourers, and, since he worked it himself, he was hardly tempted to change them into serfs, whereby his revenue would have been diminished. If, moreover, trade and industry offered resources in addition to agriculture, the Thetes could find sufficient free work and need not all rush into servile tenure. Such was the case in Attica. But the crisis which precedes the reforms of Solon is so dramatic only because it puts the question whether or no the nobility will succeed in obtaining legal sanction for the economic dominion which it exercises over the Hectemors—in short, whether the Thetes shall be serfs or citizens. But for the *seisachtheia* Athens was becoming a smaller Sparta.

While serfdom remains localized, the development of slavery is one of the most general phenomena which the collapse of the patriarchal system has produced. The family in its reduced form no longer furnished either the amount of labour or the variety of talents required to satisfy the wants which grew up with habits of well-being. To make up the deficit recourse must be had to slave labour.

More slaves were needed for house-work than formerly. Xenophanes said to Hieron, who asked him how many he owned, "Two only, and I can hardly feed them." If a philosopher minstrel, the enemy of luxury, and with good reason, speaks thus at the beginning of the Vth century, we may suppose that for a long time no Greek had been able to do decently without domestic servants. Nevertheless agriculture, the last refuge of patriarchal economy, employed very few slaves. The countries which would have needed them most used serfs in their stead. Elsewhere the small peasant took a farm lad and girl from the poor folk round about, and the big land-owner preferred free men to slaves in his own interest. In the fields as in the private houses slavery tended on the whole to maintain the household system while altering it.

But it helped to ruin it by giving a great power to the new organization of industry. The slaves who worked for the maintenance of the family could produce a surplus for sale. Thus began the manufacture of textiles on a large scale. In every house the servant-girls span, wove, and sewed. If there was a surplus it was taken to the market. So the women's apartment was quite ready to be turned into a workshop. Industrial slavery was at first distinguished from domestic slavery only by its greater output. At Miletos, for example, the wool industry procured its slaves in Phrygia and worked for export. Once the road was opened all industries rushed along it.[1]

It was in Asia Minor that slavery first expanded, keeping pace with industry. Chios was at that time the great slave-market. The traffickers in human flesh had no more scruples about exporting Greek slaves than about importing barbarian slaves. They bought families of insolvent debtors from their creditors; they sought out children to make eunuchs of them for the harems of Sardis or Susa. The prophets of Israel call down the divine wrath upon the Greeks who bring slaves to Tyre and on the Phœnicians who deliver children of Judah to the Ionians.

Impartial science is obliged to note the historical necessity and the useful effects of an institution which alone could enable the Greeks, when they had hardly emerged from the

[1] Industrial slavery made such progress that at an early date it suggested most ingenious methods of running a concern. Here is a story which has a fair substratum of truth. At Cyme there lived the slave of a cart-wright. One day an embassy came and asked him to be king of Lydia. He compensated his master and obtained his liberty. But a citizen of the town, who had ordered a chariot from him, opposed his departure, saying that he simply must have a chariot built by a king. This slave, then, was established on his own account; it was he who took and executed the orders. His master left the management of the house to him. The association of a free sleeping partner with a slave working partner is very usual in the classical period; it is curious to see it so early in a town which was very much behind its neighbours in Ionia.

family system, to soar to such heights immediately. But morality has its revenge. At once those sores of slavery appear, the gangrene of which spreads to the whole of society. The sight of the slaves at their drudgery modified ideas about work in a deplorable way. Already the aristocracy of the wealthy had only disdain for the craftsman and the agricultural labourer. All free men now felt contempt for slaves' tasks. To pass your days as a workman, to resign yourself to the trade of a *banausos* ! It was far better to earn your living as the nobles did; men rushed after adventures, and since piracy was no longer possible and colonization would not be so for ever, they enlisted as mercenary soldiers. And indeed the disastrous influence of slave labour on the position of the free worker justified the prejudice more and more. Periandros knew what he was about when, to fight the privileged classes in Corinth, he limited the number of slaves. Slavery lay like a load on the condition of the craftsmen and labourers. It tended to create ever greater inequality in the distribution of wealth, to make the situation of the middle class more precarious, and to change wealth to opulence and poverty to destitution.

CHAPTER III

# THE ECONOMIC AND SOCIAL LIFE OF SPARTA

NOWHERE in Greece did the economic system of the new times meet with such obstinate resistance as in Sparta. It is there that we must go to see what the system of family ownership can become in a state which is firmly resolved to maintain it in the midst of societies which grow more different every day.

But in making herself thus unique Sparta made herself a riddle for history. The other Greeks had difficulty in understanding a constitution by which the past claimed eternal life. How can we at this day distinguish the reality under a layer of biassed anecdotes? The historian who speaks of Spartan institutions must apologize beforehand for possible errors and almost unavoidable discrepancies.

Down to the VIIth century Sparta seems to have followed much the same evolution as the other cities, or at least those which owed their origin to the Dorian conquest. The conquering people established itself on the banks of the Eurotas and took possession of the whole of Laconia. The land was shared like booty; once provision had been made for the kings, the warriors drew lots for equal portions, the *kleroi*. Just as everywhere else, these estates belonged to families collectively. But, just as everywhere else, the decay of the patriarchal system and the search for greater wealth led to grievous inequalities which necessarily drove men to outside enterprises. In the time of the poet Tyrtæos " some were rich and others very poor." In countries which faced the sea the disinherited could take to piracy or colonization. But landsmen, who were accustomed to live in a compact group and to fight in close ranks, could not change themselves into sailors and scatter far afield. The discontented demanded a new distribution of land. Beyond the lean pastures of Taygetos they were shown the fat plains of Messenia, stretching as far as the eye could reach. At the end of the VIIIth century the Messenians were reduced to serfdom, " like asses laden with heavy burdens, forced to bring their masters the half of all their fruits." The conquerors proceeded to a new distribution of lots. This time everybody in Sparta declared himself satisfied.

They wanted things to be so to the end of time. By the constitution which they adopted the Spartiates hoped to perpetuate the state of ownership. The laws attributed to Lycurgos were forged by the logic of the conservative spirit. Before all it was necessary to keep intact a warlike organization which had passed the test, and should forestall or put down revolt. For that a fixed number of soldiers must be ensured an ample existence. Therefore at all costs a fixed number of sufficiently large estates must be maintained, they must be subject for ever to the system of family ownership, and all future generations must be bound to them by an indissoluble tie. The security of the State was guaranteed by providing its defenders with landed revenue. Thus the economic system of Sparta had no free play, for it had its end not in itself but in a political and military conception, and this is what gives the rigid lines and the unnatural aspect which it presents for hundreds of years.

The soil was henceforth divided into two parts, the ownership of which was governed by absolutely different rules— in the centre the *civic land*, and round it the *Perioikis*.

The *kleros* assigned to the family on the *civic land*, or, as it was still called, the " ancestral portion," was an inalienable patrimony, an entailed estate. The father could leave his other goods, if he had any, to the younger sons; the land must of necessity go to the eldest. This prohibition against selling or dividing a landed property is not peculiar to Sparta; we find it in Locris, in Elis, in Corinth, and in Thebes. But in other places the legislator has an economic and social object; here the predominant idea is that of common defence. Elsewhere the maintenance of the " Land Code " consecrates inequality; here absolute equality reigns, at least on the civic land, and, if the proprietors who hold it regard the other citizens merely as " Inferiors," the upper class which they form is that of the " Equals." Every precaution is taken against the smallest infringement of this equality. The lots are equal, and it is on the workers attached to the lots that

# SPARTA

inequalities in the return fall, for the rent is the same every year for all lots.

In the *Perioikis*, on the other hand, property underwent the same transformation as in the rest of Greece. It was individual, and so became alienable and divisible. While the Periœci held the greater part of it, the Spartiates acquired a large number of domains there. It was there that the younger sons, who were excluded from the entailed land of the family, could obtain a share of the inheritance.

Being sure of drawing their revenue regularly, the Spartiates did not need to take any part in the economic life of the country. For all occupations but those of the fields they had a profound contempt. Herodotos remarks that this attitude is common to all aristocratic cities except Corinth. But in Sparta it is a formal prohibition, and not merely an instinctive distaste, which prevents the citizen from working. The law does not allow him to ply a trade. It provides for his subsistence " in order that he may not put his hand to any work." Even agriculture, the noble profession *par excellence*, is forbidden to him. He owns land but has not the right to cultivate it. There is no instance of a Spartiate living in the country.

If the Spartiate had " abundant leisure," it was not that he might indulge in idleness. His life, which was very hard, was a perpetual training for war. This began in childhood and only ended in old age. At the age of seven he was " called up," went into a " herd," and had a course of gymnastic and musical training. Later he learned to handle arms and to perform more and more complicated movements; he belonged to a section (*enomotia*), a battalion (*lochos*), and a division (*mora*). Until he was thirty he slept in barracks; until he was sixty he took his chief meal at the mess. His whole time was taken up with route marches, manœuvres, and guard duty, when it was not spent in war. The Spartan people was an army perpetually mobilized and concentrated in advance. Sparta was like a camp.

The most characteristic feature of this life was the *pheiditia* or common meal. *Syssitiai*, or messes, existed in other places, but in Sparta the institution had a more aristocratic and military character. In Crete the State paid the expenses and the " comrades " or *hetairoi* had no subscription to pay.

## 90 ARCHAIC PERIOD

In Sparta all the expenses fell on the members of the association. The law, which assigned to each Spartiate a permanent income in kind, also laid down the quota of provisions which he must supply monthly in order to take part in the collective meals—an Æginetan medimnus (2 bushels) of barley meal, 8 *choes* (gallons) of wine, 5 minas (6¾ lb.) of cheese, 2½ minas (3⅔ lb.) of dried figs, and finally, for the meat, 10 obols (1*s.* 8¾*d.*). The burden was relatively heavy. The man who ceased to subscribe was excluded from the messes and lost the rank of citizen. And wealth was not enough; to be admitted to a table you must be co-opted by vote of the existing members. Thus the true Spartiates formed groups which, according to Plutarch, " had all the organization of secret societies and aristocratic clubs." But this political club was still a mess. Everywhere the Spartiate remained a soldier. " The messes and the training," Plato says, " were both alike invented by the law-giver with a view to war."

Being vowed for life to the god Ares, the Spartiates could not devote themselves to any professional, productive work. The heralds, the flute-players, and the cooks were taken on the hereditary principle from the same families; but this curious instance of Demiurges constituted into castes does not prove that a Spartiate could earn his living outside the army. On the contrary, it establishes that the Spartiates reserved to themselves the military offices of ambassadors, bandsmen, and army cooks. The other trades were not for them.

What, then, were the classes of workers which enabled the Spartiates to live without producing, to be land-owners without knowing anything of the land, to be soldiers without material cares ? For agriculture they depended on the Helots, and for trade and industry they had the Periœci. We must think of a country with 400,000 inhabitants, in which 25,000 members of the aristocracy are maintained by a serf population ten times more numerous and the trades give a livelihood to nearly 100,000 free men.

The Helots were " slaves of the State " allotted to individuals, and the law fixed their condition for ever. Each had his master, who could not send him away, nor sell him, nor change his personal status, nor increase or diminish his yearly rent. The State alone was competent to alter the

# SPARTA

clauses of a contract which it alone had dictated. The rights of the master were limited, and in regard to him the Helot was a serf, but the rights of the State were without limit, and in its eyes the Helot was a slave.

Since everything was arranged in order that the *kleros* might bring the Spartiate his fair revenue, it was necessary that the Helot should own a field, or rather that a field should own him. He cultivated a portion of ground in the way he pleased, but he could not detach himself from it. The same lot awaited his descendants to perpetuity. The rent to be paid was the same for all Helots. It did not vary according to the harvest; it was a fixed amount. The State knew what share of the produce a citizen required, and guaranteed it to him for ever. Each year the Helot must bring his master 70 medimni of barley for himself and 12 for his wife (altogether nearly 165 bushels), with a proportionate amount of wine and oil (probably 660 gallons of wine).

Since revenues had only a consumption value in Sparta this rent was quite enough to enable a family to live. The daily ration of the Spartiate was two chœnices of barley meal, that is, 15 medimni a year. With her 12 medimni the wife was well provided. So there were 55 medimni (100 bushels) for the children and servants. We see that the rent constituted a supply of food for a large family.

The Helot had in addition to supply his own seed and the food of his family. The system clearly did not allow for a large ration for these folk. However the Helot in the country got half the ration of a Spartiate, and less could not have been allotted to an agricultural worker. Moreover, if the Helots were not allowed to multiply beyond the demand, the demand was enormous; for the Helots must not only cultivate the fields but follow the army as servants, seven to a Spartiate and one to a Periœcos. In these circumstances the portion allowed for all the Helots on the *kleros* must have been at least equal to the portion due to the owner. After the first Messenian War the conquered were compelled to deliver half of the produce to their master every year; this is the tribute which was probably consolidated by law after the second war. In short, in an age of extensive culture, when hardly more than eleven bushels were obtained per acre and for every acre under corn there was an acre of fallow, the *kleros* which fed the proprietor and the workers must have been of a good size.

We must imagine the Helot as a large *métayer*, a tenant-farmer paying part of his produce as rent. His house is a centre of considerable activity. His land can only support the master's family if it also feeds a large staff of labourers. The Helot's family provides this labour; it is therefore a family whose head has many children or several households under his orders. The *kleros*, inalienable and indivisible, keeps up the family system not only among the absentee landlords but among the tenants.

Under this system one result of the absolutely fixed rent and of the wide extent of the domain was that the Helot fairly often attained to quite comfortable means. The rent had been laid down at a time of low returns. Therefore all the improvements done to the land were to the advantage of the man who tilled it and his children. If he took part in an expedition he had an opportunity for pillaging and could sell his booty. In the long run the development of agriculture brought about a twofold result in Laconia—the landlords, with an invariable income in natural products, were poor, and the tenants swelled their private earnings. In the IIIrd century, when King Cleomenes sold freedom to the Helots at five minas a head, he took 500 talents—6,000 Helots were in a position to pay a relatively large sum.

Even from the moral point of view Sparta, in spite of herself, raised the condition of the tenants. She was compelled to employ them in the army as servants, and sometimes as combatants. At Platæa there were seven Helots to a Spartiate; during the Peloponnesian War they frequently took part in military operations. By their acts of gallantry they several times obliged the State to make use of the right which it reserved to itself of freeing them.

But the more they were needed the more it was felt necessary to keep a strong hold on them. The sinister reputation with which posterity surrounds the institution of the Helots is not at all justified by their economic condition; it is, fully, by their legal situation. Nowhere, it has been said, is the free man freer than in Sparta, nor the slave more a slave. In fact the law hardly ever protects the Helot except where it is maintaining the rights of the

## SPARTA

State; it forbids the master to increase the rent, but also to grant liberty.

The numbers of the Helots, their aptitude for work, their comfortable means, and their courage as soldiers were an immense advantage and an immense danger. The Spartiates, lost among this multitude which they kept bowed over the sod, held them in obedience by fear. They felt themselves surrounded by enemies, and they could no more do without them than they could win their loyalty. They tried to debase them by ignominious treatment. If the Helots became too numerous man-hunts were organized and blood-letting was effected by means of the *krypteia*. They were watched unrestingly. If looks of more than usual hatred were surprised, or if bad news arrived from the war, at once brutal or secret executions were ordered. But Sparta spied and murdered in vain—the thought of her Helots always made her tremble.

Between the Spartiates and the Helots the Periœci held an intermediate position. They occupied a very extensive territory, but were scattered about the countryside and formed compact groups only in a few large towns. Nevertheless they were four times as numerous as the pure Spartiates. They were free men. They did not enjoy Spartan citizenship, but they counted as Lacedæmonians; their townships, although subject, ranked as cities, and there at least they were citizens. They were liable to military service and supplied the personnel of the fleet, but they could not attain the higher ranks.

Though subordinate to the Spartiates politically, the Periœci were their equals civilly. They even had an advantage, which, in reality, was a disability: neither their persons nor their goods were subject to the slavery endured by the nobles. They had the right to alienate the ground and to exercise such trade as suited them. So the Periœci were the only class in Laconia who showed activity, initiative, and independence in all the things of economic life. Difference in fortune divided them into " good men " and " base men." All professions were open to them. But the land did not attract them. The " civic " lots comprised the best-watered parts; even in the *Perioikis* the best hollows were reserved for the gods or for the State. Therefore those Periœci who took to agriculture were for the most part poor peasants.

Others went in for stock-breeding, which was more profitable. But the majority lived by the professions forbidden to the Spartiates and unattainable for the Helots, manufacture, trade, fishing, and navigation.

Now we must not imagine that Sparta was always hostile to industrial and even to artistic work. For a long time she was reckoned among the largest cities of Greece, and among those most adorned with monuments. It was only late that militarism put a stop to a development which till then had been normal, and gave Sparta the countrified, second-rate appearance which was to be remembered by posterity. The past was quite different.

Within a vast enclosure stood the temples of Artemis Orthia and Athene Chalcioecos. Hard by the potters made the *Lakaina*. They decorated it first with strokes and dots, then with animals and various figures, and finally with pomegranates. When they had completed their education they produced vases which were as good as those of Cyrene in wealth of form and beauty of ornament. After that came decadence; the beautiful white ground, the decorative motives, and the purple colour went, one after another.

With its iron-mines Laconia was a metallurgical centre from remote times. Sparta had its smiths' quarter, where they made arms, utensils, celebrated keys, and the national iron coinage. In the ruins of one single sanctuary 35,000 lead figurines have been found, which enable us to follow the development of industrial and artistic metal-work from the period of the Geometric style to the IVth century. The bronze-workers of Laconia early won a renown which archæology fully justifies. Gitiadas executed tripods surmounted by statues and adorned the temple of Athene with the bas-reliefs which earned it the name of "the House of Bronze." Theodoros of Samos was called to Sparta to decorate the Scias; there he taught the process of hollow-casting, and perhaps the most ancient specimen of it which we possess comes from Sparta. To do honour to Crœsus the Lacedæmonians sent him a magnificent mixing-bowl from their country.

For wood-work, as for pottery and metal-work, an artistic period was followed by a dull industrial period. From the earliest times the Spartiates had furniture—beds, tables, and chairs—of excellent workmanship. But the carved litters which would still appear in the classical period in processions would be no more than the last vestige of a once flourishing art. Nothing, of course, has remained of it but memories and names; we know that the old sculptors of Laconia, Hegylos, Theocles, Dutas, Doryclcidas, all disciples of the Dædalids, carved ebony, cedar, and olive-wood. But we can obtain an idea of their talent from the carved ivories of the VIIth century and even from the marbles, for the statuaries applied to stone the style which wood had given them.

Finally, the flocks and herds of the *Perioikis* supplied abundant raw material for the manufacture of woollens and for the leather trade. There was, too, the purple of Cythera, with which the uniform of the Spartan hoplites was dyed red. In the Vth century old-established industries were exporting Laconian cloaks and shoes of Amyclæ.

All this work was, by the deliberate will of the Spartiates, given over to the Periœci. It was fairly extensive. Spartan simplicity was not such as romantic morality on the war-path was to imagine it. In Sparta as in other places wealth could procure luxury, and the craftsmen were by no means reduced to making absolutely indispensable articles.

It is, however, quite true that Sparta never did anything to encourage foreign trade, because she intended to be self-sufficient and to ask other cities for as little as possible. For a long time she lingered with the system of exchanges in kind. The home market never needed any coinage but lumps of iron, so that the scales continued to be necessary for payments. At the epoch when Greece was beginning to strike coins of precious metal for international transactions Sparta decided to close her doors to outsiders. The Ephors had the right to pass an administrative act driving out passing or resident foreigners, and they used this right habitually and with rigour. Inhospitality appeared to be a necessary condition of self-sufficiency. Every stranger who could not justify his presence in the country was deported; the system was designated by a special word, *xenelasia*. In such an atmosphere foreign trade could not develop greatly. Plutarch exaggerates when he says that the Spartiates bought no foreign commodity and that no merchant ships came into their ports. But the constant, deliberate restriction of dealings with abroad prevented the Pericci from making profitable use of the monopoly which they enjoyed in law.

So the Lacedæmonian state was based upon the existence of classes one of which lived at the expense and impeded the activity of the two others. By thus surrounding themselves with enemies the masters condemned themselves to perpetual watching. For a long time all they had to fear was the hatred of the serfs, and by methods of secret ferocity they were able to quell it. But bloody wars, the abuse of civic degradation, and Malthusianism were not long in diminishing the number of the privileged class. From one generation to another the disproportion between those who exploited the social system and their victims became more glaring, and the domination of a caste reduced in numbers was less justified on the battle-fields. At Platæa (479) the Spartiates are still 5,000, like the Pericci; among the prisoners of Sphacteria they are only as two to five; at Leuctra they are only 2,000 hoplites, one to three. However, the Pericci resigned themselves to their position until the middle of the Vth century. But as the aristocracy diminished in numbers it grew proportionately more suspicious and more severe; the political and material position of the Pericci became worse, while they were filling the growing gaps in the army. At the same time the expansion of democratic ideas in the Greek world aggravated the evil by contrast. Then the Spartiates had almost as much to fear from the Pericci as from the Helots. In them too they wanted " slave souls "; they only succeeded in driving them to extremities. At last discontent entered the group of the Spartiates themselves; for, once it has been set up as a rule, inequality invades everything. The inalienability of the *kleroi* was meant to perpetuate the equality of the Spartiates; in reality, after a few centuries, what do we see ? " Property," says Aristotle, " is quite unequal among the Spartiates; some own domains of vast extent, the others have nearly nothing; all the land is in the hands of a few." The reason was that the citizens who had nothing but their *kleros* could not keep themselves on a revenue which remained unchangeable under the law. Being compelled to borrow, they pledged their revenue, and when at last they obtained the right to alienate their land it was to abandon it to their creditors. The class in whose

# SPARTA

favour the inequality had been created found that things did not turn out as it expected. A few families overwhelmed with their opulence the descendants of those whom the constitution ironically called the "Equals." Everything was turning against the ideas of an oppressive legislation. Sparta had committed herself to an undertaking which could not be realized; she had tried to resist changing manners, to fight against human nature, to maintain an obsolete system by deliberate violence and unrighteousness.

## CHAPTER IV

## COLONIZATION

OF all the economic facts which from the VIIIth to the VIth century give the Greek world a new aspect none is so characteristic in its origins or so important in its effects as the colonial movement.

When the ancients relate the foundation of a colony they generally show either the inhabitants of a city compelled to emigrate in a body after an unsuccessful war or a plague, or else a defeated faction forsaking the city of their birth to form in a free land the constitution of their choice. But a movement as general as this, which shifted a great part of the Hellenic race, taking a large population from nearly every Greek land and transporting it to nearly every barbarian country on the Mediterranean, can only have been due to remote, deep-seated, and universal causes. If this phenomenon had been the result chiefly of political troubles it would not have ceased to occur in the Vth century. It is rather with an economic situation as a whole that we must connect it. Even in antiquity certain thoughtful spirits discerned its true causes in over-population and shortage of land. Plato, for example, lays weight on the " narrowness of the soil," on the " territories which no longer suffice to feed the inhabitants." We must not, be it said in passing, think of things by the measure of our own day. The excess of population was relative, because the lack of land was largely artificial. If the Greek cities contained so many men without landed property the fault was with the land system. So long as the land had belonged collectively to the *gene* the man who did not belong to them, or left them, had no other resource but to occupy waste land or to take to brigandage or piracy. After the breakdown of the patriarchal organization the big properties were divided, but still land-owning was prohibited to those who did not belong to the great families or were not descended from men who had taken part in

## COLONIZATION

reclaiming the waste, and the splitting up of properties on death created a class of land-owners who could not support themselves. Even more than in Homeric times, Greece fills with adventurers and vagabonds running after every promise of an easier life. If there is a chance of crossing the sea and taking possession of a fertile bit of land, or of making a fortune in any way whatever, they are ready.

Thus the history of Greek colonization presents to us various types of emigrants. Legend places the royal family of the Neleidæ at the head of the Greeks who settled in Ionia, and attributes the foundation of Locri to the first hundred families of Locris. A Heraclid of Argos, Tlepolemos, was said to have led the Dorians to Rhodes, and a Heraclid of Corinth created Syracuse. On the other hand Hesiod's father presents an example of the more ordinary man who is ready to uproot himself. He was descended from a Locrian who had settled at Cyme in Æolis. Not having enough land to keep himself over there, he returned on a small boat to the mother country, and did a little business, until one day he settled in the neighbourhood, in the village of Ascra, where he continued to labour on a barren soil. Among the Parians who occupied Thasos there was a bastard, Archilochos, son of the nobleman Telesicles and the slave Enipo, who, in the course of a life full of ups and downs, had known penury and eased his bitterness in passionate iambics; but the poet had for fellow-emigrants a number of those poor fishermen whom he exhorted to " leave Paros behind, with its figs and its shell-fish."

What the Greek especially sought in the lands beyond the sea was a bit of land to cultivate. From the days when Homer described the arrival of the Phæacians in Scheria to those in which Athens multiplied, under the name of *Cleruchies*, settlements of colonists, and allotted numerous *kleroi* in order to increase the number of citizens owning land, the first thing which these emigrants did was to distribute the lands. Archilochos dreams of settling down in the rich plain of the Siris. The Megarians are not drawn to the shores of the Bosphorus either by the easy connexion between the Euxine and the Ægean or by the fish which abound in the bays on the European side; they occupy the Asiatic shore, which alone appears desirable to them with its wide stretches of fertile ground. Love of the soil was for the Greeks the chief stimulus to colonial activity.

But although Hellenic colonization had such a pronounced agrarian character, the acquisition of fields was not its only object, nor were farmers its only pioneers. As a rule, certainly, its prime object was to win land; industrial and commercial prosperity and urban activity were further developments which came when the extension of cultivation was stopped inland by the opposition of the natives, and circumstances became favourable to enterprise on the sea. But it is impossible that the Greeks should not have been led to a certain number of places by the pursuit of movable wealth.

We must not forget that at a very early date, to make up for the shortcomings of the agrarian system, recourse was had to piracy as a convenient method of procuring metals,

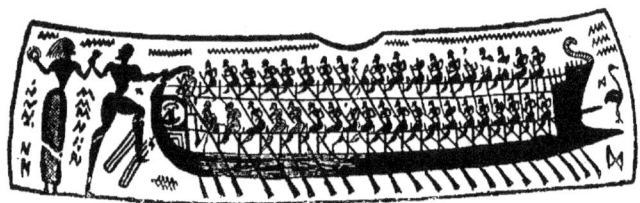

FIG. 7. A PIRATE SHIP. DIPYLON VASE, IN THE BRITISH MUSEUM.
(*J.H.S.*, Vol. XIX, Pl. viii.)

precious articles, and slaves. But this mode of acquisition had to be adapted to the new conditions imposed on it by money economy and the strengthening of public power. It took the most various forms. In time of war piracy remained almost exactly what it had been, but in time of peace it underwent profound changes.

In the monarchies of the East you could no longer think of taking booty; there was too much risk. Already in the *Odyssey* Pharaoh's army teaches the Cretan gangs a disagreeable lesson. Those who were only out for mischief enlisted in the very troops which kept them respectful. The pirate became a mercenary, the brigand turned policeman. With their head covered in a helmet, their cuirass rising over the neck, their kilt of straps lined with metal, and their greaves, shield, and spear, the "men of bronze" plied a lucrative trade. They left poor or over-populated regions

# COLONIZATION

for the great countries where the kings were rich. They were Cretans, as ever, Parians, Rhodians, Ionians, and above all Carians. Most of them went to Egypt. Towards the middle of the VIIth century King Psammetichos took into his service shipwrecked pirates, and sent for a multitude of their fellow countrymen; they all received pay, prizes, and land. Apries was so pleased with these auxiliaries that he collected as many as thirty thousand of them. The Greek mercenaries enjoyed an equally brilliant success with the kings of Asia. A brother of the poet Alcæos went into the service of the king of Babylon. In Lydia Gyges owed his throne to the Carians, and Alyattes, to conquer Caria, raised an army in Ionia. We see what glorious openings the trade of mercenary offered to the descendants of the pirates.

By a development which was also fruitful, but in another way, trade superseded piracy, and was to contribute to the foundation of the colonies. The more peaceable of the bold spirits who ventured to the east were content to do business. The Cretan bandit of the *Odyssey* already resigned himself to a tradesman's life. Even in the savage countries commerce, blended with rapine in various proportions, often presided over the birth of the colonies. Even in Homeric times men went to the Sicels to buy or sell slaves. When the Greeks occupy reefs in sight of a much used sea-way, a port on a strait surrounded by mountains, an islet off a big country, or an isolated promontory, it is not in order to follow agricultural pursuits, but to devote themselves to pillage or to unload their goods. The Cnidians and Rhodians who take possession of the Lipari Islands divide themselves into two groups, of which one works the land while the other falls upon Etruscan ships. The founders of Zancle, the future Messina, are pirates. Syracuse has its birth in the little island of Ortygia, and Cyrene in that of Platea, after the manner of the Phœnician "factories." Most of the settlements created by the Milesians along the Euxine are in their origin only such trading stations, and some of them will never be anything else. When the territory of a Greek colony comprises a fertile plain between two promontories there is nothing to show whether agricultural life there came before or after commercial life. It is quite true that the main object of a Greek colony was only exceptionally trade; but the colonies intended for the settlement of a population were not all exclusively agricultural, even at the beginning. The emigrant who set forth without hope of return was not always looking for land; he was also thinking of trade.

A glance over a map of the Greek colonies is enough to show the kind of service which this maritime empire was to do. Here and there excrescences appear, jutting inland from the coast. These are the agricultural colonies, which have a comparatively large territory. Chalcidice supplies land to the masses driven out of Euboea by the privileges of the Hippobotæ. Cyrenaica offers its oases and its pasturelands to Dorians from every source. In Sicily the Geomori of Syracuse are the lords of over 296,500 acres, which their serfs cultivate. In Italy Locri, Croton, and Sybaris come to occupy all the Œnotrian country to the Tyrrhenian Sea, and grow rich as much by agriculture as by portage across the isthmus. But on the whole the Greek colonies form a fringe, which is almost unbroken. Before Alexander the Great hardly any but the Cypselidæ of Corinth and King Battos of Cyrene dreamed of a land empire. The Greeks do not feel easy unless they can see the sea; they are saved once they can shout " *Thalassa !*" They gather round the Mediterranean like " frogs round a pond."

In the earliest cases colonization was done at a venture, without pre-conceived plan, by the mere coming together of individuals who were discontented with their lot. At the end of the Mycenæan period Asia Minor had seen a disorderly invasion of bands from all the conquered countries; so too, at the end of the VIIIth century, Sicily and Italy saw an influx, often to the same place, of men of different cities and races. Sybaris was founded by Achæans and by Dorians of Trœzen. Cyrene was occupied first by Peloponnesians and Thessalians and then by Dorians of Thera. The first generations of colonists formed a heterogeneous multitude driven by a common hope of a better condition. Eubœan and Locrian colonization in Italy in particular had this individualistic and almost anarchic character. Nevertheless even in the *Odyssey*, when the Phæacians leave Hypereia to seek a second home, they are led to Scheria by the godlike Nausithoos, who makes them build the ramparts, temples, and houses and goes on to share out the fields. It is the first example of emigration directed by the public authority. A time comes when it is almost always so. The city, having become stronger, organizes colonization and makes it national. It will no longer allow its sons to be lost to it. The occupation of a country becomes a State undertaking. Everything is laid down by rule. The colonists depart under the orders of a chief, the *oikistes*, who surrounds himself with priests and soothsayers, and also with land-surveyors. The plan of the new town is designed in advance, and the parcels of ground are drawn by lot. After that colonization is erected into a system. The colonies crowd one on another, and the biggest of them send out a swarm. Rivalry grows up between the cities, especially when the unoccupied districts become scarcer and are further away. Then it becomes necessary that a superior authority should sanction the decisions taken and co-ordinate them in order to avoid conflicts, and that an information bureau should keep up to date a list of reserved areas and vacant land. The Delphic Oracle claims this *rôle* from the VIth century onwards, and occasionally performs it.

The Greek colonies, different in their origin, differ still more in their policy towards the natives. Such relations must perforce vary according to the numbers and strength of the colonists, but also according to the numerical force, resources, requirements, military capacity, civilization, and psychology of the populations whose masters or neighbours they have become. In dealing with primitive tribes the Greek, ever versatile, knows how to make himself welcome. He brings the gift which pleases, he finds the word or gesture which charms, he talks over the men, and he makes love to the women; he obtains by a friendly parley the agreement which he wants, the right to open a market or to occupy a strip of land; and the country is his. The Phocæans land on the territory of a Ligurian tribe, the king's daughter, Gyptis, chooses their leader for husband, and Marseilles is founded. The Theræans occupy the islet of Platea, work up relations with the Libyans, obtain permission to cross on to the mainland, and behold, the kingdom of Cyrene is made. North of the Euxine Cimmerians, Scythians, and Sarmatians receive the Ionian traders well. Once established in a country, the colonists try to expand. Often they employ force, aided by treachery. Syracuse, Leontion, Ambracia, and many other towns are built on territory conquered by arms. The Locrians when they land in Italy conclude a treaty of friendship with the natives and then resort to treachery and drive them away. But you only massacre or expel the natives in cases of necessity; it is better to use kindness and to have your fields tilled by their former owners, whom you have reduced to slavery. The land-owners of Syracuse attach to the soil gangs of Cillicyrians; the Byzantines extort labour from the Bithynians of the neighbourhood; the Heracleiotes force the Mariandynians to till the land and to row in the fleet.

But certain attempts came up against an opposition which could not be broken. There are gaps in the cordon of Greek colonies. Even outside the Eastern monarchies and the area reserved to the Carthaginians and the Etruscans many peoples were able to repel the foreigners. On the shores of the Euxine the Greeks were careful to avoid the parts where the pugnacious Bithynians had succeeded the awful Bebryces of legend. The Messapians and Salentines always prevented Taras from encroaching inland. The Sicels could never be dislodged from the mountains. Sometimes even, when in contact with a highly civilized country, the colonists were influenced by it; the influence of Lydia on the Ionians was very strong, the merchants of Naucratis were Egyptianized, and a great number of Greeks adopted Etruscan fashions.

The advantages which each colony obtained for itself were communicated to the whole of Greece, but first to the mother city. The relations of the colonists with the fellow citizens whom they left behind naturally depended on the circumstances which had determined the emigration. Sometimes they are malcontents or exiles who go abroad to make themselves a better city, like the Lacedæmonians who found Taras and the Locrians who settle in the new Locri. In such a case the rupture is complete. But as a rule the reciprocal feeling is very different. At the moment of departure the kinship of those who stay and those who leave is consecrated for ever by a religious formality. On the altar of the Prytaneion the sacred fire is lighted which will be placed on the hearth of the city to be; the gods of the old country follow their children, to protect them and to remind them of

## COLONIZATION

their duty. The colony is bound to show the mother city certain marks of respect and deference. When the colony in her turn sends out colonists, she requests an *oikistes* of her mother for her daughter. Moreover the colonists are naturally inclined to keep up the customs which they have inherited and to recall dear memories. In intellectual life there is incessant exchange; legend, poetry, philosophy, sciences, and arts unite men's minds, and currents of ideas cross the seas. It is to the advantage of both that the colony should supply the mother city with cattle or corn and obtain manufactures from her in return. But these bonds, strong though they be, do not in the least weaken the two feelings which are inborn in the heart of the Greek, a love of liberty and a passion for his own interest. Independent cities are added to the number which is already so great, and new countries offer old Greece, in their laws and their manners, admirable schools of practical individualism.

There is perhaps not one Greek colony whose history would not add some feature to the picture of the activity which ferments in Greece for more than two centuries. But it will suffice to take them in large groups, in order to remark what is most characteristic in them.

Thrace was bound to attract the dwellers by the Ægean with its corn-fields and vineyards, its forest-clad mountains, and its mines of gold and silver. Opposite Eubœa there was a peninsula with a fertile soil and a wonderfully indented coastline. Its three promontories seemed to beckon to the neighbouring island. Chalcis responded to the call; she needed land for her peasants, wood for her ship-builders and markets for her metal-workers. At the end of the VIIIth century Chalcidice contained thirty-two towns. One of them, Potidæa, which stood on an isthmus, was naturally a creation of the Corinthians. Almost immediately the Parians rushed to Thasos, rich in gold, and from Thasos on to the mainland close by. The cities of Ionia and Æolis wanted their share, and the Chians settled at Maroneia, the Clazomenians at Abdera, and the Mytilenæans at Ænos.

The Greeks of Asia already overlooked the great route to the Euxine. It was a domain which they reserved for themselves. Æolian Lesbos took up position on the two shores of the entrance. She was followed by Miletos, which went on and on, from harbour to harbour, and by her example drew after her Phocæa, Teos, Colophon, and Samos; the Propontis became an Ionian lake. Then Megara appeared on the scene, and founded Chalcedon, and then Byzantion; the Bosphorus was hers. Now the Greeks saw lying open before them a vast sea whose storms, fogs, and frosts they regarded with dread. On the other side, according to vague rumours, there lived hideous and cruel peoples. For a long time they stayed there, before the " inhospitable " sea, not daring to brave it. But gradually stories went about of lands where wealth lay in heaps and the Golden Fleece was hidden. The Milesians took the risk. Their daring made the sea " hospitable " and won the treasures of the Euxine. On the southern shore, from Sinope to Trapezus and Phasis, they found timber, fruit, iron, and the trade-routes of Asia. On the northern coast, which offered them an inexhaustible store of grain and fish, they settled at Olbia, Panticapæon, and every point favourable to trade and fishing.

While the Greeks did not occupy any territory in the great countries of the East they did not abstain from exploiting them. They had to leave relations with Assyria, Media, and Persia to the Phœnicians, and even in Cyprus Hellenization made very slow progress. But, at the ends of the continental monarchy of which Phœnicia was the sea front, two phil-Hellenic countries were like colonies to them. In Lydia the Mermnadæ received them kindly for a century and a half (687-546). In Egypt traders were as well received as mercenaries and were able to establish permanent " factories." There too the Milesians set the example and secured the best share. About 650 they entered the Bolbitine Mouth with thirty ships, and they built a fortified trading station, the " Milesians' Wall." A little later they founded Naucratis on the Canopic Mouth and Daphnæ near the isthmus. They obtained the right to penetrate to the interior; they had their own quarters, or at least bazaars, in Memphis and Abydos. In the wake of the Milesians traders came pouring in everywhere. When Amasis ascended the throne (569) the Greeks might hope for everything. The monarch went out of his way to please them. He allowed the Samians to trade in the Great Oasis. Then he took a step of capital importance; he concentrated the Greeks of Egypt in Naucratis. Thus there

## COLONIZATION

was in the Delta a city administered in the Greek fashion, with its "nations" grouped round a sanctuary and an emporium. Special temples and quays were reserved for the Milesians, who enjoyed undisputed pre-eminence, the Samians, and the Æginetans. Nine other cities shared the Hellenion. Naucratis very soon became the chief market in Egypt, and one of the chief markets in the Greek world. The prototype of the future Alexandria, it accomplished down to the Persian conquest a remarkable work of Hellenization.

In Cyrenaica, again, conditions were favourable to colonization. From the earliest times the Greeks had known this coast of Libya; the north wind drove their ships there when they wanted to go to Egypt. Cyrene, founded by the Peloponnesians and Thessalians, did not attain its full importance until it had received a new influx of immigrants. Then it became the thriving capital of an African Greece.

While the cities of Asia Minor and the isles had almost a monopoly of colonization in the eastern Mediterranean, Greece proper took a leading part in the colonies of the west. Everything drew the Greeks to Italy and Sicily—an almost virgin soil, forests near the sea, and a convenient voyage which, after a crossing of forty nautical miles, simply followed the coast. Even in the Mycenæan age the Messapians and Sicels bartered hides and slaves for vases and arms from the east. In the Homeric period strangers appeared more often as pirates than as merchants, and the natives had to take refuge in the first lines of hills in order to receive pottery with Geometric pattern. Soon the pillagers found the country to their liking. The Eubœans of Chalcis were the first to found colonies in the west, as in Thrace. They first settled in Sicily, from Catane to the Straits, the two shores of which they commanded from Zancle and Rhegion. At once they sent out their ships into the Tyrrhenian Sea and founded Cumæ.

Peoples better situated and greedy for land followed in their footsteps. The Achæans, and then their neighbours the Western Locrians and the Laconians, poured the surplus of their agricultural population on the shores of Basilicate and Calabria. There anchorages are very rare but land is fertile. Towns arose, and soon shaped a brilliant destiny for themselves. Taras had the advantage of possessing the one good harbour on the gulf. Croton, Sybaris, and Locri expanded at the expense of tribes which were ready to be Hellenized or resigned to serfdom. Between the Ionian Sea and the Tyrrhenian they organized the transit of Ionian and Etruscan goods. Thus they were at the head of small empires. The wealth and power of these cities made a deep i pression. It was said that Sybaris, with its 300,000 inhabitants, ruled over twenty-five cities and four native peoples. The enormous quantity of the objects heaped in the ruins of Locri indeed suggests a considerable town.

The commercial cities of the Isthmus, Corinth and Megara, situated between the Chalcidians and the peoples of the Ionian Sea, could not renounce all interest in the West, and once the Dorians of the mainland had taken the road those of the islands, Rhodians and Cretans, refused to be left behind. Corinth took a strong position on the island at the starting-point of the sea-routes to Italy and to the Adriatic countries, Corcyra. All along Ætolia, Acarnania, Epeiros, and Illyria the sailors of the mother city and those of the colony took possession of the alluvial plains and the native markets. But already the Corinthians had been to reconnoitre the safest and widest harbour in Sicily; they founded Syracuse, which was soon mistress of an extensive territory, many slaves, and boundless wealth. The Megarians installed themselves in a new Megara; the Rhodians, uniting with the Cretans, founded Gela. It was then that the Sicilian cities began to send out swarms of their own, one after another. The Megarians, cramped for room, made for Selinus, the people of Gela for Acragas, and those of Zancle for Himera. East, north, and south, the whole Sicilian seaboard belonged to the Greeks.

With their cities crowded one on another Italy and Sicily were an extension of Greece proper. But in these countries everything happened on a bigger scale, with greater freedom of movement, less respect for tradition, more practical intelligence, and also more inclination to bluff. In the West Greece found its Americas. The well watered valleys yielded grain in masses while the highlands fed countless herds. The export of corn, live-stock, hides, and wool counterbalanced the import of manufactured goods and artistic objects. An active transit business carried textiles, vases, and metals to

## COLONIZATION

and fro between the Greek seas and the Etruscan. Sybaris and Syracuse were far bigger than any town in the old country, with streets and avenues at right angles stretching over the plain, and these crowded cities, rolling in money, called on the architects to produce monuments which should be the "biggest in creation." The art which in Sicily was the most original in character and the most perfect was that which is most typical of a mercantile society, the engraving of coins. Even philosophy, transplanted into the West, took on a local flavour; it became practical, in the form of political theory, rhetoric, or applied science, with a pronounced tendency to advertisement and ostentation.

Beyond the Tyrrhenian Sea lay the fabulous lands of Liguria and Hesperia, the "Far West." From there the

Fig. 8. Coins of Syracuse, signed Cimon and Euænetos.
(*D.A.*, Figs. 5120-1.)

precious metals came. But from Cumæ and Cyrene to the Pillars of Heracles the whole seaboard was reserved territory, for the Etruscan and Phœnician navigators allowed no others to visit the Ligurian tribes, the Iberian empire, or the kingdom of Tartessos. At length circumstances became favourable for the entry of new rivals on the scene; Tyre was ruined and Carthage was no longer at the zenith of her greatness. The Greeks seized the opportunity. About 630 a merchant of Samos, Colæos, was driven by storms to Tartessos; he came back with a cargo, the sale of which brought in sixty talents. The Greeks now knew where to look for the land of silver, and knew, too, that it had a friendly population and a generous king. The sailors of Ionia and Rhodes crossed the Sardinian Sea. The most fortunate were the Phocæans.

## ARCHAIC PERIOD

Living on fishing, trade, and piracy, they roamed about in their fifty-oar ships, the penteconters, slender, swift, and armed for war. As clever as they were bold, they so pleased the king of Tartessos that they obtained from him all the gold needed to build for their city a circuit of ramparts. After hovering about the coasts of Iberia and Liguria, about the year 600 they fixed their choice on a roadstead near the Rhone, perfectly safe and ending in an excellent harbour at the mouth of a fertile valley; there they built Massalia (Marseilles). The Massaliots, aided by the Phocæans, swarmed in their turn. In the west they founded Theline the fertile Pap (Arles), Agathe of Good Fortune (Agde), Pyrene (Port-Vendres), the new Rhodes (Rosas), the market of Emporion (Ampurias), Hemeroscopion or the Day Look-Out, and Mænace (Malaga) near the " springs of silver." To the east they occupied Olbia, Antipolis (Antibes), Nicæa (Nice), and Monœcos (Monaco). Greek money went far, and from far the products of the mines came pouring into the Greek ports. In the west a Phocæan thalassocracy menaced the peoples who had hitherto ruled there. About 560 it invaded Cyrnos (Corsica); from Alalia it overlooked the Italian coast. Twenty years later, when the King of Persia had subdued Ionia, the people of Phocæa emigrated in a body and made Alalia into a great city.

After two centuries of uninterrupted progress Greek colonization was bound to provoke a general reaction. In the east the land monarchy of the Persians took from the Greeks the markets of Lydia and Egypt, set up a barrier to their enterprises in the Scythian country, and annexed Ionia itself; the Phœnicians were avenged. In the west the Etruscans, combining with the Carthaginians, compelled the Phocæans to evacuate Corsica and to recognize Cape Artemision (De la Nao) as the limit of their zone in Iberia. The Persian Wars were extended over the whole Mediterranean. But Hellenism, attacked on all sides, revealed its strength; Salamis and Platæa had their pendants in Himera and Cumæ. Greater Greece was saved.

From the Caucasus to the Pyrenees the Greeks maintained on relatively large territories and in towns with a dense and composite population those innumerable types of autonomous, original cities in which everything favoured social experiment

# COLONIZATION

and political progress. From the posts where they had stationed themselves they continued to radiate their civilization over all the surrounding countries. They no longer had to fear stifling for want of room or dying of starvation; for they possessed all the land they needed, they could provision themselves with corn from the most productive countries, Scythia, Egypt, and Sicily, and, lastly, they held the markets in which the wealth of the whole world was concentrated.

## CHAPTER V

## TRADE

WHEN the Greek race was dispersed all along the Mediterranean it formed a whole wonderfully organized for developing its commercial qualities. The consciousness of national unity was strengthened by pan-Hellenic festivals, by a common education, and by the perpetual opposition between barbarism and Hellenism. Moral unity brought with it economic unity; goods were exchanged together with ideas. But, far from preventing variety, this unity favoured it. The creation of a Mediterranean market encouraged the international division of labour; in one place the object was wholesale production of wine or oil, in another foodstuffs were procured in exchange for manufactured articles. While multiplying their relations among themselves, the Greeks reached the markets of the East and of the barbarous countries, from Lydia and Egypt to the Ligurians and Iberians.

Nevertheless, the inveterate particularism of the Greeks was long in establishing for commerce the moral and legal conditions which it requires. No progress is so slow in Greece as that of international justice. Between men of different cities there often existed no common body of law. On sea, force must often be met by force. The vases of the Dipylon and the ivories of Sparta represent the kidnapping of women as quite a familiar scene (see Fig. 7). Piracy was only put down when a large number of cities had a war navy. Even then each took sides with his own countrymen without troubling about the rights of the case; each side felt itself justified in taking reprisals on all goods and all persons it could seize. There was no contract which held. When a Spartan carries off the flocks and shepherds of a Messenian and kills his son, the injured man has only one resource—to fall on every Lacedæmonian who comes within his reach. How, then, did Hermes the cattle-stealer become the herald

# TRADE

with the tutelary caduceus, the guarantor of peace and truce, the inventor of measures and scales, the patron of trade ?

The agora, the town market, was originally a neutral, sacred ground where the members of different *gene* met for peaceful transactions such as exchange and arbitration. When the sovereignty of the city was extended over a larger territory there were " border agoras," protected against violence by religious laws. These markets did the same service as the Celtic *magus* or the forum of Italy and Cisalpine Gaul. The regulation of the markets, so important in our Middle Ages, was no less so in antiquity. Everywhere festivals ensured for trade the protection of the gods. The temple regulations, confirmed by the laws, protected all who took part, whatever their country. It was forbidden to do them wrong, on pain of excommunication and death. Once the Truce of God (*ekecheiria*) was proclaimed, the pilgrims could count, sometimes for a month, on freedom from disturbance and anxiety. To the Ionian gatherings at Delos, to the pan-Hellenic celebrations at Olympia, Delphi, the Isthmus, and Nemea, the Greeks came pouring from afar, trusting to the safety of the seas and the roads. Their tents sprang up as far as eye could see. This multitude required food, victims, and objects of piety; everybody wanted to take away souvenirs, gifts, and useful commodities. The stall-keepers did a roaring business. Olympia, a sanctuary which came to life every four years, had to strike a coinage, in order to establish a relation between all the different currencies. Long afterwards, in obscure little towns, at Tithorea in Phocis and at Andania in Messenia, the festivals still had an economic importance. What, then, must the great assemblies have been like, to which the Greeks of every country flocked ? A hymn of the VIIth century gives us a glimpse of the luxury fostered by the gathering at Delos, describing " the men and the women with fair girdles, the swift ships and the wealth which they display."

The protection which foreigners enjoyed in the markets and near the sanctuaries was often extended to them in the harbours, which were generally situated on the edge of an agora and in the neighbourhood of a temple. In the *Odyssey* the slips at Scheria and Pylos are built along a public place dominated by a temple. At Naucratis every emporium had its guardian deity. At Ephesos, in the " sacred harbour," near the warehouses and the market, stood the temple of the goddess of the city, Artemis. This consecration of the harbours and their appendages made them into veritable places of asylum. The exercise of the right of capture, authorized on the high seas, could be forbidden in the harbours.

Overland transport had not made great progress. The old roads, with their ruts cut centuries ago, were still used. However, the importance assumed by the great sanctuaries increased the number of sacred ways. They ran from Cyllene through Elis to Olympia, and from Elis over the Isthmus to Eleusis and, by Athens and Thebes, to Delphi. Argos and Athens perfected the administration of their roads in order to come out of their peninsular seclusion, and Sparta did likewise to facilitate her military organization and defence. In their care for material interests the tyrants gave their attention to the ways of communication; the Peisistratids staked out the Attic road system with herms indicating distances. On all these roads goods were carried on muleback or in fragile vehicles, while man went on foot. In spite of all these difficulties wheeled traffic and peddling were fairly active. The Bœotian peasant went to market with his waggon and took care not to overload it, for fear of accidents. The Æginetans went all over the Peloponnese with their packs.

But the great road of the Greeks is the sea. The development of shipping was slow but steady. Naval architecture adhered to the two traditional types, but gave them greater power. The cargo-boat, which first appeared as a small tubby craft suitable for coasting, became a powerful vessel with an enormous spread of canvas, adapted to heavy loads and long voyages. In the battleship, which was also used by merchants who feared encounters, the transformation was more thorough. The *penteconter* made her appearance at the end of the Homeric period; she was now armed with a ram. Soon, towards the end of the VIIIth century, the Corinthians invented the *trireme*, the beautiful ship with three tiers of rowers, which could hold a crew of two hundred men. Ships could increase in size; an invention of the VIIth century, the anchor, made them safer.

To appreciate the changes effected let us recall the sailing directions in which Hesiod summarizes the experience of the farmer-seaman. Strict rule—stay at home in winter. " If the perilous desire to go sailing tempts you, do not yield to it in the season when the Pleiads have cast themselves on the dark sea, when from all quarters the winds blow unchained. . . . Wait for the good season." This season is very short. " Fifty days after the solstice, when the summer, too arduous a season, nears its end, comes the favourable moment for embarking. . . . Then the wind is fair and the sea without

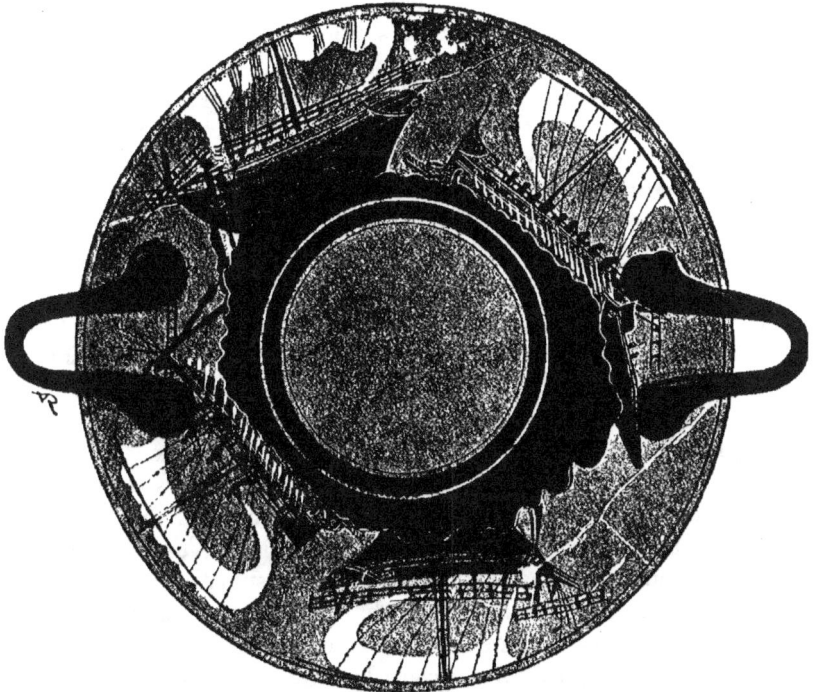

Fig. 9. Warships and merchantmen. Black-figure cup from Vulci, in the British Museum. (*D.A.*, Fig. 5284.)

danger. You can in all safety trust your swift boat to the winds and put out to sea. Sell all the cargo well, and make all speed you can to return home, not waiting for the new wine, the rains of autumn, and the surprises of the storm." Those who are impatient put out in spring; but it is unwise. " This sailing in spring, I do not approve of it and I do not regard it with a favourable eye; in that season it is hard to escape the sudden blows of misfortune." It is this last counsel which shows the extent of the progress achieved; in the VIIIth century wise folk sailed during only one month, after the dog-days; in the VIth everybody set forth in the first fine days.

Already, too, the Greeks were endeavouring to do away with the natural obstacles which impeded navigation. The harbours were protected by moles; that of Samos, built in the VIth century, was nearly 440 yards long and 38 broad. Defying the gods, man rectified the outline of lands and seas. The strait of Leucas became sanded up, so that Corcyra-bound ships had to make a detour and stand out to sea; the Corinthians deepened the fairway. Periandros, it is said, thought of cutting the Isthmus of Corinth in order to avoid the storms of Cape Malea and to shorten the voyage from the Ægean to the Ionian Sea. But such an undertaking was beyond the art of the engineers of that time. However, a timber road was laid across the Isthmus, a *diolkos*, along which the ships were dragged on rollers. Moreover, the Greeks continued to concern themselves with the cutting of isthmuses long before Xerxes made the Mount Athos canal, a mile and a quarter long.

By carrying out public works and looking after the safety of merchants, the State did great service to trade. It took care to be paid for it. The gifts which strangers once used to present to kings had become tolls, customs duties, and harbour dues. In Lydia the roads, bridges, and caravan-serais poured money into the public treasury, and it was for the benefit of his tax-collectors that the Pharaoh concentrated Greek trade in Naucratis. In Ionia, and all over Greece, import and export duties were levied. The *naulon* brought in considerable returns at Ephesos, and, in spite of the Amphictionic regulation, Crissa held to ransom the pilgrims who landed there.

If money affected the whole economy of Greece, it above all transformed commerce. Another invention, which was to revolutionize the intellectual life of Greece, had an almost exactly similar origin. Writing, the use of which had been spread by the mercantile civilization of the Minoans, was almost unknown in Greece in the time of patriarchal institutions. But when the Greek traders saw how useful good book-keeping was to the Phœnicians they hastened to imitate

# TRADE 117

them. By the IXth century the Greeks had a good number of local alphabets; here again the autonomy of the cities asserted itself. In the VIIIth century the cities and temples began to preserve the official documents. Even then the history of writing remained intimately bound up with that of trade. About 650 the economic preponderance of Miletos greatly extended the use of its alphabet, and the alphabet of Chalcis conquered Italy through Cumæ.

The intensity of Greek trade before the Persian Wars can only be estimated in comparison with the following period. According to Aristotle, *emporia*, or business in the big sense, is divided into three branches: (i) *naukleria*, ship-building, (ii) *phortegia*, the carrying trade, and (iii) *parastasis*, the mediæval *commenda*, especially loans on bottomry. This division of labour does not yet appear in Hesiod's day. If the poet of the farmers talks about the sea, it is because navigation is an additional occupation for the farmer " who wishes to escape debts and deadly famine." This kind of sailor goes to sea after the work which follows the harvest, and comes back before the vintage for the autumn ploughing. He is a countryman who goes by sea to sell a part of his produce; he is both husbandman and trading boatman. The type, which must have been frequent in the VIIIth century, did not disappear very quickly. But the merchant class became so large that in the VIIth and VIth centuries we can distinguish the elements recognized later by the acute eye of the philosopher. The expansion of certain earthenwares, the export of these receptacles for oil, wine, and scent in whole boatloads (Fig. 10), could not go on without middlemen between the producers of one country and the consumers of another. To Naucratis came Corinthian and Attic vases; the former were brought by Æginetans, the only merchants of Greece proper who were admitted to the Egyptian trading station, and the latter, covered with Ionic inscriptions, were manufactured for Ionian customers served by Ionian or Æginetan merchants. From Naucratis vases and scarabs were sent out for the Euxine; it was the Milesians who acted as brokers between their emporium on the Nile and their northern colonies.

Before it reached this point Greece had to recapture its own market by driving the Phœnicians out of the Ægean.

5

# ARCHAIC PERIOD

The Delian festivals consecrated the commercial independence of the Ionian race. Cyprus, which had become strongly Semitized, underwent a new influence. The Greeks even succeeded in reversing the *rôles*; they appeared in the ports of Phœnicia. In the time of Ezekiel the Ionian cities on the Euxine were supplying Tyre with metal and slaves.

Greek trade for a long time remained dependent upon Lydia. The sovereigns of this country had organized a powerful market, intermediate between Assyria and the western world. Roads ran from Sardis to the Euphrates

FIG. 10. CORINTHIAN SHIP LOADED WITH POTTERY. TERRA-COTTA PLAQUE. (Duruy, *Hist. des Grecs*, Vol. II, P. 481.)

and from Sinope to Tarsos. On these roads *stathmoi* were established, caravanserais which were part stronghold, part hotel, and part bazaar. Lydia was already rich in itself, with its gold-washings and its mines; transit business made it the wealthiest country in the world. Sardis became the great *entrepôt* of the East. Business and banking created fabulous fortunes. Following the example of the king Crœsus, private individuals amassed prodigious quantities of precious metals; at a time when Lydia was in its decline one Pythios was able to offer Xerxes over four million pounds in gold. This Asiatic Eldorado sought an outlet to the sea in Greek lands.

# TRADE

Cyme was the first to play this profitable part, but the Æolians were too fond of rural life, and they left to the Ionians the benefits of relations with the interior. Ephesos offered the protection of Artemis and the advantages of its harbour; it carried the day. Then it was the turn of Miletos. With the support of the reigning house of Lydia the Ionians were able to receive the goods of Sardis freely, to use the *stathmoi* themselves, and to take the road to Babylonia. Of all the wealth which came pouring into Lydia, which a Milesian dangled before the eyes of the Spartans as he showed them the map, " the gold, the silver, the copper, the embroideries, the beasts of burden, and the slaves," Ionia had its share. It was acquainted, too, with every kind of technical process and artistic motive.

When its weavers and embroiderers, its metal-workers and goldsmiths had completed their education, they were able to combine the qualities of their models with those of the Greek genius; in their turn they received orders from Lydia and sent their choice work thither. By their industrial and artistic superiority no less than by their experience of navigation and their colonizing activity, the Ionians became the masters of Hellenic trade.

The prosperity of Naucratis was particularly the work of the Milesians. What this city was like we may imagine when we think of the *fonduks* of the Italians in Alexandria. Situated on a navigable arm of the Nile, communicating by canal with the capital Saïs, well administered by Greek *prostatai*, Naucratis, with its four warehouses dominated by temples, its maze of lanes about the harbour, its manufactures of pottery, faience, and terra-cotta, and its quarters reserved for the natives, appears like one of those cities with a motley population, full of life and movement, which trade has in all times caused to spring up on the shores of the Mediterranean. From 650 to 550 the Greeks made it one of their chief staples. To it they imported pottery with wine and olive oil. From it they sent perhaps grain, certainly vases of local manufacture, linen stuffs, alabaster, natron, alum, scents and ointments in faience bottles, and the products of Africa and Arabia, gold, ivory, and frankincense. When these relations extended all over the Mediterranean, from Olbia to Etruria, Naucratis was one of the most thriving cities of the Greek world.

Merchants and sailors bragged of its luxury, and told in distant countries tales of its rich courtesans. The most marvellous things were related of the country itself, its monuments, its cults, its ancient civilization. Philosophers and students came there to seek lessons; craftsmen learned technical processes there, and there, no doubt, the Samian metal-worker Rhœcos was initiated into the secret of hollow casting.

Through Cyrenaica the Greeks could enter into direct

FIG. 11. ARCESILAS VASE, IN THE CABINET DES MÉDAILLES.
(*D.A.*, Fig. 4925.)

relations with Africa. They took to stock-breeding and the cultivation of silphium, a spice which was in demand all over Greece. Cyrene manufactured vases which were considered among the most beautiful. Its harbour stood at the end of two caravan lines, one from Egypt and the Oasis of Ammon and the other from the Sudan. A vase made in Cyrene and found in Etruria (Fig. 11) gives a complete notion of the

colony; there we see Arcesilas, king and tradesman, presiding
over the weighing of silphium near a ship, while slaves heap
sacks in the hold and a monkey gambols among the spars.

Nowhere was the commercial success of the Milesians so
complete as on the Euxine, among the Scythians. The Greeks,
especially those accustomed to the fair sky of Ionia, would
never have exiled themselves in that foul climate, in the face
of the boundless plain which harboured hordes of redoubtable
warriors, if they had not hoped to make their fortune quickly.
But what wealth there was to be had, if you only put out your
hand! Fish for smoking or drying, good corn, skins, furs,
slaves, gold, amber; all the products which came in abundance
from the fields of the Chernozyom, the mines of the Samland
and the Ural, the forests of Siberia; all the griffin-guarded
treasures, the mysterious journeyings of which were tracked
by the explorer Aristeas. To gather them, a group of traders
stationed themselves among the fisheries at every *liman* on
the coast. Of the ninety colonies with which Miletos encircled
the Euxine, the greater number were crowded in the Crimea
or about it. The smallest of these settlements had its value.
Big towns like Olbia extended their connexions, by river-
boats and caravans, to the Hyperboreian countries and to
central Asia, sending vases, filled with wine and jewellery,
to what are now the Kiev region, Silesia, and Brandenburg.
On these shores the necessities of material existence and the
cares of business made the Hellene a dull fellow. Nevertheless, at Berezan, an island of fishermen supplied with food by
the Milesians, almost everybody could read and write, and
among the merchants who covered themselves with gorgeous
jewellery it was the correct thing to give orders to Ionian
artists.

In the Greece of the West trade was not of such general
importance from the outset. The predominant interests in
Sicily and Italy were for a long time agriculture and stock-
breeding. In Syracuse, Locri, Metapontion, almost everywhere, the owners of the ground are the masters of the State.
But, thanks to the extent and the fertility of their territory,
these rural cities soon attained a very comfortable standard of
life, and formed an excellent market. In exchange for corn
and hides they demanded manufactured goods. Corinth
appropriated the best share of Sicilian trade. On the main-

land, though unable to repel the competition of Miletos, she obtained the acceptance of her money, the standard of which fitted both the Euboic system and the Æginetan; the coins of the tyrant Periandros even circulated, with a surcharge, in the Achæan cities. But presently the colonies themselves took to business. Some sent the surplus of their production to distant countries; Acragas sent oil and wine to Carthage. Most of them supplied the peoples of the interior with manufactured goods; at first they obtained them from overseas and resold them at a great profit, and later they started to manufacture them on their own account. The cities of Italy in particular organized themselves thus for trade.

Taras, which lived largely on agriculture, stock-breeding, and fishery, disposed of its wines, oils, and wool in Greek cities and barbarian countries; then it sent vases of Cyrene and Sparta into the depths of Italy; and finally it worked its

FIG. 12. SILVER STATER OF CORINTH. (*D.A.*, Fig. 6576.)

own wool and had textile works and dye works. A deposit of coins found at Taras gives a great idea of its commercial connexions; it contained six hundred coins coming not only from every town in Italy and Sicily, but from Corinth and Corcyra, the Cyclades, Cyrene, Athens and Ægina, Thrace and Macedonia, Chios and Phocæa.

The fame of Sybaris is legendary. It had an immense population and possessed a veritable empire. Its resources were inexhaustible; in the plain it had excellent wheat land, extensive vineyards, and meadows which fed the great oxen which it made into an emblem for its coins, and in the Sila were wood, resin, and wax. Sybaris chiefly exported wine, which the growers led down to the coast by a system of underground channels. It imported pottery, generally filled with oil, luxury articles, and Milesian textiles, such as the famous embroidered *himation* which was the pride of the Lacinian

Hera. Although it had only an open roadstead, Sybaris was able to force its good offices upon international transit. Being the friend of the Milesians and Etruscans, it served them as intermediary. To sail from the Ionian Sea to the Tyrrhenian Sea ships made a long and dangerous round; moreover Rhegion and Zancle allowed only Chalcidians to pass. Just at Sybaris the peninsula narrowed to an isthmus. From one shore to the other, from Sybaris to Laos, portage was organized. This traffic was the principal cause of an unprecedented prosperity. Sybaris became celebrated for its wealth. When the tyrant of Sicyon, in order to choose a son-in-law, organized a competition in luxurious display, it was a Sybarite who won. Austere folk raised their voice against the softness of a city spoiled by fortune, but Zeus at Olympia and Apollo at Delphi regarded with a friendly eye the tokens of its opulent piety. However, terrible jealousies broke out. A rival confederation tried to cut out the Sybaris and Laos route by the Siris and Pyxus route; Siris was destroyed. But the hatreds did not disarm; in 511 Sybaris vanished in its turn. Its fall shows the length of savagery to which commercial competition could go in the Greece of the VIth century.

At the advanced posts of Hellenism, facing the hostile Etruscans and the distrustful Italians, the Chalcidians of Cumæ played the part of heroic merchants. While they imported clay and bronze vases, arms, and tripods into Etruria, and procured for the tribes of Latium and Campania corn and certain Eastern goods, they were doing, without knowing it, work of the greatest historical importance. The Etruscans imitated the beautiful articles brought from Cumæ, and with goods of their own manufacture and from abroad they made themselves the suppliers of more distant peoples. They received the Chalcidian alphabet and passed it on to the Umbrians and the Oscans, with some modifications. Meanwhile, under the influence of Cumæan trade, there was awakening the civilization of the little tribes of Rome.

By the two sides of Northern Italy, by Venetia and by Liguria, Greek trade sought the routes which led into the heart of barbarism. Miletos monopolized the road which ran from the Hyperboreians to the Euxine. But there was another further west; along it the parcels packed in straw

## ARCHAIC PERIOD

came to Dodone and Venetian horses were brought to Sparta. A parallel route was afforded by the Adriatic. The Phocæans darted up it. At the mouths of the Eridanos they founded the city of Adria and perhaps planted the vine. There they collected the amber tears shed by the Heliades, and thither they took jewels, bronze situlas, and pottery. Since the Picentini and Veneti of the neighbourhood were in communication with the Sigynnes of the Ister, the pottery of Chalcis and Corinth made its way into the regions of Upper Germany. Phocæa must be destroyed, Corinth must decline, and above all amber must lose the popularity which it had always enjoyed before the Greeks would abandon the Adriatic.

The commercial relations of Massalia developed in another way, and were to last. The Greek East found there a valuable outlet, witness the many sites containing Rhodian, Ionian, Corinthian, and Attic pottery in successive strata. But the Massaliots were not content with a passive part. They made their colonies into commercial branches. By sea, however, they must halt in face of the Etruscans and Carthaginians, and the road to the Hesperides was closed by the Pillars which, in the name of Melkarth, marked the bounds of the accessible world. To reach the Atlantic they must pass by the overland route. By flashing their pretty coins before the eyes of the natives the Greeks brought into their ports, by caravan, the tin and amber which the Carthaginian mariners sought for themselves in Cornwall and at the mouth of the Elbe. The Col of Naurouze was infested by a warlike tribe. One current of trade was led down by the Ebro to Emporion and another by the Rhone to Massalia. The future Burgundy, where the roads from the English Channel and from the North Sea converged, attained in the second Hallstatt period (VIIth and VIth centuries) an importance which is partly explained by bronzes of Greek origin.

From the gold mines of Asia to the Tin Islands, from the frankincense coast to the amber coast, Greek trade secured itself a wonderful field for expansion. This trade rested on a solid foundation, for exports counterbalanced imports, and this would be the case so long as the progress of industry kept pace with the increase of population. Before all, the Greek cities needed corn; they provisioned themselves in Sicily and Italy, perhaps at Naucratis, and especially at Olbia. An

Ionian geographer saw in the Euxine the belly of Asiatic Greece, just about the time when Athens, to command the sea-route of the corn, was establishing herself at Sigeion and in the Chersonese. For food, too, the Greeks needed preserved fish from the Euxine and the Bosphorus, and spice from Libya for seasoning. For building, they required wood from Thrace, for metallurgy, copper from Cyprus, tin from the west, and iron from the Chalybes, and for the artistic industries, the precious metals of Lydia, the Euxine, Thrace, Egypt, and Iberia, the amber of the Hyperboreians, and the ivory of Africa. Slaves came chiefly from Scythia, Lydia, and Syria. The luxury articles most in demand were the carpets, stuffs, and embroideries of the East and the linen and perfumes of Egypt. In exchange for the foodstuffs which it obtained from the barbarians, Greece supplied them with its wines and oils. For the import of raw materials there was a corresponding export of manufactured goods. Miletos sent its woollens as far as Italy; Chalcis, and then Corinth, fed every market with arms, ornaments, and vases of bronze; Greek jewellery penetrated into the countries of legend; and the pottery of Ionia, Naucratis, and Cyrene, then that of Corinth, and finally that of Athens made its way, by land and sea, along every route in the world.

By the VIth century commercial prosperity had greatly changed the general aspect of Greece and contributed greatly to its power. The commercial system prevailed in most of the ports of Asia, in many islands near by, in the cities of the Isthmus, and in a large number of colonies. It exercised a strong influence on the distribution of the population and on the very constitution of society. The sight of fortunes rapidly acquired, of Colæos coming home with piles of money, set men's minds on fire. The love of the fields where he was born had long kept the peasant in the village, and he came back to it even when he went to sea for a bit of business. But now poor and energetic countrymen made for the nearest town more and more. From the acropolis the agglomeration spread out along the roads or down to the harbour. A merchant class grew up, active, keen, and enlightened. It formed guilds, like that of the *Aeinautai* at Miletos, which stoutly defended their interests. It demanded written laws, and brought democracy into the constitutions; when it met with too strong resistance it set up a tyrant. It even placed its stamp on the intellectual life of the new Greece. Philosophy, strong in the positive data brought back by the navigators, replaced the old cosmogonies by scientific systems. To demonstrate the practical value of the loftiest speculations, Thales, relying on his meteorological forecasts, formed the oil-press trust in Miletos and Chios in a year when he counted on a big oil harvest. If the focus of this civilization lay in Ionia and all the great movements which gave Greece its permanent aspect were initiated there, it was because there the resources which nature gave in abundance were augmented by the wealth created by industry, and went by the valley roads and innumerable ports to be exchanged for commodities of the East, the Euxine, Egypt, and the western lands. Finally the traders, and not only those of Asia Minor and the islands but also those of Chalcis, Ægina, Corinth, and presently Athens, not only those of the mother cities but also those of the colonies, caused Hellenism to radiate beyond ethnic frontiers. With their cargoes they carried the poetry, the legends, and the art of Greece. Through them barbarous peoples attached themselves to civilization, and civilized peoples underwent an influence which penetrated them on every side. Lydia, Egypt, and Etruria were Hellenized; in Phœnicia, Aramaic, the official language, gave way before Greek; and Carthage, which received oil and wine from Sicily, imitated the type of its coins.

## CHAPTER VI
## INDUSTRY

IF the export of manufactured goods progressed in the archaic period it was not because the manufacturer was urging the ship-owner to find markets for him. For a long time necessaries were supplied by the work of small craftsmen added to that of the family, while luxury was satisfied by beautiful articles from the East. Industry remained thus behind trade until the middle of the VIIIth century. Then, however, the mother cities had to supply their colonies, constantly growing more numerous and wealthier, with arms and utensils, textiles and vases of every kind. Soon, with the colonies serving as warehouses or manufacturing on their own account, Greece had to supply the increasing demands of the barbarian peoples. It was colonization and trade that set industry in motion.

There was no lack of raw materials. The extension of agriculture had left the poor pastures to sheep-breeding, so wool was found everywhere; it was abundant and excellent in quality on the plateaus of Asia Minor. The purple-shell had been fished from the earliest times in Crete, and the beds of Cythera, once worked by the Phœnicians, were at the disposal of the Peloponnesian dye works. Greece proper was losing its timber, but Asia Minor had the woods of Ida, the peoples of the Ionian Sea provisioned themselves from the thickets of Zacynthos and Italy, and the forests of Thrace were inexhaustible. Potter's clay appeared on the surface in many valleys. The marble quarries in Paros, Naxos, Attica, and Bœotia were worked more and more. Whereas the Greeks of the epics were ignorant of mining, their descendants extracted copper in Eubœa, where Chalcis the city of bronze became great, and obtained iron in the same island and in Laconia, Bœotia, and the Cyclades.

To take advantage of these resources the Greek craftsmen

needed a very thorough training. The civilization of Mycenæan times had not perished utterly. Crete had preserved the secret of the purple and had not forgotten metal-working, the potteries of Melos had not closed, and the immigrants had brought to Asia Minor ideas of craftsmanship which could bear fruit. Even Bœotia had kept something of the education received long ago. But the skilful hand and the inventive mind were lacking. It was then that the Phœnicians brought to the islands the embroidered stuffs of Sidon and the shields of Tyre or Cyprus. It was then that Lydia made known its skill in founding copper, tempering iron, casting and beating gold and electron into jewels or coins, and dyeing wool to weave into carpets or gaily patterned fabrics; Lydia brought into fashion in the rich cities of Ionia long purple garments, elegant footgear, jewels, and perfumes. Cretans and Ionians imitated the foreign products. When they were able to manufacture similar articles they became the suppliers of the other Greeks, who, in their turn, copied their models. The ancients remembered that Cretan artists had worked for Tegea and for Delphi, and that others had left their island for Argos. To confirm this, archæology follows a certain type of sculpture from Crete to Tegea and Delphi, and even finds it in Ionia and in Attica. The island which had received from outside the pictured shields of Idæan Zeus soon made plating and armour; it sent some to the mainland and thus helped to make good workmen in the forges of the Peloponnese. In the meantime metallurgy was progressing in Miletos, Ephesos, Samos, Chalcis, and Bœotia. These currents, uniting, reached Corinth and Sicyon, Ægina and Athens. From the mother cities the movement spread to the colonies, and from the colonies to the barbarian lands. The bronze-workers of Cumæ were the pupils of those of Chalcis and the teachers of those of Capua and the Etruscan cities. The goldsmiths of Miletos taught those of Olbia, who created a Græco-Scythian art.

Technical education was assisted by the fact that experience was handed down within the family. The son helped his father and succeeded him. Theodoros the bronze-worker of Samos made a statue with his father Telecles. In Chios the sculptor Micciades signed one of his works with his son Archermos, and the tradition was carried on by the two sons of Archermos, Bupalos and Athenis. In Athens the painter

# INDUSTRY

Eumares lived on in the sculptor Antenor, Ergotimos bequeathed his pottery works to his son Eucheiros, Nearchos did likewise to his two sons Ergoteles and Theson, and the potter Amasis I was the father of the vase-painter Amasis II. Thus schools of art and workshops were founded in which progress once achieved was permanent.

Industry, thus organized, might have degenerated through routine, but it only inspired initiative and invention. In Corinth the potters thought of mixing an iron oxyde into their clay so as to obtain the fine colour which made their goods so popular. In the same city the naval architects established the plan of the trireme. The Samians, after having a squadron of triremes built by a Corinthian, made a further advance and launched the biggest vessel which had ever been seen. Towards the end of the VIIth century metallurgy was revolutionized by iron-welding and hollow casting. The discovery of a process made the fortune of an individual and contributed to the power of a city.

The progress of technical methods brought into industry a specialization which grew stricter as time went on. The number of trades increased. At the beginning of the VIth century Athens was not yet a big town, yet a list of trades drawn up by Solon shows the ground covered since the time of the *Odyssey*. Agriculture, which was once the occupation of all, had become a profession, and the growing of trees, that is of the vine and the olive, is mentioned separately. Sea trade had its recognized place. The arts of Athene were no longer reserved to the family; the textile industry was a separate trade. If the division of labour had gone so far in a medium-sized city it must have been much further advanced in the great urban centres. Many buildings of the period show, for example, how many trades combined in the building industry.

Nevertheless we see from the artistic industries how difficult it still was for the higher occupations to form themselves into specialized professions. The quarryman who extracted the marble was also a stone-mason, who retailed it, and even a sculptor's assistant, who rough-hewed it on the spot. Even if it was not the same man who did all the work, he worked or made others work in the cuttings themselves, whether he was a statuary assisted by a quarryman or a quarryman employing a statuary. We still find, lying in the quarries of Naxos, Paros, and Pentelicon, *kouroi* badly roughed in, unfinished gods, and sometimes, beside them, a model. The greatest artists did not yet confine themselves to a narrow speciality. Consider the bronze-workers of Samos: Theodoros, the author of several statues, chased mixing-bowls of gold and silver, a golden vine with jewels for grapes, and the famous ring of Polycrates, which consisted of an emerald set in gold; Rhœcos, who also cast statues, is none the less described as an " architect," as a ship-builder. In general, sculpture and painting were not distinguished; this was true in the Vth century of Pythagoras of Rhegion and Micon, of Pheidias and Polycleitos, and before them the painter Eumares was the teacher of his son, who is known as a sculptor. One industry, however, seems to have been ahead of the others. In the manufacture of pottery, a very active artistic industry, each kind of work was sufficiently perfected to require a special apprenticeship. From the VIth century onwards the potter made the vase, the painter decorated it, and both added their signature.

The increasing importance of industry can be seen in the position assumed by the workshop. In the Homeric period the Demiurges had gone from one town to another. Even now poets and lyre-players, sculptors, painters, and architects responded to the summons of private individuals, tyrants, or cities. But in industry a considerable change had taken place. To make a shield for Ajax the leather-worker Tychios went from Bœotia to Locris; to-day the famous Bœotian shields were sent out by the manufacturer. This practice was general. Swords came from Chalcis, woollens from Miletos, terra-cottas from Cyprus, vases from one or other of the Ionian towns, from Corinth, or from Athens. The international demand was met by an international division of labour. The craftsman did not leave his residence; he needed apparatus concentrated in the workshop or studio and it was the finished article which travelled.

There were, however, exceptions, which show exactly how far industry developed. At the beginning of the archaic period the small crafts could still carry on with a travelling work-bench. In the Altis at Olympia there have been found, among the bronze statuettes offered *ex voto*, unsuccessful and

# INDUSTRY

unfinished pieces; these were left by the itinerant bronze-casters who came and worked at the temple doors during the festivals. The oldest of the " Cyrenaic " vases were perhaps made by the same hands in different places, for it has been maintained with some probability that the potters went from Sparta to Cyrene with a light apparatus, like the Siphnian potters who in our own time do the round of the islands. In most industries, it is true, the amount of production soon required a permanent plant in fairly large premises. But even then Polycrates summoned to Samos the Corinthian Ameinocles, to build him a flotilla of triremes. Ship-building,

FIG. 13. EMBROIDERY OF A CLOAK, FROM THE FRANÇOIS VASE.
(Perrot, Vol. X, Fig. 94.)

which could not have become organized and modernized without huge yards, numerous employees, an elaborate plant, a large stock of raw materials, and, in short, a considerable initial outlay, remained faithful to the system of executing contracts at the place of the customer. Medium industry worked actively for export; big industry was not yet born. There were plenty of studios and workshops, but no factories on a big scale.

Among the most remarkable conquests of the new economic system was the textile industry. But, while breaking away from the domestic occupations, it allowed them to continue. It produced hardly anything but luxury goods as yet, and did not yet show any intensity of industrial work. No doubt the long full garments demanded by the Ionian fashion required much material, and the colonies constituted a *clientèle* which was always ready to give good prices for beautiful work, but, since common stuffs were still woven in the house, the workshops, even those of Miletos, did not aim at quantity. They supplied the aristocracy with fine tissues, artistically decorated, and with many-coloured embroideries which had formerly been imported from Sidon and Lydia. The importance attached to the beauty of the material made dyeing an essential industry. When, later, Sybaris wished to manufacture its own textiles, it began by exempting the fishers and importers of purple from taxation. Fulling was a prosperous trade, practised even in the smallest towns.

The marble industry, which included extraction, cutting, and even sculpture, developed suddenly. It supplied great quantities of blocks, columns, flags, and tiles for building, and basins, steles, statues, and pedestals. While the quarries of Pentelicon and Bœotia hardly sufficed yet except for local needs, the manufacturers and artists of Naxos and Paros supplied the other islands and the great sanctuaries. From the end of the VIIth century the statuary made a point of the difference between himself and the stone-mason, and the oldest signature of an artist which is known to us is that of the Naxian sculptor Euthycartides.

It is very difficult to judge of Greek metal-working in the archaic period. Rust has corroded the iron. Of the bronze, chiefly works of art have survived. But those old metal-workers of Crete, Ionia, Bœotia, and Chalcis give a high impression of their craft. For a long time they knew only the processes of Homeric times, hammering the sheet of metal over wooden forms and incising details with a point, or else casting the metal solid in hollow moulds. In this way only small pieces could be produced; to compose a large object these had to be put together with clamps and rivets. At the end of the VIIth century Glaucos of Chios invented or imported iron-welding. Shortly afterwards the Samians Rhœcos and Theodoros employed a process, used since the XVIth century in Assyria, which one of them may have learned in Egypt—hollow casting. The bronze-workers of Samos, Ægina, and Corinth were henceforward in a position to execute

# INDUSTRY

big pieces in thin metal and, in consequence, to produce pieces of finer workmanship more cheaply. Long before this the Ionian forges had turned out all kinds of objects decorated in the Oriental manner, fittings for furniture and chariots, basins and tripods for which Greeks and barbarians contended from Armenia to the banks of the Saône. The most prized articles of armament were the Bœotian shield, the Chalcidian sword, and Cretan specialities, the *mitra* and the belly-plate, until Corinth applied quite scientific anatomy to the manu-

Fig. 14. Warrior wearing the Corinthian helmet. Bronze from Dodone. (*D.A.*, Fig. 3452.)

facture of defensive armour, cuirasses, greaves, and helmets fitting all round the head. The metal-workers of Corinth also made beds, and probably, too, a great part of the mirrors which were sold in the west. It is in these industrial surroundings that we must place the work of the great artists in bronze, the bas-reliefs of the Spartan Gitiadas, the marvellous mixing-bowl which Colæos dedicated at Samos, the offerings enumerated in the Lindian Chronicle, and the statues ordered for Olympia from the Æginetan artists Glaucias and Onatas.

But the industry on which we must lay most stress is pottery. It had to meet an extremely large demand. The great mass of it consisted of household ware and receptacles for wine, oil, and ointment. Moreover, the temples required a stock, the size of which can be gauged from the deposits of broken objects. Rich families wanted valuable vases to display at feasts and *symposia*. Huge *pithoi* were set on the tombs, or else a supply of clay articles—often very large—was placed inside. In the island of Rhodes one single dead man had by him seventy-nine Corinthian *aryballoi*, apart from other things. So the pottery trade had to provide for an enormous output. How was this work distributed?

Common crockery was made nearly everywhere, sometimes being merely baked in the sun. But certain centres were engaged in supplying what others lacked. Ægina, for example, was called the "pot-seller."

Even the manufacture of fine pottery was for a long time scattered over various places. In the days when clumsy, inexpert hands decorated vases with geometrical lines intercourse was rare, and every district had its potters. A few Attic Demiurges made and painted the Dipylon vases for the Eupatrids, while the potters of Laconia and Argolis, Thessaly, Phocis, and Bœotia had a limited *clientèle*. Other little workshops carried on in the islands, Eubœa, Delos, Myconos, Thera, Melos, Crete, Rhodes, Cyprus. There were some, too, in Asia Minor, at Stratoniceia, Miletos, Ephesos, Larissa in Æolis. In those days but few cities sent their goods over the sea, as Miletos did to its colonies on the Euxine.

Everything changed when a healthful wind came out of the East. In the course of the VIIIth century the Greek potters set themselves to imitate the patterns traced on carpets, hangings, bronzes, and jewels from abroad. The Geometric style was succeeded by the Oriental style. Buyers of vases would now have nothing but friezes of animals, and then epic or legendary scenes with human figures. This revolution chiefly benefited the cities from which it had started; types grew diverse and production was concentrated. Miletos was no doubt the source of the ware of reddish clay with a light yellow coating which was so much sold from the Euxine to Italy. Samos, excluded from the Milesian markets, disposed of its *alabastra*, shaped like female statuettes, everywhere else. Clazomenæ found outlets for its grey pottery, and the black ware, the *bucchero nero* of Lesbos, went to supply models to the Etruscans. At Naucratis the Ionian manufacturers added Egyptian motives to the usual ornamentation, and sent their vases of clay or faience and their ointment pots of opaque or translucent glass into every country visited by the Greeks. Finally, the artistic phials, which have been given the name " Proto-Corinthian " but indicate an Eastern origin by their pretty shapes and the sure tastefulness of their ornament, conquered a wider market than any other pottery of the time. While Asia thus increased its production, the

FIG. 15. EXTRACTION OF CLAY. CORINTHIAN PLAQUE OF TERRA-COTTA. (Perrot, Vol. IX, Fig. 280.)

island workshops closed down, except those of Melos, which saved themselves by the perfection of their workmanship and kept the custom of the Cyclades. In European Greece manufacture was no longer as dispersed as it had been; but the decrease in competition at home did less good to the potters of Bœotia and Eubœa, and even to those of Corinth and Athens, than to their Ionian rivals, and the beautiful Laconian ware with a white ground had to be imitated at Cyrene before it spread on the market.

Not until the middle of the VIIth century did the pottery of Corinth make its way to the front rank. There is every sign of a highly organized industry at that time. Between the clay-pit and the workshop, pottery provided a great part of the city with a living. The quarryman attacking a side with his pick while his assistant gathers up the lumps in a basket, or the potter turning the wheel with his foot as he shapes the clay with the paring-chisel, poking the fire with the

FIG. 16. POTTER AT THE KILN. CORINTHIAN PLAQUE OF TERRA-COTTA.
(Perrot, Vol. IX, Fig. 283.)

firing-iron, climbing up a ladder with a hook to break up a flaming kiln, or looking at the batch of pots as it cools—all these scenes were popular, and the men of the trade loved to depict them on the plaques which they hung in the chapels of their quarter. The general public, including the poets, knew the demons which the corporation feared—Syntrips the

FIG 17. POTTER AT THE KILN. CORINTHIAN PLAQUE OF TERRA-COTTA.
(Perrot, Vol. IX, Fig. 281.)

Smasher, Smaragos the Cracker, Asbetos the Sooty One. To achieve this development the manufacturers of Corinth had been obliged to specialize. In the earliest times they used the common yellow clay provided by nature, and made vases of every shape. When they learned to redden the clay by an

# INDUSTRY

admixture of oxydized substances and to depict scenes with many figures, they preferred the big-bellied forms, especially the crater. But they did not trouble about providing delicate

Fig. 18. Demolition of a kiln. Corinthian plaque of terracotta. (Perrot, Vol. IX, Fig. 282.)

satisfactions for the sense of beauty. Fine execution and careful detail are not in their line; they produce by the dozen for customers who are easily pleased. The drawing may be

Fig. 19. Kiln full of pottery. Corinthian plaque of terracotta. (*D.A.*, Fig. 3038.)

slovenly and the lines may be incised—it's so easy! If the colours run and lose their brilliance, it can't be helped! All that is wanted is that they should be varied and showy. To explain the subject to the ignorant buyer a few words of legend are scribbled alongside. If the potters of Corinth were the first to sign their work, it was for business motives rather than from the pride of artists. They must keep on opening up new markets to the boats which sailed packed with vases from deck to hull. The result was magnificent. No Hellenic product was ever so popular or found so many markets as the pottery of Corinth. From 650 to 550 it was exported in quantities to all parts of European Greece, to the islands, to the cities of Asia Minor except Miletos, all along the Euxine, to Syria, to Cyrene, to Carthage, and above all to the western

FIG. 20. THE SUICIDE OF AJAX, ON A CORINTHIAN CRATER, IN THE LOUVRE. (Perrot, Vol. IX, Fig. 335.)

colonies, to the Etruscans, unequalled customers, and even to the barbarian countries north and west of the Alps.

Spoiled by success, Corinthian pottery made no effort to improve its style. After enjoying for a century the supremacy which it had captured from Ionia, it had to surrender the market to a rival which had been working for this victory for more than two hundred years. Attica contained excellent clays, which took minium well. The craftsmen of the Cerameicos who had made the *pithoi* destined for the neighbouring cemetery had already proved their technical skill and their spirit of invention by the huge dimensions and varied decora-

# INDUSTRY 139

tion of these vases. When their successors, by imitating the Oriental type of fauna and flora, had acquired absolute sureness of hand, they made admirable use of the fine glaze which they possessed, contrasting it with the colour of the fired clay. They created the red vase with black figures and, later, the black vase with red figures. With their conscientiousness, their lightness of hand, and their gift of observation they re-instated art in industry, and in the representation of mythical or popular scenes they displayed an originality which was full of power. It was a revelation. Wherever

Fig. 21. The François vase. Black-figure crater, signed Ergotimos and Cleitias. (Perrot, Vol. X, Fig. 123.)

taste had become refined these vases were wanted, and no other. Attic pottery perhaps did not spread so widely as Corinthian, especially since it was more expensive; but the total demand was not less, nor, above all, were the profits. The oldest of these vases were still exported by Æginetan and Ionian middlemen. But from 560 or 550 the Athenians took it upon themselves to place wares signed by Ergotimos and Cleitias, Nicosthenes, Execias, Andocides, and many others. They captured the whole market of the Euxine, Cyprus, Egypt, Etruria, Liguria, and the Iberian country.

## 140 ARCHAIC PERIOD

The workshops of Ionia and the islands disappear; the painters of Corinth can get no more work. All the men of the craft who in other times would have founded a firm in their own country, Amasis, Phintias, Cachrylion, and the like, settled in Athens as Metics and contributed to a prosperity based on the complete monopoly of the trade.

It is Attic pottery, then, which gives us the best example of a strong industry before the Persian Wars. The Cerameicos, the quarter which Athene reserved for the fire god Hephæstos, continually spread out into the country. There, in the fire of the kilns, a whole population of workers was busily employed. As a rule they were men of low birth, even the most renowned; their spelling is deplorable and they often bear the names of slaves or freedmen. The increase in number

FIG. 22. POTTER'S WORKSHOP. BLACK-FIGURE HYDRIA, IN THE MUNICH MUSEUM. (*D.A.*, Fig. 3034.)

of slave workers is a certain sign; the master potters needed a fairly large staff. They must have labourers to mix the clay, specialists to shape the bodies and handles (two men to a wheel for the big vases), assistants at the side of the painter to prepare the colours and varnishes, to spread the black lustrous paint, and to finish off the work with a glaze all over, and strong and conscientious workmen for the double firing. Nevertheless a dozen men, or fifteen at the most, were enough to do all this work. A hydria (Fig. 22) represents a workshop opening on a yard. The master or foreman, leaning on a staff, supervises seven or eight workmen; the painter and his assistants are absent, probably because they stay in a closed room away from the noise, dust, and soot. So there is nothing to show that the work which the whole world demanded of the

# INDUSTRY 141

Cerameicos was concentrated in big factories; on the contrary, everything suggests that it was distributed among a multitude of small or medium craftsmen.

Although the signed vases are in a minority, we know about a hundred different makes, covering a hundred years, several dozens being contemporary. The most ancient potters, such as Execias and Amasis, did both the making and the decoration; they had no painter in their employment. No doubt there was not enough work for two masters in the pottery of Nearchos, for his sons, instead of forming a partnership, had each a firm under his own name. In the latter part of the VIth century the most important firms, those of Nicos-

Fig. 23. Amphora of Nicosthenes. (*D.A.*, Fig. 7296.)

thenes and of Pamphæos, had quite an industrial character. One reproduced the same type of amphora incessantly, and the other supplied all shapes at all prices, while both followed the changes in public taste and abandoned black-figure for red. Nevertheless, Nicosthenes was able, with his own paint-brush, to decorate almost all his output, and Pamphæos did his own ornament when he had time. Sometimes several painters worked for the same firm, but they were not attached to it. The vase-manufacturer Hischylos published the work of three painters, but with at least two of them his connexion was only occasional. Siconides decorated black-figure vases for him, as he did for Tleupolemos, and Epictetos, the painter of red-figure vases, went and worked for him as he did for Pamphæos, Nicosthenes, Python, and Pistoxenos. The celebrated Euphronios, after decorating cups for Cachrylion, established himself on his own account and did the whole work in person; only at the end of his career, in the middle of the Vth century, did he take the painter Onesimos into partnership. The intensity of ceramic production in Athens was, in short, an extension in place. This industry was just like the others ; the head of an undertaking did not need to collect as much capital and labour as possible, because he was not driven by the necessity of getting the biggest possible return out of expensive machines, in order to diminish his general costs and to obtain a progressive increase in profits.

However it was organized, industry, supported by active trade, seems to have brought in great profits. The craftsmen dedicated rich offerings to the gods. These expressions of pious liberality were subject to a tariff laid down by tradition; the tithe was given. Just as Rhodopis the courtesan sent a tithe of her fortune to Delphi, so the Telchines of Rhodes dedicated to Athene Polias and Zeus Polieus a caldron as " a tithe of their works," and the potters of Corinth or Athens were no less generous. To pay such dividends to the gods, they must have done splendid business. And we are not much surprised to see a vase-painter representing himself as taking part in an orgy in a sumptuous apartment among gay companions.

In these flourishing industries competition is already keen and bitter. The sculptor proudly puts his name on his work; as he becomes conscious of his talent he desires to distinguish himself from his rivals. The potter and the vase-painter do the same, for the signature is a certificate of origin which will carry the make far. At first the manufacturer signs alone, for customers are only interested in the name of the firm; then he adds to his name that of the painter, which receives increasing consideration; in the end it is generally the artist alone who recommends himself to the public. Personal pride and advertisement. To capture the fashion, an illustrious person is asked for his patronage, and a choice vase is dedicated to him, with a salutation inscribed on it. Sympathies and interests combine; Phintias on a hydria pays a compliment to two *confrères*. But fighting is not always quite fair; Pamphæos copies the style of Hischylos or Nicosthenes

## INDUSTRY

without scruple. A little trumpet-blowing comes in useful, and all the better if you can discredit the shop opposite. On a second-rate amphora Euthymides writes beside his signature " Euphranios will never do as well."

From individuals, competition extends to cities. It becomes international, keeping pace with the division of labour. The reputation won by the products of a city benefits all who make them. When a modeller of figurines signs himself " Sicon of Cyprus," or obscure potters add " Athenian " to their name, they give their address and recommend their goods. So keen rivalry sets all the ports capable of contesting the universal market flying at each other's throats. As long as the Milesians are masters they prohibit access to Asia Minor to Samian pottery, and only allow a few such cargoes into the Euxine, they keep out Corinthian ware so effectively that not the smallest potsherd of it has been found in the ruins of their city, and they manage for a long time to exclude it from Naucratis. When Corinth triumphs, the rivals whom she has ousted vainly copy her shapes and industrialize their methods after her example; she maintains her superiority, and in certain regions, for example at Delphi, she hardly tolerates any goods but her own. By this time the economic struggle is so fierce that it leads to acts of violence and bloody strife. When the Spartans, to show Crœsus what their bronze-workers can do, send him a valuable vase, the Samians, out of jealousy, capture the ship which carries it. An insignificant conflict between Eretria and Chalcis is enough to kindle in every part of Greece, one after another, a war without end: Samos declares war on Eretria, Miletos on Samos, Corinth on Miletos, Ægina and Megara on Corinth; soon, on the Propontis, the Megarian and Milesian colonies are colliding with the Samian colonies, while in Italy Croton, supported by the Samians, commences an inexpiable war against Sybaris, the ally of Miletos. All this time Athens, which cannot favour either Corinth or Ægina, works and prospers. By their honest, artistic design her vases make Corinthian pottery look cheap and nasty. In vain the threatened manufacturers try to hold their own, in vain Argos and Ægina defend their market by measures of prohibition sanctioned by religious law. Athens is ready, from the middle of the VIth century, to take possession of an industrial and commercial monopoly.

# PART THREE
# THE ATHENIAN PERIOD

### CHAPTER I
### DEMOCRACY AND PROPERTY

FOR centuries Greece had been moving from patriarchal institutions, which knew only collective ownership and household economy, towards an order of things which proceeded to split up the land, added the resources of trade and industry to the fruits of the earth, and found a supreme guarantee for personal liberty in the omnipotence of the city. The work was on a way to completion when it nearly perished under the repeated blows of the Persians. Greece was victorious. Henceforth it would act entirely in the line of its natural development, and would direct all its political and social forces towards the ideal of a democratic city.

But for Greece to be able to fulfil its destiny one city must march before the others, a city capable of initiative and taught by her past what road to follow. This glorious and profitable mission was assumed by Athens.

She had been preparing herself for it from the beginning. The Athenian people was vowed to equality. Since its origin it had combined the material and moral conditions needed. The *autochthony* of which it boasted gave it the advantages of racial unity, and the *synoecism* which grouped all the small towns in one city established its territorial unity. Within the *gene*, unalterable custom, which admitted no right of primogeniture and required unanimity for important decisions, safeguarded the rights of each member. Outside the *gene*, the commoners at an early date formed a class of peasants and another of craftsmen, in which individuals were remunerated according to their work, and grew accustomed to treating their common affairs. But meanwhile the agrarian nobility maintained the family system on their great domains, and even contemplated absorbing their tenants into it as serfs. In 622 Dracon divided up the *genos* into groups of different kinship;

in 594 Solon broke down the barriers which the law of the family still maintained between the individual and the State. The ground was freed and mobilized. The person was liberated; *Habeas Corpus*, the prohibition against the pledging of the body for a debt, became the immovable foundation of citizen dignity. These principles found political expression in a flexible organization of classes, in which the citizens were ranked not in families, by birth, but each according to his income. But the family organization, abolished in law, persisted in fact, especially in the great families. It was in vain that the tyrant Peisistratos fought the aristocracy, distributed waste land to the peasants, enriched the craftsmen by public works, and made the merchant navy take the road to the Hellespont ; the *gene* kept their place, and some of them their influence, in the *phratries* and the *tribes*. Finally Cleisthenes suppressed all that survived of the institutions based on the *genos*, destroying the traditional groups and creating new government districts in which he forced topography to adapt itself to the decimal system. His skilfully violent combination of political arithmetic with political land-surveying made one fact visible to all eyes—the city is composed of equal citizens.

The democracy was coming to birth. Hardly born, it was strengthened by the ordeal of the Persian Wars and the victory. Patriotic union and general emigration before the enemy had mingled the ranks. Athens and Greece were saved at Marathon by the hoplites and at Salamis by the sailors; the middle and lower classes had won glorious titles to support their claims. At the same time the discovery of new veins at Laureion, the building of a large harbour at the Peiræeus, the foundation of a sea empire, the upkeep of a strong fleet, and the colossal development of trade and industry set up another power against landed property, and displaced the centre of gravity of the commonwealth. The democracy was in full force.

1. THE STATE AND THE INDIVIDUAL.

The sovereign people has all rights and possesses all powers. Being absolute master of the laws and of justice, it is equally master of property, for it makes no distinction

## DEMOCRACY AND PROPERTY 147

between politics and economy nor, consequently, between public and private goods. In theory the Assembly can dispose of private fortunes as it will. But in practice there is no opposition between the sovereignty of the people and individualism; on the contrary, they support each other. Far from sacrificing the man to the omnipotence of the State, the democracy makes it its principle that the omnipotence of the State should serve for the protection of the greatest number, while injuring as few rights as possible.

Such was the basis on which the government of the people was founded. All citizens must be able to go to the Assembly, all in turn must form part of the Council, and all must have access to the magistracies and a place in the juries. Since they numbered only forty thousand, this meant almost continual occupation; the citizen was taken up entirely with public affairs. How could he fulfil such an arduous function without pay? Yet if unpropertied men abstained oligarchy would rule. Therefore, to maintain the democracy, it was absolutely necessary that the State should compensate the citizens who gave up their time to it. Payment of public services, *misthophoria*, was the essential condition of the system.

Out of the six thousand Heliasts on the register three thousand, on an average, sat every day; each received, at various dates, one, two, or three obols. In the Assembly no compensation was required for a long time; craftsmen and shopkeepers, fishermen and rustics gladly left their work to take part in the forty meetings of the year. But when abstention became general the members of the Ecclesia were given presence-tokens which were at first worth one obol and in the end, according to the meeting, one drachma or one and a half. The five hundred Councillors (*Bouleutai*), who sat all the year round, drew five obols a day in the IVth century, and the Prytaneis one obol more. To the highest magistrates, the Archons, the State was less generous; they received only four obols. The subordinate offices, those of the clerks, heralds, guardians of the arsenals, and guardians of the Acropolis, gave a living to a crowd of small folk. The rowers of the fleet were allowed a daily salary of two obols, and later of three. The hoplites, who had served without pay at the time of the Persian Wars and had had to bring three days' rations with them, now had their expenses paid, and were entitled to their drachma on distant expeditions. When the cavalry ceased to be drawn exclusively from the wealthy classes, the keep of the horse was ensured by a permanent allowance. *Misthophoria* was, under the democracy, a State obligation.

No more would have been needed, if the organization of the sovereignty of the people had been a purely political question. But, since the upper classes represented wealth rather than birth, the lower classes aspired to social equality, and endeavoured to make the omnipotence of the State serve their material interests. To ensure good order and the peaceful enjoyment of property was not the sole duty of the city; it must provide for the most general needs. It was fair that each should share in the advantages of the association. The principle of liberty and equality would be an imposture if the contrast between possessors and non-possessors was too great. The citizen, says Aristotle, must not be "degraded" by extreme indigence; it prevents him from attaining the magistracies and does not allow him leisure to think of the public good. Everywhere those who held the power enjoyed the profit of it, and why not the multitude in Athens as much as the few great men in other cities ?

The enemies of the democracy said that the mob wanted not only to improve its lot but to reduce fortunes. Plato fiercely condemned *ochlocracy* as "a re-awakening of Titanic nature," and turned aside from the crowd as from a "monstrous beast." Certainly the Athenians would have been a people of demigods if they had never known the feeling of envy. More than one of these little potentates drew himself up at the entrance to the law-court, as he murmured, like Philocleon in the comedy, " Now I can with a glad heart make fine rich folk see what I am." Yet as a rule the people used its power only to make the common good prevail. It was Pericles, an aristocrat by birth and a great land-owner, who laid the foundations of their social policy. He set out to assist the one side while preserving the property of the other. And he succeeded. While countless other cities flowed with the blood of struggles in which the stakes were all the land and all debts, Athens ever held the right of property sacred. The Athenian people declared goods confiscated by judicial sentence or by decree, but not once in the whole course of its history did it effect a general confiscation. To satisfy appetites which seemed to it legitimate, it clung to the common law. In Athens the principle that all power lay in the State was, if one may use such terms, a rather socialistic radicalism with conservative tendencies.

The idea of providing for the existence of the poor citizens manifested itself in the most various forms. It gave *misthophoria* an economic significance. The small employee lived on his salary; the citizen in straitened circumstances obtained appreciable assistance from the allowances. As the good old Heliast goes home with his two or three obols, he rejoices beforehand in the welcome which he will get from his wife and daughter. Moreover, so long as the presence-tokens were distributed only in the law-courts, they went only to the men of a certain age, the old soldiers; it was their pension. But later, when the treasury poured out its " milk " to all members of the Assembly irrespective of age, the *misthos* became an unemployment dole, that is to say an encouragement to remain unemployed. The financial misdeeds of the *misthophoria* have been greatly exaggerated; it has been called the bird-lime of the city, and represented as a bottomless cask. What is true is that it was disastrous in its economic and social effects. By creating pauperism which it only half satisfied, it paralysed initiative in the citizen class and caused the greater part of work and business to be left to Metics and slaves.

Yet the State had no intention whatever of encouraging the citizens to idleness. On the contrary, it intervened to supply them with the wherewithal to earn their living usefully. In order to provide land for the farmers, it sent them in thousands into the *Cleruchies*. These colonies had at first had a military and political object; Athens gave them a social purpose. She divided the soil of them among her Thetes and Zeugitæ, using them as outlets to relieve the congestion of poor peasants. " They send away," says Plato, " those who, having nothing, desire the goods of those who have something; they get rid of them, as of an ill engendered by the city, and they cloak this discharge with the respectable pretext of founding a colony." Unfortunately these emigrants had too often lost the inclination for effort, having been spoiled by politics. They let or sold their allotment and came back to town to eat up their rent or capital. This practice became so regular that the abuse was consecrated by a decree—for military reasons, it is true; in 427 it was decided that the land-owners of Mytilene should henceforward cultivate their land as tenants paying rent to Cleruchs who were established in the city as proprietary settlers.

Something had to be done also for the craftsmen and traders. For a long time they had benefited by the great works of public utility without the city having any deliberate intention of favouring them. When the harbour, arsenals, and Long Walls were completed, the enterprising State elaborated vast schemes of embellishment, this time with a view to providing the workers with employment. This, according to Plutarch, is how Pericles explained his idea. " The working class does not go into the army at all. I did not want it to be deprived of the same advantages, nor yet to enjoy them through idleness. I therefore carried out, in the interest of the people, these great building schemes, work which should keep various industries busy a long time. In this way the stay-at-home population would, no less than the fighters, have their share of the public funds. . . . Every trade, like a general commanding an army, employs an ordered multitude of salaried workers and labourers, an organized corps of labour. Thus the public service spreads and distributes prosperity among all ages and all conditions of men."

If the State assumed such obligations as these, it was still more natural that it should provide public assistance for invalided workmen and the children of citizens who had died for their country. In application of the same principle the treasury was charged, in grave circumstances, with the relief of the general poverty. In years of dearth it took steps for corn to be sold cheap or even distributed free, and in years of war and distress it granted indigent persons the *diobelia*, the two obols a day which a man needed in order to live.

What was more remarkable was the keenness with which the people, after satisfying its material needs, demanded its share of the intellectual and moral delights provided in abundance in a great city by a highly developed civilization. *Panem et circenses.* On feast days the citizens thronged to the religious ceremonies, processions, and sacrifices. They also wanted their seat in the theatre. The rich bore the cost of

## DEMOCRACY AND PROPERTY 151

the performances, but the lessee who was responsible for the building and scenery took an entrance fee. It was inadmissible that the shows should be closed to the poor. The State allowed them the two obols demanded at the door. Subsequently these sums, known as the *theorika*, were distributed at all the great festivals, to enable the poor to improve their fare and to have a good time. The fund of the *theorika* was fed by the surplus of the budget; the people must have its official amusement grant.

In short, at the cost of certain waste which caused the doctrinaires to growl with some reason, the Athenian democracy of the Vth century had succeeded in reconciling the general interest with individual appetites. The power of the city and personal liberty stood in stable equilibrium. The State recognized as the limit to its omnipotence the obligation of ensuring the well-being of the citizens; the citizens, rich or poor, admitted that their rights were bounded by the common utility. Public and private prosperity resulted from political concord, which had for its foundation social duty.

This, at bottom, was the principle which governed ownership. Property belonged to the individual, under the control of the city. There was neither communism nor anarchy. The maintenance of each in the use and enjoyment of what belonged to him, under conditions determined by the law—no system could be imagined more favourable to society. All goods were at the disposal of the State without belonging to it slavishly, and its demands detracted nothing from the pride or activity of the citizen.

The public domain was not essentially different from what it is in modern countries. The rights of the " Crown " reached beneath the ground. In all times the Greek cities had reserved to themselves the wealth of the mines. Siphnos was able, with its production of gold and silver, to build marble monuments, to consecrate a magnificent " Treasury " at Delphi, and yet to distribute every year among all the citizens a substantial balance. The Thasians produced 150 talents a year, and even 250, with which they could build themselves walls and ships without paying any taxes. Then

Athens suddenly found that it was her duty to regulate the working of the mines. In 483 veins of unprecedented richness appeared at Laureion. What was to be done? About the right of the community there was no doubt. But should the people divide up the windfall or use it for some work of public interest? Themistocles caused the question to be settled in favour of the State and a fleet to be built. How was the working organized for future times? The prospector who discovered a vein had to declare it and was entitled to one twenty-fourth of the output. Concessions were given out on contract, those in which shafts had to be cut for ten years, and those which were already in full bearing for three years. The right of the concessionnaire was very extensive; he was said to " buy " the mine, he organized the working as he pleased, the ore was his, and he could cede his concession to a third party, complete with surface and underground plant. The right of the State was asserted by the contract in which it appeared as lessor, by the measures which it ordered to prevent abuse in the working, and by the part of the output which it levied every year; public registers showed the name and boundaries of every concession, the name of the contractor, and the amount of the rent. Quarries were subject to two different systems. Hard-stone quarries were worked by the State, while pits of soft stone belonged to the owner of the ground, on the principle that he who owns the surface owns what lies beneath.

Restrictions on landed property were little known in Greece. Sparta forbade the sale of the hereditary allotment, but Sparta was always an exception. The chief limit to the liberty of alienation of real property—and this was general, because it was inherent in the very conception of the city—was the prohibition against foreigners acquiring such property. Athens never abolished this traditional bar. To prevent the land occupied by citizens from passing into foreign hands, and also to prevent the citizens from deserting their post and swelling the crowd of unemployed townsmen, she compelled the Cleruchs, as far as she could, to live on their allotment and to work it themselves. These restrictions were of an exceptional nature, and are explained by a political necessity, not by an eminent right over the soil inhering in the State.

Nothing brings out the principles in force so well as the

# DEMOCRACY AND PROPERTY 153

procedure of expropriation in the public interest. In such a matter Greece moved towards an increasingly explicit recognition of the right of the owners. On this road Athens seems to have gone ahead of the other cities. In Eretria, towards the end of the IVth century, the State still determined the value of the lands which it required, without amicable agreement or arbitration. On the other hand, in 403, when imperative reasons of high policy required that certain properties should be ceded to new owners, a commission of experts appointed by the two parties decided upon the price in case of disagreement. Already the State was conforming to the rule which Dio Chrysostom formulates in these terms: " The law requires that he from whom something is taken should receive from those who take it the money which he paid for it."

But it is very true that in many cities the social revolutions dealt property some hard blows. From the days when the poet Theognis waxed wroth against the villeins installed in the nobles' houses in Megara to the time when Agis and Cleomenes supported the extreme demands of the agrarian proletariat in Sparta itself, we constantly find, from one end of Greece to the other, a party rising to demand the distribution of land and the abolition of debts. When these measures are not imposed by violence they are effected by roundabout ways; debts are not cancelled, only priority is given to new debts. But Athens never dispossessed either owners or creditors, by open force or by chicanery. After putting down the Thirty, the victorious democracy caused these words to be added to the oath of the Heliasts: " I will not vote either for an abolition of private debts or for a distribution of the lands and houses belonging to Athenians." Every year the Archon, as soon as he entered office, had proclamation made by the voice of the herald: " What each possesses, he shall remain possessor and absolute master thereof."

Everything, even the financial policy of Athens, shows the same anxiety to consider the interests and feelings of the taxpayer. Much evil has been said—and there is plenty to say—of the fiscal system which the Athenians adopted in the Vth and IVth centuries. But to be fair we must look at its origins and understand its spirit. When Athens already held the hegemony in Greece, she had neither regular taxes nor a treasury. Being forced to ensure herself a permanent revenue, all that she devised was the customs duties, the duties on sales, and the proceeds of fines and confiscations. The dignity of the citizen could not submit to personal taxes; it allowed only the " liturgies," because these contributions, which were required of wealthy men, were a small burden to patriotism or vanity. But it is in days of distress, when special resources are needed, that Athens shows in brilliant fashion what respect she has for acquired goods. Other cities may rob the treasures of their temples without shame: Athens borrows " from the Goddess and the other gods " in time of war and repays them with the first money which peace brings her. Elsewhere the treasury wrings forced loans out of individuals, laying hands on land, slaves, crops, jewels, securities; it accomplishes *coups d'État* in the most off-hand way imaginable. An ancient economist has drawn up an interminable list of these acts of legal violence, and nowhere in it do we see the name of Athens. That democracy, so often charged with greed, distinguished itself by its upright dealing. It knew that the faithful observance of engagements is the foundation of credit. Hardly was it rid of the Thirty, but it made it a point of pride to repay the sums which they had borrowed from Sparta—a meritorious promptness at a time when, out of thirteen cities which had obtained loans from the Delian Amphictiony, on the day of payment eight paid only instalments and three paid nothing at all. This honesty was not merely intelligent understanding of its own interest; its source lay deeper. The Athenian people respected property because it respected personal liberty.

2. SOCIALISM.

So history teaches us that Athens always refrained from any attempt against private property, and that even in the least scrupulous of the Greek cities neither the spoliations ordered as an emergency measure nor the displacements of wealth effected by the parties aimed at permanent socialization. But the eager Greek mind could not be content with explaining and justifying the economic and social state of things as they were; it had to soar above realities on the wings of dialectic. Every great theory made its first flight in Greece. Greek

## DEMOCRACY AND PROPERTY 155

thought, going centuries ahead, created socialist systems and invented communism.

We must not, however, let ourselves be deceived by similarities which are so striking because they are so unexpected. Greek philosophy is much less detached from its environment than it seems. Even its Utopias are not independent of time or space. The spring-board from which it flies into the empyrean rests on a base of historical conceptions. When it draws the distinction between what is and what should be, when it strives to give the city an eternal organization, the absolute ideas which it expresses only become precise in the light of the doctrines, the institutions, the passions, and the conflicts of the day. It is enough to look carefully to see radical differences between the socialism of Greek antiquity and that of modern times. While the theorists of to-day, even when they demand the nationalization of the land, chiefly attack movable and industrial wealth, the ancients hardly considered anything but the ownership of the soil. Whereas the former propose to reduce the share of capital in the profits of labour, the latter wished to improve the situation, not of all the poor, but only of those who enjoyed citizen rights, and, since their object was to increase the number of privileged persons, they laid all the heavier a burden on the class of born workers, the slaves. Greek socialism is in its essence agrarian and aristocratic.

That the object pursued should have been the redistribution of real property is easily explained in a period in which the overwhelming majority of the population lived by the land and big industry did not yet exist. But that these plans of general recasting should have been almost always the work of friends of the oligarchic system may indeed appear more surprising. Let us bear in mind, however, that great schemes for social reform are always and necessarily conceived by parties in opposition. The men who were disgusted by "ochlocracy" and its consequences turned from a hated present to a radiant past; they loved to play the airs of a rustic pipe to sweet archaistic words. Being full of contempt for the merchants, craftsmen, and slaves, they set out to lead society back, by salutary constraint, to household and natural economy, their highest ideal.

This explains how it was that for a long time there was

no one to demand a new, complete distribution of property but the philosophers who were hostile to democracy. In the exuberance of the ideas produced by Greece from the VIth to the IVth century, those systems which seek social equilibrium end in an equality which becomes stricter as it is confined to a more limited circle, and when they go as far as communism they impose it as a regulation upon a select few.

The oldest of these systems are perhaps the most characteristic. Pythagoras, in order to make justice reign among his disciples, imposes on them perfect equality and community of goods; but his order is only a sect, half religious and half political, and when he tries to extend his rule to the whole city the democrats of Croton rebel and drive him out. Hippodamos of Miletos distinguishes three classes in society, the good, the strong, and the hard-working, and divides the soil into three parts, sacred, public, and private; but only the warriors live on the collective property, and the tillers of the soil, the craftsmen, and the traders all have a right to personal property. Phaleas of Chalcedon legislates for a purely agricultural society. He knows only landed property, which he would make equal for all, but individual, and he makes the craftsmen into public slaves.

With Socrates more general ideas come to prevail. The city is an organic group of moral beings; the object of politics is to seek the common welfare; the art of government comprises all the virtues, and therefore all branches of knowledge. These ethical principles, which henceforward dominate Greek thought, do not however introduce any essential change into the plans for economic reorganization.

Plato may vary his conclusions in the *Republic* and the *Laws*, but for all that his idealistic communism and his practical socialism are both equally an aristocrat's ideal of the sovereign State. The mission of the city is to realize justice. This is opposed by the selfishness of individuals, bringing with it the corruption of riches and the degradation of poverty. To remedy the evil, to prevent divisions and to create perfect unity, the only way is to sacrifice the person to the State; the State must combine in one coherent whole those atoms which are individuals. Therefore it is first necessary that the city should assign to each his rank according to his aptitudes, and, consequently, that the son should be

## DEMOCRACY AND PROPERTY

tied to the position of his father by education. There will be three classes, three castes, the philosophers who govern the city, the warriors who defend it, and the producers who feed it. Next, the city must distribute property in such a way as to set up on a foundation of equality an unchangeable order. The only system which is absolutely just is communism, complete communism which applies to wives and children as to material objects. But this system is suited to the upper classes alone; the workers are only there to provide for the needs of the true citizens. Platonic communism starts not from the observation of economic facts but from an *a priori* moral principle; it results in the setting up of a group of consumers, equal among themselves, above the vile producers; it depends entirely upon privilege and slavery. Yet Plato deigns to cast his eyes on reality, to consider man as he is, as the artificial manners of democracy and money economy have made him. Making allowance for prejudice, he imagines a transitional system which shall make humanity better and prepare the way for the ideal system. Communism is brought down to a patriarchal system modelled on the institutions of Sparta. Since private property is necessary, let it at least be family property and not personal. There shall be as many allotments as citizens—5,040. These lots are inalienable and indivisible, and, that there may be no excess of citizens, severe laws keep down the birth rate. The fruits of the earth are divided into three parts, of which two are reserved to citizens and slaves while the third alone, that of the craftsmen and foreigners, is used for trade. There is no concession to the commercial system—no coined gold or silver, no lending at interest, no one allowed to possess more than four minas in movable wealth, all commodities and salaries placed on an official tariff. The comparison of this legislation with that of Lycurgos is enough to reveal its tendencies; they are definitely opposed to democracy.

It was inevitable that the ideas of intellectual men should find their way into the popular masses. A Syracusan demagogue told the mob " Equality of wealth is the beginning of freedom, as poverty is the beginning of servitude." We see in Aristophanes, through the theatrical caricature, the dreams in which the imagination of small folk indulged when they pictured the abolition of poverty and community of goods.

In *The Assembly of Women* Praxagora expounds her system. " All goods must be held by all in common, so that all live from an equal portion. It must not be allowed that one should be rich and another wretched, that one should have a great farm and another not enough ground to bury him, nor that one should keep many slaves and another not a single servant. No, I shall make one common life for all, the same for all. Land, money, and movable goods shall form a pool, the common property of all. Then no one will need to work any more; your only concern will be to scent yourself before going on the spree. The women will belong to all the men, and the children will regard as their fathers all men older than themselves." The enthusiastic Praxagora has an answer for everything. The rogues will not give their share to the community ? They will gain nothing by it. Who will cultivate the earth ? The slaves. All the men will want the same women ? That will be arranged in the regulations. But the conservative poet laughs at these fads in his own way. He brings on two citizens who have been told to add their goods to the common stock. The simpleton hastens to obey, but the sceptic waits, determined " not to give up the fruit of his sweat and his saving until he is quite sure what there is to it." As for the organization of love, we can imagine the stupendous fun for which it gives scope.

In the *Plutos* Aristophanes' criticism is more general and more profound. Here he shows what would happen in a society which restored sight to the blind god of wealth and drove out Poverty. Give Plutos his sight ! What madness ! " For if Plutos gives himself to all equally there will be no one left to ply a trade or to learn an art." Drive out Poverty ! But she is so fertile in good ! " I am the sole cause of all your blessings," she says, " and it is through me that you live. . . . I compel the craftsman, by indigence and need, to work for his living." Although the comic author does not pretend to write plays with a purpose, he sets in effective contrast, like a good showman, the representatives of the two economic systems. On one point, at least, the opponents agree; neither party can imagine a city without slavery. The people has vague desires for equality in welfare—it asks to eat, drink, and so on, with the right to leisure. Free men aspire to a socialism in enjoyment which would have slave labour for its

# DEMOCRACY AND PROPERTY 159

foundation. Whether socialist or not, Greek democracy cannot dispense with slaves, and is never anything but a wider aristocracy.

So the communist theories, born in the restricted circles of a haughty philosophy, kept their original exclusiveness when they spread in a democracy which was more greedy than logical. They could assume a universal character only in the schools which renounced the conception of the city and rose to the notion of humanity; but the Cynics and Stoics left the crowd indifferent, when they did not shock it. That is why, in the whole of Greece, practical socialism never goes beyond a revolutionary individualism. It never demands the abolition of property, but a transfer which shall give each of the victors his share, until inequality is born again and rouses against them a new generation of property-dividers. Athens escapes these vicissitudes by keeping the rights of private property secure, while taking from it in the name of the public interest enough to give some relief to poverty. With the pure wine of democracy, which she pours out without stint, she mixes a small dose of socialism, just enough to act as a tonic on the poor without having too lowering an effect upon the rich.

CHAPTER II

IDEAS ON LABOUR

THE divorce which we have remarked in Greece between the cities with an agricultural society and the commercial cities appears definitely when each type is asked what it thinks of labour, and especially manual labour.

Herodotos had already observed that the difference of opinions obtaining on this subject was a question, not of race, but of government and economy. He said that the contempt of the barbarian peoples for the mechanical arts was shared by the warlike aristocracies of Greece, and that Corinth, as a trading and manufacturing city, distinguished herself from the other oligarchies by her ideas about the craftsman. And indeed the cities in which the nobility was in power had nothing but disdain for the labouring classes. Often the name of citizen seemed to them incompatible with the exercise of any trade whatever. In Thebes the shopkeepers were excluded from the magistracies and were only admitted to them ten years after retiring from business. At Thespiæ every profession was a disgrace, even that of farmer. At Epidauros the infamy attaching to manual tasks was such that the State had to form them into an administrative service entrusted to public slaves. In application of the same principle, the law forbade the Spartiate to descend to any occupation. But as a rule aristocratic prejudice did not go so far. It admitted that the citizen could earn his living in an independent and self-respecting way by agriculture, and even by the higher forms of business and banking; but it regarded retail trade and manual labour as dishonouring. Even art was not excepted. The hereditary pride of the Bœotian nobility was one day to find a faithful spokesman in Plutarch. Even a literary man of his knowledge dared to say that no man of high mind would wish to be Pheidias or Polycleitos, who after all were just craftsmen, and were in the same case as perfumers and dyers; their products gave

160

# IDEAS ON LABOUR

pleasure but they were none the less low and contemptible persons.

Even in the cities won over to democratic ideas the minority held obstinately to the notions beloved of oligarchy. They lived on their land, aloof from the tradesmen and manufacturers, on whom they looked down. The craftsmen are indispensable, but why make so much of them? Think what you like of the work, the workman is a degraded being. He will never have the full worth of a man. His sedentary life, far away from the free air and the palæstra, warps his body as he stoops over the bench or the counter. The passion for gain prevents him from cultivating his mind, and the habit of executing small work makes him small. His whole soul, absorbed in the pursuit of sordid lucre, is closed to great and beautiful thoughts, and through submission to the will of others it becomes flat and stunted. *That* a citizen? No, nor a free man either. The artist or scholar preserves his dignity only if he refuses pay. Let him aspire to honours but turn aside from wealth. Genius merits esteem provided that it does not turn glory into cash. Polygnotos, who covers a portico with paintings and does not accept money, is worthy to obtain citizenship; Gorgias, who levies tribute on the enthusiasm of his audience, is only a vile trader in eloquence.

These prejudices had their theorists. Most of the philosophers were led to defend them by their mania for things Spartan and their tenderness for the manners and constitution of their forefathers. They had a personal reason for attaching themselves to them still more in the repugnance with which intellectual labour regards manual labour, as keen as that which landed property feels for trade and industry. The belief in the superior dignity of science dug a trench between the elect and the mass, between those who had leisure for meditation and those who had not.

Socrates was an exception. He loved to go into shops and works and to chat with the traders and craftsmen. When men who lived on their income were reduced to poverty, he encouraged them to work. He persuaded Aristarchos, not without a struggle, to fit up a work-room in his house for his womenfolk and to sell the cloth which they wove. He exhorted Eutheros to take a post as steward, but did not succeed in bending a pride which would not brook servitude. His opponents reproached him with teaching that all work is good. In reality he only recommended those occupations which do not deprive a man of leisure, the source of liberty. But even that was enough to distinguish him from the other philosophers and from his immediate disciples.

Plato sets above all others the inventors, poets, and artists, whose soul emanates from divine Eros. Among these privileged ones he allows a place, on principle, to the craftsmen who are able to maintain the liberty of the gods in production and the moderation of the wise in the acquisition of property. But how can labour follow the right road, that is to say create beauty without any other object than the common good ? In the ideal city, it is true, a life of labour can still be honourable. But in real life it is almost impossible for the craftsman to master all the wild-beast element which he contains within himself. The body and soul of the *banausos* bear the stamp of his gross life. Between the exercise of a mechanical profession and the duty of a citizen there is a radical incompatibility. And, since the craftsman cannot be a good man, it is necessary that the good man should lead the craftsman.

In bringing the Platonic dream to the ground Aristotle does not allow even as a metaphysical hypothesis that the craftsman or the trader can be virtuous. He condemns without mercy every occupation which does not derive direct from nature and has the remotest connexion with *chrematistike*. Like a good Macedonian, Aristotle is ready to include under the head of natural labour the working of forests and mines, but he disapproves of all other industries, because of the wages which make craftsman and labourer alike dependent upon the customer or the employer. Not one of the manual professions escapes his censure. The most mechanical are those which most deform the body, the most servile are those which take up the most time, the most degrading are those which require the least virtue—*i.e.*, intelligence and morality; but even the most elevated are both degrading and servile. Whatever he may do, the *banausos* has in him " a certain element of slavishness." If the exercise of a paying profession is a disgrace even to the musician, the pedagogue, and the sophist, still more is this so with the occupations which warp

## IDEAS ON LABOUR

the body and the soul. The man who takes to them is unworthy to count among the citizens, and the worst democracy is one of craftsmen and workers.

These systems were the joy of little circles in which they consoled vanities weary of waiting and ambitions run to seed. But they did not spread very far. The bulk of Athenian society remained strongly attached to the idea of equality. Public opinion was favourable to labour. Old traditions supported and fortified the very logic of the democratic system. The Athenians had a law against idleness; it applied to citizens who had no regular means of livelihood. Another law exempted the son from providing for the maintenance of his father if the latter had not caused him to learn a trade. Finally, the laws on slander punished anyone who insulted a citizen by reproaching him with his trade. The ideas of the Athenians upon labour are expressed by Thucydides, in the mouth of Pericles. " Among us it is no disgrace to acknowledge your poverty, but more disgraceful to do nothing to escape it. Here the same men are at once concerned with their own affairs and those of the city, and those who have taken to a profession are none the less acquainted with political matters." There was a kind of pact between the trades and the city; they devoted a part of their time to it, and it placed at their disposal a part of its resources. If the social programme of Pericles gave work to all the corporations of craftsmen, it was because the Assembly of the people was composed, as Socrates says, of fullers, cobblers, carpenters, smiths, farmers, retailers, pedlars, and dealers in old goods. Here it was, with a vengeance, the system which the philosophers detested, " the worst democracy," that of the workers. Merchants and manufacturers pushed into the highest posts of the State, and to make these offices accessible to the humble a salary was attached to them. Even the Metics, despite their foreign origin, were by no means despised when their calling was not wholly despicable; they could obtain citizenship after making their fortune. Some were surrounded with respect, like the armour-manufacturer Cephalos, who enjoyed personal relations with Pericles and is given a place of honour by Plato himself in his *Republic*.

The obligation to work, the law of Zeus which Hesiod preached to the peasants, now fell on all men and made all trades creditable. Listen to Socrates, exhorting Aristarchos to have weaving done in his house for sale. " Because these ladies are free women and your relations, do you think that they should do nothing but eat and sleep ? Why, does happiness for free men consist in living in idleness rather than in following a useful occupation for which one is qualified ? . . . Who are the wiser, the lazy ones or those who are usefully employed ? Who are the more righteous, those who work or those who fold their arms and dream of means of subsistence ?" These were the ideas current in Athens. Later, the New Comedy, the mouthpiece of popular sentiment, made commonplaces of it. " Earn your living in any way, provided you do nothing evil." " Laziness does not feed a poor man." " A shipwrecked man would not save himself if he did not reach land; nor can a man fallen into poverty be sure of his living if he has no trade.—But I have wealth, lands, houses.—You know the turns of fate, which in a night make a well-to-do man into a beggar. You must shelter in the haven of the trades, to lower your anchor in all security." The Athenian submitted to this necessity without grumbling. He felt it no humiliation to have a profession; he spoke of it without embarrassment. When Euphronios dedicates an *ex voto* he does not omit to call himself a potter. On the tombs the reliefs show the dead man heroized with the tools of the blacksmith or shoe-maker, and the inscriptions declare without false shame that the deceased was a goldsmith, teacher, actor, steersman, shepherd, or bath-keeper, or, if a woman, was a salt-merchant, clothes-dealer, wet-nurse, or " good dancer." When in 401 the people conferred honours on the Metics who had fought for the democracy, it did not feel that it was vulgarizing its decree by mentioning the profession of each, or even by putting a journeyman before a statuary. The blending of arts and crafts, which led aristocrats to despise the artist as much as the craftsman, led these democrats to honour the craftsman as much as the artist. Even the *banausos* was a man of the arts, a *technites ;* he exercised a " manual art," a *cheirotechne*.

Nevertheless, in a country in which the classes were mingled by their daily life, the theories in favour among the philosophers spread from the circles which welcomed them out of interest to those which affected them out of snobbishness.

# IDEAS ON LABOUR

The agrarian system had left a hereditary stamp on the whole population, and still formed men's minds in the country demes. The merchants and manufacturers for their part differentiated between the professions according to the chances of fortune, the degree of independence, and the facilities for work. While abolishing political and legal distinctions, the democracy did not prevent social distinctions. Thus a rough order of precedence among the trades became established. Between one profession and another either there was a certain feeling of envy or airs of superiority were assumed. The self-satisfaction of the "best" people, the vanity of upstarts, and the conceit of intellectuals are the same in all times.

The small land-owner had for the city worker feelings akin to those of the great land-owner for the rich business man. The instinctive antipathy of the peasant for the townsman was enhanced by the dull irritation felt by the farmer against those who sold him manufactured goods so dear, and by the contemptuous pity of the truly free man for the unfortunates who were compelled to toil in a prison. Aristophanes, who loves to talk the language of the countryside, makes fun of the women who combine many small trades, or with an offensive laugh accuses Cleon of stinking of leather.

In the town public opinion did not regard important merchants and small shopkeepers as of the same rank. Still more, then, were the retailers who sat in the Agora or hawked their goods in the streets held in low esteem. They were mostly foreigners, and Aristophanes dealt Euripides a hard blow when he said that his mother was a greengrocer. We shall see how hard it was for an Athenian to defend his honour and his citizenship when an enemy reproached him with his mother's profession. A client of Demosthenes would like to appeal to the law forbidding insulting allusion to a profession; he does not dare. He seeks for excuses, and finds them, with blushes, in his poverty. "It is true, we do sell ribbons; we do not live in the manner we should wish. . . . They say, too, about my mother that she was a wet-nurse. Yes, at the time of the national misfortunes, in the midst of the general ruin; the fact is true, we do not deny it. . . . But let none of you take that in bad part. We often see free persons reduced by poverty to servile and low occupations. You should pity them; that is fairer than to crush them.

Many Athenian women have been forced by the distress of the time to go as nurses or as weavers or to hire themselves out for the vintage. . . . But be careful not to speak hardly of the poor—it is bad enough already to be poor—especially of those who have a trade and earn their living honestly." At every word of this confession we feel how strongly manners, even in democratic Athens, opposed the laws of equality, and how much they differentiated between professions.

In industry the distinctions established were for a long time of a moral order. Solon had forbidden respectable people to manufacture perfumes; when the prohibition disappeared a prejudice survived. But from the Vth century the heads of great factories, men like Cleon or Cephalos, were in a different rank from the mere craftsmen, and labour in the workshop was considered superior to that in the mines. However, the difference cannot yet have been perceptible between the master and his men, any more than between the skilled worker and the labourer. All wages alike were one drachma a day, for the man who carried the scaffolding as for the architect and the sculptor, for the slave as well as for the citizen. Later, in the IVth century, when the labourer still drew his old salary and the skilled worker or craftsman got one and a half, two, or even two and a half drachmas a day, these differences in remuneration were clearly related to the consideration in which the various trades were held, and, within each trade, the various classes of worker.

There are no definite lines of division. In the depths we discern a crowd dedicated to the hard drudgery, the repulsive and degrading tasks; there the waste of society crouches together with the slaves. Above them are all the professions suitable to free men, Metics or citizens. But a further division soon came into being in this class. After a few generations the citizens lost the inclination for work on the land or in trade or in industry. Those who could, ceased to take a personal part in their business. Pericles had a steward to manage his properties; chiefs of industry and craftsmen hired out slaves whom they had trained, and sometimes even a mine or workshop complete with staff. Thus the Athenians tended to become *rentiers*, men without profession living on their income. For them the great attraction was politics. The party leaders, who had at first been land-owners, and later

## IDEAS ON LABOUR  167

merchants or manufacturers, were in the end orators without any other profession. Plain citizens left their field or shop for whole years to serve in the Council or in a magistracy. A time came when it was no longer true that in Athens every one was equally able to attend to the affairs of the State and to his own business. Furthermore, the sons of craftsmen and merchants aimed at professions which gave less work to the hand than to the head. Sophocles' father was a blacksmith, that of Socrates a stone mason, Lysias and Demosthenes were the sons of armourers, and Apollodoros deserted the paternal bank for the bar. As time went on, from the mass of " liberal " professions certain arts which are especially " liberal " became more and more detached, and the citizens of Athens were more and more disposed to confine themselves to these. They did not despise the commercial or industrial careers, but they insensibly abandoned them for art and letters, administration and politics. Athenogenes sold his father's perfume-works to a farmer, to live by the art of oratory. A woodman named Timomachos had a woodworker for son and a Strategos for grandson. Here we see clearly the stages through which many families in Attica passed; the countrymen, allured by the town, go into trade and industry, and the sons of successful merchants and craftsmen turn to the liberal careers.

CHAPTER III

# THE CITIZENS

IT must not be supposed that Greek democracy established equality among all free men. Athens refused citizenship to the foreigners domiciled on her territory. At first she was not very particular; an Athenian formed a line of Athenians, whatever the country of his wife. But when the development of trade drew masses of foreigners to Attica mixed marriages became frequent. At the same time the triumphant democracy was increasing the material and moral advantages attached to citizenship. The more keenly these were sought by those who were excluded from them, the more resolutely those who enjoyed them defended their privilege. In 451 a law proposed by Pericles himself provided that to be a citizen a man must be born of a citizen father and a citizen mother. The Athenian who presented a son to his phratry must swear that his wife was an Athenian; if not, the child was impure, a bastard, a *nothos*. Six years later the usefulness of this restriction became manifest; because they had demanded their share in a distribution of corn, thousands of men born in Attica were sold as slaves. One of the first steps which the people took after the civil troubles was to bring the law of exclusion into force again. As soon as it was suspected that illegitimate entries had been made on the registers of citizens, a decree ordered a general revision of all registers. Athens consented to confer citizenship on a foreigner only as a national reward for distinguished services. The democracy guarded its golden book with jealous care.

The distinctions established by Solon between the citizens themselves were never cancelled by a formal law. Officially the classes based on income still existed. For the Pentacosiomedimni the minimum was fixed at five hundred measures, or, in practice, at five hundred drachmas, for the Knights at three hundred drachmas, for the Zeugitæ at two hundred drachmas; finally, the Thetes were those citizens who did not

## THE CITIZENS

possess this last minimum of income. Honours and duties were divided among the four classes in exact proportion. The three upper classes held the public offices, and the first alone had access to the highest magistracy, the Archonship; the last was only admitted to the Assembly and to the courts of the Heliasts. But the Pentacosiomedimni and Knights also bore the cost of the " liturgies " and served in the cavalry, providing their own horse; the Zeugitæ paid the ordinary taxes and went into the heavy infantry of the hoplites, supplying their armour; the Thetes, exempt from taxation, formed the light infantry battalions on general mobilization and served in the crews of the fleet.

Little by little, almost without any new law, by the combined action of economic and political forces, the class system was transformed. In fifty years the numerical relation of the Thetes to the higher classes changed greatly. In 480, out of 30,000 citizens, there were about 12,000 hoplites and cavalry, and therefore about 20,000 Thetes; so the possessors represented a third of the city and the proletariat two thirds. In 431 the total of citizens was over 40,000. But the number of Thetes had not changed, while that of the hoplites and cavalry had doubled. These two phenomena, the stationary condition of the proletariat and the enormous development of the well-to-do classes, are easily explained. A prodigious increase of wealth raised a great number of Athenians in the class scale. We know, for instance, that one Athemion dedicated a statue on the Acropolis because he had risen from his rank among the Thetes to that of Knight. The increase in the circulation of coin and the resultant diminution of the power of money lowered the real value of the fixed minimum rates of the classes. Imperceptibly the class of the Thetes emptied itself into that of the Zeugitæ, and the latter into the two classes above. The State further expedited this movement by giving the Cleruchs allotments of lands which ensured them an income of two hundred drachmas, and by so turning Thetes into Zeugitæ. Thus there was a perpetual rise in the social scale.

Meanwhile the victories of the democracy were breaking down the scientific balance of rights and obligations which the constitution was supposed to maintain between the classes. Political privileges disappeared. The Archonship was opened to the Knights in 487, and to the Zeugitæ in 457; it became impossible to refuse it to the Thetes. From that time the classes ceased to exist save on the recruiting-rolls and taxation registers; but there each chose his own place according to his resources and his vanity. Soon war mingled the ranks still further. When necessary the Zeugitæ and Knights embarked in the fleet. Since the hoplites' service became too heavy, they were granted pay; then Thetes could be called to this duty and, to force them in, the minimum income was reduced to a hundred and fifty drachmas. Henceforward the system of classes based on income was practically abolished. All citizens were nearly equal.

Equal in law, but not in fact. Social differences still existed. No doubt there was nothing resembling castes. The citizen employed his activity as he wished and changed his condition as he could; the farmer's or craftsman's son passed by a normal stage to a liberal profession. But opinion and wealth kept class distinctions alive.

The aristocracy, which in the IVth century would be only the rich *bourgeoisie*, still preserved in the Vth century some features of the old nobility. It was the right thing, in the well-born class, to adorn your name with your patronymic, as a title of nobility. The heads of the great families held it their duty to preserve the estate of their fathers intact and to compel their heiresses to marry their nearest kinsman. They no longer lived on their land and they made a steward take their place, but for a long time they regarded their town-house in Athens as a mere temporary lodging which it was useless to decorate luxuriously. Their sons, the *jeunesse dorée*, invited flute-girls to smart wine-parties, ordered vase-painters to inscribe greetings in their name on choice vases, devoured treatises on horsemanship, and exercised on the plain of Colonos previous to parading on their thoroughbreds in the Panathenaic Procession. They supplied the army with officers and the fleet with trierarchs. Magnificence, says Aristotle, is a virtue, the virtue of the noble. Each of them took a pride in offering to the gods fat victims on which the people would feast, in causing his tribe to win in the gymnastic contests, in producing in the competitions of tragedy and comedy the most sumptuous choruses in the finest plays, and in commanding the best crew in the best-fitted trireme. For a long time these great landlords remained the masters of the commonwealth and guided the democracy; after Aristeides, Themistocles, and Cimon comes Pericles of the Alcmæonid house.

As for the citizens of the working classes, they were mostly farmers. When it was necessary, for fear of the Spartan invasion, to concentrate the country population within the fortifications, they were terribly distressed; "for," says Thucydides, "most of them had always been accustomed to live in the country . . . and when they left their homes and the worships which had been handed down by their fathers . . . each felt that he was bidding his native city farewell." This strong race of peasants had acquired, through work and through attendance at their village assemblies, a sense of realities, practice in affairs, and the spirit of freedom. Their democratic convictions were tempered by an innate respect for tradition and an invincible distrust of sensational oratory, furious debates, and fantastic ideals. Aristophanes found among these rustics some of his favourite characters, Trygæos of Athmonon, "a good vine-dresser, no informer, and no lover of politics," Strepsiades, "who had such a happy life in the fields, slovenly, growing mouldy, just living heedlessly on, where bees and sheep and pressed olives abound," and Dicæopolis, one of those Acharnians who leave their big village to cut down the green oaks in the mountains or to drive their donkey, laden with charcoal, to town, and, at the call of the Strategos, drop the axe for the spear and give the city a thousand hoplites, all "close-grained and stubborn, made of ilex and maple wood," Marathon men. Most of the peasants, owning moderate or small farms, just managed to earn their living and were classed among the Zeugitæ. Some, however, owned no land, or not enough to keep themselves. These hired themselves out as farm labourers or shepherds, and sent their daughters out by the day for the harvest or olive-picking.

The urban democracy was supported by the shopkeepers, craftsmen, and workers. The keenest of them were the Peiræeus men, ship-builders and fitters, sailors and dockmen. Coming into contact with foreigners and being used to distant ventures, they had bold ideas in politics as in business, and were ambitious each for himself and all for the public good, which was their own. Rowdy and turbulent, they were always ready to rush to the Pnyx. They made the fortune of socializing and imperialist radicalism. For forty years they accepted, not over cheerfully, the lordly leadership of the "Olympian." When he died they wanted their own men as chiefs, Eucrates the tow-seller, Lysicles the sheep-dealer, Cleon the tanner, Hyperbolos the lamp-maker, Cleophon the harp-manufacturer. In this way they could obtain from the system of government material profits and moral advantages. Theirs were the presence-tokens, the salaries, and the allowances, theirs were the shares of corn from the free doles and the allotments of land in the Cleruchies, theirs were the pleasures for which the *leitourgoi* and the *theorika* fund paid the bill.

When politics become an ordinary occupation for a people and a means of making its life easier, the system must inevitably in the long run affect the organization of labour. Its effect in Athens was a great reduction of the activity of the citizens in every trade.

This is a fact which is quickly seen in the accounts of public works. The part taken by the citizens in the building of the Erechtheion in 409-408 is not at all what one would expect.[1] By the side of the Metics and slaves they have a very small place. Out of 71 contractors and workers whose condition is known, they number 20, that is 28%. Their inferiority is established in almost every profession. The only exceptions are the architect, who is an official, and a potter who happens to be the sole representative of his corporation. The citizens still hold their own in the wood industries; out of 14 carpenters and joiners they are 5, perhaps 7; the reason is that these trades are a continuation of that of the Acharnian woodmen. But out of 40 stone-workers they are only 10 or 11. They abandon the rougher tasks altogether; among 14 labourers and 2 sawyers there is not one citizen. Even in artistic industry their share is secondary or nil. Out of 8 sculptor's roughing assistants they number 3; among 10 carvers of decorations there is perhaps one; neither the goldsmith nor the painter is of them.

[1] See *C.I.A.*, Vol. I, no. 324 *a, b, c*.

# THE CITIZENS

Are we to suppose that the citizens made up for their numerical inferiority in industry by the size of their workshops? This seems to be true of some. Phalacros of Pæania, a stone-mason, contracts for the laying and shaping of stones and does the fluting of a column with three of his

FIG. 24. THE ERECHTHEION. EAST FRONT, WITH FLUTED COLUMNS. Five columns remain standing out of six.

*Photograph by M. Burthe d'Annelet.*

slaves. But several Metics execute at least as many contracts at prices at least as high. It is true that Antiphanes of the Cerameicos, Phyromachos of Cephisia, and Iasos of Collytos deliver statuettes for 240, 180, and 90 drachmas, but three of their Metic rivals get exactly the same sums. There is not even any indication that the citizens employ more slaves than the Metics, individually or, a fortiori, collectively. But there are quite a number of citizens entered for minute sums, small craftsmen or plain workmen. If the citizens allow Metic competition in this way it is because it does not hurt them. Otherwise they would have been quick to demand protection of the city. Now, they fight on an absolute equality. A day's wage for a workman is one drachma, and the pay by the job or the piece is fixed in advance, without any distinction. Fair play is good enough for the citizens, because they are not anxious to do more than they do. The fluting of six columns is done, at 300 drachmas a column, by six gangs comprising thirty-four men in all. Among these there are seven citizens, three of whom are foremen of their gangs. Of the 1,800 drachmas paid they earn 390 with their own hands. Only five slaves can be attributed to them with certainty, and these earn a further 300 drachmas. For laying certain stones two citizens earn 40 drachmas, out of 157. For the carving of some figurines 1,207 drachmas are paid, out of which three citizens get 510, leaving the rest to five Metics. It even happens, and that in the wood industries, in which they are relatively numerous, that the citizens do less work and obtain less remuneration than their rivals. Three of them are employed, with two Metics, on shaping beams at so much a foot. They take things easily and do 9, 47, and 68 feet respectively, earning a total of 31 drachmas for the three, while one of the two Metics disposes of 84 feet and the other of 180, making 66 drachmas between them.

Far from increasing, the activity of the citizens rather slowed down in the IVth century. Such at least is the aspect which it presents in the accounts of Eleusis, in 329-328.[1] Out of 94 professionals only 20 are citizens; the proportion has come down from 28% to 21%. Let us eliminate the slaves: in 408, out of 55 free men, 36% were citizens; in 328, out of 74 free men, they are only 27%. Naturally the citizens continue to disdain the work of the mere labourer, which the Metics themselves are now abandoning. Those occupations which they accept are not all equally suited to them. Among 27 heads of undertakings and small employers we find 9 citizens (33%), among 41 merchants they are 11

[1] See *C.I.A.*, Vols. II and IV, no. 834 *b*.

# THE CITIZENS 175

(27%), and among 15 works-contractors they are 2 (13%). The method of direct orders is to their advantage and they drop off as soon as it is a matter of tenders. The only trades in which they have the superiority are pig-breeding, transport by mule or ox, the extraction of lime, and brick-making, but this superiority is not at all great, and is due to the exclusive right of citizens to own land. In all other branches of trade and manufacture their inferiority is manifest. They hardly touch mason's work and stone-cutting. Metal-working they renounce altogether. They only just hold a place in the wood trade, which now obtains its supplies from Macedonia by the Peiræeus, and they give up carpentry and joinery. One would think that the citizen only consents to adopt a trade when he is absolutely driven to it.

This does not mean that he makes this decision only under stress of poverty. Some of these contractors and merchants are important personages. There is Arrhineides son of Charicles, of Pæania, who sells three cart-loads of lime for $12\frac{1}{2}$ drachmas; he is a contractor who plays a part in public life, thanks to his wealth. We find him holding the trierarchy, standing security for ships lent to Chalcis, and facilitating the food supply of the people by his generosity. Ergasos son of Phanomachos, of Icaria, sells bundles of reeds for eight or for two drachmas; but he bears the costs of the *choregia*. Neocleides of Cephisia, who undertakes to extract, cut, and lay stones and imports them, is the son of a contractor Antimachos, who had an important share in the Eleusis contracts twenty-five years ago. A manufacturer like Lycurgos of Melite, who takes an order for 26,000 bricks, the transport of which alone costs 390 drachmas, must have a fairly large personnel under him.

But among the citizens who live by a trade there are many who earn but little. Among the shops of the Theseion that in which Ameinias of Cythadenæon sells his baskets at a drachma each makes a poor show beside that in which the Metic Philon, iron-merchant, receives one order after another. Dieitrephes of Potamos, house-breaker, who accepts a job at 45 drachmas, supplying his own scaffolding, compares badly with the Metic Philocles, who asks 300 drachmas for the removal of rubbish. Artemon of Thria works with the freedman Tibeios; they make their living together as they can, chopping straw and riddling sand for the mortar-plashers and carrying washes and colours for the painters. Bion of Pæania combines with a Metic from Megara for a job at 14 drachmas; Lyces of Perithœdæ gets 4 drachmas for opening the offertory boxes of the sanctuary; these are humble supernumeraries to whom one day's pay is a windfall. On the whole the small number of citizens engaged in trade and industry is not counterbalanced by their turn-over. When they are manufacturers or merchants their houses do not appear more notable than those of the Metics, and often, citizens as they are, they are small, very small workers.

In truth the situation of the citizens appears even less brilliant in trade than in industry. Go through the speeches of Demosthenes; not one of the ship-owners or bankers who have retained the great advocate is a citizen by birth, and at the most one of them has become a citizen because he did big business as a Metic. Not one of the great firms known to us belongs to a citizen. The Athenians are still more reluctant to carry on a petty retail business. They must be driven by poverty. In such business they are quite lost, especially the women; mingling with Metics and freedmen, you expose yourself to being confused with them. The enemies of Euripides reproach him with having had a greengrocer for a mother; they hope that they will thus deprive him of his citizenship. A litigant whose mother was obliged to sell ribbons entreats his judges " not to regard as foreigners all those who work." If the law punishes the man who insults an Athenian, man or woman, for plying a trade on the Agora, it is not so much in order to defend their honour as merchants against a prejudice as to defend their citizenship against a slanderous doubt.

Two privileges determined the part played by the citizens in the economy of Athens. They alone enjoyed political rights, and they alone possessed the land. They devoted a part, often a great part, of their time to public affairs, and obtained in compensation allowances which made a supplement to their means of existence. But their chief resource, and also their pride, was their bit of land. Industry attracted them little, except the working of quarries and mines, which came more or less directly within their monopoly of land-

## THE CITIZENS

owning. They did not like commerce, and confined themselves to investing money in big business and banking concerns, and to living by a small trade in case of necessity. It was on others than the citizens that the greatest part of industrial and commercial work devolved, on the Metics and the slaves.

CHAPTER IV

## THE METICS

THE condition of the foreigner, which was so hard at the beginning, had greatly improved in the Vth century. The old hostility might survive in the aristocratic cities which despised work, but it had disappeared from the cities which grew rich on trade and industry. The Athenians were proud of the good reception which they gave to the foreigner, and especially to the resident alien or Metic. Guided by interest as much as by democratic feeling, they ensured for him a situation which, through the progressive mitigation of the law, was excellent in fact.

Once entered on the register of the deme where he elected to reside, the Metic had his personal status. He was excluded from real property and could not, even by a mixed marriage, create a line of citizens. In respect of justice he was less protected than the citizen in his person, but not in his goods. He paid the ordinary taxes and the " liturgies " as well, and had no special burden but a residence duty of a few drachmas. According to his wealth he served in the army as a hoplite or in the fleet as a rower or sailor. He lived where he liked, worshipped what gods he pleased, and spoke to Athenians as an equal. The general opinion is expressed by Aristophanes in a striking simile; as good bread is made of flour and bran, the thriving city mixes pure citizens and solid Metics.

In return for her kindness Athens expected valuable services of her Metics.

All the mass of craftsmen and labourers whom we saw in Homeric times wandering from town to town, and later settling in Miletos, Chalcis, Corinth, and Ægina, now concentrated in the city which aspired to economic supremacy. They came from everywhere. At first they had been chiefly Greeks from Europe and Asia. Now barbarians appeared; a colony of Thracian miners settled at Laureion, a Phrygian town was set up on the Bœotian border, and Paphlagonians, Galatians, Lydians, and Syrians were followed by Egyptians and even Arabs. When we know whence they came, these thousands of foreigners, we guess for what points they made —for the working quarters, the port, the market. They lived

Fig. 25. Head of a Semite, on a vase from Phaleron.
(P. Girard, *La Peinture antique*, P. 247.)

in crowds in the urban demes and in the outskirts. In a list of 246 Metics 159 are domiciled in the city and in the Peiræeus (65%). The Metic class, cosmopolitan in its origins, was essentially industrial and commercial.

In the city those Metics who had neither personal resources nor profession drifted about in the depths. But the majority, poor or rich, lived by regular work. They filled every industry. Free labourers, craftsmen, and manufacturers were mainly of their class.

Let us re-examine the accounts for public works which we have already consulted for the citizens. In the accounts of the Erechtheion, among the 71 professionals whose condition is known, we find 35 Metics (49%) as against 20 citizens (28%) and 16 slaves (23%). All jobs suit these Metics; they take on several trades at once; when they can find no work for their professional skill they offer the strength of their arms. Some chisel the fine flutings of a column, but it is not because they are afraid of doing a day's work as common labourers and giving a hand to take away a scaffolding. Another, who does the drudgery of a labourer and works at his own trade in placing battens and affixing delicate mouldings, accepts an order for rosettes which he causes to be carved by his paid men. And what workers they are! Here are two Metics shaping beams with three citizens. The citizens earn $2\frac{1}{2}$, $11\frac{3}{4}$, and 17 drachmas; the Metics go off with their 21 and

45 drachmas. In almost every profession the Metics are more numerous than the citizens and the slaves. They beat the slaves as labourers and the citizens as sculptors' assistants, and they monopolize the professions of sawyer, decorative sculptor, goldsmith, and painter. They fill all the trades, not only as labourers and small craftsmen, but as foremen, contractors, and employers. Manis the carpenter, Sisyphos the goldsmith, and Dionysodoros the painter are paid for the work done by their men. Ameiniades and Simias direct each a gang of stone-masons; the former works with his slave and three other labourers and keeps for himself two shares out of five, while the latter works with four slaves of his own and two slaves of Axiopeithes, another Metic, and takes five sevenths of the total price, two sevenths going to Axiopeithes.

The energy of the Metics had not died down in the IVth century—quite the contrary. In 328 the Eleusis accounts give them a still greater importance. Out of 94 professionals, the Metics number 45 and, if we add foreigners, 54. While the proportion of citizens sinks from 28% to 21%, and that of slaves from 23% to 21%, that of Metics and other foreigners rises from 49% to 58%. If we count only free men, the citizens fall from 36% to 27%, and the Metics from 64% to 61%, but if we include foreigners, the Metics rise to 73%. The activity displayed by these Metics is intense. They are obliged to leave to the citizens the working of the subsoil, the extraction of lime, and the manufacture of bricks, and to the public slaves the menial tasks which were not beneath their pride as free men in the times when the day's wage of the common labourer was equal to that of the skilled worker. Apart from that, their keenness and versatility are amazing. They do everything. A contractor tenders for a work of quarrying, transporting, and laying stones, for which he charges over 800 drachmas; the same man sells a pot of glue for 4 drachmas and five baskets at 5 obols each. Such energy deserves to succeed. The Metics do the removal of rubbish, mason's work, and plastering, they capture the wood trade, timber construction, and rough carpentry, metal work and all subsidiary occupations are in their hands, and they hold the clothing industries, the sale of colours and varnishes, and in short every small trade.

That the Athenians should have felt some jealousy of this, and that the Government should have tried to give an advantage to the citizens, was very natural. So we notice at Eleusis that the treatment of Metics and other foreigners varies slightly in the case of orders, friendly contracts, and tenders. On the list of contractors and employers chosen by the commissioners or *epistatai* and the architect without other formality, the proportion of the citizens is one third. The system of direct purchase gives less opportunity for favouritism; on the list of suppliers the citizens are not quite so numerous. And in the case of the tenders, where all compete on the same footing, the Metics and foreigners carry the day easily; out of 15 contractors they number 13, and of the total value of the work given out in this way their share is 79%.

So the building-yards of Eleusis in 328 present the same spectacle, only intensified, as those of the Erechtheion in 408. The citizens turn from the industrial and commercial professions, leaving the field free to the Metics.

While we have more information regarding those industries which are more or less closely associated with building, we know enough about the others to be able to give this conclusion a general import. Petty industry suited the Metics who had no money, as big industry suited those with capital at their disposal. We know from their epitaphs the miller Gerys, the bath-man Callios, the dyer Onesimos, the painter Leptines, the gilder Gurgos. Other Metics were barbers or muleteers. Cleanthes the philosopher served as baker's man. Comedy had a special mask for the character of the foreign cook, Tettix.

The textile industry afforded the Metics the most varied employment, and they went into it in crowds. The women were attracted by the weaving and sewing, and often sold the product of their work themselves, like Thettale who supplies bonnets for the public slaves at Eleusis. The men took readily to fulling; a dedication made by that corporation contains names of freedmen alone.

Leather, hides, and furs provided the freedmen with one of their favourite occupations. From the Eleusis accounts alone we know of the house of Attos, where goat skins are bought for slaves, and the shop of the cobbler Charias, where their shoes are resoled.

The ceramic industry was at an early date monopolized by foreigners. Many master potters and painters, in the Vth century as in the VIth, bear foreign or servile names, Amasis, Sicelos, Duris, Brygos, Syriscos, Mys, The Lydian, etc. The inscriptions painted on the vases always indicate an imperfect pronunciation of Attic or even a total lack of education in Greek. Common crockery becomes a monopoly of the non-citizens; for the orator Andocides, to manufacture lamps is to do the work " of a foreign barbarian." When the *epistatai* of Eleusis, to encourage the national production, prefer paying more for " Corinth style " tiles to importing the genuine article from Corinth itself, they give the order to the Metic Demetrios.

In metal-working, too, the Metics were the masters; with good reason they were given a special place in the festivals of Hephæstos. They were founders, smiths, nailers, locksmiths, manufacturers of tools and instruments, cutlers, and armourers. For work or trade in gold, lead, or iron there is not a man mentioned in the accounts of public works, whose condition is known, who is not a Metic. In 408 they are three, all established in the quarter of Melite, Adonis who sells gold-leaf, Sisyphos who does the gilding of the ceiling, and Sostratos who sells lead. In 329 they are six, Apollodoros who makes the nails, Menon who provides the locks, Hedylos who fits the door with iron, Sophilos who supplies the cutlery, Hephæstos who makes the tools, and Philon who does a little of everything. The two biggest workshops known in Athens are the shield factories founded by Cephalos of Syracuse and the freedman Pasion.

Only one industry was an exception, that of the mines. There the Metics had practically no chance. Inability to own the land involved inability to excavate beneath it. To obtain a concession the Metic must have obtained *isoteleia*, assimilation to the citizens in fiscal matters. So Xenophon advised the Athenians to be generous with this useful honour, in order to revive the prosperity of Laureion. As a rule the pitmen were slaves and the concessionaires citizens; the Metics, excluded from the advantages, disdained an arduous and humiliating employment. But very occasionally one of them was granted the privilege which allowed him to compete with citizens. Then he brought into the mining business the

# THE METICS

boldness of ideas and spirit of initiative peculiar to his class. The only mining concern which we see in the hands of a Metic is the most important which has come to our knowledge; Sosias the Thracian employed a thousand slaves at Laureion.

In trade the Metics enjoyed the same supremacy as in industry. There was almost complete freedom of trade in Greece. Athens demanded of foreigners a small market duty from which citizens were exempt, but it was not enough to hamper business. There was no idea of protection. Goods paid one fiftieth both on import and on export. When a big undertaking was put in hand, merchants from other cities were allowed to come when they were not actually entreated. According to the Eleusis accounts the *epistatai* buy the tiles and boards in Corinth for large sums. They allow a share of the orders for the work and the materials to two Metics from Megara, three Bœotians, a merchant from Samos, and another from Cnidos. Some bring the products of their own country, cypress logs and garments of special shape; others supply articles which are found in Attica, timber, lime, a basket; some undertake transport, and one Bœotian carries off the two biggest orders of this kind.

If freedom of exchange was to the profit of passing foreigners, it may be imagined that resident foreigners took advantage of the freedom of internal trade. At the docks, in the street, on the market, at squalid booths and in grand bazaars, the Metics held the retail trade. There were thousands of them peddling and dealing in old goods. Often they sold the goods which they had manufactured themselves; the iron-merchants had a sale-room and workshop together. Still more often they acted as middlemen; the greengrocers and corn-chandlers did not sell their own produce, since they owned no land. They insinuated themselves between the producer and the consumer, ever ready to divine interests and to anticipate demands. The accounts of the Erechtheion give a significant example of this. Two talents of lead are wanted for a piece of running-in. The Laureion mines belong to the State, they are worked by Athenian citizens, and to whom is the order given? To Sostratos, a Metic domiciled in Melite. The daughters and wives of the Metics had an equal instinct for business. We see them among the contractors at Eleusis; beside Thettale with her bonnets there is the Egyptian Soteris selling colours, and Artemis comes from the Peiræeus with bundles of reeds. One must know how to make the most of every opportunity.

With their genius for business and their foreign connexions, the Metics were in a perfect position for appropriating the higher branches of business, and especially import trade. Eastern goods had been captured by men of Syrian origin, and the merchant who sold gold-leaf for the decoration of the Parthenon bore the Phœnician name of Adonis. Thrace and Macedonia sent to Attica wood, hemp, and ropes, and these markets, too, were concentrated in the Peiræeus in the hands of Metics. Salt fish came from the Euxine, and the biggest house in this line of import business was that of Chærephilos and Sons, the four chiefs of which were raised to the rank of citizen for services done to the State. But the merchants whose transactions most affected the prosperity and the very existence of the Athenian people were those whose business extended from Sicily, Egypt, and the Euxine to the Peiræeus, and from the Peiræeus to every port in Greece—the corn merchants. Whether importers or brokers, they were almost always Metics. Their business did not enjoy complete freedom or an altogether excellent reputation, but neither Government control nor popular hatred distinguished between citizens and foreigners. Certain Metics, although wheat kings, even managed to disarm prejudice by their generosity. Chrysippos and his brother, who owned an important corn business with a branch on the Bosphorus, were well known for their patriotic philanthropy; on one occasion, among others, when the price of corn had gone up to 16 drachmas, they distributed at the cost price of 5 drachmas over 10,000 medimni. Heracleides of Salamis in Cyprus, another corn *euergetes*, earned five honorary decrees and a special ambassador was sent to a tyrant who had molested him.

Through the import trade the Metics controlled shipping. Moreover, ever since the law ordered that every ship laden with corn should come to the Peiræeus, it had hardly been possible to distinguish between the importer and the shipowner. It was not that the Metic was always the owner of the ships which he freighted; there was too much risk. He

# THE METICS 185

much preferred to share in the profits of a bottomry bond, secured on ship and cargo. Four of the speeches ascribed to Demosthenes refer to loans of this kind; all four show us Metics at work.[1] The Metics were thus masters of the fleet which made Athens the mistress of world trade.

But the holders of bottomry bonds were generally bankers. Traffic in money was almost entirely in the hands of the class which tapped movable wealth at almost all its sources. So the majority of the *trapezitai* established in the Peiræeus were Metics. Being well informed of all business that was going on, they fed by loans the commercial and industrial undertakings by which they profited. The great banks were often managed by former slaves who had become Metics. In the IVth century Pasion and Phormion are sufficiently well known. Demosthenes praises, not without a touch of irony, the bankers who " owe their success in business to good fortune," and " are absolutely obliged to watch after the preservation of their wealth." These great financiers saw things on a large scale; they knew that confidence was a security which was quoted on Exchange; they had enough patriotism, or at least acumen and vanity, to place their wealth and credit at the service of the commonwealth and to raise themselves by creditable means to the rank of citizens.

Thus in all branches of industry and trade the most important firms, the record of which has been preserved, had Metics at their head. The only mine concessionaire employing at least a thousand slaves, as we have seen, was Sosias the Thracian. The largest manufacture of which the Attic documents speak was the armour business of Cephalos the Syracusan. The most renowned firm on the salted food market was that of Chærephilos and Sons. The most celebrated bank was that of Pasion and his successor. These facts, taken together, are eloquent. Above the herd of

[1] The Metic Protos loads at the Peiræeus a ship commanded by two Massaliots, to carry goods to Syracuse and to return with corn. Three Metics, Chrysippos, his brother, and Theodoros the Phœnician, advance money on bottomry to the Metic Phormion for a voyage to the Bosphorus and back. The Metic Antipatros of Cition in Cyprus and the citizen Androcles lend money to two Metics, Artemon and Apollodoros of Phaselis, for a voyage to the Euxine and back, mortgaging a cargo of wine. Lastly, two Metics of Egyptian origin, Pamphilos and Dareios, lend money on the bottom to Dionysodoros and Parmeniscos, skipper-owners and corn-brokers of the same origin.

labourers and men of small earnings who had come from the four corners of the earth and swarmed in the populous quarters, a cosmopolitan aristocracy of manufacturers and merchants was growing up, whose highest ambition was to be assimilated into the Athenian people.

⊧ Their strength lay in their wealth. They held the capital. The citizens had the land, the houses, the public offices. For the Metics, movable property was everything, and they owned a great part of it. We can make an inventory of certain big fortunes. When Pasion realized his business he had as assets a capital of 60 talents (about £14,000), 20 being in real estate and 40 in bonds; on a basis of 8% for the real property and 12% for the bonds he could reckon on an income of about 40,000 drachmas. For Sosias to be able to hire a thousand slaves at an obol a head per diem, and thus to incur for labour alone an expenditure of 10 talents, which must have been trebled by the costs of feeding and maintenance, he must have had for the working of his mines sums which were colossal for the time. These are no doubt exceptional cases, but they are not so very rare. The group of the rich Metics changed continually according to the freaks of fortune, but it was always fairly numerous. These upstarts enjoyed life in the grand manner, throwing their money about lavishly. Their sons shone in the front rank of the gay younger generation. Among the companions of Alcibiades (what more need one say ?) there was a Metic from the Peiræeus, Cephisodoros. Comedy came to scoff at the arrogance of these foreigners who had their meals served on plate. But as a rule the Metics resembled the true Athenians who, according to Thucydides, " appreciate wealth for its practical advantages rather than as a means of display." They gratified their taste for ostentation by more intelligent and more useful actions. They readily accepted the costly " liturgies "; when the city needed voluntary gifts they were always there. Chrysippos gave up a profit of 100,000 drachmas, to assist the food supply, without his generosity bringing him the citizenship; what must have been the munificence of those who obtained that supreme honour !

It was impossible that a class which imported goods, and with them ideas, from all over the world, which was able to

## THE METICS

display the effort of its intelligence in every direction and to guide its instinct for success on every course, should never know any other means of action than money, and should confine all its ambition to gain. The liberal careers also attracted the Metics. From the humblest stations to the highest, they made themselves a place there which was very respectable.

To art it was but a step from industry. The master potters and the vase-painters were not common craftsmen, the statuaries who executed marble figurines at 60 drachmas apiece for the frieze of the Erechtheion were not plain roughing-assistants; they belonged for the most part to the Metic class. Among the great sculptors we may name Nesiotes, Styppax the Cypriot, Agoracritos of Paros, Cresilas of Cydonia, and the bronze-worker Mys, him who executed the reliefs on the shield of Athene Promachos. For decorative painting and easel-pictures the most illustrious names are those of foreigners, Polygnotos of Thasos, a lordly individual who refused money and obtained the citizenship, Zeuxis of Heracleia, and Parrhasios of Ephesos, the Oriental who loved to show himself off in purple garments and golden crown. Lastly, the architect of the Peiræeus, the creator of the cosmopolitan town on a rectangular plan, was that vigorous spirit who would have brought peoples into line as he did his streets, Hippodamos of Miletos.

The intellectual professions offered to many Metics the opportunity of making a great reputation and to some of leaving a glorious name.

Among the doctors there are Hippocrates of Cos, who had an immense success in Athens, the Acarnanian Euenor, who earned by his services the *proxenia* and the citizenship, and Pheidias of Rhodes, who opened a free hospital and received a crown as a reward. Among the scientists we find the astronomer Phaeinos, the master of Meton.

Most of the philosophers who taught in Athens before Socrates and after Plato came from abroad. They exercised a powerful influence on the moral and social evolution of the Athenian people. Already Anaxagoras of Clazomenæ had set the mind of Pericles working, when from the heterogeneous multitudes a new teaching arose. Sophists appeared from every side; Protagoras came from Abdera, Gorgias from

Leontion, Prodicos from Ceos, Hippias from Elis, Polos from Acragas. They brought with them all the ideas which were being worked out in the Hellenic world, but especially those which best suited men who were emancipated from local prejudices and eager for practical novelties. As professors, lecturers, living by their profession and anxious to live very comfortably by it, they frankly presented themselves as importers of intellectual commodities and dealers therein. So the Metics, as they invaded the economic domain in Athens, at the same time caused their ideas to penetrate into public and private life. They systematically occupied all the avenues of thought which radiated from the centre of sophistry.

Their fruitful initiative created the great systems of the IVth century. The Academy was an exception; it was for the old true-blue Athenians that Plato laid down the principles of aristocratic idealism imbued with religion. But the keen-eyed realist, who knew and thought again all that the Greeks of all times had ever known and thought, was Aristotle the Stageirite. His successor was a fuller's son, Theophrastos of Eresos. The doctrine which most strongly called for the abolition of slavery, that of the Cynics, was born in the Cynosarges, the gymnasium reserved for half-Athenians; this sect was founded by Antisthenes, the son of an Athenian and of a Thracian slave-woman, was popularized by Diogenes, an insolvent banker from Sinope, and had for its *scholarches* Crates of Thebes. Lastly, it was a merchant from Cition, Zeno, who based human dignity and personal liberty on Stoicism, and the audience which he collected in the Porch was amazingly cosmopolitan. The schools of Athens, the supreme glory of the city in her decline, owed to the Metics of the IVth century the international character which enabled them to last.

The sophists also created a line of orators. Certain Metics, who were pure Attic, were not content with teaching eloquence; they took part in the debates of the Assembly and law-courts, in spite of their condition; they composed speeches to order as a profession. These were *logographoi*. Thus among the eight orators of the IVth century who were placed in the Canon there are three Metics. Lysias son of Cephalos, after having helped in the restoration of the democracy in 403, and having failed to obtain the citizenship thereby, spent

## THE METICS

the rest of his life in writing speeches for all the great political trials, and this son of a Syracusan has remained the complete model of Atticism. Isæos, who was born in Chalcis, was in his time the leading commercial advocate, and none knew the civil law of Athens more thoroughly. Deinarchos of Corinth succeeded in worming himself into party politics and in obtaining the name of the last of the great Attic orators.

Being allowed to pay the expenses of *choregia*, the Metics could also present their works at the musical and poetical contests. They did not fail to do so. From the very first they turned to the form in which the words had the least importance and the music predominated, the dithyramb. They deprived even the music of its Greek character, and Orientalized it; the Dorian mode was replaced by the Lydian, plaintive or voluptuous. The Athenians, faithful to tradition, were loud in protest; this sort of thing was only fit for " workmen, journeymen, and suchlike." This mixed public had for its purveyors in 398 Philoxenos of Cythera, Timotheos of Miletos, Telestes of Selinus, and Polyidos—three foreigners out of four, and born in the most opposite quarters of the Greek world.

The drama did not at first appear to lend itself to the enterprise of the Metics. Tragedy, religious or patriotic, was a sort of national priestly function; comedy, which took its themes from politics, was reserved to citizens. Athens had tragic poets who were not Athenians, but none of them reached the front rank. The Old Comedy remained closed to the Metics. But after the civil wars the public spirit and taste changed greatly. The need for pacification and the moral amnesty prohibited the introduction of statesmen on to the stage; manners, growing more refined, turned from Gargantuan fantasies and dirty jokes to psychological analysis and the subtle observation of the realities of every day; but above all a social difference in the mass of the spectators, the departure of the peasants to their homes in the country and the growing numbers and influence of the Metics, obliged authors to represent other subjects and other characters, to replace citizens, absorbed in harvests, assemblies, and law-courts, by the popular types of the craftsmen and merchants. There is not one Metic name among the comic poets of the Vth century; in the IVth all who are of any value, except Aristophanes in his later period, are Metics. Antiphanes, the pioneer of the new style, was not an Athenian, nor were Anaxandrides, Alexis, and Philemon. To show the circles in which these writers lived and the life which they wished to depict, we have only to read a list of the plays of Antiphanes. At the top comes this title: *The Metic.* The list includes *The Epidaurian*, *The Corinthian Girl*, *The Girls of Lemnos*, *The Carians*, *The Carian Girl*, etc., etc. We seem to see here the crowd yelling and gesticulating on the quays of the Peiræeus. Then come *The Peasant*, *The Shepherd*, *The Gardener*, *The Miner*, *The Fuller*, *The Painter*, *The Mending-Woman*, *The Hairdressing Girl*, *The Masseuse*, *The Flute Girl*, etc., etc. Now we are in Melite, looking on at the comings and goings of the working world, and hearing the melancholy cry of the unfortunate " who die of hunger all the year round, and are always hopeful."

In art, science, and literature, then, the Metics showed the same qualities of practical intelligence as in manufacture, trade, and banking. They founded the principal schools of rhetoric, they created philosophical systems with realist tendencies, they were the best advocates, they brought modern music into fashion, and they attained great popularity as writers of comedy. They invaded, transformed, and appropriated every sphere in which, while making money and a name for themselves, they could express their feelings and spread their ideas.

The lasting alliance of the Athenian people and the Metics was therefore extremely fruitful. The organization of a powerful fleet, the creation of a sea empire, the works of public utility and beauty, the vast extension given to industrial and commercial undertakings, all these great achievements required the active co-operation of the Metics. There was no doubt of that. The success of the democracy had both for cause and for effect the prosperity of the craftsmen, traders, and seamen of foreign origin. To break the last resistance of the oligarchy the Peiræeus conquered Athens, and the Metics at once resumed the economic supremacy. But in making money they did not work only for one party; they contributed greatly to the power and glory of the city. They made the Peiræeus the centre of Greek trade, and they placed vast resources at the disposal of the treasury. It was largely due to them that Athens appeared as the capital of Greece and of the world. And by their participation with their special qualities in the splendid development of art and letters they laid in the schools the foundations of that University which was to be for Athens the dear consolation of her old age.

Athens was the city which, before the Hellenistic epoch, contained most Metics and gave them the most favourable position. But the institution existed in Greece wherever trade and industry were sufficiently developed. The class which was excluded from real property was always on the search for movable property. As soon as a city wished for its share in the flow of riches drawn by international trade, it appealed to the professionals. These landless men transplanted and acclimatized themselves easily wherever they found lucrative work. To show their gratitude for the blessings which their adopted country ensured to them, the Metics had only to make money. There were always some who made big fortunes in commerce, ship-owning, or banking. These held in their coffers the greater part of the metal reserves and paper securities. They brought about the concentration of capital.

Thus, beside the class which is invested with political rights and is attached to the soil, there exists a class which represents movable wealth, and, by the nature of its transactions and its realist spirit, is extremely mobile. From almost every city traders and manufacturers pour into almost every other city. The Metics may grow fond of the land where they have been well received and where they earn their living, but none the less they remain apart from the citizens and form a heterogeneous group in their country. The city could easily have absorbed these vigorous elements; they were, practically speaking, already assimilated. But the citizen could not agree to a sharing of privilege which would have seemed to him a diminution of his advantages and a profanation of his rights. Thus there was formed in Greece in the Vth and IVth centuries a kind of international nation which was preparing, chiefly in economic interests but also in the domain of ideas and in the very framework of society, for the cosmopolitanism of the Hellenistic period.

CHAPTER V

THE SLAVES

IN the eyes of the Greek no healthy, lasting society could dispense with slaves. To devote his forces and intelligence to the city, the citizen must be relieved of domestic occupations and manual labour. Slavery was a necessary institution. That it might be a legal institution there must be creatures made for servitude by a natural inferiority. These born slaves existed; they were the barbarians. So the life of the city necessitated and justified slavery. No one would see, neither philosopher nor common man, that the rights invoked were merely wants.

1. THE RECRUITING AND CONDITION OF THE SLAVES.

Slavery came from three sources—birth, war, and judicial condemnation.

The slaves " born in the house " were not very numerous. In the deeds of manumission found at Delphi, out of 841 slaves freed there are 217 of this class; and it should be noted that a master was more willing to free servants whom he had known since their childhood. The reason was that the breeding of human live-stock was not a good speculation. Most of the new-born infants were killed or exposed; those who had the most chance of surviving were those who owed their birth to a caprice of the master.

The vast majority of slaves came from war. After a pitched battle those prisoners who could not buy their freedom were sold; after the assault of a city the men were put to the sword and the women and children divided among the victors by lot. To barbarians these laws were applied in all their brutality; after the Eurymedon campaign Cimon threw more than 20,000 prisoners on the market. Towards Greeks certain scruples were felt, and neutral public opinion made mercy necessary. Furthermore, in barbarian countries slave-raiding

# THE SLAVES

was always allowed, and occasionally a little poaching was done on Greek soil. Wherever the power of the State did not make itself felt with energy, in Thessaly, in Ætolia, brigands and pirates acted as purveyors to the dealers in men. Lastly, private law itself contributed to the recruiting of slaves. Athens caused individual liberty to be respected in almost all circumstances, but elsewhere subordination easily became servitude. Even in philanthropical Athens the father had a right to expose his children, and new-born infants were hardly ever picked up on roads and public places except to be made into slaves. In most cities a father could get rid even of the children whom he had brought up (a horrible temptation in time of need); Athens forbade this abominable traffic, but authorized the sale of a guilty daughter. The insolvent debtor fell into the power of his creditor, with his wife and children; Athens almost alone forbade loans on the person. Everywhere the State, arrogating to itself the right which it allowed to individuals, maintained penal slavery in the code of law; Athens confined this to the Metic who usurped the rank of citizen, but most cities made much use of it, and some made civic degradation or *atimia* an ingenious preliminary to slavery.

In general, most slaves came into their master's house by way of purchase. They were of very varied origins. Few were Greeks; these were often wastrels, criminals sold abroad. In 415 one set of sixteen slaves was composed of five Thracians, three Carians, two Syrians, two Illyrians, one Scythian, one Cholcidian, one Lydian, and one Maltese. To meet the increasing demand the recruiters gradually extended their field of operation, and procured Bastarnæ and Sarmatians, Persians and Arabs, Egyptians and Libyans. In origin the slaves were more or less equally distributed between the rude countries of the North and the more civilized East. In other words, the Greeks had almost as much need of strong arms for the mines and workshops as of pliant natures and quick wits for domestic service and business.

So the slave trade was very busy in Greece. Dealers rushed after the armies or entered into relations with the pirates. They operated chiefly in the neighbourhood of the barbarian lands. Chios, Ephesos, Byzantion, and Thessaly, these were the great markets of supply. The recruiters sometimes formed a syndicate covering a district. The importers sent almost all the goods to Attica. A monthly fair was held on the Agora of Athens. Part of the cargoes was sent to Sunion for the mines. The surplus of imports was re-embarked for Sicily. So Athens was the centre of this business. The slave-dealers there were very rich; they ordered their bust from the fashionable sculptor, and would one day be sufficiently powerful to give financial backing to a revolution.

The price of slaves varied according to the period and, in the same period, according to sex, age, origin, and accomplishments. It followed the fluctuations of supply and demand; after a war, for example, it fell considerably. We know, however, that from the end of the VIth century the ransom of a prisoner of war was commonly 2 minas (£7 15s.), that at the beginning of the IVth it rose in Sicily to 3 minas, and that later it oscillated between 2 and 5 minas, settling at this last figure (£19 8s.) after the period of Alexander. The average ransom of a prisoner should be equal to the higher price of a male slave. In any case the continual increase of the ransom was certainly connected with a general rise in slaves. In 415 a sale by the legal authorities yielded on an average 167 drachmas per full-grown male. Thracians cost about this amount. Less value was attached to the Cholcidian, the Scythian, the Illyrian, the Carian, and the Messenian; these were apparently rough creatures, and their price could be as low as 105 drachmas. Rather more was given for a Lydian or a Cephallenian, and two Syrians, no doubt clever and well-trained, were run up to 240 and 301 drachmas. For women the price varied between 135 and 220 drachmas, with a rather higher average than that reached by the men.

In the IVth century the mine-workers, who counted as labourers, cost 184 or perhaps 154 drachmas. We even find average prices of 150 and 125 drachmas, but these were for field workers. Skilled workers, on the other hand, were worth a great deal. Twenty cabinet-makers were given as pledge for a debt of 40 minas; therefore they were worth over 2 minas a head. According to a legal speech, an armourer for two minas was a gift; between three and six should have been paid for him. A building-labourer was worth between five and six minas. The foreman of a workshop brought in a profit,

## THE SLAVES

and therefore cost half as much again as his subordinates. So prices were more variable in the IVth century than in the Vth, and, while the minimum was still almost the same, the average had increased greatly.[1]

The ideas of the Greeks on the necessity and lawfulness of slavery determined the legal status of the slave. He was a living instrument. He belonged to another man, he was his chattel. But this chattel was alive and had a soul. According as the master's right was absolute and uncompromising, or took into account the exceptional nature of this kind of property, there were notable differences in law, and still more in practice; for we can hardly say that slavery had a legal position in the city; it was subject to household law, which the master interpreted according to his own ideas.

On principle the slave had no personality. He had no real name of his own. If two slaves cohabited this union, though tolerated, was not a marriage. Their issue was merely an increase in live-stock which belonged to the owner of the woman. Not being a person, the slave had not the free disposal of his body. He might be made over to another or confiscated; he might become immovable property through the use to which he was put. Being property himself, he was incapable of exercising the right of property. He was allowed to save his earnings; sometimes he plied his trade outside and had the use of part of his salary; he might even make a fortune and show off his wealth. But his enjoyment of his property always depended on a permission which might be recalled. In law the master's authority came between the legally disqualified slave and third parties, whether they were private individuals or representatives of the State. The slave could not lodge an accusation without the master. But his responsibility also was very limited. He was covered by the orders which he had received. Since he owned nothing in law, he could not be subjected to pecuniary penalties; for him

[1] In the Hellenistic period the prices of slaves are still higher. A mime of Herondas mentions a slave costing 3 minas. At the siege of Rhodes in 304 a slave's ransom is fixed by an agreement at 500 dr. The lists from Delphi confirm these figures. Of the men's ransoms, numbering 223, about three-quarters come between 3 and 5 minas; only 10% are below 3 minas and 19% above, the maximum being 20 minas. The ransoms of 378 women give almost the same proportion of average prices, but 17% lower prices and only 10% higher prices, with a maximum of 15 minas.

there was, instead, the whip. If a sentence for damages was given, it fell on the master; he paid the damages, or else gave up the slave altogether by noxal surrender.

The interest of the master was the slave's only safeguard. For Aristotle the slave is an instrument, and " one must take care of the instrument in the measure which the work requires." If a man has a good servant he will be wise to feed and dress him better, to allow him rest, to let him form a family, and to hold out a prospect of the supreme reward, freedom. Plato is hard enough on the " brute " who revolts against a natural inequality; but such a difficult piece of property must be treated well, " for our own advantage rather than for his."

One might suppose that in societies in which the law kept down the slaves with implacable logic, and philosophy sought no alleviation of their lot but in a better utilization of their labour, nothing could lighten the weight of their chains. Yet the Athenian people had the merit of introducing humane contradictions into its law and improving the condition of the slaves. It acted in obedience to economic and political necessities. In a country where there were many slaves, public safety required that they should not be kept in a permanent state of exasperation. But above all the democratic idea had its own special virtue, that thoughtful tenderness for the humble which is designated by the essentially Athenian word " philanthropy." From the citizens this idea went on to shed its blessings on those who had not the right of citizenship, nor any right at all. Aristotle observes contemptuously that " democracy is adapted to the anarchy of slaves "; but, an Athenian retorts, " it was not for the slaves that the law-giver felt so much concern, . . . he considered that the man who in a democracy does outrage to anybody whomsoever is not fit to take part in civic life." So the slaves had a better time in Athens than in any other city, and it was said that they enjoyed there an amount of freedom which the poor citizens of many an oligarchic State might have envied them.

By a series of fine inconsistencies the law of Athens went so far as to regard the slave as a human being. The master had a very extensive right of correction, but he had no longer the right of life and death. The slave was armed against arbitrary and continuous cruelty; he could take refuge in certain sanctuaries and, under the ægis of the deity, call upon his master to sell him. Elsewhere the slave was exposed to the violence of all free men. Plato thought this an excellent plan. There was nothing like it in Athens. There the aristocrat was furious because he could not thrash the swine in the street and make them get out of his way.

The criminal code safeguarded the life of the slave. It was one of the boasts of the Athenian. " Among you," the Hecuba of Euripides says to the Greeks, " the free man and the slave are alike protected by the laws of murder." It is of the law of Athens that the poet is thinking. Incidentally he exaggerates its range. The murderer of a slave could never be tried by the Areiopagos, nor condemned to death. He was sentenced to temporary exile, and might be dispensed from this by the legal champion of his victim; he was at the mercy of the slave's master, and had only to pay him for the necessary permission to settle the blood price. But the eulogy bestowed on the Athenians at least proclaims the ideal at which reality, still imperfect, was aiming.

Athens protected even the honour of the slave. Every grave act coming within the definition of " outrage " was a menace to public order, and the penalty was made very severe if it appeared that the cause of a weak man was that of the whole city.

But the most novel idea, that which was most full of promise, was that of giving the slave guarantees even against the officials who embodied the State. All over Greece the police regulations carried as penalty the fine for free men and the whip for slaves. As a rule the length of the flogging was left to the magistrate or the executioner. In Athens the slave received fifty strokes, as the citizen paid fifty drachmas; both penalties were alike limited. The law recognized that the slave had a right, even under the whip of the city. This was the beginning of a legal revolution, and the Greeks were so well aware of it that the people which dared to set foot on this road was never followed along it.

In law, then, the condition of the slave was comparatively good in Athens. But it was not good enough to make his life other than abominable. Everything depended on the master. Everywhere there were despots whose every word was accompanied by a lash. But on the whole manners were mild in Greece, especially in Athens. " Philanthropy " would not have been in the spirit of the law if it had not pervaded the whole soul in private relations. When he came into the house the slave was initiated into the family worship. Showers of figs, nuts, and other fruit were poured on his head as a presage of the joys which his work would bring him. Henceforward he was one of the family. Nothing in his costume distinguished him from the free worker. He talked in his free way with everybody. He sometimes overdid this, and in the comedy Daos is appallingly impudent. But, take it all round, freedom of speech, which did not damage industry or loyalty, was preferred to silent, hypocritical hostility. A " boy " born in the house and his master who had played with him might be bound by genuine affection; a nurse might be surrounded with tenderness and deference. Many slave families were formed without opposition, and the parents kept their children. The thrifty worker heaped up his savings without fear of filling a money box for his master. An intelligent land-owner or manufacturer knew that he had every interest in giving a decent position to the men who worked his land or ran his factory. In certain cases manumission was no more than a moral satisfaction.

All these features together give a picture which is no doubt too idyllic. Beneath the few slaves who were on familiar terms with their masters there were thousands of squalid creatures vegetating, especially in the mines, fed just enough to prevent their strength from diminishing, and resting from work only when they were beaten. We cannot forget that the slaves of the Athenians used to flee to Megara, that the appearance of the Spartans was for the workers of Laureion the signal for desertion in a mass, and that in Attica itself many wretches bore on their forehead the brand of the runaway. But it is something that, in a realistic theatre, we hear slaves uttering grateful praises of their masters.

2. SLAVE LABOUR.

It would be very interesting to be certain of the number of slaves in the various cities of Greece. We hear of 470,000 slaves in Ægina, of 460,000 in Corinth, of 400,000 in Athens. The exaggeration is obvious. It may at least be taken as a rule that in the commercial and manufacturing cities the

## THE SLAVES

slave population was greater than the free. On the other hand, those districts which still lived by agriculture and stock-breeding had few slaves. When in the middle of the IVth century a land-owner in Phocis had a thousand there was an outcry. Slavery, then, appears in Greece as a concomitant of trade and industry, varying according to their development. At the same points, once in Ionia, now on the Saronic Gulf, economic life and slave labour were concentrated.

If we cannot know the number of the slaves we should at least like to know the proportion of the sexes in this class. We should then have exact information for the relative importance of the servile occupations; we could compare the total amount of domestic labour with that of industrial and commercial labour. Unfortunately the information which we possess on the subject refers chiefly to freedmen. Now the slaves who most easily obtained their liberty were those who had most opportunity for making themselves pleasant. In this the women were at a great advantage, for they attended to the cares of the household and had still other means of winning the good graces of the master. Of the 1,675 manumissions known from the inscriptions 927 refer to women (55%) and 748 to men (45%). It does not follow that the female element predominated among slaves. Moreover, even in the deeds of manumission, the preponderance of the women is not constant. At Chæroneia it is enormous; out of 104 slaves freed 65 are women (62·5%) and 39 are men (37·5%). It is almost as great at Delphi; figures covering 841 cases give 510 women (60·6%) as against 331 men (39·4%). But in Athens, according to the vases dedicated to the Goddess by former slaves (the manumission *phialai*), the proportion is the other way; out of 233 donors the women number 105 (45%) and the men 128 (55%). Moreover, on the lists of slaves confiscated by the Athenians in 415 the women are not many; a set of 16 slaves contains 4 or 5 females (25 or 31%). Therefore it seems that in Greece as a whole domestic service and family industry required rather more women than the fields, workshops, and commercial houses required male slaves. But, although the female element of the slave class was in a considerable majority in communities which got their resources from the soil and remained attached to the economy of old times, the male element predominated in the same proportion in cities where trade and industry were highly developed.

The whole of Greece needed slaves for domestic service. Almost all the work of providing food was done by the women. The maidservants made the bread and did the cooking. For big dinners special dishes were ordered from professional cooks, or else one of these artists was engaged for the day; and one or two great personages had a chef of their own. We hear of the chef of Alcibiades; and the story goes that the cook of Demetrios of Phaleron made enough in two years to buy three tenement houses. Round about the master cook there was a busy staff of slaves, scullions, bakers, and pastry-cooks.

The clothing of the family was also made at home. Under the eye of their mistress the slave-girls span, wove, and embroidered. Their chief occupations were the manufacture of materials and sewing; that is why, once free, they generally lived by the textile industry.

Women in easy circumstances had several slaves in their service, and even the humblest always had one. The speeches of the orators give us some typical examples. Ciron, a landowner with a fortune of more than twenty-thousand drachmas, had three domestics. An honest farmer, whose wife had one single child, kept a cook (a woman), a chamber-maid, and a nurse maid. The ordinary middle-class townsman had a serving man and women of two classes, those of the ground floor, who did the house work, and those of the first floor, who made the clothes. Diogenes Laertios takes us into the homes of the philosophers. Plato freed a woman in his will and left four slaves to his heirs. Aristotle, who found that with too many servants it was hard to organize work, nevertheless had nine slaves, not including children. Theophrastos, too, had nine. Straton's will mentioned seven, and Lycon's twelve. In sum, a man of average fortune employed in his house from three to twelve slaves of the two sexes. But three was on the small side. There were families in very difficult circumstances who could not do with less. Stephanos, who lived on his wits with his concubine and three children, placed at the disposal of this household a male slave and two servant women. In the *Plutos* of Aristophanes, when poor old Chremylos groans over his wretched lot he confides his

# THE SLAVES

woes in his serving man. People used to point out, as "characters," Diogenes, who did not need any one to keep his tub in order, Hippias, who made his own clothes and shoes, and Chrysippos, who took Odysseus for a model in the art of fending for himself.

The rich were obliged by the progress of luxury to live in great style, with chamber-maids, wet-nurses, dry-nurses, housekeepers, lady's maids, valets, footmen, coachmen, grooms, and pedagogues. "Use slaves like the members of the body, one for each purpose." The precept comes from a philosopher. The division of labour which it proclaims produced in very wealthy families an extreme diversity of servile functions. That servants might be well trained they were sent to take lessons at the school of housekeeping or from a certificated master in the culinary art.

In houses with a large domestic staff it was found necessary to place a trustworthy person over them. Pericles had a steward who managed his estates and had charge of the personnel. Big land-owners even had a female housekeeper in addition to the steward. Such a post was well suited to slaves; it was easy to get back from them anything which they should take improperly. For this very reason citizens looked down on it. Eutheros, to whom Socrates suggests this means of earning a living, thanks him for nothing. It was an important and delicate decision, to choose out of your slaves the man or woman who should be put over them. Xenophon gives minute advice on the subject. As housekeeper you must choose "the woman who seems least inclined to gluttony, drink, sleep, and running after men; she must also have an excellent memory, and she must be capable of either foreseeing the punishment which neglect will cost her or of thinking of ways of pleasing her masters and deserving their favour." But the masters too must treat her with sympathy, and interest her in her work and in their property, "by keeping her informed of their position and sharing their happiness with her." As steward, also, you must reject the idler, the drunkard, and the dissolute man, and look for intelligence, industry, loyalty, experience, and authority, without being too much afraid of love of gain, which is a stimulus.

Apart from this, the Greeks never attained the frightful squandering of labour of which the Roman town houses and villas were to boast. It is true that in the VIth century a Sybarite appeared at the court of Sicyon with a retinue of a thousand slaves; but these Greeks from the colonies wanted to dazzle the old world. It is also true that, two centuries later, a man in Phocis formed a troop of slaves who were likewise reckoned at a thousand head, but he meant them to work in the fields; the proof of it is that he was accused of taking the bread from the mouths of so many free men, and in the same country the wife of Philomelos attracted attention the first time she walked out accompanied by two servant-women. So it is not in thousands, nor even in hundreds, that we must count the slaves in the houses which were most largely supplied with them. It was even held, with Aristotle, that too many servants spoiled the service. Plato compares to " tyrants " (we should say, to princes) those private individuals who own fifty slaves or more. We find one rich Metic, in 415, with only sixteen slaves. In the next century the ostentatious Meidias perhaps owned more; he had three or four footmen following him and kept a number of servant-women; but if he had had a " tyrannical " household staff his opponent Demosthenes would have made the most of it, and he says nothing about it. The Athenians, who loved money in order to employ it usefully, took good care not to sink large capital in an over-grand style of house-keeping.

Agriculture did not make a very great use of slave labour. In the countries of big estates, Laconia, Messenia, and Thessaly, the lords of the land had it worked by serfs who must pay a fixed revenue. Countries of small farms are notoriously ill-adapted to slavery. Corn-growing furnished only intermittent work. To feed slaves all the year round in order to employ them usefully for about seven weeks is bad business. If costs of this amount are not to absorb the return in advance, the estate must be extraordinarily fertile and very extensive. In Greece, where the soil was poor and the fallow in alternate years reduced the sown land by a half, the production of corn by slave labour could not be remunerative. The cultivation of the olive and vine requires great care and knowledge. It suited the small proprietor working his own land. One or two slaves, employed in the house when there was no work in the fields—no more were needed. And indeed, as Aristotle says,

" with the poor, the ox takes the place of a slave." In other words, to have more than two slaves the farmer had to be in comfortable circumstances.

Therefore the slave population was insignificant in the agricultural districts. In the Vth century there were hardly any slaves in central Greece. In 431 Platæa could not make up a troop of a hundred and ten female slaves. In the IVth century the slave element barely came to one third of the total population in Bœotia. Even at Thebes, in 335, the number of slaves was far from being equal to that of free men. In Locris and Phocis slavery was almost unknown until the looting of Delphi brought gold pouring into those rural districts. In agricultural regions, then, slavery was a late institution. Sometimes it progressed suddenly through the sudden development of wealth; but wherever the development took place naturally it was very slow. Here and there an isolated agriculturist turned to slaves for the help which was indispensable, and sometimes for the family which he lacked. If, in the environs of Delphi, the farmer is very ready to free his slaves, and if the freedman in one case out of ten bears the name of his master, it is because work in common and concubinage brought master and slaves together.

Even in the manufacturing and commercial countries the abundance of slave labour was of no benefit to agriculture. Attica had few rural slaves. Xenophon's model farm employs slave labour almost entirely, but it is economical with it. Not number but quality was sought; for the difference in productivity between the good and the bad worker was reckoned at nine tenths. Agricultural science already fixed the return to be expected per team of oxen and per worker; each knew exactly how many beasts and men he needed. Among the condemned men whose goods were sold in 415 only one possessed sixteen slaves, and he was a Metic from the Peiræeus, who could not own land. All the others, those whose lands or crops, standing or ingathered, had been confiscated, either had no slaves at all or had one, two, three, or at the most four. In a list of 131 freedmen whose occupations are known there are 62 women, none of whom worked on the land, and 69 men, of whom 9 were farmers (almost all market-gardeners) and 2 vine-growers. A wise land-owner did not keep permanently the whole staff needed at the time of the oil-pressing; he took on hired men by the job or the day. They were not always free men, it is true; they were often slaves, but they were hired out. Going from one farm to another, and doing different tasks as the seasons came round, these slaves brought their masters a return which was sufficiently regular to be remunerative. One Arethusios had two men whom he hired out for all agricultural tasks; his own part was confined to making the contracts and drawing his share of their wages. The organization of labour by the hiring of slaves, which did great service in industry, was also applied, but in a limited form, in agriculture.

For industry was what required far the most slaves. The industrial system was such that it could not work without the motive power of slave labour. The division of labour in the crafts required an ever greater variety of manual operations. But for want of machines, " instruments working by themselves " as Aristotle calls them, all the work was done by man power. The slave was an animated tool; a gang of slaves was a machine with men for parts. The more arduous or delicate a task was, the more need it had, failing powerful or ingenious machines, of numerous or skilful slaves. An Athenian could not imagine that any industry could keep going without them.

The smallest craftsman had a few slaves as workmen or at least one slave as mate. Whether the work was done in the workshop, on the site, or at the customer's place, whether the master worked with his men or no, it was to him that the fruit of their labour came. One Athenian who sends mattress-makers to private houses lives on their salaries. In a comedy a mother and daughter have no means of subsistence but the money earned by their slave. A craftsman must be very badly off to say, like Lysias' cripple, " I have a trade which brings me a small income, and I carry it on myself, for I cannot afford a slave to whom I could entrust it."

The building industries employed slaves in the most varied fashion. In the accounts of the Erechtheion we find slaves of all kinds. One is a labourer at a drachma a day. Others are skilled workers, but are told off in case of need to set up or remove scaffolding. The majority work only at their own trade. Out of thirty-five marble workers about twenty are

# THE SLAVES

slaves; half of these work with their master, and one is the foreman of a gang. All are paid at the same rate as the free men and their master himself; but, if their pay is entered under their name, it does not follow that they keep it.

Slave labour, extensively used by small employers, held an almost exclusive place in those industries which were organized in workshops and factories. In Socrates' day the miller Nausicydes, the baker Cyrebos, the chiton-maker Demeas, and the cloak-maker Menon made their fortunes without employing one free man. Timarchos owned a shoe-making establishment with workers and foreman of slave condition. The orators tell us of slaves plying the trade of metal-workers, embroiderers, druggists, and perfumers. Sophocles' father had them in his forge and Isocrates' father

FIG. 26. SLAVES IN A POTTERY WORKS. COTYLE FROM ABAE IN PHOCIS, IN THE ATHENS MUSEUM. (Walters, *Hist. of Ancient Pottery*, Vol. I, P. 218, Fig. 70.)

in his lyre manufactory. On a vase painting the potter is surrounded by slaves whom he threatens or chastises. The patrimony of Demosthenes included a bed factory and an armour works, which were chiefly valuable for the personnel with which they were supplied. Manufactories of shields like those of Cephalos and Pasion owed their importance less to the premises and the stock than to the human machinery. There are abundant examples of the kind from Athens, and they are not lacking from other cities. In Megara dress-making was done entirely by barbarian labour.

But, though the total number of industrial slaves was large, they were never grouped in masses. There was nothing comparable to the great factory of the present day. The absence of machinery, the necessity for keeping the permanent staff proportionate to the constant, certain demand, the difficulty of keeping effective control over workmen who had not the incentive of pay, everything prevented the concentra'ion of industry and the collection of large bodies of labour. The shoe-makers of Timarchos numbered nine or ten, Demosthenes' workshops contained twenty cabinet-makers and thirty-two or thirty-three armourers, and the great factory of Cephalos employed a hundred and twenty men.

The only industries which could employ multitudes of workers were those which required neither vast buildings nor skilled labour, the transport business and the mines. The transport of heavy material needed an enormous train of waggons and oxen; to load the waggons and to drive the beasts at least one man was needed for each team. At Laureion, both for extraction and for smelting, labour was entirely servile. A concession or a workshop was hired, complete with personnel. The normal concession included a gang of thirty miners, but a man could obtain a large number of concessions and employ a whole army of slaves. Nicias hired a thousand to Sosias, Hipponicos hired out six hundred, Philomenides three hundred. When the Spartans occupied Deceleia twenty thousand fugitive slaves came running up to them. Xenophon proposed that the State should buy and let out miners up to ten thousand; the project may be fantastic, but the figure is significant.

To sum up, industrial slavery is inevitably confined within fairly narrow limits. It assumes a certain development only when the division of labour ceases to be rudimentary, and it does not progress beyond a certain point. For the tasks which require only physical strength the number of slaves can always be increased until it is sufficient. But if complicated articles have to be manufactured in quantities, it is indispensable that each man should specialize in one operation, in one motion. This is only possible with machinery, for to turn the human tool into an automatic machine a course of training would be necessary, which would cost too much for too little result. Now so long as a society enslaves man power, being ignorant of the use of machine power, it has such opportunity for obtaining plentiful, docile labour that it does not feel the necessity of supplementing it artificially. The absence of machinery is at once the cause and, to a certain

## THE SLAVES

extent, the effect of industrial slavery; the result is that slavery is an obstacle to industry and even prevents itself from extending indefinitely.

### 3. MILDER FORMS OF SLAVERY.

The hiring of slaves, a practice of which we have seen several examples, is worthy of our consideration. It will show us how readily the institution of slavery could be adapted to the most varied requirements.

The slave is an instrument which is expensive to keep, a machine which must be fed even when it is not working. Farmers and craftsmen had every interest in not buying more than the number of hands strictly necessary for current work. But casual tasks, to meet which no permanent organization could be adopted, were distributed fairly evenly over the aggregate of the agricultural and industrial concerns. So there was a large place in the economic system of Greece for slaves who passed through the hands of several employers at intervals. The use of these transient folk was even a convenient way of obtaining the personnel which was needed permanently. It was a very costly matter to rear a slave and teach him a trade; it was still more costly to buy a skilled worker. Allowance had to be made for passing sickness, chronic infirmity, old age, and death; in a word, out of the return of the human capital a big reserve had to be set apart as a sinking-fund. Moreover, no industry was secure from unemployment; the most careful estimates of the labour necessary might be suddenly upset. Therefore the head of a business who wanted slaves often had every interest in paying hire day by day rather than in sinking a large capital.

There were, then, a great number of employers prepared to take their labour on lease. To whom were they to turn? Certain farmers and manufacturers let out their men in the dead season. But from the Vth century, and especially in the IVth, the hiring of slaves constituted a special profession or at any rate a mode of investment; the owner and the employer of the labour became distinct. The heads of concerns, especially when they were the sons of their fathers, soon grew tired of the cares entailed by the management of a big house and the supervision of a large staff. "All who can spare themselves this trouble," says Aristotle, "hand over the charge to a steward, and themselves plunge into politics or study philosophy." Even then you had to have a confidential slave under your control. It was better, as a rule, to relieve yourself of all trouble and simply to draw from your human capital the reasonable interest which so many people were ready to offer. The hirer out of slaves supplied labour almost as the banker supplied money.

Certain masters placed luxury slaves at the disposal of the public. In a city like Athens, rich and filled with foreigners, slaves could be hired like carriages. Cooks, footmen, lady's maids, flute-girls went out to the house of the customer. Theophrastos' miser gets the slaves of his friends to wait on him and lets out his own. When slaves had a trade, as soon as their master had no work to give them he sent them to the Agora to look for an engagement. They brought him their pay, unless he went in person to collect it. But the hiring out of slaves was a much bigger business when a contract for a long period made it a permanent investment. The provision of keep and the responsibility for accidents were left to the employer, and the return was steady. Contracts referred not to single individuals but to gangs and sometimes regiments of workers. They could even be leased out with the premises of which they were a part, and then the hire of the men could hardly be distinguished from the rent of the buildings. Phormion let his shield manufactory, all complete, capital, premises, and personnel, for a talent. Pantænetos took a mining concession, provided with thirty slaves, for a rent of 12%. As a rule the mining slave brought in an obol a day. Nicias made a thousand obols in this way (about £2,400 a year), Hipponicos a hundred drachmas (about £1,440 a year), and Philomenides half as much. To get good interest from your money, and to have a guarantee that the men would be returned in good condition, was a first-class transaction, offering complete security. What could be more tempting, even for modest fortunes? Euctemon's inheritance, assessed at three talents, comprised a piece of land, a wood, cattle, a town house, and "slave workmen." Ciron's consisted of a piece of land, two houses, three servant women, and "slaves earning wages." Even for mine labour there were small men who hired out slaves, like Diocleides who went

to Laureion to collect his rent for a single slave. There was no business better suited to women, after investment in real property, than the purchase of slaves for letting out. Socrates asks the courtesan Theodote with affected simplicity " Have you land ?" " No." " Then you have a house which you let ?" " No, I have no house." " Then you have workmen."
This was the valuable resource which Xenophon wanted to secure for the State. His plan is grand in its simplicity. The treasury shall first acquire 1,200 slaves, which it will hire to the mine concessionnaires. By constantly making new purchases with the rent collected, it will multiply its human capital by five in five or six years. It will even raise this capital to 10,000 head, which will bring in an annual income of 100 talents. The author of this magnificent scheme has no doubt that by socializing the hiring of slaves it will always be possible to find a market for a constantly increasing quantity of men, without the price ever falling. He is unaware of the relations of supply and demand; he only sees one thing, that money invested in slaves brings in as much as 33%, and that that would be a good thing to take for the State.

The hiring of slaves detached them more or less from their master; the practice of letting them work in their own way had a far more important effect on their life and status. Those who went out to work necessarily enjoyed a fair amount of liberty, especially when their master was not in the trade himself or they belonged to a woman. Others, established in a shop, placed in command of a ship, or entrusted with a big piece of business, naturally escaped being subject to meticulous control. There was thus formed in industry, and still more in trade, a class of slaves whose situation was very greatly improved.

The fundamental advantage enjoyed by these privileged ones was permission to live where they pleased; hence their name of *choris oikountes*. Thereby they were already partly freed, and that is why the slave " living out "was often confused with the freedman, who was included among the " resident aliens." The slave and his master alone knew the exact tie which bound them; for others it was not always easy to distinguish the slave who had this amount of freedom from the ex-slave, who just might not have it. We see, for example, in the Erechtheion accounts, a workman who sometimes calls himself " Crœsos slave of Philocles " and sometimes " Crœsos domiciled in Scambonidæ." He was a slave who had permission to live in his own domicile. This right of living out must have been highly appreciated by the slaves. It gave them complete independence in their daily life, and they were free to form a family.

Their material situation varied greatly. There were some to whom their master left the task of seeking work, making them pay him to perpetuity the rent which he would otherwise have demanded from the men to whom he hired them. Timarchos allowed his shoe-makers to form a co-operative society of production, on condition that they paid him a daily sum of two obols per workman and three per foreman. This system of fixed payments was even suited to petty trade. Theophrastos' miser establishes his slave in a stall, and when the latter pays in copper the rent which by the agreement should have been paid in silver he exacts an exchange fee from him. Being free to move about, certain slaves made quite a good position for themselves. Some became master potters. Some acted as deputies to the kings of Athenian business. A slave of the firm of Chrysippos and Brother managed the Bosphorus branch, holding power of attorney and keeping the money. Phormion, the proxy of Pasion's Bank, was for a long time a slave before he was freed. In this way there rose out of the slave class personages who were wealthy, lavish, and proud, happy to prove themselves in their own eyes and to show their power to all.

At bottom the condition even of the most independent slaves had a weak point. Liberty enjoyed on sufferance is never anything but precarious. The slave who was obliged to pay a regular return was in practice a serf who paid a subscription, a freedman burdened with a perpetual tribute; but if he did not pay the return regularly, or if his master changed his mind merely out of caprice, he became once more a plain slave, in the strict sense of the term. When a merchant left the running of his business to a slave, he was responsible even for obligations of which he knew nothing;[1] therefore he was

[1] We gather the amount of liberty which could go with slavery from the history of Midas, the slave of Athenogenes. This Athenogenes, the son and grandson of perfumers, decided to leave bottles and washes and to go into politics. He entrusted his three shops to Midas. The latter managed the business with full powers. Being free to contract

# THE SLAVES 211

absolutely compelled to exercise some control. Even when he gave the slave his head the master still held the reins.

It is sufficiently remarkable that trade and industry should have caused some slaves of strong character to rise above the mass. It is perhaps still more surprising to see a whole class of these men without rights attaining a very decent position in public life.

The State had slaves of its own. Indeed it had two kinds, workmen and subordinate officials.

In a great city like Athens many public services which needed workers bought them. The mint employed a fairly large staff, and the roads officials had gangs of sweepers and road-menders under them; these departments had recourse to slave labour. The commissioners of public works did not call upon private industry alone; they also had squads of slaves at their disposal. So in 329-328 seventeen public slaves were employed in the yards of Eleusis, with a foreman who was likewise a slave.

Certain theorists and even some politicians thought of developing the institution of the State slave on a grand scale. Plato would have all trades carried on by slaves in his republic. One Diophantos tried to put part of this scheme into practice; and then Xenophon proposed that the treasury should acquire ten thousand miners and hire them to the concessionnaires at Laureion. Athens did not fall to the seductions of these two systems, knowing how dangerous they were for her finances, for the free workers, and for the slaves themselves. More daring was shown in certain distant and obscure cities, in which aristocratic contempt for manual labour prevailed and the proximity of barbarians made the recruiting of slaves cheap and easy. At Epidamnos, near Illyria, all public works were carried out by slaves grouped by trades. At Chalcedon, near Mysia and Lydia, the tyrant Phalcas decided that every professional man should be a public slave. We see what lay behind the suggestions of a man like Plato, and why they were rejected by the democracy.

---

debts, he proceeded to do so. But, since the slave had no civil personality, it was the master who in such cases found himself the debtor. To save the situation Athenogenes sold Midas, hoping to pass the responsibility on to the guileless purchaser.

The Athenian State did not feel the same scruples about the allotment of minor employments. Many slaves held posts in which they had nothing in common with the workmen. Such were the Scythian archers, policemen who by their office had some authority over the citizens themselves. Such were the agents of justice, the executioner and his assistants. Such, too, were the guardians of the public stores and the inspectors of weights and measures. Such, above all, were all the multitude of heralds or beadles, registrars, scribes, and accountants attached to every magistracy.

We know from an inscription from Eleusis the material condition of the slave employed on public works. For his food (*trophe*) he got three obols a day, or 180 drachmas a year, enough for him to feed well without spending everything. He was clothed; the State gave him every year a working garment or *exomis*, an outer garment or *himation*, a goatskin cloak, a felt cap, and a stout pair of shoes with right to three resolings, representing in all 45 drachmas. This salary, then, came to 225 drachmas a year (£8 14s.). The foreman received the same ration allowance, but instead of being clothed he was given an allowance of 100 drachmas (£10 18s.). Over and above their ordinary allowance all these slaves received gratuities in kind. At certain sacrifices there was a good hunk of mutton or pork for each. At the Feast of the Pitchers a gang of eighteen men was given a victim worth 23 drachmas and two metretæ of wine ($16\frac{1}{2}$ gallons). The most deserving received a reward of a higher kind; they were employed inside the temple, and were allowed 15 drachmas to obtain admission to the Mysteries.

For its subordinate officials the State did more than for its workmen; it gave them an assured moral standing. Except the archers, who lived under canvas, and the executioner, whom prejudice kept outside the walls, they lived where they liked. They could have their own house; their furniture was their own; they kept their savings. They were free to take a wife and to bring up their children. They were present at sacred ceremonies and appeared in processions. Being ranked as foreigners, they could not appear in the law-courts, but they could defend their interests by obtaining the help of a patron. We know one of these slaves, named Pittalacos, who

# THE SLAVES

was quite a little personage, living in great style and going to the law-courts like an Athenian.

On what were the privileges of the public slave ultimately based? The only law which protected him was that which protected every slave against ill-treatment by any other person than his master. The master of the public slave was the State, a rational being. He was under the orders of a magistrate, but the latter could exercise his authority only to enforce respect for the regulations; his slaves were subject to administrative discipline, but that was almost all.

How could their chief treat them with severity? He needed them. They alone were fully acquainted with his accounts; indeed it was once suggested that they should be made responsible for the army funds. He did not know what was in his stores; when an inventory was made of the bronzes preserved on the Acropolis, it was one of the slaves that was publicly given credit for it. The magistrate was appointed for one year; the slaves were always there, looking after the archives, keeping up the traditions and the forms, suggesting ways out of difficulties. On the Pnyx, from which they were legally excluded, they sat behind the president, ready to pass him the relevant document for any question; their names sometimes appear in the official list of the members of the office. When it was found desirable, after a revolution, to put the legal code in order and to cancel obsolete or contradictory clauses, the work of editing was confided to one Nicomachos, who had become, in his servile capacity of registrar, the most learned jurisconsult in Athens. These registry clerks certainly inspired some jealousy in the poor Athenian, who was not quite sure whether he should despise or covet posts intermediate between slavery and middle-class citizenship; they were often accused of using their competence in the interest of the highest bidder. But on the whole their class was treated with much consideration, which they thoroughly deserved. It was this body of unassuming, trustworthy servants which caused the hidden machinery of the State to work and, in a commonwealth which was ever moving, ensured the continuity of the government.

## 4. THE FREEDMEN.

So there were many degrees in slavery, from the misery of the miner, toiling in the darkness, to the magnificence of the banker, flaunting it in the company of the highest-born citizens, and the dignity of the official, conscious of the service which he rendered to the city. But in law the position of the slaves was the same throughout. The only improvement of their lot which was not revocable was the recognition of their liberty by a formal deed, manumission.

The methods of manumission were various. As a rule the slave was released by repurchase. But the master was not obliged to accept the ransom offered; his good will must be won or he must be tempted by an alluring offer. Freedom might be purchased direct by the slave himself, but it was generally a third person who did this; the slave handed the ransom to him, and was bought and set free. In the beginning the gods, i.e., the priests, had really bought the slaves; manumission was effected by dedication to a deity, and the manumitted man, free in respect of men, became a sacred slave, a *hierodoulos*. Later the god came in as a witness and not as a party; he gave his guarantee to a contract between the master, the freedman, and the buyer. Gratuitous manumission was an exceptional case, the spontaneous act or the last wish of a grateful master, or a favour bestowed by decree in return for service done to the commonwealth.

In most cities manumission was confirmed by solemn formalities. It was done inside or in front of a temple. It had sureties who were morally responsible, the god, the priest, and other persons of a priestly character; what was still safer, it had sureties who were materially responsible, who undertook, should any one infringe the liberty thus sold, to pay one and a half or two and a half times the purchase price. Witnesses to the deed were present, who would be able to certify all. The terms of the deed were generally carved on a wall of the sanctuary. But the Athenians hated any excessive formality. In Athens, to make the deed of manumission valid, an oral or written declaration was enough. The name of the slave liberated was proclaimed in the law-court or in the theatre. For choice an original document was drafted before witnesses; usually it was a will. Religion now came in only as a subsidiary witness, to solemnize the moment when the freedman was born to a new life; he received baptism in " the Water of Deliverance."

Athens did not cast the freedmen into a separate class, like other Greek cities and Rome. She simply placed them among the Metics. The freedman at once took a new name, a name which was his own for good. Like the Metic, he had civil personality but no political rights. Like the Metic, he must have a legal representative with the city, who was naturally his old master. Like the Metic, he paid, in addition to the usual taxes, tribute, the sign of his condition. In the army, in the law-courts, in religious ceremonies, everywhere the freedmen were ranked with the Metics, beside but below the citizens.

Their only inferiority in relation to the other Metics came from the private obligations which still bound them. Their former master had a right to their inheritance, if they died childless. Moreover, the same contract which created their liberty might restrict it. When a slave was liberated gratuitously it was natural for his benefactor to make certain demands. At Cos a slave was released on condition that he and his descendants cultivated a sacred garden and contributed to certain religious ceremonies. It seems more curious, at first sight, that manumission against payment should not have been an absolute release. But sometimes the savings of the slave did not come up to the desired amount, or the master was content to release him on credit, or a third party advanced the ransom and acquired a right over his debtor. Thus many slaves only obtained their liberty in virtue of a burdensome engagement; they would pay it off either in kind or in money or in both. While there were slaves who lived where they wished, there were freedmen who were bound to reside near their former master and owed them their service for a fixed period or for the rest of their life. A manumitted woman might find herself deprived of all right over her future children; she was refused the option of strangling them at birth, and one or two were taken to replace her in the house which she had left. When the freedman had a trade, he was sometimes made to work without pay for his master or to give him a part of his wages. Sosas will learn the trade of fuller, to do all the work which his master gives him; another will practise medicine as his master's assistant, and will have a right only to bed, board, and clothing. Some masters even reserved the right to hire the freedman to third persons, as if he were still a slave. And the penalties contained in the restrictive clauses were severe. Attic law provided for a private suit against the ungrateful or criminal freedman. If the accused was acquitted he was released from all obligations to his master, and had only to thank Athene by offering her a silver *phiale* weighing a hundred drachmas. But if he was found guilty he relapsed into slavery and became the chattel of an exasperated master.

The great concern of the freedmen was to obtain an endurable position in the society into which they entered. Those of Athens almost all settled in the city quarters or the environs; in a list of 177 freedmen, 158 live in the urban or suburban demes and about ten by the sea. Agriculture did not attract them; they could only lead a poor life on the land of others. A few, however, obtained work as day-labourers with market-gardeners. Others remained attached to their offices. But it was in commerce and industry that the freedmen found their chief resource. From the cook to the banker, they continued at their old trade, often with their patron. Most were hawkers, shop-keepers, labourers, craftsmen, porters, or transport agents. In a list of 69 freedmen, 11 live by agriculture (9 farmers, 2 vine-growers), 15 by trade (2 big merchants, one iron-merchant, one tow-merchant, one dealer in salted goods, one greengrocer, one sesame-merchant, one frankincense-merchant, one merchant of uncertain character, one retailer), 7 by minor trades (2 servants, one footman, one baker, one cook, one barber), 24 by industry (one tanner, one leather-dresser, 7 saddlers-and-shoemakers, 2 shoemakers, one bed-manufacturer, one lead- and silver-founder, 2 blacksmiths, 2 gilders, 2 gem-engravers, one book-copyist, 3 manufacturers of uncertain goods, one labourer), 10 by transport (one ox-hirer, 2 donkey-men, 2 muleteers, 2 baggage-porters, one amphora-carrier, one wineskin-carrier, one porter of uncertain goods), and, lastly, two in administrative employment (one registrar, one assistant registrar).

Above the general mass, certain freedmen attained a good

position. Mylias was manager of the armour works bequeathed to Demosthenes, and Lampis, a skipper-owner, directed the business of Dion & Co. Several master potters bear names which betray their servile origin. Banking was monopolized by freedmen, Pasion and his successor Phormion, Socrates and his successor Satyros, Timodemos the successor of Socles, Cittos, Eumathes, etc. There were even freedmen who made a name in letters and philosophy. Step by step, one of these former slaves would rise by his exceptional qualities and distinguished services to the realization of the highest dream, the citizenship. Nicomachos, who was charged with editing the laws of Athens and held their fate in his all-powerful hands, rose " from slave to citizen, from beggar to rich man, from assistant registrar to legislator." The bankers Pasion and Phormion obtained from public gratitude their certificate of complete naturalization.

The women had far greater difficulty in benefiting by their regained liberty. Many of them, poor servants, did not even make use of it. Some had no choice; the deed of manumission laid on them the obligation to continuing in service. But others resumed their customary tasks of their own free will, prisoners of their habits and glad to protect themselves from need. When they tried to earn their living outside, the first work which offered itself was that which they had learned in the gynæceum, the manufacture of clothing. In a list of 46 freedwomen plying a trade, 35 are weavers, one is a shoemaker, and one a cobbler. They had no other resource but the minor street trades; the same list gives 3 retailers of odd goods and 4 sellers of frankincense, sesame, and tow. The married woman often helped her husband in his business. The freedwomen who lived as free-lances were not afraid of any profession; they were inn-keepers, citharaplayers, flute-girls, acrobats, courtesans, procuresses.

Compared with the slaves, the freedmen were not numerous. At Delphi we find from nine to twenty manumissions in various years. In Athens, towards the end of the IVth century, the freedmen who dedicated a *phiale* to the Goddess numbered sixty a year; but these catalogues of dedications cannot be taken as complete lists of manumissions. It is nevertheless certain that, in the most generous city in Greece, masters were not very ready to give their slaves liberty, and that there, as elsewhere, the owners of human cattle knew that business was business.

The infrequency of manumissions was chiefly due to economic reasons. There was no advantage in releasing a slave at the trade price. One worker must be replaced by another. Now, you knew what you were losing; the man who was going away had shown himself capable of making money and saving expense. On the other hand, you did not know the productive value of the man whom you were getting. Except in rare cases, the decision to release a slave was inspired by sentiment or a large sum. The State quite sympathized with this. Athens needed Metics, but she recruited them among the foreigners of free estate. It was useless to diminish the amount of slave labour. On this point public interest was at one with private interests.

Economic motives were reinforced by a moral reason. The freedman was held in low esteem. He was reproached with keeping the manners and mentality of slavehood. Poor wretch, for years he has been the butt of ill treatment and contempt, keeping his hatred down in the bottom of his heart and cringing in order not to leap up, he has never had another pleasure in life but occasional bouts of lewdness, the satisfaction of his hunger by pilfering, and the crabbed joy of swelling the hoard which is to bring him freedom; in short, in him the vices inoculated by society are aggravated by heredity and slavery; and people are surprised because he does not grow a new soul in a night. He is greedy and coarse; he thinks only of material needs. All trades are good to him, and all means of succeeding in them. He obtains wealth by fraud and position by adulation. He marries his master's daughter. He dazzles the town with his ridiculous ostentation. There is no harder despot to his slaves than the upstart from slavery.

In short, the same beliefs which for the Greeks made slavery a legal institution led them logically to be sparing of the favour of manumission. Being convinced that in recruiting slaves they were obeying an unavoidable necessity, they could not dismiss the army of labour at the rate at which it was formed. Being persuaded that every barbarian was condemned to serve by a natural inferiority, they told themselves that nothing could raise him from his degradation.

## THE SLAVES

So, though the Athenians might improve the condition of the slave, they did not go so far as to make freedom easy of attainment. By a remarkable departure from its principles, the law protected him against third persons, including the magistrates, and against his own master. In practice the slaves of private individuals were treated kindly, were free in their actions, and were sometimes rich, while the slaves of the State were secure for the morrow. There were, therefore, many who advanced by stages on the road to freedom. But to very few was it given to reach the goal. Athens made slavery endurable, but did not try to abolish it. It was not that, amid the chorus of traditional declamations on the necessity of slavery, certain discordant voices did not arise to call for its suppression. In the days when the frequency of international relations widened the intellectual and moral horizon, sophists and Cynics boldly proclaimed the superiority of natural law over positive law. Alcidamas utters a striking maxim. " God created us all free; nature makes no slaves." Comedy, the echo of the popular conscience, sets the stage ringing with the pathetic words of Philemon: " Though one is a slave, he is a man no less than you, master; he is made of the same flesh. No one is a slave by nature; it is fate that enslaves the body." But to translate such words into acts and to abolish slavery it would have been necessary to overthrow all institutions and to destroy the city. The time was not come; Athens could not think of suicide. At least, carried along by her democratic tradition and by her " philanthropy," she did not cease to make in favour of the slaves partial reforms, which, by the logic of principles, might one day have led to a decisive reform. But the Macedonian was watching. The liberation of the slaves was one of the measures which the conqueror of Athens hastened to forbid.

## CHAPTER VI

## THE DIVISION OF LABOUR

IN ancient Greece social phenomena are more apparent in political than in economic form. This rule applies even to the division of labour. Thus Athens in the Vth and IVth centuries shows us a progressive specialization of public offices. The splitting up of powers increases the number of offices. " In great cities," says Aristotle, "each magistracy has special duties. The great number of the citizens makes it possible to have many officials. It cannot be denied that posts are much better filled when the attention of the magistrates is thus limited. In small cities, on the other hand, many various duties must be concentrated in a few hands. In that case we may compare the public offices to certain instruments which serve several purposes."

But the development which brings about a multiplication of offices, corresponding to the complexity of requirements, acts with equal force on the division of labour in the economic sphere. The professions which had broken loose from the family occupations split into many branches in the great commercial centres, especially in that formed by Athens and the Peiræeus. In the countrysides and country towns several small trades were still exercised by one man, but in the city a man like Hippias, who wanted to be dependent on no one but himself, inspired general mirth. The genius of a Plato came to give the economic sciences for the first time a theory of the division of labour.

Already the *Sophist* and the *Politics* sketch out a classification of crafts and trades. One of these dialogues distinguishes between the creative and the acquisitive arts, the other between the principal arts, which make articles of consumption, and the auxiliary arts, which supply the instruments necessary for this manufacture. The acquisition of raw materials includes the extraction of ores, the felling of trees, the stripping of bark and papyrus, the cutting of osiers

# THE DIVISION OF LABOUR 221

the flaying of beasts, and the tanning of hides. The principal arts supply man with house, clothing, and arms, provide for the maintenance of his body (agriculture, hunting, cooking, gymnastics, medicine), satisfy his need for play (painting, music), etc. The instruments are of various kinds—tools, different utensils, and means of transport, i.e. vehicles and ships.

But it is in the *Republic* that we find an exposition which has all its doctrinal value at this day, and constitutes a document of the first order on the economic condition of Athens in the first third of the IVth century. The primal necessities are food, housing, and clothing; the most primitive society needs husbandmen, house-builders, weavers, and shoemakers. "But must each do for all the others the work which is his own? Must the husbandman, for example, provide food for four, or should he, without thought of the others, spend a quarter of his time in seeking sustenance and the rest in building his house and making his coats and shoes?" "I think that the former way would be more advantageous to him." "Which would be better—that each should ply several trades, or that he should confine himself to his own?" "He should confine himself to his own." All the advantages of specialization are resumed in these words: "More is done, and done better and more easily, when one man does one thing according to his capacity and at the right moment."

Here the principle is laid down, and the consequences are drawn in the *Laws*. "Let no iron-worker work in wood; let no wood-worker have iron-workers under him; let each practise one single trade, by which he will live." With marvellous discernment Plato goes still further. What is true for one city is true for the whole aggregate of cities. None produces all that it needs; each has to obtain from outside what it lacks, and, in compensation, to produce above its own consumption. In addition to the merchants who act as middlemen within the city there must be agents for export and import. The law of the division of labour is universal in its action.

Without Plato's philosophic penetration, but with a gift of observation which makes his words remarkably precise, Xenophon not only tells us of the specialization of trades,

8*

but shows us the true division of labour within the same trade. At the same time he informs us of the great difference which existed in this respect between various places. " We must not be surprised," he says, " to find that articles, of whatever kind they be, are better made in big cities than in small. In small cities the same workman makes a bed, a door, a plough, and a table, and often he builds a house too, happy to have enough work from all these crafts to earn his living. Now it is impossible that the workman who does so many things should be equally successful in all. In the big cities, on the other hand, where there is a large population with the same wants, a man can live by one single trade. Sometimes, indeed, he practises only a special branch of a trade. One makes men's shoes, another women's, one lives entirely by the stitching of the shoes, another by cutting the leather. In the making of chitons one is a cutter and another only fits the pieces. A man whose work is confined to such a limited task must necessarily excel at it."

Several documents confirm the words of Plato and Xenophon on the specialization of trades. In a speech attributed to Pericles we are told of work done on the Acropolis. " All kinds of raw materials, marble, brass, ivory, gold, ebony, cypress, have been put in hand by craftsmen of all classes, carpenters, moulders, bronze-workers, marble-workers, goldsmiths, turners, painters, enamellers, and metal-chasers. For carriage we have needed merchants, sailors, and pilots on the sea, and on land cartwrights, oxhirers, waggoners, rope-makers, sail-makers, leather-dressers, road-menders, and miners. And every trade . . . employs an ordered crowd of workers and an organized body of labour." In the comedy of the *Peace* Aristophanes shows us how far metal-working was split up, when he brings on craftsmen who made each one single article, the sickle or the mattock, the javelin, the helmet, the crest, the cuirass, the shield, or the trumpet.

To obtain a more lively picture of the division of labour let us cast an eye on the different branches of industry.

The provision of food still held a large place in family life, especially in the country. Many households made their own flour and bread from their own corn. The slaves wielded the traditional pounder or turned the quern. A model

## THE DIVISION OF LABOUR 223

establishment possessed a bake-house. Almost everywhere the mistress of the house did the cooking with the servant-women. In town, however, these occupations passed more and more into the hands of professionals. The importer put foreign corn on to the market; the merchant sold it to the miller, who supplied the baker. We hear of millers and bakers in a large and in a small way, citizens who performed frequent " liturgies " and freedmen established in low quarters on the outskirts. Pig's flesh and salted goods brought fortunes to big merchants or a livelihood to retailers. Fruiterers, greengrocers, and sesame-sellers of both sexes went about the streets or had stalls on the market. An official document mentions a walnut-seller. Cooking, too, became a profession. It was the boast of the great houses to train each slave for a special duty. Xenophon, in his reflections on the division of labour, speaks of the art of cooking. " The man," he says, " who has only one single man to make his bed, lay his table, knead the bread, and prepare the meal, must take everything as it is offered to him; but where each has his special task, one boiling the meat, another roasting it, one doing the fish in spiced sauce, another frying it, and another making the bread, not of different kinds, but of the one kind which suits the master, it seems to me that everything will be quite perfect." Metics sold exotic dishes to the public. Even citizens plied this trade, which was considered highly respectable. For big dinner-parties outside help was called in, buyer, scullions, waiter, etc., up to twelve cooks sometimes. A place was reserved on the Agora for chefs waiting for an engagement, with their assistants and their paraphernalia. Some of these artists were masters who conveyed their teaching far and wide or wrote cookery-books. There were specialists in pastry. There were others who enjoyed a pan-Hellenic reputation for black puddings, stews, lentil soup, fish, and above all congers. Itinerant cooks and keepers of cook-shops sold modest portions of meat to the common people.

For clothing old customs were not abandoned. The women made the clothes of the family and kept them in order. The wool was still carded and spun at home; on a vase painting a woman sits preparing it over a basket. In the gynæceums ladies and young girls spent their days at the embroidery frame. On the other hand, the washing, dyeing, and fulling of the wool constituted so many separate in-

FIG. 27. WOMAN PREPARING WOOL. CUP FROM VULCI. (*Jahreshefte des archæol. Instituts*, Vol. XIII, Pl. i.)

dustries. Common materials were woven partly by the family, partly with the help of women engaged by the day, and partly in factories. Finer fabrics came from special

FIG. 28. WORK IN THE GYNÆCEUM. ATTIC PYXIS, IN THE NEW YORK MUSEUM. (*American Journal of Archæology*, Vol. XI, P. 419, Fig. 3.)

workshops, or else, if a private individual had a slave-girl who was expert in this work, he sent all that he did not use to the market, and thus practised a subsidiary trade. The

# THE DIVISION OF LABOUR

garments were easily made at home because of their extreme simplicity; but for this very reason it was not difficult to organize work in the gynæceum for sale. Sometimes slave labour was used for making a single kind of garment. Demeas made the chlamys, the sleeveless military overcoat, Menon the chlanis, the light cloak of fine wool. The making of the chiton even needed special workers for the cutting and putting together. Every style of headgear had its specialists; one Conon made ladies' bonnets.

Leather and hides were prepared in great tanneries, like that which Cleon the demagogue inherited from his father and that owned by another party-leader, Anytos. Leather-dressing formed a separate industry; we see it practised by the father of the Strategos Iphicrates. Work in leather was divided up in a fairly unequal way. There were men who were at once saddlers, harness-makers, and shoemakers, and there were shoemakers who both made and repaired shoes. But each of these trades might also exist independently. Certain saddlers produced only one class of article, for example the bridle. Men's shoes and women's shoes, which were made by different firms, required different hands for the cutting and the putting together.

Work in the mines was already highly organized. For the extraction the master miner commanded three gangs; the strongest men handled pitching-tool and pick, the lads carried the ore out, and the women and old men were employed on the sifting. In the workshops on the surface the master smelter supervised the work of the crushers (the strongest at the mortar, the weakest at the hand-mill), the washers, and the smelters.

On the division of labour in the metal works we have not much information. But we know from Aristophanes the extent to which the manufacture of agricultural implements and arms was specialized. Demosthenes' father ran a sword factory and procured hilts ready-made from other firms. Artistic bronze-work required the co-operation of the rough-ing-assistant for the industrial part and th' artist for the finish and chiselling. We are a long way from Homer's *chalkeus*.

In the potteries shaping, firing, and decoration were separated from the VIth century onwards. Nicosthenes might still sell vases of all shapes, but soon distinction was made between the makers of cooking-pots, jars, *lekythoi*, *kothones*, goblets, etc. Among the vase-painters, the difference grew more and more marked between the workman who merely did the ornamental bits and the master, such as Duris or Meidias, who treated a subject and executed figures.

It is not easy to obtain a clear notion of the division of labour in the building industry, for sometimes big contractors obtained orders for very different works and left the execution to foremen, free workers, or slaves of specialist professions. But if we consult the accounts of public works we at least are in no danger of exaggerating the progress made. Already towards the end of the Vth century the Erechtheion accounts show different men working in wood and in stone, and the rough carpenter is distinct from the sawyer and the decorative wood-worker. This does not prevent the word *tekton* still being used to designate the stone-cutter and the mason just as much as the man who sets the beams, the sawyer, and the decorator who makes the panels of a ceiling. One Micion who lays rafters and battens also does mason's work; Manis, who fits roof timbers and fastens mouldings, also carves rosettes in marble. So, too, there are men who not only do the laying of the stones but also do the plastering of the walls and the fluting of the columns. In 329, at Eleusis, further progress is to be seen. The *tekton* still combines the tasks of repairing pavements and making roofs, Agathon quarries, transports, and lays stones, Euthymides lays foundations and makes bricks, and Parmenon is both mason and plasterer; but even among these employers, who have a large number of workmen, work in stone excludes that in wood, and the small craftsmen specialize in mason's work, brick-laying, or plastering. We find just the same change taking place at Epidauros. In the first quarter of the IVth century the contractors, great or small, perform different tasks. The Corinthians Euterpidas and Lycios cut the stones, and one cuts cross-beams while the other supplies deal. Aristæos does the mason's work, the roofing, and the varnishing, and carves an inscription. In the second half of the century Saunion of Paros obtains an order for all kinds of work, extraction and laying of stones, sculpture,

# THE DIVISION OF LABOUR

and inscriptions; but all his contracts are connected with marble.

Work in wood, while breaking away from that in stone and in brick, itself became split up into more and more trades. The woodman of Acharnæ made charcoal which he took to market. Plato tells us how important the barking of oak-trees and the cutting of osiers had become, and Aristophanes mentions Diitrephes the basket-maker. The accounts of the Erechtheion rank the wood-worker among the *tektones*, but designate him by a special name. At Eleusis one craftsman undertook to make doors, a clothes chest, and a winch, but others made doors alone, and one merchant sold door-jambs by themselves. Even among the cabinet-makers there were several trades; those who made beds were distinguished from those who made chairs, and a street in Athens took its name from the box-makers. Cart-building had long been a speciality. Ship-building, so important in the Peiræeus, employed several different professions. The manufacture of oars was an independent industry, and so was rope-making, which was distinct from the tow-trade.

In the manufacture of musical instruments the lyre-maker was distinguished from the flute-maker. But it is hard to say whether this distinction was rigid, and whether Cleophon, the *lyropoios*, really sold nothing but lyres, or was like the modern French *luthier* (musical instrument maker), who would be in a bad way if he was limited to selling lutes.

Between high art and industrial art the difference became clearly marked from the Vth century. In the IVth, Isocrates says " Who would venture to compare Pheidias to a modeller in terra-cotta, or Zeuxis and Parrhasios to painters of *ex votos ?*" The industrial arts became more and more split up; the encaustic painter was distinguished from the distemper painter, the gilder from the goldsmith. In a list of freedmen we find two gem-engravers and one book-copyist.

In the transport business a great number of small trades is not a sign of progress. For the works at Delphi and Epidauros sea transport was separate from land transport, and the prices paid give a poor idea of both. But at the Peiræeus the organization of transport appears to have been admirable; goods and passengers had their special wharves and ships. For transport the great cities had a multitude of different agents, ox-hirers, donkey-men, muleteers, and porters. Among these last, specialists appear as carriers of amphoras and carriers of wineskins.

So the Greece of the Vth and IVth centuries presents, on the whole, a remarkable specialization of trades. But we must not see in this phenomenon the significance which political economy usually attaches to it. In modern times a great division of labour goes with the development of capitalism and large-scale industry. In ancient Greece it was just the richest manufacturers who directed dissimilar industries at the same time and produced several kinds of article in the same works. The great miller Nausicydes makes use of his bran and mill-sweepings for breeding pigs. Anytos attaches a shoe factory to his tannery. Demosthenes' father is both armourer and cabinet-maker. One Conon leaves in his will slaves who are druggists and others who make ladies' fashions. At Epidauros, a contractor from Paros goes into partnership with one Athenian for the extraction of marble and with another Athenian for the sculpture of it, and in addition obtains the order for carving the inscriptions. At Delphi, a quarryman from Argos undertakes to build a colonnade, to set triglyphs and lintels in place, to supply models for the sculpture, to cut steles, to make iron clamps, to saw beams, and to rig up a crane on a jetty. The variety of these undertakings is no proof that professional specialization did not exist among the craftsmen and workmen. But the men who thus specialized were humble individuals, working independently or in little groups. The cleverest slaves were employed in a domestic workshop and took the products of their labour to the market. The armourers and makers of agricultural implements whom Aristophanes introduces to us one after the other, do indeed show us that work in metals was very much divided; but they were craftsmen who went on to the public road to offer each article as they completed it. The division of labour does not authorize the same conclusions in antiquity as in contemporary societies, because it was not associated with machines. It was a feature, not of great factories, but of a small or medium-sized industry dealing direct with exacting customers.

It is true that competition was not exclusively local. The Greek world was acquainted with international division of labour. Many cities sent their products abroad, Corinth her hangings and carpets, Megara her common clothing, Pellene her plushy cloaks, Miletos her chlamydes, Argos her caldrons, Chalcis her swords, and Athens the vases of the Cerameicos and the silver of Laureion. But labour, though so intense in the exporting cities, was not concentrated in establishments provided with monstrous engines; the labouring classes swarmed in the ports and the quarters of the city, but were not dependent on a few all-powerful firms.

CHAPTER VII

MONEY

1. THE MONETARY SYSTEM

IN the great centuries of Greece natural economy retained much vitality. It more or less governed life in remote districts. The Spartiate continued to live on the harvest brought in by the Helots. Thasos in the IVth century appropriated the enjoyment of a piece of land to the remuneration of a public service. When Delphi opened a subscription in 360, the Apolloniates sent 3,000 medimni of barley. The Thessalians still paid their taxes out of their harvest, and Syracuse exacted the tithe from her Sicel subjects. In the great cities, it is true, all institutions were based on money economy. When Aristeides taxed the cities of the Delian Confederacy in 478, he demanded only money. Nevertheless, even in Attica, natural economy was far from having disappeared. Before the Peloponnesian War most of the land-owners lived on the revenues of their estates. When Pericles sold the whole of his harvest together, and obtained his provisions in the city market, this method of domestic economy was remarked as a novelty. About 412 an Athenian invested capital in the Chersonese and obtained the interest in corn. In the leases of the period rent was paid in barley; on this point contracts were the same at Eleusis as at Olympia or Heracleia. Even in town, wages were for a long time paid in food; towards the end of the IVth century contracts still specified that a craftsman or labourer should feed himself " at home." All over Greece the priests received as stipend a part of the tithe and as perquisite a part of the victims sacrificed. The importance of the trousseau in a bride's portion continued to recall the days when the dowry was not made up in coin.

All these exceptions do not prove that the economy of classical Greece was not monetary, but they show the exact meaning which must be given to the general rule. We are not in a period in which the monetary system, fully developed, can give birth to indefinite credit and to the wild extremes of capitalism.

At the beginning of the Vth century the minting of money was hampered by the scarcity of metals. The mines of Thasos, the Thracian coast, and Siphnos were the only ones from which the Greeks obtained gold and silver before the Persian Wars. It is true that the Thasians extracted gold on their own island and at Scapte Hyle to the amount of 150 talents a year. The Siphnians, indeed, grew so rich that with the tithe of their revenue from the mines they set up one of the finest of the "Treasuries" which were the pride of Delphi, and about 524 Samian freebooters came and forced them to pay a tribute of 100 talents. But in the Greek lands as a whole the yield was too small to supply great quantities for coining. Suddenly there was a revolution. In 483 the prospectors at Laureion made marvellous finds; work was started on the rich veins of Maroneia; and in a year the State took 100 talents for its share. Shortly afterwards the mines of the Strymon were bringing the king of Macedon a talent of silver a day, and the gold of Mount Pangæos was attracting the Athenians. The precious metals spread over Greece.

But as fast as they came into circulation they were withdrawn from it, especially gold, by the practice of hoarding. This primitive method of capitalization persisted in several forms. About 480, in Phrygia, Pythios kept in his cellars 2,000 silver talents and 3,993,000 gold staters—over four million pounds. At the same epoch Architeles of Corinth owned so much gold that people came from distances to buy it. The temples above all drained the precious metal. Bullion and pieces of jewellery came to the gods from all parts as *ex voto* offerings, tithes, fines and shares of booty. Delphi received gifts from the whole world without ceasing; about 360 her reserve was assessed at 6,000 silver talents and 4,000 gold, and it was sufficient to maintain a mercenary army for ten years. On the Acropolis of Athens the Goddess amassed as much as 9,700 talents of coined silver, in addition to the offerings, the sacred vases, and the Persian spoils, worth another 500 talents, and the cloak of the chrysele-

## ATHENIAN PERIOD

phantine statue, which weighed 44 talents of fine gold and was worth 616 talents of silver. The extent to which the circulation of gold was reduced by mortmain is shown by certain facts. When the Lacedæmonians decided to gild the statue of Apollo of Amyclæ, they could not obtain the required metal in Hellas and had to ask Crœsus for it. Hieron I of Syracuse had great trouble in obtaining the gold for a tripod and a Victory intended for Delphi; only Architcles the Corinthian helped him out of his difficulty.

While the sanctuaries thus held back the gold in Greece, in Persia the Great King kept piles of bullion hidden in his palace. Therefore in the course of the Vth century the value of gold went up steadily. Darius I had fixed the ratio of the yellow metal to the white at $1 : 13\frac{1}{3}$. About 438 this ratio had risen to $1 : 14$. The King hid away his gold bars more jealously than ever, and suspended the coining of darics.

FIG. 29. CYZICENE OF ELECTRON. (*D.A.*, Fig. 2270.)

The disappearance of coined gold left the field open for the electron stater; save for the extraordinary popularity of the " Cyzicenes " there was for some time complete silver monometallism.

Towards the end of the Vth century an inverse movement commenced. Persia, intervening in the struggles of the Greek cities, poured out enormous sums to the Spartans, the Athenians, and the Bœotians, while mercenaries enlisted in their tens of thousands in the service of the King and the satraps. The gold of Susa was beginning to circulate. The disasters of the Peloponnesian War compelled the Athenians to empty the coffers of the Acropolis and to melt down the Victories and the mantle of the Goddess. The Arcadians mobilized the treasure of Olympia, the Phocians laid hands on that of Delphi. Trade brought the darics flowing in. Philip of Macedon developed the Pangæos workings and drew

# MONEY

from them 1,000 talents a year. Finally Alexander opened the secret coffers of Persepolis.

So gold currency spread very rapidly. In an Athenian house in 409 a sum of 3,000 drachmas contained 30% of gold; six years later, in a fund of 32,000 drachmas, the gold was 44%. The coining of gold became so general that the ratio between the two metals altered with unprecedented speed. At the beginning of the IVth century it had come down to 1 : 12. To set bi-metallism on a solid basis Philip established the Macedonian system on the ratio of 1 : 12⅔. But the law of supply and demand overturned the obstacle which he tried to erect against it. " Gold, become common, falls as it raises the price of silver." These words, written in 355, hold good for a long period. From 336, before the conquest of Asia, the officials placed in charge of the building of the Delphic temple take one stater of gold for ten staters of silver. This ratio of 1 : 10 is final. A comparison of it with the original ratio of 1 : 13⅓ gives a notion of the great mass of gold previously held in the Greek temples and the Persian palaces.

In brief, silver supplied Greece with its national currency. But each city clung to its right to strike its own coinage. Political autonomy had as a result monetary anarchy. Serious difficulties ensued in commercial practice. Every international exchange entailed a money-changing transaction. Now the majority of the cities obtained scandalous profits from their issues. The coining of electron encouraged fraud. This white gold contained a proportion of silver which varied, in the natural state, between 20% and 48%. Between two electron staters of identical appearance the real value could differ in the same proportion as between an Euboic drachma and an Æginetan drachma. The silver currency was debased almost everywhere by unscrupulous alloying. " A great number of cities," says Demosthenes, " use silver which is obviously mixed with copper and lead." Indeed the existing specimens of the coinage of the Italian and Sicilian colonies sometimes contain only 910 thousandths of real silver. Often the city did not give itself so much trouble, and merely made its coins under weight. In case of need the mint adopted extreme measures. Hippias of Athens withdrew from circulation all the money issued, and replaced it by a new currency of half the weight, and Dionysios of Syracuse ordered his creditors to present themselves with all their coin, doubled its value by means of a surcharge, and wiped out the debt while keeping a large balance for himself.

All these methods, debasing, clipping, and fictitious valorization, can only succeed by the forcing of the exchange within the limits of the territory in which a law obtains. On the international market money is merely a commodity subject to the law of supply and demand, with its price fixed by its intrinsic qualities. While suspect coins were sent back to the city of issue, certain cities by their honesty secured universal acceptance of their currency. The Cyzicenes, the staters of Lampsacos, the *hektai* of Phocæa, and the " Philips " enjoyed as good a reputation as the darics. Down to the first quarter of the Vth century, wherever coined money was

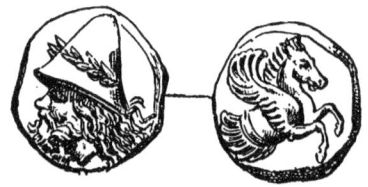

FIG. 30. GOLD STATER OF LAMPSACOS. (*D.A.*, Fig. 6581.)

needed, people accepted the " tortoises " of Ægina and the " foals " of Corinth, which contained 961 thousandths of real silver.

Just then Athens rose to the head of Greece in coinage as in everything else. She had a peculiar advantage in the silver mines of Laureion. Yet the very abundance of the white metal presented a serious danger, that of depreciation. Silver soon went down 5% in relation to gold, and, after being for a long time worth between two and three hundred times its weight in copper, in the IVth century it was worth only 120 times as much. Athens safeguarded her currency by her unfailing honesty. On this subject she had the same ideas as the advanced states of modern times; no temporary gain could compensate for the least diminution of the public credit, and there was no better policy than honesty. No precaution was neglected. The pigs of silver brought to the mint there underwent another last refining, before they were cast into the moulds. Since the blank had to be pared in

# MONEY

order to have a good finish, it was at first given a weight over that of the standard. Thus no coin was issued which was not declared good by the touchstone and the assay balance. The alloy is extraordinarily pure, reaching as much as 985 thousandths. It is often lower, but it never goes below 966 thousandths, and in this case the alloying is not artificial, for it sometimes contains two thousandths of gold, so that the coin has a higher value than the standard.

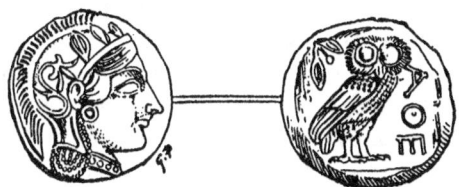

Fig. 31. Attic tetradrachm (archaic style).

Nothing could detach Athens from a tradition which was part of her honour. In the most terrible years of her history, when the treasury was empty, when the galleries of Laureion were abandoned because of the invasion, when sacred vases and pious offerings were thrown into the melting-pot one after the other, she was indeed obliged to strike emergency currencies of gold and of bronze; but never, not even when she was fighting for her life, did she consent to debase her silver

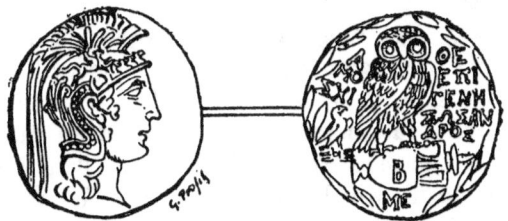

Fig. 32. Attic tetradrachm (late style).

coinage. This uprightness had its reward. The " Laureiot owl " was recognized as " the best of all coins." It was current on all markets. Neither passion for autonomy nor political hate could resist it in Greek lands, and it was well received among all the barbarian peoples. So the Athenians only touched the type of their coins with extreme prudence. Long after art had been given a new life by the genius of Pheidias, the coiner's hammer was still reproducing the archaic stamps of Athene with the fixed smile and of her bird with the large round eyes. Old established habits must not be disturbed. The Attic tetradrachm, a universal object of exchange, even became an article of export. While the coinage of Laureion encouraged foreign trade, inversely foreign demand gave a useful impetus to mining and minting.

By her monetary supremacy Athens seemed to be leading the Greece of the Vth century towards monetary unity. The Confederacy of Delos opened a vast field of expansion to the owls. How could Athens admit that the federal tax should be assessed and paid in different currencies, and that the pay of her sailors should not be good everywhere ? The capital must give her money an official character. Political power was aided by commercial preponderance. Without any coercive measure, by the mere force of circumstances, independent minting ceased in the Cyclades, and in the cities of Asia Minor it was reduced to supplying small cash for local requirements. Later, in the days when the Athenians centralized their empire by arms and laws, the confederate cities were formally ordered to adopt the Attic coins, weights, and measures. But Athens no longer had the means to impose her will. It was ordained that never, in anything, would Greece attain unity.

After the fall of Athens a great number of cities returned eagerly to striking coinage: it was for each of them a proof of her liberty. But monetary anarchy had such drawbacks that attempts were made to remedy it. Special agreements, limited unions were composed. Olbia, by a one-sided measure, gave legal currency and favoured treatment to the Cyzicenes, fixing the rate of exchange. Mytilene and Phocæa agreed to issue identical currencies. The federations which gave such a special character to the constitutional history of the IVth century always had a common coinage, and some of these political experiments are only known to us from their issues of money, remarkable effects of autonomy in a widened form. But for all this an instrument of exchange was necessary on the international market. Athens remained mistress of trade and still watched over the good alloy of her money. An Athenian could write, towards the middle of the IVth century, " In most foreign cities the merchant captains are obliged, for want of current specie, to take another cargo in

# MONEY

exchange for that which they unload. Among us, if you do not want a return freight, you sell your cargo for money; you take excellent merchandise, and wherever you sell it you get more than your capital." Thus Attic money was at a premium on every exchange. The administration of Delphi was forced to obtain some for its payments at an exchange fee of 6·66%. In theory the ratio of the Attic drachma to the Æginetan drachma was 7 : 10, but in actual business it was 3 : 4. No disaster, not even the Macedonian conquest, could prevent the universal diffusion of a currency which owed its good name to its intrinsic value.

As a general rule greater circulation of money causes a decrease in the purchasing power of precious metal, i.e. a general rise in prices. Was this so in Greece ? No doubt it is difficult to argue about the price of commodities in antiquity. There were enormous differences between the producing and the importing countries; there were considerable differences between wholesale and retail trade; and the price of certain goods, particularly cereals, was subject to extraordinary variations in the same year and sometimes on the same day. However, we have sign-posts which enable us to observe a continuous rise. At the end of the IVth century Demetrios of Phaleron reckoned that since Solon's time prices had been multiplied by five. They are even six times as much, if we stop a little earlier, at Alexander's conquest. After having increased by about 50% during the VIth century, they doubled between 480 and 404, and doubled once again about 330; a commodity which was worth 1 about 590 rose, at the dates given above, to 1½, 3, and 6.[1]

---

[1] Wheat is worth 2 dr. a medimnus (1s. a bushel) towards the end of the Vth century; about the beginning of the IVth it is worth 3 dr. in the retail trade; fifty years later the normal price is from 5 to 6 dr. (2s. 8d. to 3s. 2d. a bushel). But dearth often doubles this price; a crisis brings it to 16 and even 32 dr. (8s. 5d. and 16s. 10d. a bushel). Barley is sold retail at 2 dr. at the end of the Vth century, and wholesale at the same price in 360; in 328 the price oscillates between 3 dr. and 3 dr. 5 ob. (1s. 7d. and 2s. a bushel).

Oil costs in Attica, about 380, 12 dr. per metretes (1s. a gallon), retail price; later thrice as much is paid at Lampsacos.

An ox, assessed at 5 dr. in Solon's time, is still about this price in Sicily at the end of the Persian Wars, and in 368 Alexander of Pheræ promises the Athenians meat at half an obol per mina (½d. per lb.). But for a long time very different prices have been in force in Attica. Oxen for sacrifice cost 51 dr. a head on an average in 410, and 77¼ dr. about 375. There is a rise of 50% in thirty-five years. (*Cont. on p.* 238.)

## 2. INVESTMENTS AND INTEREST

To the end of the Persian Wars Greek society had not advanced beyond hoarding. Money was amassed and did not work. The temples had their reserves and individuals filled their coffers with their surplus. A wealthy Milesian comes to Sparta to deposit his whole fortune in a temple; he can find nothing better to do with it than to place it in security. The Phrygian Pythios, who counts his silver talents in thousands and his gold staters in millions, does not use them, and offers them all to King Xerxes. In the house of the Corinthian Architeles the bars of gold lie idle. Herodotos rediscovers the wisdom of old times when he makes Solon say that the only advantage of opulence is that it allows a man to gratify certain whims and is an insurance against bad times.

But from the middle of the Vth century, and especially in the IVth, wealth circulated and the available money was turned into productive capital. About 410 one Diodotos left 80,000 drachmas; of these, 48,000 were invested, 46,000 for a short period and only 2,000 (true, it was war time) more permanently. In the second quarter of the IVth century the statement of a fortune of a third the size, which, however, was very carefully managed, contained only 900 drachmas of ready money; the bulk of the assets comprised furniture, live-stock, ingathered harvest worth over 5,000 drachmas, a building valued at 15,000 drachmas, two houses out on lease together worth 3,500 drachmas, 4,000 drachmas on loan

---

The price of copper at least doubles in a hundred years. We have seen that silver, which in the Vth century was worth between 200 and 300 times its weight in copper, is worth only 120 times in the IVth century. Thus the price of copper, which used to vary between 26 dr. and 41 dr. per talent (35 dr. in Athens about 420) rises to 69 dr., that is from between 28s. 2d. and 44s. 4d. per cwt. to 73s. 9d.

From the prices of worked iron we can reckon that the price of raw iron varied until about 336 between 5 dr. and 5¾ dr. per talent (between 5s. 2d. and 6s. per cwt.); the rise was very slow within these limits, when, about 330, a boom quadrupled the price.

The *himation* or outer garment, plain quality, costs 16 dr. in 392; the wholesale price of 18½ dr. paid in 329 for the commonest quality seems to indicate a fairly serious rise. An unworked ox hide costs 3 dr. about 380, and twice as much at Troezen in the second half of that century. So shoemaking becomes expensive. In 388 a young blood is luxuriously shod for 8 dr.; in 329 slaves' footgear costs 6 dr. wholesale.

bearing interest, and over 1,000 drachmas in other loans. If Lysias in 404 had in hand 3 silver talents, 400 Cyzicenes, and 100 darics (about £1,280), and Demosthenes' father left on his death 80 minas of ready silver, it was because both directed industries which required much floating capital. The times had gone in which men allowed the wealth which they had acquired to lie dormant. A moderate sum was kept for daily needs and the remainder was invested.

If this transformation had happened abruptly, capital in all its forms would have gone down in value. But it did not take place with such rapidity. Whatever the investment might be, the returns were at a high rate. It was not infrequent, in the IVth century, for the fortunes of minors, when managed well, to double or treble in a few years.

Above all the capitalist wanted to acquire land. But he could only do this if he was a citizen. These two factors, the importance attached to ownership of land and the disqualification of the Metic, cancelled each other from the economic point of view, for the latter prevented the former from inflating the price of land and consequently from reducing the income yielded by it. There was therefore nothing to impede the free action of the law that the safer investment should be the less remunerative and that it should nevertheless remain in proportion to other investments. Before the middle of the IVth century the rent of a property was assessed at 8% of the purchase price. But the fall in the value of coin caused the rate of capitalization to rise to 12%. In 300 a farmer who rented an estate at 600 drachmas a year reserved the right to buy it for 5,000 drachmas. In emphyteutic leases referring to land which was not highly productive, an anomaly appears; future improvements were taken into account in the book value but not in the rent, which thus remained far below the ordinary rate, sometimes between 2% and 4%.

In big towns like Athens many houses were leased. In normal times the income from house property was almost equal to that from land. A certain Stratocles, who owned one property worth 3,000 drachmas and another worth 500, obtained 300 drachmas from them in rent, about $8\frac{1}{2}\%$.

After the leasing of houses the most popular investment was the letting of slaves on hire. At first sight it seems a splendid business. For an average slave, whose price varied between 150 and 200 drachmas, the employer paid the owner one obol a day and provided keep. If a slave worked the whole year round he represented a gross income of 60 drachmas (between 30% and 40%). But we must deduct for deterioration and unemployment. In the mines, it is true, the slave was hired by the year and must be returned undamaged; but in practice he was soon used up, and then no one would take him. Wastage was at least as high in this kind of lease as in the others. The hired slave was therefore a capital which brought in a big return because it could not be invested permanently, or because, diminishing very quickly, it must be reconstituted very quickly from the interest; he was a stock which did not yield regular dividends or was only partially repaid. As always, the rate of the return rose in inverse ratio to the certainty.

Land, rented houses and capable slaves—these were the usual investments of the Athenian *rentier*, and Socrates pretends to take these to be the courtesan Theodote's source of income. There was, however, another use of acquired wealth which increased in importance—loan at interest.

It was not universally admitted. The ideas of the philosophers on the subject were behind the times. They agreed in declaring usury detestable, because it made money produce money and constituted the least natural of modes of acquisition. The customs of the family were still strong enough for the free loan or *eranos* to be a constant practice, even outside the family. The *eranistes* asked only for his capital to be returned. A friendly loan, a debt of honour, and gratitude as interest. But if the free loan was held in some esteem, it was because the lender parted with a sum which might be useful to him and might never come back to him. To decide the possessor of property to deprive himself of it, to allow an indifferent party to profit thereby, the attraction of a compensation was necessary. Nothing was more legitimate than a surplus value for the capital thus risked, a share in the increase of productivity which it caused. No doubt the professional money-lender was in

# MONEY

bad odour. But he was regarded as different from the honest man who lent money "to do a service and in order not to see his capital melt away in his hands." The public usefulness of loan at interest was proclaimed, as a necessary method of feeding trade, and the popular courts were asked to visit the full severity of the law upon fraudulent debtors.

In practice the supply was at least counterbalanced by the demand. On the one hand, the increase of wealth and of coin encouraged investment; individuals made use of their savings and sanctuaries of their reserves. On the other hand, the growing activity of the market encouraged borrowing. Money transactions became so numerous towards the end of the Vth century as to necessitate intermediaries, the bankers. At the middle of the IVth century the inventories of legacies and the lawsuits show us fortunes invested entirely in loans. To provide his stock the trader borrowed. Nicobulos, who was in business for a long time, often had recourse to credit, and when he had capital he employed it in the business of others. Æschines the philosopher kept his perfume-works going by means of borrowing. Pantænetos and Mantitheos worked mines with the support of money-lenders.

What could be the demands of capital here? The general rise in prices proves that the supply of precious metal increased to a greater extent than the articles of consumption. It therefore seems that there should have been a corresponding fall in interest. But too many factors were working in the opposite direction. The largest treasures were slow in being mobilized. The requirements of trade and industry became ever more pressing. The undertakings which especially asked for credit were those in which the risks were greatest and control most difficult, enterprises of import and export by sea. In this class of business the interest on money had to be swelled by a big share in the profits and a big insurance premium. The rate fixed for loans which were frequently required and were very risky could not remain without influence on the normal rate, but tended to raise it. It is true that the lender's security was multiplied and reinforced in every way, by mortgages for double the amount lent, by the pledging of workshops with slaves and goods, by penal clauses giving right of seizure without an order of court, or by bonds in the form of absolute conveyance with a right of redemption, under which the rent represented interest, all without prejudice to securities being demanded which were coupled with strict conditions. But this wealth of securities was not always effective. The law of humanity, which forbade the pledging of the body as security for a loan, destroyed the most serious guarantee which small men could have offered. Another obstacle to the liberty of contracts made their conditions harder. The Metics, who possessed movable fortunes, could not lend on mortgage over real property because they could not enter into possession of their security. Most loans had therefore to be guaranteed by movable property or slaves. The best security was still the borrower's word and sureties jointly and severally liable. So the Athenians perfectly understood the power of personal credit. "Of all kinds of capital," says Demosthenes, "the most productive in business is confidence, and if you do not know that you do not know anything." It was not enough to prevent the rate of interest from being very high.

The State, which by its laws worked unwittingly to raise it, never held it its duty to intervene to restrict it. Solon imposed restrictive laws in respect of guarantees, but recognized none in respect of interest. On one single occasion, to our knowledge, the Athenian law fixed the rate of additional interest on default of payment, and made it 18%; this rate may perhaps represent a penal measure, but in any case it is not lower than the normal rate. Moreover it is practically certain that the principle of unrestricted liberty was common to the whole of Greece. It is very surprising to find, at Delphi, a decree which forbids the exaction on any loan, public or private, of interest over 6%; the fixing of a maximum, and that so low, can only have been a revolutionary measure taken by a political party. The general rule was one of *laisser faire*.

A system of frequent payments of interest is suited to a market on which the law is dictated by small capitalists; the lender cannot wait to draw the interest due or he wants compound interest. This was the system in Greece. In short-dated contracts, like marine loans, the interest was paid with the principal. As a rule the interest was reckoned at so much per mina per month, thus making twelve or

# MONEY

thirteen dates of payment in the year. Every debtor dreaded "the end of the moon."

The normal interest was one drachma per mina (12%). The rate of 5 obols (10%) was only granted as a favour. We see mortgage loans at 8 and 9 obols (16% and 18%). Xenophon proposed that the Athenians should create a public fund which should lend to individuals at 10 obols (20%). The highest rates were imposed on industry. A perfume-manufacturer borrowed from friends at 9 obols in order to repay bankers who were taking twice as much from him.

For commerce the usual rate was 8 or 9 obols, but bottomry bonds were much more productive. The lender advanced his money on hull and cargo; in case of shipwreck the borrower owed nothing, neither interest nor principal; if he reached his destination, either outward or homeward according to the terms of the agreement, he repaid the capital with the specified interest. So we have here a genuine case of partnership *en commandite*, which produced in part the effects of an insurance contract. But the creditor ran more risk than the debtor; in addition to the perils of the sea he had to fear all the frauds usual in a world of illicit traffic, such as barratry, misappropriation of the security, and failure to obtain a freight for the homeward voyage. Bottomry was an excellent business if all went well, but it was an extremely hazardous transaction. So the interest was very high. It varied according to the person of the borrower, the place of destination, the duration of the sea voyage, and the political situation. For a single voyage from the Bosphorus to the Peiræeus in war time loans are given at one eighth ($12\frac{1}{2}$%), a nice premium to make in a few days. For the same voyage, outward and homeward, 30% is asked. At other times the conditions were somewhat milder; for the crossing from Athens to Thrace and the Bosphorus, with the option of going as far as the Borysthenes, and the homeward voyage without excessive delays, $22\frac{1}{2}$% is accepted; for the whole sailing season, about seven months, 30% is demanded. A capitalist who is happily inspired can employ his money twice in the same season and make 40% and even $66\frac{2}{3}$%. Some of them unblushingly ask for 100% for ventures in the Euxine and the Adriatic.

It is needless to lay stress on the enormities of the money-lenders. The 36% required by the bankers from a suspicious client, the 25% *per diem* which Theophrastos' miser collects in person as he goes from shop to shop, are almost without importance except in the history of manners. On the other hand, what we must remember, as a sign of an economic and social situation, is the high rate of normal interest and above all of marine interest.

## CHAPTER VIII

## LANDED PROPERTY AND AGRICULTURE

XENOPHON in his *Œconomicus* places in the mouth of Socrates a superb eulogy on agriculture. Work in the fields is not merely a source of pleasure; it gives strength to the body and hardihood to the soul, and it teaches even the free man justice and solidarity. " It is the most honoured profession because it gives the community the best citizens." The most beautiful of the arts is also the most useful. Agriculture provides sufficiency, if a little will-power is exercised. " She opens her arms to all who come to her and offers them all they wish, knowing how to receive her guests with magnificence. . . . She is the mother and nurse of the other arts; when Agriculture thrives all the others thrive with her; wherever the land is left untilled almost all the other arts perish, on land and on sea." A purpose lies beneath Xenophon's words. He is contrasting the riches drawn from the earth, which in his eyes are alone a reality, with the riches in money displayed by commerce and industry. He is expressing the Physiocratic prejudice, like Plato and Aristotle. But most of the Greeks, and probably most of the Athenians, thought the same as the philosophers on the subject. Landed property still retained much of the almost exclusive importance which it had had for so many centuries; by the very fact that the foreigner was debarred from it, it kept all its old prestige. No doubt agriculture found itself losing ground in an economic world invaded by commercialism. It suffered more and more, in an age of international competition, from having no asset but a small portion of meagre soil. For all that, the land remained the sole means of livelihood in many countries, and the chief resource of the citizens even in a country which had so definitely embraced marine trade as Attica.

## 1. The Distribution of the Land

The distribution of the land differed greatly in the various cities. In many parts individual appropriation had been only incompletely carried out, or else it had not rendered the land easily transferable and divisible, or else it had allowed rich men to round off their estates by purchase and the realization of mortgages. Pindar constantly shows us the great land-owner, devoted to horses, chariots, and physical exercise, the great lord of the high mien and the open hand, who is glad to invite poets to sing the nobility of his race, the wonders of his mansion, and his own great achievements. In Thessaly the Scopads displayed royal opulence, and a cavalryman from Pharsalos, before taking the field, offered a contribution of twelve talents (£2,800), with two hundred serfs raised on his land. Gellias of Acragas had in his wine-store three hundred tanks in which he could keep 30,000 amphoras of wine (260,000 gallons). In Laconia the law made a vain pretence of maintaining for ever the *kleros* of moderate size with its human live-stock. When victory had heaped gold and silver in Sparta, alienation by deed of gift or will had to be authorized; the creditors had means to legalize evictions, and the women, to whom the law against making use of movable capital did not apply, prepared the way by very one-sided loans for inevitable expropriations. The valleys of the Eurotas and the Pamisos offered the agrarian capitalist a magnificent field of operation. The concentration of property was effected there with unprecedented rapidity; at the time of Aristotle, as we have seen, " some owned immense fortunes, the others had almost nothing."

While Laconia was becoming a typical country of large properties, Attica presented a particularly remarkable example of the opposite state of things. It had changed much since the days when it, too, had belonged to a small number of Eupatrids.

We know from the census of the classes how small, medium, and large property were regarded in Solon's time. The small holders or Thetes were those who did not obtain from land of their own more than 200 measures of solid or liquid, i.e. 285 bushels of corn or 1,716 gallons of wine and

## LAND AND AGRICULTURE

oil. To be classed as a medium proprietor or Zeugites it was therefore sufficient to own between 7 and 10 acres of vineyard; the farmer who grew only corn must, with the fallow in alternate years, have between 30 and 50 acres; the man who produced his own wine and bread had not more than 25 acres. Thus the lower limit of medium property in Attica is the same as that given in the official documents in France; the reason is that it depends on physiological needs rather than on economic phenomena. But this is by no means the case with the upper limit. In France it is fixed at 40 hectares (98·8 acres). The Athenian rose into the class of the Knights, the great land-owners who had to furnish a horse to the State, when he had 300 measures, i.e. 429 bushels of corn or 2,574 gallons of wine and oil. A vine-grower counted as a big proprietor if he had 12 or 15 acres, a corn-grower, if he had 45-75 acres, and the man who grew an equal amount of corn and wine, if he had 30-45 acres. Above these came the very greatest land-owners, the Pentacosio-medimni, whose land had to yield 500 measures, 712¼ bushels of solid or 4,268 gallons of liquid. It could well do this with 20 or 25 acres of vineyard, or with 75-125 acres of corn-land, or with 50-75 acres of mixed land. Thus, at the time when the Athenian people was still groaning over the appropriation of the land, it regarded as a very large property an estate which in the countries of our time would be placed in the middle class of medium property.

Later the rule of dividing up an estate on succession and the progress of vine-growing split up the land without ceasing. In the IVth century the legal speeches of the orators give us the value of eight estates. They are assessed or sold at between 2,000 and 15,000 drachmas, and the only two which are quoted at two talents and two and a half talents, with an income of 800 and 1,200 drachmas, are situated in the exceptionally fertile plain of Eleusis and Thria. The *poletai*, whose duty it is to collect the tax on sales of land, record estates of small and sometimes very small value; there are plots worth 50 drachmas, and, though the maximum reaches 15,000 drachmas (just as in the orators), the average for sixteen lots is below 2,100 drachmas. The inscriptions on the mortgage-stones tell the same story. In a series of twenty-four loans only one is for a sum of 8,000 drachmas, secured on a house and a field; on unbuilt property the average is about 1,830 drachmas.

But we must see what was called a big estate at that time. The son of Aristeides received as a national gift 100 *plethra* of plough-land and as much under trees, 45 acres in all. In those days, says Demosthenes, the State must have been rich in land to indulge in such munificence. Apart from one exceptional case, the largest property which Attica could show as against the vast domains of Laconia measured 300 *plethra*, or 64 acres.

This state of things was common to the democratic cities. It seems to have prevailed in Asia Minor and the islands. In the Vth century Chios divided confiscated land into six lots and sold them at prices varying between 1,700 and 5,340 staters or double drachmas. At Halicarnassos, out of fifteen estates, four were sold for between 50 and 342 Phœnician drachmas, six for between 500 and 1,000, and three for between 1,000 and 2,000; only two reached a higher price, the dearest attaining to 3,600 drachmas, and the average price was 990 Phœnician drachmas (£32 8*s*.). In the IVth century, at Iasos, confiscated goods were sold at prices varying between a minimum of 98 drachmas and a maximum of at least 6,720 drachmas; but three men had to combine to secure the big lot, and several joined forces to obtain a lot worth 1,120 drachmas. The dividing up of land is regarded by Aristotle as a general phenomenon. With the Utopias of Plato he contrasts reality. " In fact," he says, " no one is destitute, because properties are divided indefinitely."

And yet, by the very excess of a process of division which was gradually pushed to the point of pulverization, new facilities began to offer themselves for a slow, unseen reconstitution of the large property. While estates of medium size were being divided and subdivided, the mass of countrymen found it more and more difficult to live by their labour. Their difficulties became manifest in Attica when the Peloponnesians had destroyed their vines and olive-trees, and above all when the distress following the defeat had taken from them the resources from public offices, trade, and industry with which they used to eke out the meagre return of their tiny lands. With time the evil became worse. The proprietor who could grow for sale might profit by the rise in

## LAND AND AGRICULTURE

farm produce, but the peasant who was obliged to consume his production suffered from the general increase of the cost of living. To avoid further splitting up many families revived the system of undivided property in new forms; one sole heir kept the farm and paid rent to the others, or a father gave to his daughter as dowry a mortgage-bond bearing interest. In bad years the small farmer borrowed money from his rich neighbour or from the banker. Once again the land began to be burdened with debts. It is by no mere chance that the oldest steles inscribed with mortgages and with sales with right of redemption date from the IVth century. Often the mortgage ended in eviction, and the sale with right of redemption became a final alienation. In other cases the peasant in desperation made over his bit of land and left the country. The speculator who bought for resale and the land-owner who wanted to round off his estate were in clover.

It happened fairly often that an Athenian owned several estates in different parts of Attica. Let us run through the list of properties confiscated in 415. Under the name of Pherecles we find a small estate at Bate, two between Athens and Eleusis, one at Cycala, and two the situation of which is unknown. From Euphiletos we have a house in the deme of Semachidæ, a field at Gargettos, and two other fields. A third condemned man owns 35 drachmas' worth of standing harvest at Thria and Athmonon. Similar examples are plentiful. Plato had properties at Iphistiadæ and Eiresidæ. A client of Isæos, Theopompos, owned land at Œnoe and Prospalta. Timarchos, who had inherited a house in Athens, a field at Alopece, and a grazing at Sphettos, bought other land at Cephisia and Amphitrope. In the official registers of sales the same purchaser is entered for several lots.

This accumulation of small properties in the same hands cannot be regarded, outright, as an equivalent of large property. In the Vth century it took place in normal ways, by dowry and inheritance, perhaps at least as much as by systematic purchases. Even in the IVth century it was perpetually counteracted, in the former case by the equality of apportionment and in the latter by the frequency of transfers of real property, by which the buyer of to-day became the seller of to-morrow. But in spite of these obstacles landed property tended to a kind of concentration. The ruling commercial system attacked the land. Transactions of this kind increased in number and size; speculation became " cornering " In 415 the four estates of Euphiletos were together worth 425 drachmas; fifty years later the two estates of Theopompos were valued one at 5,000 drachmas and the other at 3,000. In spite of the splitting up, or rather in consequence of it, it was easy for a rich man to become a large estate-owner, if not to form a large estate.

So Attica was almost unacquainted with the agrarian system which consists in the formation of one vast continuous domain in order to reduce general costs and to organize cultivation on a large scale. When a litigant represents his opponent as an upstart who owns more land by himself than all the judges in the court together, it is a piece of malice, the vagueness and exaggeration of which are perhaps explained by the impossibility of knowing the precise extent of scattered properties. Only once in Attica do we quite clearly find what we should call a large estate to-day. A contemporary of Demosthenes named Phænippos owned an estate with a circumference of 40 stades (over 4 miles) and an area of 3,600 *plethra* (778 acres). On it he grew, in a bad year, 1,000 medimni (1,424 bushels) of barley and 800 metretæ (6,820 gallons) of wine, and he obtained from it timber worth 3,600 drachmas (£140). But this case is unique, as far as we know. If an Athenian found himself a big proprietor at any given moment, it was because his investments happened to have turned out well. He was in the position of the banker Phormion, who lent large sums on real property and kept it in the event of non-payment; he was like the father of Isocrates, who bought neglected land, improved it, and sold it at a profit. Whether it was split up or concentrated, the soil was commercialized.

2. THE RURAL POPULATION

The great majority of Athenian citizens lived on their land or from their land. In the VIIth century they almost all dwelled in the country and seldom went to town. At the beginning of the Peloponnesian War, when the villagers were collected within the walls, " this change," says Thucydides,

# LAND AND AGRICULTURE

"was very hard for them." A century later, when this measure of public safety was revived, on the approach of Philip, it had to be enforced by pain of death.

Between these countrymen we must make distinctions. In 431, out of about 42,000 citizens, a thousand counted as big land-owners, 22,000 Zeugitæ lived decently, almost all on an estate of medium size, and lastly there were about 20,000 poor workers, many of whom had a bit of a field.

The great land-owner, like the small farmer, worked his land himself. It is to him that Xenophon, in his manual, the *Œconomicus*, offers Ischomachos as a model. He must possess the "royal art," the art of command. To convince his staff of his superiority, he must set an example of industry. Ischomachos and his wife, helped by a steward whom they have trained themselves, have an eye for everything and do not waste a moment. It is not enough to find the most suitable crop for each piece of land, and the most remunerative method for each crop; the good farmer must also be a good man of business. To dispose of your produce is a good thing, to buy corn where it is plentiful and sell it where it is scarce is better; but nothing is as good as the system of buying badly kept land cheap, putting it into good condition, and selling it, and then beginning over again. Intensive farming and speculation, that is the ideal. Demosthenes shows us a good specimen of the business farmer; while small farmers were obliged to sell their land in plentiful years on account of bad markets, the resourceful Phænippos profited by dearth to obtain for his wine and barley as much as four times the normal price. These people, says Socrates, love their land as corn-dealers love their grain—for the profits.

The great land-owner for a long time led the life of a country gentleman. In the Vth century the most splendid houses were not found in Athens, but in the depths of the country. Even in Demosthenes' time Apollodoros, the son of the wealthy Pasion, lived on his land, while recovering the money invested by his father and taking part in politics. An Athenian who had his banker in the city managed his slaves in the fields and reared sheep with fine wool. But the rich were more and more drawn to the centre of business and social pleasures. The unambitious squire allowed himself to be dragged from his estate by the clamourings of a wife who felt herself too fine a lady for an obscure deme, and by anxiety for his children's future. All in vain Strepsiades loves his delightful peasant's life and dreams of his son " bringing home the goats down the rocks, as Grandfather did in his goat-hide cloak." He has married a lady of high degree, a niece of Megacles the son of Megacles, who, ever since their wedding-day, has reproached him with " stinking of tubs, cheese-crates, and wool," and thinks of nothing but " scent, saffron dresses, waste, and guzzling," and wants her son to have a name with " something horsy in it " and " to drive his chariot in town, like Megacles, all dressed in purple."

How could this tendency be resisted ? Of the families which were won over to the town the more sensible continued to concern themselves with their land. Ischomachos leaves on his horse the first thing every morning and comes back tired out at night. But the rich disliked such a fatiguing life; they had better things to do. They took to the habit of not visiting their estate except at long intervals, for the sowing and the harvest. So arose what Aristotle calls " Athenian economy." The true head of the farm was the manager. For this work a faithful, honest, hard-working slave was chosen, who was expected to have understanding and experience in farming, the gift of command, and a high sense of responsibility. Thanks to the manager, the landowner became a *rentier*. Absenteeism was to be the feature of the new conditions. Some, like Criton, caused their harvest to be sent to them in kind. But Pericles, who had trained the pattern of a steward, Euangelos, already adopted a more convenient system. He caused all his produce to be sold, and the provisions necessary for each day to be bought as required from a big firm; he kept an exact balance between receipts and expenses, without becoming wholly taken up with the details of a complicated administration.

But the mass of farmers worked with their own hands. The peasant as Hesiod described him reappears in the *Electra* of Euripides. He sets out at dawn with his beasts and comes home at dusk. His wife makes the clothes and prepares the dinner. His barn furnishes him with all he needs. The only value of money in his eyes is that it enables him to offer travellers better hospitality—his only pride—and insures the worker against sickness—the only danger to be feared.

# LAND AND AGRICULTURE

When he is exiled into Athens, this man will sigh, like Dicæopolis, " Oh how I miss my village ! It never said to me ' Buy coal, or vinegar, or oil '; it did not know the word ' Buy '; it produced everything itself."

In the Vth century, then, the small farmer found no cause for complaint. The plains of the Mesogæa, of the Cephissos, and of Eleusis gave a good yield in corn and vegetables, the Diacria was covered with splendid vines, all along Parnes pasture and underwood were plentiful, in the hills the hives were full of bees, and everywhere the olive-groves produced oil which rose to wonderful prices. When Aristophanes praises country life his poetry is compound of truth, taken from the life and redolent of good things. All over Attica the husbandman, having sown his corn, leaves the rest to God, and goes off to have a drink and gorge himself on beans and figs. Thousands could see themselves in Trygæos, who loves his vines and hates politics. When the Acharnians went into the woods, axe in hand, they were proud to read on the tomb of one of themselves " Never, by Zeus, was better woodman seen ! Death to the enemy." Everything gives us the impression of a man content with his lot, even this letter, written by some highland shepherd. " Mnesiergos sends his love to all at home and hopes that this letter finds you in good health, as it leaves him at present. Please send me a blanket, sheepskin or goatskin, as cheap as possible, without hair, and some boots. I shall pay as soon as I have a chance." Farmers and vine-growers, woodmen and cattle-raisers, whether they lived comfortably or made just enough to keep alive, all had a profound sense of their dignity; they were land-owners and citizens.

But after the great war, when the countryman could go back to his village, he found his house in ruins, his fields run to waste, and his olive-grove and vineyard destroyed. With a few advances he could restore his corn, but it would be longer before he could think of drinking his own wine. As for selling oil, that was all over; with shoots from the olive-trees which had been cut down, the very quickest rate of reproduction could not give even sparse fruit for ten years, nor trees in full bearing for half a century. Many gave up the struggle; others fell into debt. And all the time land was being divided up. Aristophanes' rustics sing a very different tune now; in the *Plutos*, Chremylos and his friends toil hard and live on onions. It is worse in the New Comedy. The farmer speaks of his lot with nothing but bitterness. In Menander he says with doleful irony " The earth has indeed a sense of justice; it returns just as much barley as you have given it." In Philemon he complains with even more violence of his field. " For twenty medimni it gives back only thirteen. It is a thief." The poor peasant " lives on hope alone."

Unable to exist on their scrap of land, or destitute of all property, many farmers resigned themselves to the condition of tenants. But, though leasehold was fairly important in Greece, the system was applied almost solely to public or sacred properties. In Attica the State, the tribes, the demes, the phratries, and the temples constantly leased their domains; on the other hand it was rare for a contract to mention an individual as lessor. The big landlord would rather trust to a slave than to a free man; in any case the citizens did not want to be under a master as tenants any more than as stewards. The small land-owner who gave up his field would sell it and obtain capital rather than lease it out for a meagre rent; in either case his lot was not alluring. Lysias has preserved for us the instructive history of a field at the end of the Vth century. The owner sells it after six years; the purchaser leases it out, but very soon sells it again; the new purchaser establishes four tenants on it, one after another, of whom one remains two years and the others one year only. Three owners and five tenants in five or six years—that does not give the impression of a paying concern.

The public or sacred leaseholds did not inspire the peasant with the same aversion. In dealing with a purely conventional personality he did not feel that he was subordinate to an individual, free man and citizen that he was. Even the forms in which the authorities wrapped up the deed of lease were of a kind to elevate it in the eyes of the public and to encourage competition. At Eleusis the Goddesses let out their fair corn-fields and demanded 8% or 10% of the harvest. But it was waste land that was leased, the tenant undertaking to enclose it, to erect the necessary buildings, and to reclaim it for corn and vine or olive. In this case leases were for ten, twenty, or forty years. Sometimes they were for

# LAND AND AGRICULTURE

an unlimited period; the clause providing for planting trees led to "emphyteusis." The reasons which made leases longer also made rents lower. The tenant must at least be allowed to recover his outlay; the lessor recovered on the enhanced value of the land. In the classical period it was the long leasehold which permitted agriculture to continue the work of the previous centuries, the conquest of unproductive land.

In the service of the landlords and tenants lived a whole rural proletariat. We are not speaking here of slaves, but of free workers. For the most part they were Metics and freedmen, especially on the outskirts of Athens, where market-gardening prevailed. This class of workers gladly accepted engagements by the year. Citizens disliked any lasting engagement, which would have made them the fellows of foreigners and slaves. If they refused the post of steward, even when pressed by poverty, it was not in order to sink still lower. They preferred to hire themselves out for the day. The harvest, the olive-gathering, and the vintage offered poor men and women an opportunity of earning a few drachmas. But such windfalls did not take you far. You struggled through in summer, but that was all.

### 3. Rural Economy

The changes which occurred in the distribution of property and in the condition of the rural population inevitably extended to the methods of agriculture.

With its hard climate and its poor soil, Greece too often gives the agriculturalist " poverty for a foster-sister." Nevertheless, the ancients tilled the earth of well watered valleys and alluvial plains with fruitful results, and they had drained large areas of swamp and conquered many terraces on the mountains. From the Vth century, and especially in the IVth, the scientific spirit of the Greeks devoted itself to the things of the earth and sought, as Plato says, " to co-operate with nature." Agricultural treatises became numerous; the Roman Varro consulted over fifty Greek works. Xenophon's Ischomachos, who boasts his practical experience, rather laughs at these arm-chair farmers, but he profits by their teaching and communicates his experience to them. The plough was improved, being given a metal share. The farmer examined the nature of the soil; he made a "*dokimasia*" of it, by the natural vegetation and the colour of the sods. To give his land rest, he still divided it into two breaks, but on that which he once left fallow he now planted vegetables. He even commenced to practise the three-field system, with winter sowing, spring sowing, and fallow. The question of improving the soil occupied attention. One Chartrodes classified manures in order of value. In the first rank, as in the Flemish system, he placed night soil, which was confined to garden produce; on the fields stable manure was used, being spread according to the ground and the crop; weeds, dry grass, twigs, and dead wood were carefully burned. In addition to the three ploughings of the year, wise men recommended supplementary ones, and the new three-field system with sowing at varying seasons raised complicated questions on the number of dressings and the

FIG. 33. PLOUGHING AND SOWING. BLACK-FIGURE CUP, IN THE LOUVRE. *D.A.*, Fig. 5968.)

time for them. For the spring sowing precocious varieties found in Sicily and acclimatized in Eubœa were chosen. The amount of grain was in proportion to the quality of the soil, being sown thick in rich earth and thin in poor. In every way the methods of agriculture were improved, and gave better returns.

In Attica intensive, scientific agriculture had to contribute to the feeding of a great city. But the surface was insufficient. Of 630,000 acres over a third was forest and pasture-land unsuited for cultivation. In the very midst of the arable land the sand appeared at every step, or a patch of limestone which defied the plough. Water was often lacking. Once a great crown of forests had ensured a certain regularity in the distribution of rains and running water. But ruthless deforestation, due to the demands of building, metal-working, and the ship yards, had denuded the higher ground. Plato knew mountains, from which fine timber had once come down, which now fed only bees; he no longer saw in Attica trunks

# LAND AND AGRICULTURE

which could be compared to the beams in the old houses. These general conditions, aggravated by the competition of better-supplied countries, were an obstacle to working the fields and pastures on a large scale; but they were not such as to hamper the development of market-gardening and fruit-growing.

In Attica the cultivation of corn never occupied more than 16%, or at the very most 20% of the total area. The practice of the fallow reduced the ground under corn in any year to between fifty and sixty thousand acres. But wheat was grown only in the best land of the Mesogæa or the Rarian Plain; elsewhere they were content with barley. In 328 Attica produced 387,325 medimni of barley (552,200 bushels) and 39,500 medimni of wheat (56,375 bushels), i.e. a total corn production of 426,825 medimni (608,575 bushels), of which 90% was barley. We may reckon the yield per acre at nine or ten bushels, and the return at five or six to one. In that year, it is true, Greece was suffering from a general dearth; but the average production of Attica hardly exceeded thirteen bushels per acre, and did not rise above five or six hundred thousand medimni. We can understand the ecstasies of men accustomed to such a low yield when they saw the glorious harvests of Egypt, Babylon, and Sicily.

So long as the population was not dense Attica was almost self-sufficing in cereals. But, as an agglomeration of consumers who were not producers grew up, the public food-supply caused anxiety. Solon, even at his early date, forbade the export of farm produce, and the Peisistratids encouraged the extensive development of agriculture as well as relations with the corn countries of the Euxine. But it was later, when Athens and the Peiræeus were big towns, that the food problem became very serious. The landowners still lived on their harvest. They even sold their surplus; for agriculture did not cease to be profitable, the exorbitant cost of carriage acting as a protective duty. But the small quantities which they brought to the market were far from meeting requirements.

We can make a rough estimate of the amount consumed. We must allow an average of six medimni of corn per head per year. For a population which in prosperous times must have numbered 350,000 souls the yearly total attained

2,100,000 medimni. In 328 about 1,600,000 medimni had to be imported, four times the home production. As a rule the amount imported must be reckoned at one and a half million medimni. Attica produced at the very most a quarter of its requirements. It partly made up the deficit with the aid of its colonies. In 328 the three islands which it still owned produced 413,875 medimni (590,018 bushels) of grain, of which 26% was wheat. But out of this only half could go to trade. So, in an average year, Athens must obtain from twelve to thirteen hundred thousand medimni of grain from abroad. Half was sent from the Euxine; the rest came from Egypt, Sicily, and Italy.

Nor did Attica offer very favourable conditions to stock-breeding. There were no moist valleys, no grassy uplands,

Fig. 34. Peasants taking pigs to market. Attic vase. (*D.A.*, Fig. 5977.)

and very few natural meadows. Plants fit for fodder only began to spread in the Vth century; lucern was brought from Media by the Persian invaders. There was not overmuch for the saddle and race horses which were the joy of the ephebi, the luxury of the rich land-owners, and the object of speculation for men with their eyes open. So the mule and ass were a great help. Oxen were rare; they were used as draught-animals, and when they were fattened by the millers with mill-sweepings they supplied the sacred butcher with choice victims. Vast stretches of pasture and underwood were at least suited for sheep and goats. The small live-stock had above all to supply milk and wool. The Attic breeders had succeeded in producing a sheep with a fine wool which was highly valued. The Athenian's liking for pig's flesh is therefore easily explained by the lack of rich pastures and the scarcity of other meat. Every house, if possible, had its pig. The swineherd, according to Plato, is as indispensable as the baker. In spite of all, Attica had not enough live-stock to feed itself. It made up for it by fishing. It also called upon the countries of great stock-farms. From Bœotia it took draught oxen; from Olbia it imported quantities of salted goods such as hams and dried fish.

From the Vth century, as we have seen, the Athenians no longer found enough timber at home. Parnes still furnished ilex and maple to the woodmen and charcoal-burners of Acharnæ. We even hear of a land-owner who sent six asses laden with wood to town every day. But, though Attica

FIG. 35. SATYRS GATHERING GRAPES. (Duruy, *Hist. des Grecs*, Vol. II, P. 238.)

had enough wood for fuel, it must turn for carpenter's and joiner's wood to Asia Minor, Cyprus, Italy, and above all Macedonia. The great timber-merchants lived at the Peiræeus and in Corinth.

To see the progress of intensive cultivation we must look at the vineyards, orchards, and kitchen-gardens. It is a known law that big towns attract fruit-growing and vegetable-growing. Athens was no exception. The Greek agriculturalists were above all tree-growers, and Ischomachos is especially concerned for his plantations. In leases the lessor was ready to forego an immediate return in order to enrich his estate by putting in vines and olives. If we find in the IVth century estates doubling or trebling in value in a few years, it is because new methods were intelligently applied to them. This was done by small and big land-owners alike. Look at the peasants of Aristophanes. Strepsiades dreams only of sheep and bees, oil-presses and wine-tubs; Dicæopolis, who produces his own charcoal, oil, wine, and vinegar, buys pigs and asks the price of corn; a vine-grower who has just sold grapes runs off, with his mouth full of small change, to buy flour.

The dry, rocky soil favoured tree-growing. All that was needed was proper regulation of the distribution and use of water, and the law-givers provided for that at an early date. The fig-tree grew everywhere, to the joy of the "fig-eating" people. Athens could almost do without Thracian and Ionian

FIG. 36. OLIVE-GATHERING. ATTIC VASE, IN THE BRITISH MUSEUM.
(Duruy, *Hist. des Grecs*, Vol. I, P. 716.)

wines. The olive-gathering became as popular as the vintage. Gnarled old trees, protected by the Goddess and defended against the axe by a ferocious law, made the wealth and the glory of Athens. From the time of Solon she manufactured more oil than she required. By pressing none but perfectly mature fruit the Athenians obtained a product of incomparable purity and exquisite flavour. The amphoras which held Attic oil were in demand in every country, and deserved to be offered as prizes at the Panathenaic contests.

Antiquity went for its sugar to the bees. On flowery hills, scented by the sun, the hives were set up in such crowds that the distance to be observed had to be fixed by regulation.

## LAND AND AGRICULTURE 261

The bee-masters of Attica collected a honey of the first quality, which was the object of an extensive trade.

Lastly, there were the luxuries. In the Vth century Athens attracted the fruit and vegetables of the neighbouring countries and the islands. She saw on her Agora the peasants of the Megarid and even of Thebes, a city completely surrounded by market-gardens. The ships brought to the Peiræeus the pears and apples of Eubœa and the raisins and figs of Rhodes. But, thanks to irrigation and the improvement of the soil, the market-gardeners soon organized cultivation in Attica, almost on industrial lines. On market days they brought in cabbages, lentils, peas, onions, and garlic. By careful tending they acclimatized the cucurbitaceous

FIG. 87. SALE OF OIL, WITH THE LEGEND "ZEUS, LET ME GROW RICH!" ATTIC AMPHORA FROM CAERE, IN THE VATICAN MUSEUM. (*D.A.*, Fig. 5394.)

plants of Egypt. The development of plantations made nursery-gardening into a special profession. There were even flower-growers. In the IVth century rich people indulged in the strange fancy of pleasure-gardens, "Paradises" in the Asiatic style. But long before that flowers were grown on a large scale in the environs of Athens. Numerous rose-gardens kept the florists of the town supplied. There was a big demand in days when no religious ceremony and no private entertainment was complete without a supply of wreaths.

All these kinds of cultivation, which drive a man to exercise his wits on soil and water, were admirably suited to the ingenuity of the Greek. They gave good profits and increased the value of landed property to an extraordinary degree. But there were risks attached to them. The big land-owner could modernize his methods without fear; he was certain of obtaining an immense advantage. An estate of 300 *plethra* might reach a price of over 250 minas; 64¼ acres at £1,000 means a net return of at least 25*s*. per acre. But the small farmer who wished to improve his property went through a difficult time. He required a fairly large outlay; if he borrowed, he entered on a very dangerous road. Besides, a revolution in methods of cultivation does not take place without crises. Bad sales played their part; according to Xenophon, growers abandon an "unfruitful" labour for commerce, not in consequence of a bad harvest but, on the contrary, "when the abundance of wine and corn makes these products cheap." Intensive methods certainly helped the small vine-grower or the small market gardener to keep himself on his land, if he triumphed over these obstacles; but they did not succeed in preventing the disastrous results of excessive division of the ground, and they might aggravate them. The transformation of agriculture thus had its effect on the distribution of property and the condition of the rural classes. It brought more well-being to the small men who could hold out; it caused the others to go under the more quickly. The mobility of agriculture gave more mobility to the land. It also tended to convert landed estates into a kind of floating capital, and facilitated the formation of great domains.

CHAPTER IX

INDUSTRY

1. THE SITUATION OF INDUSTRY

IN the Vth and IVth centuries industry in Greece assumed an economic and social importance which did not escape attention. When Socrates would indicate the composition of the Athenian Assembly, before mentioning the husbandmen and the small tradesmen he enumerates the fullers, the shoemakers, the masons, and the metal-workers. The men of the crafts can form the majority; their chiefs become the masters of the commonwealth. Demos gives himself into the hands of lamp-merchants, turners, leather-dressers, and cobblers, and Aristophanes puts this statement into the mouth of a sausage-seller. Moreover, the citizens abandon the lower kinds of work, and in the accounts of public works they appear as an aristocracy of labour, lost in the multitude of Metics and slaves. Nor was Athens an exception. The little towns of the Peloponnese swarmed with craftsmen; their military contingents were almost entirely formed of men with professions. The industrial callings even attracted women. Many freedwomen and daughters of citizens reduced to need devoted themselves to the works of Athene Ergane. They wove for custom, they sold yarn, ribbons, clothes, and bonnets of their own making, or they plaited wreaths.

But, if a great part of the population lived by industry, it does not follow that it was industry on a large scale. First, we must not be misled by the concentration of many workshops in the same city or in the same quarter. We involuntarily think of the great manufacturing towns of modern times when we see the Cerameicos in Athens entirely occupied by the potters, the tanneries collected outside the city, the Peiræeus filled with workshops which manufacture imported raw materials and work for export, and Laureion inhabited by a whole people of miners and metal-workers. In order not to misinterpret this concentration, it is sufficient to recall analogous facts. There are also in Athens a Street of the Box-Merchants and a Street of the Herm-Sellers, and the craftsmen teem round the Agora. The workshops are innumerable. Some are big enough to be called factories, but none is a huge concern of the modern kind. Rival manufacturers live next door to each other; they are jealous of each other, but the struggle is not bitter, for there is work for all and the weak are not crushed by the strong. Small

FIG. 38. SPINNING-WOMAN DRAWING OUT HER YARN. CUP FROM ORVIETO. (*D.A.*, Fig. 3382.)

industry predominates; medium-sized industry plays a certain part; large industry barely makes a vague appearance.

The first cause which prevented one whole class of industries from developing indefinitely was the persistence of work in the home. At the time when the miller Nausicydes and the baker Cyrebos were each amassing a great fortune, housewives were still employed, like their grandmothers, in pounding the corn and kneading the dough. They kept the manufacture of clothing in their hands from the moment when the fleece was brought to them to the moment when they gave their menfolk the finished chiton. The greatest ladies of Greece taught their daughters everything connected

INDUSTRY 265

with the making of clothes. Like the wise Arete, Queen of
the Phæacians, the mother of the tyrant Jason span and
wove in her palace. Everywhere the mistress of the gynæ-

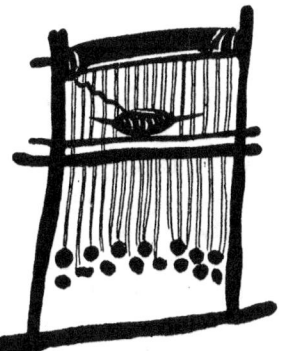

Fig. 39. The weaving-loom. Bœotian vase of the Vth century.
(*D.A.*, Fig. 6845.)

ceum held, in Plato's words, "the government of shuttles
and distaffs." Indeed it was in these home work-rooms that
an industry which worked for the public was born. For that

Fig. 40. The web of Penelope. Vase from Chiusi. (*D.A.*,
Fig. 6844).

it was sufficient that the output should exceed the requirements of the house and that the surplus should be sold.
This might happen without fixed intention, but it was also

done with the deliberate purpose of practising a profession. In this way Athens manufactured men's clothing; Megara specialized in the worker's *exomis* ; Corinth put on the markets its blankets, its *kalasireis* of fine wool, and its linen cloth; Pellene made cloaks which were in great demand; Patræ was filled with women, thanks to its byssos weaving-works; Cos had a name for its bombyx silk goods; Chios, Miletos, and Cyprus sent their hangings, their embroidered garments, and their carpets far and wide; Taras grew rich on its linen stuffs; and Syracuse transformed the wool of Sicily into textiles of many colours. But the textile industry, even when it had become a special profession, produced in small quantities. For common materials, the families only turned to it for a supplement to their own output, and preferred to call in women by the day. For the finer qualities manufacture was scattered and the demand limited.

Even those industries which were entirely in the service of the public kept some traces of the family system. The son fairly often succeeded his father. In the liberal careers the case was very frequent; the schools of medicine and music were family groups, the history of sculpture and painting is that of a few houses, and the architects of Delphi were, in succession, two Agathons, then Agasicrates, the son of the second, and lastly Agathocles, the son or brother of Agasicrates. In the same way the industrial art of the potters was handed down in the family. " How long," says Plato, " the potter's son helps his father and watches him at work before he touches the wheel himself!" In the other industries we find similar examples, but they are far fewer. Cleon inherited a tannery from his father, Anytos left one to his son, Lysias and his brother Polemarchos began by manufacturing shields like their father Cephalos, Athenogenes made perfumes like his father and grandfather before him, and among the contractors at Eleusis we see Antimachos son of Neocleides succeeded by Neocleides son of Antimachos. But each chose his own profession freely, and we see manufacturers' sons eager to escape from the paternal mill and to plunge into politics. The exodus of men from the country contributed to the recruiting of the industrial class, while the sons of craftsmen became artists, doctors, and orators. Individuals went from one profession to another with extreme mobility. Hereditary professions were not the rule.

In any case there was nothing like the great factory with countless hands. The largest establishment of which we know in Attica was the shield factory which the Syracusan Cephalos founded in the Peiræeus in 435 and handed down to his sons. In 404 it contained 120 slaves. After that come the two houses managed by the father of Demosthenes. For the people of the time these " were neither of them small industries." Now the arms factory had 32 or 33 slaves, the bed factory 20. A shield factory bequeathed to Apollodoros did, it is true, produce twice the output of the armoury bequeathed to Demosthenes, and therefore may have contained twice the personnel. Even then we have only one industry which employed more than a hundred workers, and those which employed more than twenty were considered very large. The celebrated potter Duris probably had not more than a dozen men about him. The gang of shoe-makers inherited by Timarchos consisted of nine or ten slaves, and in a mime of Herondas the fashionable shoe-maker has thirteen. The mines, it is true, present a very different aspect; there slaves were hired by the hundred. But when a man needed a big staff of working miners it was because he had obtained by auction a large number of small concessions. The State only gave out small lots. The typical mine employed about thirty men underground, about the same in the washing-room, and far less in the foundry. We know of one concessionnaire who put his hand to the pick and had for total capital a sum of 4,500 drachmas; with such initial assets he cannot have had more than fifteen or twenty workers under him.

Athenian industry, then, never involved a great agglomeration of workers in one undertaking. What is typical of this industry is not the factory in which Cephalos collected over a hundred hands, but rather the hovel in which the Micylos of the poet Crates cards wool with his wife " to escape starvation," or the workshop in which, according to an inscription, the helmet-maker Dionysios worked together with his wife, the gilder Atremis. And these are not accidental, isolated cases. The Athenian craftsman had no interest in increasing the number of his workers, Xenophon says. He was in the same position as the farmer, who knew exactly how many day-workers he needed, and that one man above this number was a sheer loss.

Whether they were conducted by the family or by a single owner, these workshops with their small personnel did not require much capital. As a rule, big fortunes, even in a city like Athens, were rare, and, being exposed to the risks inseparable from investments at high rates of interest, they were ephemeral. But industry did not attract them especially, and it did without them. A small foundry was worth 1,700 drachmas, including slaves. Even the mines could keep going without a great concentration of capital; one concession of the normal type with thirty slaves served as security for a loan of 10,500 drachmas, and another for a mortgage of one talent; and a man with 4,500 drachmas bid at the auction. It might be supposed that ship-building at least would have required huge yards and the formation of big companies. It had to supply a merchant fleet which covered the whole Mediterranean and a war navy which had 300 vessels in the Vth century and over 400 in the IVth. But what do we see in reality? One hundred and eighty-three ships, the builders of which are known to us, were launched in fifty-two years from fifty-nine different yards. It was the same with the public works contractor. With the system of giving orders in small lots and paying by instalments in advance, he did not need to have much money. When craftsmen united for big jobs it was the labour of their little firms that they were combining. Even those factories which prospered do not seem to have been capable of enlargement by the increase of capital. The banker Pasion would have had no difficulty from the financial point of view in extending the factory which was already bringing him a talent a year; yet he did nothing of the kind. Demosthenes' father obtained an income of only 30 minas from his armoury; in his bed factory he sank only a capital of 40 minas and a floating capital of 150 minas; apparently he did not see his way to developing these two concerns, since they did not prevent him from buying a house for 30 minas and drawing 177 minas interest a year on loans and deposits. Timarchos did not increase his staff of nine or ten shoemakers; he preferred to acquire a weaving-woman and an

# INDUSTRY

embroiderer, and invested in land. Conon had a bonnet-weaving establishment and a drug business, without either workshop suffering from the existence of the other. In the Peiræeus we find a workshop with dwelling-quarters rented for 54 drachmas; nowhere do we find a great factory representing a fortune.

For the soul of the great factory is the machine; and without machinery the great manufacturer does not supersede the craftsman. The slaves were quite enough for the output; there was no need to rack one's brains to cope with shortage or dearness of labour. The Greek engineers distinguished between simple machines and composite machines. The former were five in number, the lever, the wedge, the

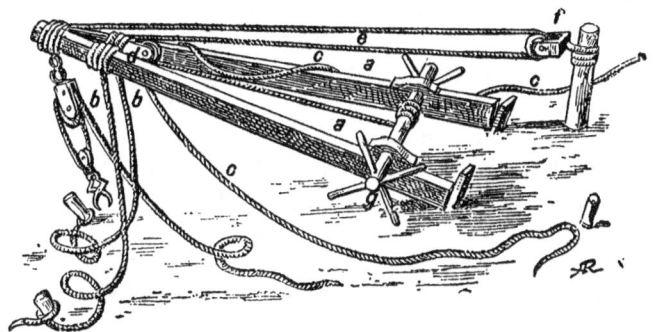

FIG. 41. HOIST, BEFORE SETTING UP. (*D.A.*, Fig. 4745.)
*a*, wooden legs; *b*, fore-stays; *c*, back-stays; *d*, upper block; *e*, gear-rope; *f*, lower block, fastened to a pile; *g*, windlass.

screw, the windlass, and the pulley or block. The latter were merely combinations of the former, and the only one known in the Vth century was the crane. Archytas was the first to apply geometry to mechanics; he caused perceptible progress to be made in the theory and practice of the lever, and solved several problems of traction, to the advantage of construction and shipping. But no advance was made beyond the apparatus invented by the architects Chersiphron and Metagenes for the land transport of heavy material. Loads were lifted with the help of two-legged machines or sheers. These were erected in yards and on harbour moles. In the mines the shortness of leases and the cheapness of labour retarded technical progress. Since the only object was the immediate return, and no one troubled about making extraction easier for future concessionnaires, the section of the galleries was small, no winding plant was installed at the pit-heads, and mechanical crushing was unknown; all the work was done by strength of arm. The smelting and refining furnaces, though not expensive, were fairly developed, but they did not make it possible to separate gold from silver. The bronze-workers obtained wonderful colour-effects, but this metal polychromy was attained by the simplest methods, incrustation, the juxtaposition of different alloys, gilding, silver-plating, or patient, skilful patination. By Callias' process certain dye-stuffs were extracted from argentiferous lead, in particular cinnabar or vermilion, but always without any expensive plant. The same is probably true of the process invented by a woman of Cos for winding silkcocoons. The vase paintings often represent workshops with a few implements hung on the walls. (See Figs. 44–46.) It is Greek industry that we see here, with its apparatus of primitive simplicity and its low output.

It made no great demands in respect of raw material, either. This was often supplied to the craftsman by his customer. The family which could not weave enough cloth for itself gave yarn to a workwoman, who wove it in the house or at her own home. In a play of Aristophanes a goldsmith and a harness-maker go to a house to mend a clasp and a strap. When he wanted some building done, Timotheos procured timber from Macedonia. When the State undertook public works, it divided them up into lots and chose in each case between two systems, either doing the work itself or giving it to a private contractor. The latter method had the advantage of laying all the responsibility on one or more contractors. The former was necessary for difficult work which required artistic perfection or, where the task could not be divided up, a comparatively large quantity of personnel, materials, and capital. For the work which it did itself the State supplied everything. It bought the gold and ivory from which Pheidias was to make the statue of the Goddess. For other statues it procured copper and tin, fuel for the casting, and the beams and planks of the inclined plane and the platform. If column-drums had to be brought to the site, it made a road, built waggons, and only asked the transport agents for beasts at so much a day. It would

# INDUSTRY 271

instal a windlass at its own cost and give the iron-work out on contract; it procured tools for the workmen and had them steeled when they became worn. It was to relieve itself of these cares that the State turned more and more to the contractor. Yet it still supplied him with scaffolding, stone, wood, lead, iron, and bronze. When an administrative body decided to adorn a temple with a monumental entrance, it began by acquiring cedar or cypress, ivory, glue, and pins. If the contractor must himself supply the materials or engines needed, if the mason was to furnish common stone for the foundations, or if the carpenter was to bring his own scaffolding, this condition had to be expressly stipulated. The ordinary rule was that the craftsman sold his labour and nothing else.

All these advantages did not, however, draw a very large number of contractors, especially of such as had considerable means at their disposal. The State tried all manner of devices to divide up the lots and to organize competition; orders were brought within the power of the humblest workers, alone or in partnership; craftsmen were summoned from one town to another, and sometimes from great distances. At Delphi an order for stone which comes to about 1,100 drachmas occupies five quarrymen, one from Argos, two from Bœotia, and two from Corinth; other work is given to contractors as far as Arcadia, and they are allowed their living-expenses so long as the contract is in hand. At Epidauros the lots are less split up than anywhere else; one of them even reaches the figure of 14,000 Attic drachmas. But on this occasion the whole of Greece was making a supreme effort. A painter came from Stymphalos, the cypress-wood was supplied by a Cretan, and the heralds went cadging for tenders from Tegea to Thebes. We even know of two contractors in Argos who bid for orders first at Epidauros and then at Delphi. Argos in her turn, to build her Long Walls, sent to Athens for skilled workmen. Athens herself always gave out small orders which small contractors could undertake. The work on the Erechtheion was the occasion of a vast number of small payments. The largest sum mentioned in the Eleusis accounts of 328, amounting to 7,087 drachmas, was paid for binding the windlass with iron, i.e. for an indivisible operation; then comes an order for quarrying, transporting, and laying stone, which amounts to 2,660 drachmas; after which only one or two items rise above 500 drachmas. And foreigners followed the contract-auctions in Attica as keenly as elsewhere; out of twenty orders put up to auction at Eleusis, thirteen were secured by twelve Metics, as against seven which went to two citizens. For such competition to be allowed, desired, and actually encouraged everywhere, each city in Greece must have felt incapable of accomplishing by her own resources any project of public works which rose above the ordinary.

Puny as industry was, it could not always confine itself to executing orders. Sometimes it produced in advance. The retailers and exporters enabled the craftsmen to work regularly without troubling too much about the demand. The shoe-maker made to measure and sold ready-made. The armourer had to provide for sudden, large demands. When the Thirty confiscated the factory of Lysias and Polemarchos, they found in stock great quantities of gold, silver, and ivory, and seven hundred finished shields. In Thebes a band of insurgents broke into the armourers' shops and fitted themselves out with lances and swords. But the craftsmen had no advantage in producing without cease and sinking capital in the shape of stock. The demand was too restricted. Even the armourer was afraid of the repercussion of political events. Demosthenes asks his guardian why his armour works have paid nothing during his minority; it is not, he says, for want of work, as is proved by the accounts of the output; then is it because the arms manufactured could not be sold? Here, certainly, we have over-production. And here we have its effects: in Aristophanes the merchants weep over the cuirasses, trumpets, crests, helmets, and javelins for which they cannot find buyers. As a rule the manufacturer made his arrangements so that production should not outstrip orders to a dangerous extent, and hired out the slaves whom he could not employ. In the IVth century he was perpetually concerned with keeping his personnel down to what was absolutely necessary. According to Xenophon, once the blacksmith or bronze-worker neglects to regulate his work by his sales, " down goes the price of his goods, and his business is ruined." If the industry of Laureion was the only one which absorbed labour

# INDUSTRY

indefinitely, it was because only the silver-market absorbed output indefinitely.

The returns of industry reached a high figure. In comparison with the natural product, the manufactured product was dear. Its price had to be in proportion to the normal interest on money and the remuneration of labour. The sums paid for the hire of slaves give valuable information on this point. Xenophon reckons that if the State buys 1,200 miners, and uses the hire paid for their labour in buying more, it will be able to raise their number to 6,000 in five or six years. If, therefore, the obol paid each day for each miner is capitalized for about five and a half years it will be possible to multiply the number of miners by five; this represents an annual profit of 33% on slaves who cost on an average 180 drachmas. For the skilful worker the hire is greater, but so is the purchasing price. Let us see what Demosthenes' father gets from his two factories. From 20 cabinet-makers he obtains a yearly profit of 12 minas, i.e. one obol per man per day. But together they are worth at least 40 minas. Thus they bring in at most 30%. His 32 or 33 armourers bring a net yearly profit of 30 minas; according to the orator, whose interest it is to exaggerate, they are worth " up to five and six minas per head, and never less than three," or an average of three or four minas; so the income is between 23% and 31%. Lastly, as daily hire for his shoe-makers, Timarchos takes 2 obols per man and one obol extra for the foreman; at 4 minas a man and 6 minas for the foreman, we again get 30%. In sum, below 25% the income from industry is on the low side, above 30% it is rather high. When Æschines the philosopher wanted to open a perfumery business he borrowed money from a bank at 36%; it was sheer madness. But to repay this debt he obtained funds at 18%. Then he might have made a success, if he had only had the qualifications of a manufacturer.

At 30% the income from industry was equal to two and a half times the normal interest. But it entailed a fairly big risk, the death of the slaves. A percentage must be deducted as sinking-fund. If the slave in the mine gave in appearance a rather higher return than the slave who made furniture or shoes or metal goods, it was just because his work was more unhealthy and his life more exposed. The difference in return did not therefore depend on the number of persons employed, i.e. the size of the concern. The plant was neither so complicated nor so expensive that concentration in a single concern would diminish the general costs. Small-scale industry was at least as remunerative as large-scale. Fortunes were made in the mines which were enormous for the time. By lucky digging, Callias made the 200 talents which earned him the nickname of Laccoplutos (*Grubenbaron*, as the Germans say); his son Hipponicos passed for the richest man in all Greece; Nicias owned 100 talents; the firm of Epicrates realized that sum in a year; when Diphilos was condemned to the confiscation of his property for illicit exploitation, 160 talents were found in his coffers. But the Athenian who invested a large capital in mining business had no other advantage over the man who risked only a few thousand drachmas than that he acquired several concessions at once. He increased his profits only in arithmetical proportion. He even added, to the expenses which would fall on several small concessionnaires, the cost of a manager, which was very heavy. This question of the return covers all the rest, in the sense that there is no industry on a large scale where the amalgamation of small concerns does not *ipso facto* cause a considerable saving.

But we should have a very incomplete notion of Greek industry if we neglected the moral aspect. In a people with a lively imagination and acute wits the crafts readily assumed an æsthetic character. Here there was no machine ruling over the man who minded it, and forcing him to repeat the same motion over and over again, as if he were himself an automatic driving-gear. Tasks were not necessarily monotonous; they might even develop a natural bent. There was no mass production, done in feverish haste, piled up in the darkness by nameless hands. The craftsman did his work in a little workshop under the eyes of the passer-by. He did not drudge at it from morning to night, but took his time to finish everything that passed through his hands. Even for export he was asked to supply articles of value. Eye and hand were exercised at leisure, *amour-propre* was aroused, and technical progress was achieved in a glad spirit. This joy in work, the collaboration of creative thought and obedient tool, the love of free play ennobling the daily endeavour, all

# INDUSTRY

this somehow shed a ray of light on the commonest object and made the workman an artist. Was he a sculptor or a mere decorator, the Thrasymedes of Paros who chiselled the chryselephantine statue of Asclepios at Epidauros, and then executed doors of cypress-wood plated with ivory and a coffered ceiling? What name are we to give to the marble-workers who earned a modest wage cutting fine flutings on the columns of the Erechtheion? When the Cerameicos potter made and decorated humble receptacles for oil and wine, he was a Greek working for Greeks. The air which blew about the working quarters of Athens had passed over

Fig. 42. The vase-painter. Attic cup. (*D.A.*, Fig. 7340.)

the Parthenon, and in it the lowest workman breathed a spirit of perfect harmony. By personal endeavour new forms and motives were invented without number; even the busiest workshops did not reproduce their models twice. Plato's contemporaries could say of industry, as of art, " Everything that we Greeks take, we transform into beauty."

## 2. Workers and Wages

Let us visit the workers in their workshops and living-quarters; let us see at close range the small men who worked with their hands.

The skilled workers were called after their trades. The labourers, "those," as Plato says, "who sell the service of their arms," were called "wage-earners" (*misthotoi*). Under them were the assistants, servants, and apprentices. One and all were either free men, whether citizens or foreigners, or else slaves, but the lower you go in the scale of labour the more Metics and slaves do you find. To act as a labourer for a few days was generally for the citizen a temporary means of keeping himself, one of the extremities to which sudden misfortune might reduce a man.

As a rule the hiring of service was not the occasion of a formal contract. One craftsman made an agreement with another for the execution of certain work, sometimes of a single task, and it is often difficult to say whether one of these collaborators was the subordinate or the partner of the other. Between the employer, whether he was a workshop-owner or a customer, and the employee, whether labourer or craftsman, the relationship was loose from a legal point of view, and the terms of the agreement were free. Plato, who was prepared to make regulations for everything, would have had officials to supervise the workers and to fix their wages. But the Athenian State refrained from entering on this path. The authorities never once thought of limiting the working day. Questions of payment, in case of dispute, simply went before the law-courts. A man could claim any remuneration due to him by legal proceedings, and cases between ship-owners and seamen or dock-workers were in the competence of the *Nautodikai* of the Peiræeus. In only one case do we find the authorities prescribing a salary; the *Astynomoi* did not allow women who played the flute, harp, or cithara to take more than two drachmas, and when several applicants wished to engage the same woman they assigned her by lot; but this was a police measure. Nor did the hygiene and safety of the workshop interest the city. The employment of a free child at turning a mill was prohibited on pain of death; but the very severity of the punishment proves that it was intended, not to protect the child against too heavy labour, but to preserve the son of a citizen from servitude. The mining laws treated as crimes the destruction of pit-props and the smoking of galleries, but this was in order to prevent the rapacious concessionnaire, not from killing his

# INDUSTRY

miners, but from destroying public property. On principle, therefore, industry enjoyed complete liberty.

Technical progress made apprenticeship necessary in almost every profession. The advantage of agriculture, to Xenophon's mind, is that, to succeed, it is sufficient to keep your eyes open and to ask questions; the other arts require a long experience before you can live decently by them. " If you want to make a man a shoe-maker, a mason, a blacksmith . . . you send him to a master who can teach him." Even the cook took lessons from a master cook. A formal contract, often in writing, fixed the amount to be paid by the apprentice's family, the length of the indentures, and the obligations on both sides. Since the sculptors and

FIG. 43. COMPETITION OF APPRENTICE VASE-PAINTERS. HYDRIA FROM RUVO. (*D.A.*, Fig. 3041.)

painters demanded very high premiums, poor men could only go into their studios as assistants. This was how Lysippos and Protogenes began. The learner was subjected to harsh discipline, and was not always sure of learning his trade thoroughly, for the fear of competition made the master distrustful, and he did not communicate his most precious secrets. The importance attached to professional education is attested by the apprentices' competitions. The vase-painters represent their pupils bent over ornamental details, while Athene and Victory come and crown them. On the pedestal of a monument dedicated by a potter we read these verses: " Among those who combine earth, water, and fire in their art Bacchios won the first place by his gifts, over every rival, in the judgement of the whole of Greece, and in all the competitions organized by this city he won the crown."

Men out of work used to look for engagements on the Agora, where a special place was set apart for them, the Colonos. So the "Colonites" were the unemployed. Engagements by the year generally ran from the 16th Anthesterion (March). There was a reason for this date in the country, where it marked the resumption of work after the winter; the agricultural workers passed it on to all classes of workers. The beginning of the new period was observed with joyous celebrations.

The worker's day began very early. He rose before daylight. Aristophanes amuses himself with a description of

FIG. 44. BRONZE-WORKER'S STUDIO: CASTING AND PUTTING TOGETHER. ATTIC BLACK-FIGURE CUP, IN THE BERLIN MUSEUM. (Perrot, Vol. X, P. 361.)

the scene. "As soon as the cock sends forth his morning song, they all jump out of bed, blacksmiths, potters, leather-dressers, shoe-makers, bathmen, flour-dealers, lyre-turners, and shield-makers; they slip on their shoes and rush off to their work in the dark." Work no doubt went on until sunset. In the mines, where it never ceased, there were successive ten-hour shifts. For night work the millers, bakers, and pastry-cooks paid wages at skilled rates.

Inside the workshops painted on the vases we often see clothes hanging on the wall. When a man was working he wanted to be comfortable. For sedentary work he bared his upper part and legs, or took off everything, wearing only a cap. In the forges and potteries, the more clothes there are hanging on the wall, the more vases hang there too. Going near the fire made a man thirsty.

FIG. 45. BRONZE-WORKER'S STUDIO: FINISHING. SAME CUP.
(*Ibid.*, Fig. 360.)

In the absence of machines, and with only a moderate division of labour, the craftsman and the labourer had relatively varied occupations. For tasks done by several men

FIG. 46. SHOE-MAKER AT WORK. ATTIC CUP, IN THE BRITISH MUSEUM.
(*D.A.*, Fig. 6688.)

together, and especially for hard or monotonous work, the time was set by music. The flute, the pipe, and the whistle governed motions and gave orders in the ship-building yards,

There were old songs for every trade, and for each operation in it. The airs which Calypso and Circe sang as they span and wove were known by all the women. Others were sung when the corn was pounded or milled. Harvesters, millers, fishermen, rowers, bathmen, all had their chanty. With the cultivation of the vine the Greeks took to Egypt the Song of the Wine-Press. Like dancing and gymnastics, manual labour was made rhythmical and gay.

Shop and workshop were open to visitors and idlers. As in Hesiod's time, men liked to go into the forge and to stand peacefully watching the workmen as they handled tongs, hammer, and polisher. They went to the barber's as the Frenchman goes to his café. Young men made appointments to meet and chat at the perfumer's. Socrates was always sure of finding an audience at the statuary's or the armourer's; when he wished to meet Euthydemos he went with a crowd of friends into a saddler's shop, and it was the leather-dresser Simon who took down his sayings in a diary.

The employer did not keep a great distance between himself and his men. On feast-days they met at the sacrifice and at the sacred meal, of which he bore the cost. The *epistatai* of the Erechtheion offer a victim " together with the workmen." At Eleusis the public slaves get each a good hunk of meat and about a gallon of good ordinary wine. It is a big present.

While labour does not appear too severe in the small workshops, it presents a very different spectacle in the mines. At Laureion each shift did ten hours' work after ten hours' rest. Five hewers, followed by twenty or twenty-five carriers, went one after the other to the face of the workings. In galleries between two and three feet wide and between two feet and a little over three feet high, they had often to crawl, and always to dig on their knees, on their stomachs, or on their backs. We can guess what the ventilation was like in these narrow passages. The heat was cruel. Heaped up bodies and smoky lamps made the air unbreathable. No hygienic precautions were taken. Nevertheless, we must not apply to Laureion the melancholy descriptions which are true of the mines of Egypt and Spain. Slaves though they were, the miners of Attica were not treated like convicts. The smaller concessionnaires mixed with the hewers, so their existence must have been endurable. Naturally the owner was prevented by his own interest from taking unnecessary risks with the health of his workers; they gave a high and steady output which he could not have got from exhausted bodies. The miners of Laureion were not shut away for the rest of their lives, like the quarrymen buried in the *latomiai* of Syracuse, who married there and begot children who fled screaming at the sight of a horse or an ox. At the centre of the district, at Thoricos, there was a theatre which could seat five thousand spectators; the mass of labourers were not denied all distractions. That slaves should flee to Deceleia, when Sparta called them to freedom, was only natural; but Laureion was never the scene of a general revolt, like Messenia or Sicily.

Where there were many workers, and the employer did not wish to manage his concern himself, he placed at their head a works-manager or foreman. Nicias had the work of his mines directed by a man to whom he had paid a talent. Demosthenes' father kept in his armour factory an overseer who, after the death of the chief, had full powers of proxy. Midas managed Athenogenes' perfumery works with all the rights which to-day are conferred by signature. The nine or ten shoe-makers of Timarchos were directed by a workshop foreman. At Eleusis seventeen public slaves, employed on the temple works, had one foreman, and twenty-eight free workers, brought from Megara, had two. The foremen were usually slaves, but sometimes freedmen or foreigners. They may have made a bit on the feeding of their men, since it was they who did the catering. They had a name for being very hard. " Slave," says a comic poet, " beware of serving a former slave; when the bull is resting he forgets the yoke." They had an agile arm and a ready whip. A vase painting shows us, in a pottery shop, a slave hung up by his arms and legs and lashed unmercifully. (See Fig. 26.) The iron rings found here and there in the galleries of Laureion speak volumes about the discipline which reigned in the mines. But such treatment was confined to slaves. The law of Athens protected the person of the free man against every chastisement and every constraint.

The return of labour varied according to the trade and according to the period. We can calculate the time taken by the marble-workers to flute the columns of the Erechtheion. The five men of the gang which was most employed needed about sixty days to do twenty-four flutings with flat ridges, 19 ft. 6 in. long. That makes about nineteen inches per man per day. It is not much. On the other hand, at Eleusis in 329-8 the gang of three bricklayers, working steadily, laid in one day 413 squares, $17\frac{3}{4}$ in. by $17\frac{3}{4}$ in. by 4 in., i.e. altogether about 300 cubic feet. In the ancient galleries of Laureion, at points where the sterile rock is of the hardest limestone, the face of the workings, which are at least two feet high and wide, is cut in at regular intervals of four or five inches; each of these cuttings shows the normal output of five hewers working one after the other, each so long as his lamp burned, i.e. two hours. Therefore each man hewed about 250 cubic inches in an hour; this result, obtained with the pick and pitching-tool, is higher than that demanded to-day on the same sites from gun-powder and dynamite.

We now have to consider the question of wages.

Certain labourers, even in the IVth century, received no other remuneration than their food for the day. Otherwise it would not have been specified in the accounts that the workers who received wages had to feed themselves " at home." But this mode of payment had almost disappeared in Attica, except in the country. We have seen above that even the public slaves received a ration-allowance of 180 drachmas a year in money, and drew nothing in kind but clothing, and that their foreman, who did not receive clothing, had in addition to his keep a salary of 100 drachmas.

Whereas the public slave was paid at every Prytany, ten times a year, the workman was paid by the day or by the job. In the last third of the Vth century the price at Athens of labour by the day was one drachma. No difference was made in view of either the social position or the trade of the worker, and the labourer was paid as much for his day's work as the craftsman. But mere assistants received only 3 obols. For agricultural labourers food was reckoned at 2 ob., and they were given 4 ob. in cash. In the IVth century wages by the day tended in general to rise and to vary. In the years 395-391 a gang of bricklayers, consisting of a master

# INDUSTRY

mason and two lads, was paid from 4 dr. to 4 dr. 4 ob., the master getting 2 dr. and the lads 1 dr. or 1 dr. 2 ob. each. At Delphi, about the middle of the century, the plasterers received 30 Æginetan drachmas a month or 1 dr. $2\frac{1}{2}$ ob. in Attic money a day. At Eleusis, in 329-8, the old wage of one drachma was only given to assistants; the labourers received $1\frac{1}{2}$ dr., and the skilled workers 2 dr. (sawyers) or $2\frac{1}{2}$ dr. (bricklayers, plasterers, carpenters).

But work did not go on the whole year round. There were many days when nothing was done. The Athenian calendar contained about sixty holidays, about as many as our own, including Sundays. On working days the citizen went to the law-court or the Assembly, which brought him the allowance of two or three obols. Moreover, there was not enough work to keep all hands constantly employed, and the free workman was not disposed to devote all his time to his trade. We find a gang of thirty-three men working full strength two days out of seven; on the other days two, four, twelve, fourteen, and even twenty-three are absent. When the marble-workers execute the fluting of the columns of the Erechtheion, the three gangs which contain citizens never do more than 22 or 23 drachmas worth of work per man in thirty-six or thirty-seven days, while the three gangs of slaves, directed by a slave or a Metic, do work worth 27, 35, and even 38 drachmas. The yearly salary of the architect was calculated on a basis of 2 dr. a day, at the time when the masons were earning $2\frac{1}{2}$ dr. a day; this proves with certainty that the latter were idle for at least one fifth of the year and probably much more.[1]

From at least the Vth century onward work was also done by the piece. In the Erechtheion accounts the sawyers are sometimes paid by the day and sometimes by the saw-

[1] The advantage of the architect and the officials over the craftsmen and labourers lies just in the fact that they escape unemployment. Their emoluments are not at a higher rate, but they are fixed by the year and paid in halves, tenths, or twelfths. In the Vth century the Athenian architect gets 360 dr., one per day. In the first half of the following century the architect at Epidauros gets $\frac{2}{3}$ more, thanks to the Æginetan drachma. In the second half, the architect at Eleusis receives 720 dr. (2 dr. per day). At Delphi the architect is paid 360 Æginetan drachmas for at least eight years, then, in 345, he gets double, and in 342 four times the amount (almost three times as much as his colleague at Eleusis). Salaries come more and more to depend on talent and reputation.

cut, the carpenters receive so much for each beam shaped or each plank laid, the decorative joiners who make the panels of the ceiling fit the frames at 6 dr. apiece and fasten the mouldings at 3 dr. apiece, and the masons wall up the intervals of the columns at 10 dr. each. For the fluting of the columns 300 dr. are paid, whatever may be the strength of the gang which does the work and whatever time they take over it. Rosettes for the soffits are ordered at the fixed price of 14 dr. The marble statuettes of the frieze cost so much per subject— 60 dr. for a full-sized figure, 30 dr. for a medium figure, 20 dr. for a child. Work by the measure, a variety of work by the piece, is also done. The stone-cutters have a tariff which takes both material and size into account. Plastering and painting are done by the linear foot or by the square foot.

Payment by the piece and by the measure seems to have developed along with the division of labour, at the expense of payment by the day. In the IVth century the cutting, carriage, and transport of stones are done by the piece. At Eleusis the moulding of bricks one foot and a half square costs 36 dr. per thousand including clay, and 40 dr. without clay, the carriage of the same bricks costs, according to the distance, 15, 17, or 25 dr. per thousand, and the laying, which in 395-1 cost between 12 and 15 dr. per thousand, may reach 17 dr. in 329-8. The measurer and the carrier of the corn are entitled to $7\frac{1}{2}$ ob. and 4 ob. respectively per 100 medimni (8$d$. and 4$d$. a bushel). Inscriptions on stone are paid at various rates. In Athens the carving of decrees is priced at a tariff which rises by tens—20 dr. for 1,000 characters, 30 for 1,500, 40 for 2,000, and so on. At Epidauros the letters are reckoned at one drachma per hundred, sometimes at round rates of 10, 20, and 30 Æginetan drachmas, and sometimes exactly, fractions being taken into account. The stone-cutters at Delphi in 338 receive one Æginetan drachma for a hundred letters.

Work by the day and work by the job gradually came to be apportioned by agreement, rough work being left to plain day-labourers, and the task which required manual skill being reserved for workers who were able to put their soul into it if they took time over it. In 408 the men working on the Erechtheion were paid a drachma a day, as labourers or as craftsmen, as well as working by the job. Towards the

## INDUSTRY

middle of the IVth century the same kind of work was remunerated in different ways, according to the amount of finish required. At Delphi we have a good example which shows that the falling off of work by the day was in proportion to the improvement of technical processes; the same contractor does the plastering of plain stones by the day and that of worked stones at 4 dr. per face. Work by the piece does not seem to have been an economy for the customer. Here, indeed, is a case where, combined with the contract system, it costs more. Three bricklaying jobs are done at Eleusis. In two of them, which are paid by the day, the laying of a thousand bricks comes to 13 dr. 2 ob.; in the third, a contractor charges 17 dr. the thousand. He thus makes a profit of 21-22%, for which he has to engage and supervise the workmen and to be responsible for bad work. Gradually work by the job tended to drive out work by the day, even for plain tasks. It was better suited to an age in which the works contract placed a professional craftsman between the workman and the customer, and the distinction between the skilled worker and the plain labourer was accentuated.

But when we speak of wages we must determine their real value. What standard of living could the craftsman and the labourer attain? That there was suffering in the IVth century there is no doubt. We have only to listen to the wail of the fuller in the comedy. "In our trade we have the earnest of a livelihood, and we die of hunger all the year round, for ever hoping." But perhaps unemployment was more frequent in a trade in which competition was keener than in others. Let us look at the question as a whole. First of all, we must remember the abstemiousness of the South. In old days, says Aristophanes, if you went out for the day, "you took a calabash of drink and some dry bread, a couple of onions, and three olives." Clothes were very simple, and were made for a great part at home. For dwelling there were a few small rooms in a house of sunbaked brick. Let us try to calculate the cost of living in these circumstances.

Food consisted of two elements: (i) the *sitos*, i.e. cereals in the form of bread, scone, or porridge; (ii) the *opsonion*, i.e. fresh or dried vegetables, meat, which was almost always pig, fresh or salt fish, and lastly fruit, chiefly olives and figs.

The usual drink was wine, very much diluted, or spring water. It is easy to calculate the cost of the *sitos*. The grown man's ration was reckoned at one chœnix of wheat (nearly two pints) or two chœnices of barley meal a day. This was the big ration, which was demanded by the Spartan soldier in the field; he regarded it as very large, since he considered that half as much was enough for his servant.

At the end of the Vth century, therefore, when wheat was at 3 dr. the medimnus, the worker's *sitos* cost him $22\frac{1}{2}$ dr. a year for $7\frac{1}{2}$ medimni. With 60 dr. a year, or one obol a day, he was well fed. With an additional 60 dr. he could meet his other expenses. A single man lived comfortably on 120 dr. in the time of Pericles. It was enough if he worked one day in three. Now let us suppose the typical case of the man with a wife and two children to keep. Allow three full rations for the four of them, and their food will cost 180 dr. Clothing may be reckoned at 50 dr., housing at 36 dr., and sundry expenses at 14 dr. This makes 280 dr. altogether. These figures agree quite well with the salary of the architect, who must have been able to maintain a family decently on his 360 dr. The workman who earned one drachma a day could feed his family, if it was not too large, without even being compelled to work on every working day.

In the IVth century, when the general rise in prices brought the cost of corn up to 5 dr. the medimnus, the single man's food came to 100 dr., and that of a family of four to 300 dr. But the other expenses had not increased at the same rate, since the public slave lived well on 180 dr. a year plus clothing. A worker could, therefore, keep a wife and two children on 450 dr. It is true that the architect now received 750 dr., and a middle-class townsman complained that he could only just live on 540 dr.; but in these times the upper classes were beginning to have expensive wants which were not felt to the same degree by the working classes. Therefore a plain assistant, getting one drachma a day, could, if he worked three hundred days in the year, ensure a good average standard of living for his wife; but he was obliged to practise moderation and to be content with reduced rations if he had children. The labourer who earned $1\frac{1}{2}$ dr. could feed two

# INDUSTRY

children, provided he worked on all days but holidays. The skilled worker with 2 dr. or $2\frac{1}{2}$ dr. could save 150 or 300 dr. if he was constantly employed, or else he could rest three days in eight, or even one in two. While the unskilled worker, burdened with a family, could only manage by dint of hard work and privations, the skilled worker or small craftsman could bring up several children and give them, according to the work he did, an average or high standard of living.

CHAPTER X

TRADE

THE shortage of agricultural commodities and raw materials perforce gave Greek trade an ever increasing importance. It was absolutely necessary to collect products on the distant markets on which they abounded, and to distribute them among the cities with a growing population in which they were lacking. Plato himself, the declared enemy of trade, well defined the social usefulness of the trader when he called him the agent who ensures the regular and measured distribution of the wealth produced by nature without measure or regularity. Aristotle recognized equally that it is impossible for a country to remain in isolation, without selling or buying, importing or exporting. It is true that the theorists understood the legitimacy of exchanges in their own way. They would have been glad to bring back the days in which each sold the surplus of his production direct, and transactions were confined to natural products. But the people, especially in the democratic cities, was ignorant of doctrines which it would have regarded as crazy. Life laughed at systems. Trade assumed a grand development in Athens and the Peiræeus.

1. MATERIAL CONDITIONS OF TRADE

At this period *kapeleia*, retail trade, or, more generally, land trade, was distinguished from *emporia*, wholesale trade, which was classed together with sea-borne trade. For both branches the Athenian market was highly organized.

The agricultural producer could always go to the consumer without an intermediary. The market-gardener came to town with his fruit and his vegetables, the land-owner sent in his asses laden with wood, the Acharnian brought his baskets of charcoal. But, whereas at Locri the law forbade any transaction through an intermediary, and even any written contract, and at Erythræ retailers were excluded from the wool-market by decree, in Attica it was the natural play of economic relations which caused direct sale to survive.

The small traders, men and women, proclaimed themselves in streets and squares by their cries. The pedlars walked along the roads beside their beast with great bundles loading his sides, or else sat on their ass with a huge bale on their own shoulders. The shops in Athens were wretched stalls, clustering in the neighbourhood of the Agora or in

Fig. 47. Ass carrying a package. Attic cup.
(Perrot, Vol. X, Fig. 364.)

sacred precincts like that of the Theseion. In all the quarters of the town the pot-houses sold drink and food to the common people. The character of the seller of corn, porridge, and vegetables, or of garlic, wine, and bread, is the joy of Aristophanes.

But the centre of home trade is the Agora. There all day long is found the throbbing life, political, social, and economic, of the great city. At the ends of the square are the offices of the magistrates, with the official placards which attract the curious. The crowd shelters under the porticoes with their slender colonnades. It passes in front of the frescoes of the great Polygnotos and flocks "to the Herms," where business men discuss prices, and political enthusiasts argue over the agenda of the next Assembly, and gapers listen to the town criers, and idlers chatter and wave their knotty sticks about, and the young bloods make their long white cloaks sweep in the most elegant manner. All who have something to sell, slaves with cloth which they have just made, craftsmen from the Cerameicos, Melite, or Scambonidæ, peasants who left their village before daybreak, Megarians driving their pigs, fishermen from Lake Copais, pass in every direction. Through alleys planted with trees they reach the places assigned to different goods, separated by movable barriers. One after another, at the hours fixed by the regulations, the different markets open; there are markets for vegetables, fruit, cheese, fish, meat and sausages, poultry and game, wine, wood, pottery, ironmongery, and old articles. There is even a corner for books. Every merchant has his place, which he reserves by paying a fee; in the shade of an awning or an umbrella he sets out his goods on trestles, near his cart and his resting beasts. Shoppers walk about; traders call to them; porters and messengers offer their services. Shouts, oaths, and quarrels; the *Agoranomoi* do not know to whom to listen. When the open-air markets are shut the customers make for the covered hall, which is like an Eastern bazaar, with counters occupying the end.

All these retailers had a bad name. Abuse was heaped on their rowdiness and vulgarity. Women who made their living in the street or on the Agora, or owned taverns, were suspected of misconduct, and the law did not allow prosecution for adultery in the case of persons of this class. But the small dealers were chiefly reproached with habitual rapacity, dishonesty, and lying. They overcharged, they adulterated their goods, they gave short weight, they swindled over the exchange.

The hucksters of the whole of Greece swarmed to the fairs which were held in connection with the great festivals. They poured in the wake of armies, some in order to sell horses or articles of equipment, others to buy booty and prisoners cheap, and most of them as sutlers. The Athenian fleet which sailed for Sicily was accompanied by a great number of merchant vessels. Xenophon draws a lively picture of the impetus given to the trade of a town by the passage of troops. Generals were obliged to take precautions against these flocks of cormorants by granting a limited number of permissions.

The chief obstacle to the development of land trade into business on a big scale was the difficulty of communication. No doubt some progress was made. Athens had the roads repaired by slaves under the orders of five surveyors. A fair number of roads started from the milestone set up by the Peisistratids. The most important of them served ports. Two ran from the Peiræeus; one, which was planted with olive trees, divided at the gates of Athens, and the other, a carriage road, passed between the Long Walls. The Deceleia road was continued by the Eubœan Way, on which the Athenians organized a transport service between Chalcis and Oreos. The road which ran from Bœotia and Phocis to Thessaly, Macedonia, Chalcidice, and Thrace was used more and more. But for all that the road system was deficient. In Attica the heads of the road administration obtained indifferent results, for want of sufficient credit, and perhaps, too, because these officials, who were appointed by lot, were lacking in competence. The roads near the temples were strengthened in great haste when the festivals were approaching, but there was no attempt to make wheeled transport easier. The Sacred Way to Eleusis was provided with a built-up portion varying between 8 ft. and 15 ft. 8 in. in breadth. Vehicles could not pass at every point on it. Moreover, for religious reasons, the bridge which made the direct route possible was made only 4 ft. 9 in. broad, so that chariots had to make a *détour* inland. It is a significant fact that, before an edifice of any size was built, the work necessary for the transport of the materials was carried out as an urgent matter. The *naopoioi* who formed the building commission at Delphi were obliged to install an unloading quay with a machine in the port of Cirrha; the *epistatai* of the temple of Eleusis entered in their accounts the renovation of a road leading to the quarries of Pentelicon. Everywhere the administration of the roads was insufficient.

Wheeled vehicles had improved; four-wheeled freight

waggons were built. But Attica had hardly enough oxen to draw them. The great transport contractors, the " feeders of oxen," were Bœotians; in 329 Eudemos of Platæa sent teams to Athens for work in progress. On the other hand, the small transport business throve in Attica. In a list of sixty-nine freedmen whose profession is known it appears against ten names. The trade of muleteer and donkey-boy is mentioned frequently. Carriers had their own speciality, either amphoras or skins.

The shortcomings of the roads and the scarcity of pack-animals caused the price of land transport to soar to incredible heights.[1] The monstrous charges for cartage for a long time prevented overland trade from developing greatly. And if land transport was badly organized for goods, it was not organized at all for passengers. Each managed as he could by his own devices.[2]

[1] The carting of blocks of marble from the port of Epidauros up to the temple costs 42% of the purchase price. And the contractors do not make fortunes. Fines rain on their heads; we know of one who makes 1,775 dr. over one transaction and another time pays 1,080 dr. for delay; on the whole he loses. In Attica, to take column drums from Pentelicon to Eleusis, after the road had been repaired and waggons had been built, teams of oxen had to be hired at from 4 dr. to 4 dr. 3½ ob. a span per day. These blocks, measuring over two cubic yards and weighing about five tons, had to be carted about 25 miles. Each drum required 20-33 span of oxen for three days. The only waggon which could do the journey in two and a half days was drawn by 40 span. An average of 342 dr. was paid per block, i.e. 2s. per ton per mile. For fragile goods transport was relatively as dear as for heavy goods. From Laciadæ to Eleusis (ca. 12 m.) a hundred tiles pay 40 dr., 40% of the cost price. For bricks costing 40 dr. a thousand, local cartage comes to 25 dr., and transport from Eleusis to Athens to 35 dr. But all this is nothing to the prices paid by the Delphic administration for the transport of materials bought in Sicyon or Corinth. From the port they had to be carried up nearly 2,000 feet. Four blocks of tufa, which cost 244 dr. (Æginetan) for cutting and 896 dr. for carriage to the wharf, then cost 1,680 dr. " from the sea to the temple." Stones which cost 61 dr. each in Corinth cost 705 dr. on delivery at Delphi ! It is fantastic. The costs of transport are never lower, except for light or divisible materials which run no risk. From Pteleon to Eleusis a medimnus of lime costs one obol for transport (1d. a bushel); from the Peiræeus to Eleusis the transport of a mixed consignment (wood, varnish, and colours) weighing about 10 cwt. comes to 7 dr. 3 ob. (about 6d. per cwt.). At Epidauros, from port to temple, 1½ ob. (Æginetan) are paid per talent of lead (5d. per cwt.). But at Delphi, even for metal, transport is still very dear; to carry up 4 tal. 5 minas of tin, 8 dr. (Æginetan) are charged (3s. per cwt.).

[2] The question of lodging, at least, was beginning to be solved in various ways. First, arrangements had to be made for housing the crowds attracted by the religious gatherings and fairs. Private hospitality was not enough. The cities hired houses at the holy places to

# TRADE 293

Posts there were none, even for the Governments. When the public safety required the despatch of an urgent message professional runners were employed; they were able to do the journey from Athens to Argos and back (160 miles) in two days, and from Platæa to Delphi and back (85 miles) in one day. Beacon signals were used in exceptional cases. The Athenian State at least had two advice-boats constantly at its disposal, the *Paralos* and the *Salaminian*. Private persons had to wait for an opportunity for sending their correspondence. However, in the big ports a whole service of commercial information was gradually developed, quite spontaneously, by means of the news picked up by ships on their way. Those firms which had correspondents at a certain number of centres could form a private information agency.

In every respect sea-borne trade was superior to trade by land. Shipping made great progress from the Vth century onwards. The trireme, the swift cruiser, carried two hundred men; war transports held still more, and some were fitted to take horses. Merchant vessels had a burden up to 10,000 talents (360 tons); they frequently transported 5,000 medimni of grain (over 7,000 bushels). But coasting vessels did not as a rule exceed 500 talents (18 tons). Navigators still preferred to remain in sight of land, and to go to Sicily they always sailed by Corcyra and Taras; but they were no longer so much afraid of the open sea as before. For long voyages they still waited for the good season, and the mariners of the Peiræeus sailed after the Dionysia and returned before the autumn equinox; but the speculators could not allow all navigation to be suspended during the winter, and did not

receive their own citizens; at Delphi Larissa had a house, and so did even a small town like Echinos in Malis. Sometimes the State opened hostels near the temples, to take foreigners and citizens; when the Thebans destroyed Platæa they preserved the Heræon and built by it a hostel 200 square ft., with two storeys of rooms; the ambassadors of Athens and Philip swore the peace of 346 in a hostel at Pheræ, in front of the temple of the Dioscuri. The sanctuaries themselves built for their own profit hospitals and caravanserais with dormitories and refectories; these establishments, at first intended for the patients in the Asclepieia, were later used by all pilgrims. Individuals followed this example. In populous quarters and on busy roads many inns and hostels were run on business lines. But they were noisome holes, nests of bugs, where visitors were mercilessly fleeced. In a big town like Athens decent people could take furnished rooms or flats, slaves, and carriages; but they were dear.

trouble themselves about the state of the weather. Forced runs were often made, without any halt at night. From the frequent use of maps we may suppose that marine charts were used. Lighthouses were still unknown, but many sea-marks and signals of all kinds were erected. Monuments of marble or white stone were built on eminences; the mariners of Athens looked out for the shining crest of the Athene Promachos, and at Thasos a sepulchral tower bore an epitaph saying that it would be " the salvation of ships and sailors."

With the means available, speeds were not yet great. They had, however, very much increased. In Homeric times it took at least three days to go from Lesbos to Argolis (240 nautical miles), five days from Crete to Egypt (300 miles), and seven days from the Cyclades to Ithaca (280 miles); with a good wind, between two and three knots were made. At the beginning of the IVth century Xenophon gives, as examples of speed, crossings done from Cotyora to Sinope (170 miles) in a day and a night, from Sinope to Heracleia (190 miles) in two days, and from Heracleia to Byzantion (125 miles) in a long day of between sixteen and eighteen hours. So high speeds varied between six and seven knots; since the days of the *Odyssey* they had trebled. On the good average speed of a merchantman, which is the important thing, Xenophon again gives us a valuable indication; a Milesian ship went from Lampsacos to the Laconian coast (290 miles) in three days and three nights. This speed of four or five knots was that of the long journey without halts and with a light wind. But, since as a rule there was no rowing at night, we must allow in the good season about sixteen hours of travelling in a day. The distance covered in an ordinary day thus comes between 65 and 80 nautical miles. Therefore the times of the most usual voyages were as follows.

|  |  |  | Naut. Miles. | Days. |
|---|---|---|---|---|
| From the Peiræeus | to | Ephesos or Mytilene | 190 | $2\frac{1}{2}$–3 |
| ,, | ,, | to Abdera | 240 | 3–4 |
| ,, | ,, | to Potidæa or Olynthos | 215 | 3 |
| ,, | ,, | to Lampsacos | 240 | 3–4 |
| ,, | ,, | to Byzantion | 350 | $4\frac{1}{2}$–$5\frac{1}{2}$ |
| ,, | ,, | to Heracleia | 475 | 6–7 |
| ,, | ,, | to Sinope | 665 | $8\frac{1}{2}$–10 |
| ,, | ,, | to Phasis or Dioscurias | 950 | 12–14 |
| ,, | ,, | to Panticapæon | 800 | 10–12 |
| ,, | ,, | to Crete | 170 | 2–$2\frac{1}{2}$ |
| ,, | ,, | to Rhodes | 250 | $3\frac{1}{2}$–4 |

# TRADE

|  | Naut. Miles. | Days. |
|---|---|---|
| From Rhodes to Egypt | 320 | 4–5 |
| ,, ,, to Sidon | 380 | 5–6 |
| From the Peiræeus to Cythera | 110 | 1½–2 |
| From Cythera to Cyrene | 200 | 2½–3 |
| From Cyrene to Egypt | 470 | 6–7 |
| From the Peiræeus to Corcyra | 375 | 5–6 |
| From Corinth to Corcyra | 190 | 2½–3 |
| From Corcyra to Taras or Croton | 160–165 | 2–2½ |
| ,, ,, to Syracuse | 320 | 4–5 |

The improvements introduced into the organization of marine trade are well brought out by Aristotle when he includes under *emporia*, or commerce, three elements, *naukleria*, *phortegia*, and *parastasis*. The two first are ship-owning and transport. The third is the *commenda* of the Middle Ages, a mixed institution, the principal varieties of which are bottomry, *commandite*, commission, and consignment. Aristotle further distinguishes, among sea-faring men, between those who go in for *chrematistikon*, who carry on trade, and those engaged in *porthmeutikon*, who transport passengers and goods. So we find sailors who go all over the Mediterranean with their cargoes, and others who maintain a regular service between two ports.

And what a difference there was between the cost of sea transport and that of land transport! It is almost incredible. Competition brought down freightage, although transport was still profitable, thanks to the abundance of demand and the increasing facilities of navigation. Passengers were not especially remunerative ; the fare from Ægina to the Peiræeus was 2 obols, and for 2 drachmas you could go to Egypt or the Euxine with wife, children, and luggage. It was goods that counted. They ensured a regular flow of consignments to marine enterprise. Freightage was comparatively low,[1] but it brought in a good profit, because the

[1] Light, easily packed goods pay extraordinarily little. The rate for the carriage of vermilion from Ceos to the Peiræeus is fixed by decree at one obol the talent (2*d*. per cwt.), which is nothing for a commodity worth 30-35 dr. At Eleusis the carriage of tiles, which by road comes to 40 dr. the hundred for about twelve miles, costs by boat from Corinth 20 ob. for a triple journey (5% of the purchase price). The Peiræeus ferry brings 67 talents of fire-wood to Eleusis for 7 dr. 3 ob. (7% of the purchase price); the rate is about 4*d*. per ton per nautical mile. When the Corinth ferry takes joiner's wood four times that distance, the cost of carriage is 17% of that of purchase; but timber goes the same distance, from Sicyon to Cirrha, without the transport

ship-owner adapted his price to the profits of the merchant, which were considerable, and to the interest on marine loans, which was enormous.

2. LEGAL CONDITIONS OF TRADE

Having studied the material conditions of trade, we shall consider its legal conditions, its relations with the State, and the special law to which it gave birth.

We should have a wretched idea of the commercial freedom of the Greek city if we judged it from Plato. Even when he compounds with realities, and admits trade as a necessary evil, he subjects it to a control which treats the merchant as a thief promised to the gaolers. Citizens are forbidden to practise any trade, and foreigners may practise only two at a time; profits are limited to the exact remuneration of the pains taken and the service rendered; the public authority must determine by categories and amounts those goods the import of which is permitted. Such are the main lines of the system. To apply it, a corps of *Astynomoi* will supervise industry, while *Agoranomoi* devote their attention especially to trade, fixing prices and tolerating neither advertisement nor bargaining nor sale on credit.

These arrangements recall the rigours of the Spartan legislation. Athens had very different principles. Her tradition went back to Solon, who allowed no legal limitation either of the rate of interest or of the right of association. For Athens the common law was liberty. But human liberty is never absolute; to define it is to mark its bounds. What, then, were the restrictions imposed on commercial freedom by the Athenian State ?

The city stepped in, in the name of the general interest, to ensure honest dealing. " The first administrative service demanded by material needs," says Aristotle, " is that which deals with the market, where there must be a magistracy to

---

adding more than 6 or 7% to the purchase price. Of course stone costs much more, especially in proportion to its value. At Delphi the contractors who specialize in " transport of stone by sea " demand prices which seem very high to us for the carriage of cut blocks of tufa from Corinth to Cirrha (about 40 nautical miles). 300% of the cost of cutting is enormous; but when we find 36% charged for cartage at the landing-quay, and nearly 700% for the journey from the port up to the temples, we are rather tempted to think it moderate.

supervise transactions and to maintain good order." This magistracy was that of the *Agoranomoi*. There was no city, however small, in which it did not exist. But its duties were not the same everywhere. The market regulations varied greatly. Some came close to Plato's favourite ideas in many points. In a decree of Erythræ on the sale of wool and waste, the exporter is forbidden to sell by retail locally, and the middleman is forbidden to sell any lot which does not come direct from the shearing; the use of the public weighing-machine is obligatory. Delos later issued similar regulations for the wood and coal trades, and added the obligation to sell at a fixed price, without bargaining. In exceptional cases the price of a commodity might be fixed by decree; at Lampsacos, to fill the treasury, an increase of 50% on corn and an equal tax on the sale were decreed. We even find the city intervening in the matter of exchange; a regulation of Olbia prescribed that foreign currencies should be exchanged publicly for the national currency in bronze and in silver, fixed the value of gold as eleven and a half times that of silver, and, to encourage the repression of fraud, farmed out the proceeds of the fines.

Athens on the whole confined herself to fulfilling the duty which Aristotle assigns to the State. Two boards of ten *Agoranomoi* and ten *Metronomoi* were divided equally between Athens and the Peiræeus. The former saw that the commodities offered for sale were pure and of good quality, the latter that the weights and measures used by merchants conformed to the public standards.

For the corn trade, however, Athens would hear no talk of liberty. The problem of the food-supply was too urgent. It dominated the whole of politics. At the first sitting of each Prytany, ten times a year, a report on the food-supply was laid before the Assembly. In the Vth century the question of imperialism was largely one of food. " Without drawing anything from the earth, I obtain everything by the sea," an Athenian wrote at the time. Above all, the countries of large production must be reserved. It was no mere chance that the two most hazardous adventures ever attempted by Athenian energy were the expeditions to Egypt and Sicily. Immediately after the failure of the first, the evicted people was thinking of the second, and in the interval it staked a claim on the Euxine. In the IVth century the Athenians obtained, through the favour of the native kings, at first priority of purchase, loading, and, consequently, sale, and subsequently an exemption from duties which was equivalent to a rebate of one thirtieth. So they had to watch over the route followed by the transports. From the beginning of the Peloponnesian War the " Wardens of the Hellespont " sent to Athens all the corn which came through. During the war with Philip the sole duty of the fleet was the *sitopompeia*, the convoying of grain. In September 340 it escorted 230 merchant ships, of which 180 belonged to Athens and her allies. In this way the food-supply was ensured outside.

But it was also necessary, by internal legislation, to encourage the import of corn and to prevent the concealment of stocks, attempts at engrossing, and artificial raising of the price. Extremely severe laws laid down the duties of the *emporoi*, or wholesale merchants, and the *sitopolai*, or dealers in large quantities, millers, bakers, and the like. No bottomry loan could be made unless it was secured on commodities of first necessity, particularly corn; no corn might be transported elsewhere than to the Peiræeus; not more than one third of any cargo which had come into the Corn Harbour could be re-exported; not more than fifty " loads " of corn could be bought at one time. The execution of these laws was entrusted to ten inspectors of the emporium, who had the supervision of the warehouses, and to the *Sitophylakes*, ten in number and later thirty-five, who saw that corn, flour, and bread were sold at the current price and in good weight. In this way the food-supply was ensured at home.

The war navy and the diplomatists, the legislators and the administrative authority united their efforts to procure for the Athenians their daily bread. There was not much commercial liberty in all this! Yet it was never considered necessary to establish a maximum on the pretext of a " fair price." Without this supreme violation of her traditions. Athens obtained bread cheap, while reserving for her trade a lucrative business, an essential element of predominance.

Besides restrictions in the interest of the corn-supply there were restrictions in the interest of the revenue. The State, which intervened in favour of the consumer, thought also of the treasury. For the object of the customs duties was to

# TRADE

procure financial resources for the people, not to hamper the free play of exchanges. Many cities previously had taken special measures to encourage an industry, to handicap a competitor, or to prevent the export of certain commodities; but these exceptional arrangements had no lasting effect. So, too, in the Vth century, the closing of Athenian territory to goods from Megara was an arm of war, like the prohibition of the export of weapons and ship-building materials. Perhaps the idea of protection was not always unknown to the Athenians, but it never went beyond the very simple form of preferential treatment of Athenians in State contracts; thus, the commissioners of public works bought at Laciadæ "Corinth style" tiles at 140 drachmas the hundred, before they brought the genuine article from Corinth, which cost only 86 drachmas 4 obols. In any case, there was no trace of protection in the *ad valorem* duties levied in the ports on all goods imported or exported. The duty was too low; it did not even make smuggling worth while. At the Peiræeus it was at first one hundredth; then it rose to the rate adopted in most Greek towns, one fiftieth. Athens, being obliged after 413 to leave no stone unturned, imposed a duty of one twentieth on the subject cities, but on the other hand she exempted them from tribute. The very moderate usual rate of 2% was levied with great strictness on all goods, even on the import of corn, even on the export of tripods and oxen sent by the Amphictions to the festivals at Delos. For the fiftieth was collected by a company to which it was farmed out; any exemption would have been a defraudation of the company. Before a cargo was taken on or unloaded, the customs officials or *Pentecostologoi* asked for the bill of lading and inspected the goods on the wharf. In case of fraud, the goods were confiscated, or the duty was multiplied by ten. So declarations were usually correct, and the customs registers gave a true account of the value of a cargo. In brief, the customs never hampered foreign trade and were not a severe burden on national trade.

Certain cities did, however, sometimes meet special requirements by exceptional violations of liberty. Formerly the great resource in emergencies had been the public and sacred domain. Then the State had taken to trafficking in its rights and to extending them in order to make more out of them. Byzantion sold to her rich Metics the right of owning land, and the citizenship. Finally the State abused its sovereign power to arrogate to itself temporary monopolies of sale. The *Economics*, wrongly attributed to Aristotle, give an endless list of these devices. Byzantion (Byzantion again) bought all the corn on the market on credit and made a great profit on the rise; Clazomenæ borrowed all the oil of the harvest and used it as security for her purchases of corn. Or, instead of itself exercising the rights which it assumed, the State ceded them to the highest bidder. Byzantion (ever to the fore) did so with the sea fisheries and the money exchange. We see that unscrupulous fiscal practices were very widespread. But Athens never, not in her worst days, descended to this general level of dishonesty. She obtained monopolies for her trades in the other cities, for example that of vermilion at Ceos, but she allowed none at home. Proposals of this kind were often made to her; one man suggested that the treasury should buy all the lead of Laureion at 2 dr. the talent, to be held until the price should rise to 6 dr.; others wanted the State to rent ships, warehouses, and hostelries. Athens found that freedom of trade had too many advantages to be subjected to such restrictions.

By the force of custom, and then by the intervention of legislation, a commercial law had become established by the Vth century. It already had all the complexity which in such a matter is the sign of progress. Plato spoke with disgust of all these regulations " about ship-building, wholesale and retail trade, commissions, customs, mines, loans, interest, and thousands of other questions of the kind."

Every agreement, however unimportant, was set down in writing. For the drafting, registration, copying, and keeping of contracts, accounts, and receipts, every precaution was taken; seals were affixed, oaths were exchanged, witnesses were present, several copies were made, documents were deposited with third persons, etc. Combinations of interests took the most varied forms, partnership, *commandite*, mandate, commission, management. In the banks especially the books were kept according to strict rules of accountancy. Bearer and order bills were unknown, but already the bottomry bond which could be ceded to a third person and realized when a declaration of safe-arrival at the port was received, constituted a kind of bill of exchange. The law regarding obligations in case of non-payment or insolvency provided for everything; there were accepted rules for protest, cessation of payment, and bankruptcy.

In spite of the frequent use of the penal clause in contracts, commercial trials were numerous. In the Vth century the court of the *Nautodikai*, or marine judges, examined and decided disputes between marine people and traders, cases of transport and ship-building, and litigation affecting the dock-workers. In the IVth century the investigation and the sentence were separated; the former devolved upon the *Eisagogeis* or " introducers," the latter on the *Thesmothetai*. About 350, commercial litigants were granted the privilege of a rapid procedure; judgement must be given within a month of the application, and execution was immediate, including arrest.

### 3. COMMERCIAL COMPANIES AND BANKS

We shall understand the intensity of Athenian trade when we know how far the grouping of individuals in societies or companies and the collecting of capital in banks had advanced.

Athens allowed complete liberty of association, on the one condition that there was no infringement of the laws of public order. This principle had been laid down by Solon at a time when there was not yet a clear distinction between the permanent brotherhood of a religious nature, such as the *thiasos*, and the temporary association of two or more persons for a business undertaking or piratical venture. It came into general practice as commerce demanded an ever greater amount of labour, capital, and credit. There were cities which restricted the right of association, in order to prevent contractors from combining when public works were given out. Athens, true to a law based on freedom of contracts and individual responsibility, allowed associations to form and act as they pleased, but did not permit them to set their civil personality against the claims made on each of the associates.

The first associations known in Greece were those which men naturally form when they are united on board a ship for a common enterprise; hence the marine trading companies. This tradition was bound to survive because the greatness of the risks made it necessary to divide them. The most usual association is that created by bottomry loans; it is a society in which profits and risks are shared by a moneylender and a ship-owner. Further to diminish his risk, each of the two parties looks for yet other associates; for example, three men combine to form a capital of 7,500 dr. In addition to the nominal partners there may be yet other partners who do not appear in the articles of association. So we have here a mixed association of labour and capital, under which are two associations, one of labour and the other of capital. The object of this association is one definite transaction; it is a *societas unius rei*. It lasts the time of a single voyage or of an outward and homeward voyage.

The temporary nature of these associations is to be seen, often in the humblest forms, in the branches of trade and industry connected with building. At Delphi the stonecutter Nicodamos of Argos by himself undertakes orders which bring him from 3 staters (6s. 6d.) to 6 minas (£23 5s. 6d.); a rival, Pasion, by himself builds a wall for 20 minas 10 staters (£78 14s. 6d.); but for an order worth 34 minas 26 staters (£133 7s. 2d.) the two combine, and when Pasion retires his place is taken by Sion and Theuphantos. So, too, Nicodamos takes a partner to build a colonnade for 1 talent 5 minas 20 staters (£254 7s. 2d.). As soon as it is a matter of more than fifty or at any rate a hundred pounds, these small contractors combine. But in Attica partnerships are very different. An account from Eleusis mentions only one name for the big orders; it is for minor jobs, sometimes very small indeed, that little traders or piece-workers combine, generally Metics or freedmen. Two combine to sell sacks of chopped straw at 180 dr. or to do a job for 20 dr. odd; for carriage four men get 456 dr., five get 225 dr., and two get 14 dr. One can hardly give the name of "associations" to these undertakings, which may end after one day.

But there were industrial and commercial companies of more imposing appearance and greater permanence. The contractors Nicostratos and Chremon of Argos were employed at Epidauros and at Delphi for years. "Chærophanes and Associates" made a contract with the city of Eretria which was valid for four years; but perhaps we have here one principal contractor backed by mere capitalists. Two craftsmen hired a workshop at Delphi for a certain time. Four impresarios combined to take the Peiræeus theatre on lease.

But where the partnership system triumphed in a truly modern form was in the mining and metallurgical industries, in banking, and in the farming of taxes. Companies took a predominant part in the exploitation of Laureion. They seem to have been remarkably powerful already, these mining companies. We know nothing of the balance-sheets of Philippos and Nausicles, nor of Hypereides, Æschylides, and Dicæocrates' Sons, but Epicrates and Co., who included among their shareholders the richest men in Athens, report an annual profit of 100 talents (£23,280). The washings and foundries were run in the same way; the best-known firm was that of the Demophilos and Co. Smelting Furnaces. In banking the necessary combination of capital produced partnerships which frequently had several chiefs. The great bankers Antisthenes and Archestratos are succeeded by Pasion, who ends by taking his freedman Phormion into partnership; after Pasion's death part of the business is carried on by Phormion, while the rest falls to the son of the deceased, who leaves the management of it to four partners. Moreover, in banking the sleeping partners and sureties appear as partners, ever ready to play an active part; when the banker Heracleides bolts, his sureties take the business into their hands. The farming out of the taxes encourages the formation of companies to exploit them. The Peiræeus customs were a big business. Since a large personnel was required for this, a society which was once organized was able to offer the fiscal authorities more advantageous terms, and easily obtained the concession. Moreover, no one had any scruple about preventing competition by collusive understandings. In certain countries the farming companies managed in this way to obtain an absolute monopoly for themselves at the expense of the treasury; in Athens there was never any question of such crying abuses as this.

As we have already perceived, the bank had become the indispensable agent of trade, the essential organ of economic life. Yet it was of very recent origin, and nothing shows better than its history the rapidity with which business developed in the Greece of the Vth century.

The cradle of the bank was in the temples. The gods

hoarded treasure. They had their own fortune, and they offered an inviolable sanctuary to the deposits of individuals and of the State. Athene stretched her guardian hand over the treasury of the Athenian confederacy, and Lysander entrusted two talents to the god of Delphi. So the great shrines had immense wealth at their disposal, and the smaller ones had some resources. Far-seeing administrators could not let all this capital lie dormant; needy cities could not neglect to call upon it. The gods lent at interest. About 375 the Amphictions of Delos entered into their accounts 47 talents (£11,280) against thirteen cities. Certain Attic demes every year put loans up to auction. The sacred administrations established the rules of good book-keeping and the conditions of a safe investment, and the funds of the *opisthodomoi* did the service demanded later of Government banks. Finance was born in the shade of sanctity.

Private individuals also learned gradually to employ their money productively. " We use our wealth," the Athenian said, " not for display but for action." In the IVth century a big inheritance always included a good number of bonds. But not everybody was in a position to make a profitable contract just at the right moment and to supervise its execution. Not everybody had, like Socrates, a friend to whom to confide the investment of his little fortune. The temple treasurers could not come into direct touch with the general public. For money and credit transactions a special profession was necessary. For a long time there had been seen, sitting at a table, at the harbour or on the market, men whose business was to exchange money. They took a fairly big premium; to obtain 100 Attic drachmas the *naopoioi* of Delphi had to give 75 Æginetan drachmas, instead of 70. As time went on, the money-changers extended their business, investing funds outside the country and lending money for all kinds of undertakings. They needed a large capital, and acted as intermediaries between the sellers and buyers of money. In addition to exchange the *trapezitai* did business in deposits and loans. They were bankers.

In less than a century the banks had developed all their operations to a remarkable extent. They made loans on personal security, on pledges, on mortgage, and on cargoes. They corresponded with foreign markets and undertook long-

# TRADE

distance payments, issuing short-dated letters of credit, money-orders, and cheques, without however rising to the idea of the true bill of exchange or of the transfer. For all these transactions the books had to be kept with the utmost care; in the bankers' ledgers each client had a page allotted to him, divided into two columns for credit and debit. Even in the law-courts these books furnished a presumption which a reputation for honesty could convert into proof. The banks, thus organized, were in constant relations with industry and marine trade; certain bankers built factories and owned ships in their own name. We know from the legal speeches of the time how much the Athenian used the bank in everyday life. Apollodoros and Timotheos keep all their money with the banker; when they are in difficulties they give him pledges in the shape of cups, a gold crown, and carpets. The execution of a sentence is effected at the bank of the condemned man. To obtain a mining concession Mantitheos and his father borrow 2,000 drachmas from Blepæos. To save his money from the risks of a voyage a foreigner, the son of a minister, goes and gets a letter of credit from Pasion. Even the Government services make use of the advantages offered to them; one commission of public works deposits the funds at its disposal with a *trapezites*. The service rendered by the banks made the usefulness of credit obvious to all; it was considered wonderful that a bit of paper could represent a fortune, and men of experience said " In the world of banking and business a reputation as a hard-working man, and also an honest one, has a marvellous power."

When we see how sudden progress was, we understand how Athens so soon had banks of the first class. The oldest, that which was founded towards the end of the Vth century by Antisthenes and Archestratos, was to be the most celebrated of all under their successor Pasion, the Rothschild of the IVth century B.C. From 394 onward Pasion did enormous business with all markets, especially Byzantion and the Euxine. He owned numerous premises and managed a big arms factory. For his patriotic liberality he obtained the citizenship. When in 371 he was obliged by ill-health to retire from business, the firm had a capital of 50 talents (£11,640), of which 39 talents were his personal property. If we want to have an idea of what this capital represented we must place ourselves about the beginning of our own century, and multiply £11,640 by at least four in order to have the relative value of the money, and again by four to obtain its productive value at a time when the rate of interest was four times what it is to-day. The importance of the banks is well shown by the care with which their chiefs chose a successor. Without regard for birth they chose the fittest man, and to attach him permanently to the house they appointed him in their will to be their son-in-law or the second husband of their widow. So, from freedman to freedman, from Metic to Metic, regular banking families were created. The most illustrious example is the ex-slave Pasion, leaving his business and his wife to his ex-slave Phormion. Demosthenes quotes a number of similar cases, and he explains the custom by the importance of the interests at stake, which must not depend on a single human life.

The *trapezitai* inspired the Athenians with the same feelings as other peoples showed later towards the Lombards and the Jews. "The trade of financier," according to Aristotle, " is rightly hated." A person in a comedy declares that there is no more execrable pest. " It is a strange and unusual thing," says Demosthenes, " among people who trade in money as a profession, to appear both active and honest." But the orator himself only talks like this to bring out the virtues of a particular banker, and on him, as on many others, the Athenian people conferred the highest token of esteem which it could imagine, the patent of full naturalization.

The union of banking and trade in the IVth century gave a sudden impulse to speculation. The free play of supply and demand was upset by veritable *coups de Bourse*. The philosopher Thales, with his brilliant operation in oil, had his disciples. The capitalists could not imagine that speculation in land had not existed in all times, and saw no other motive in the agrarian reforms of Solon. Corn and metal especially lent themselves to lucrative manipulation. Information was obtained on the state of the harvest in the producing countries, advantage was taken of political crises which impeded export or the free use of the seas, a storm, a shipwreck, the sudden arrival of a boat, everything was a pretext for rigging the market, and, failing true news, false news was invented. Since there were no time-bargains to

# TRADE

nullify variations by distributing them over a certain period, the smallest incident produced its effect instantaneously. The law prevented at least the engrossing of corn. On the metal market, on the other hand, we find a corner succeeding brilliantly. A Sicilian banker bought up the output of iron in all the factories, and made a profit of 200%. It was a similar deal in lead that Pythocles proposed to the Athenian Government. But the time had not come for the most magnificent operations; we must await the dawn of a new age to see a Greek, the master of the Egyptian granary, give the law to the world market.

### 4. THE COMMERCIAL HEGEMONY OF ATHENS

It was Athens that gave the trade of Greece its whole impetus. But she did not succeed in triumphing over her rivals until about the middle of the Vth century. Traditional connexions are not broken quickly. The Ionian cities acted as intermediaries to the Athenian market until 480. With her *diolkos* and her two ports Corinth continued to convey from one sea to the other the products of east and west. Ægina remained prosperous until the defeat of 457. The efforts of Themistocles to replace the open roadstead of Phaleron by a larger and safer harbour, the growth of a working population called up by the construction of a powerful fleet, and the skilful policy which placed Athens at the head of a confederacy which continually increased its scope, produced their full effect when at last, under the vigorous stimulus of Pericles, the Greeks, reconciled among themselves, were at peace with the Great King. Then the ships of the whole world took the road to the Peiræeus.

A vast anchorage. The western shore reserved for the war fleet; slips and arsenals on all sides. The eastern shore belongs to the merchant navy; it is the emporium. It is divided by moles; there are boundary-marks showing the purpose of each dock and the moorings of each class of ship. At the "Ferry Wharf" the ships come alongside which run to Eleusis, Corinth, and Ægina, and the one which comes from the islands, crammed with passengers. Further off, the big transports are berthed in rows. Opposite the wharves run the five porticoes, the warehouses; they receive all goods except grain. The Corn Hall, the *Alphitopolis*, where the merchants of the town obtain their supplies, stands at the end of the War Harbour, for there the triremes also take on provisions before sailing. Among the sailors and stevedores customs agents trot about. The *Deigma* or Trade Exchange serves as a rendezvous for the merchants who deal by sample; on the Agora goods are offered wholesale. The " tables " of the bankers stand between the offices of port-inspectors, *Agoranomoi*, *Metronomoi*, corn-controllers, farmers of the fiftieth, and judges of marine suits. When you have left the emporium you are in the town. Built on the plans of Hippodamos of Miletos, that lover of symmetry, it is like an American city. From the Agora broad, straight streets run, intersected at right angles by minor streets; the big thoroughfares are lined with wealthy houses, where ship-owners, business men, and bankers live. Sailors and fishermen, retailers and craftsmen, labourers and porters crowd in the purlieus. Hostelries, inns, and drink-shops come one after another; the houses of pleasure are always full. Citizens mingle with Metics, slaves, freedmen, and passing foreigners. It is a motley crowd, wearing every costume, worshipping every god, speaking every lingo in the world. Through this contact the Atticism of the Peiræeus people becomes contaminated with outlandish words and rude manners; but their individualism acquires a singular force. " The men of the sea," says Aristotle " are inclined to democracy "; in Attica they are mad for it. They throw themselves into politics and trade with the same spirit of initiative and equal energy. The Peiræeus contributes largely to forming the public spirit in Athens and to making that city the economic capital of the Greek race.

The Athenians grew accustomed to regarding their city as the centre of Greece and of the world. " If you want to go from one end of Greece to the other," says Xenophon, " you go, as it were, in a circle round Athens." The great sea routes started from the Peiræeus. Those of the north ended in Chalcidice and Thrace, or in the Propontis and the Euxine; that of the east reached Chios, Lesbos, and the ports of Asia Minor; that of the south ran by Delos to Samos, or by Paros and Naxos to Rhodes, and on to Phaselis, Cyprus, Phœnicia, Egypt, and Cyrenaica. Even towards the western seas, though nothing could deprive Corinth of the advantage of her

# TRADE

position on the Isthmus, a delay of two or three days was not enough to discourage an enterprising and dogged trader. So Athenian commerce radiated in every direction. In the immediate neighbourhood of the Peiræeus it knit lasting connexions with the markets which it had caused to decline. It attached the islands to itself as veritable dependencies. It found excellent support bases in the Cleruchies placed at the ends of the Ægean and in the confederate cities of Ionia, Caria, the Hellespont, and Thrace. Thus it was able to win supremacy on every market.

The economic importance of Chalcidice and Thrace is sufficiently shown by the stubbornness of the conflicts which took place around Potidæa, Olynthos, and Amphipolis. These ports received commodities from the interior. The Athenians came there at first for live-stock and grain. When they had markets better supplied with grain, they began to exploit the gold-mines in the region of Mount Pangæos, exported wood, flax, and pitch from Macedonia, and obtained sturdy slaves from the Thracians.

On the Euxine Athenian trade had been stopped short by the Persian Wars; there is no transition here, but an abrupt and complete gap, between the red-figure vases of the severe style and the vases of the fine style. But after the victory of Salamis the Greeks came back to obtain Scythian corn, and Herodotos visited Olbia. Athens, driven out of Egypt, sought another granary. She established Cleruchies in the Chersonese, on the Propontis, and still further, at Sinope and Amisos. She sent Pericles in person to cruise in the Euxine. When the Peloponnesian War broke out her first care was to post her officials on the Hellespont in order to watch the homeward-bound ships and to send them to the Peiræeus. In the IVth century she obtained by diplomacy what she could not exact by force. The princes of the Cimmerian Bosphorus granted to Athenian traders priority of loading and exemption from export duty. From the harvest of the barbarians the Athenians took their four or five hundred medimni; the others waited until they had done. With the corn they took cattle, fish, salted goods, hides, wool, and slaves. In exchange they imported wine and oil in common pots or painted vases, and artistic objects such as terra-cottas. To the Phasis country they went for wood, hemp, Cholcian cloth, and wax. From Sinope they got fish, chestnuts, almonds, wood, iron, and Paphlagonian slaves.

The war had closed the Persian Empire to a whole generation of Greeks. The caravans had forgotten the way to the Ionian ports. When peace was restored the broken tradition was not resumed. It was to the extremities of the peninsula that the commercial movement turned. The Propontis and Caria gained all that Ionia lost. Lampsacos paid twice as much federal tribute as Ephesos. Phaselis became a considerable centre of exchange. It was by this city that Athens obtained her Asiatic goods. Before 465 a commercial treaty was concluded between the two cities, and more than a century later Demosthenes asserted that no city gave the consular law-courts at the Peiræeus so much work as Phaselis. But at all other points in the Persian Empire Athens was able to dispense with intermediaries. Travellers and traders began to go about freely in the Eastern countries; the Greek missions to Susa formed legations of a kind; Athens secured for her citizens the protection of the phil-Hellenic princes in Egypt and Phœnicia; and she conferred *proxenia* on business men and dignitaries of Sidon and Cyprus.

The Orientals, on their side, once more visited the Greek ports. When a Phœnician ship came in people went to see it and admired the good order which reigned on board. The Egyptian and Cypriot colonies in the Peiræeus were large and influential. The Sidonian importers obtained exemption from the duty on Metics. At a time when the western colonies of the Persian Empire were using Greek as the official language, Aramaic and Persian were known by a few Athenians.

So relations with the East were very extensive. In the middle of the Peloponnesian War the flotillas of merchantmen came home regularly from Egypt by Phœnicia, Phaselis, and Rhodes, or else by Cythera. To Phœnicia the Athenians exported vases, some of which were resold to the Ethiopians, and blocks of marble, which were carved by the pupils of Greek artists. In Egypt olive oil was always sure of a market. The Greeks exchanged it chiefly for corn; they also bought carpets, linen, muslins called *sindones*, paper, sails, and ropes of papyrus, ivory, glass vases and cups, frankincense, ointments, rare animals, and nigger-boys. Athens was so successful in establishing herself as the intermediary between the East and Greece that Gaza adopted the standard and copied the type of the " owls," and the *naopoioi* of Delphi, when they wanted ivory for the decoration of the temple, were obliged to buy it in Attica. The Hellenization of the Persian Empire before the conquest of Alexander was not only the work of the mercenaries, the artists, and the doctors, but also of the traders.

In the west, as in the east, Themistocles, with his brilliant foresight, showed the Athenians the path of the future. As early as the VIth century masses of Attic vases had gone to Italy, and four fifths of the Panathenaic amphoras of archaic style were found in Etruria. But the Athenians had had to share the profits of this export trade. To cut out the middlemen and with the same blow to repel Corinthian competition was an idea which came naturally to business men and politicians. Athens had only to take up the inheritance of Chalcis in the west and to protect the colonies of Chalcis against the great Corinthian colony, Syracuse. She reserved to herself the Etruscan and Campanian market, and perhaps entered into relations with Rome; she directed the colonization of Thurii; she made alliances with Egesta, Leontion, and Rhegion. So she had supporting bases in Sicily and in Italy. The great schemes of 415 were not conceived suddenly; long before, Athens had been contesting western trade with the Sicilian Corinth. She wished to remain free to seek in the ports of Great Greece timber for construction, cattle, and, as Sophocles says, " the white wheat of Italy, blest of the gods," in Etruria metal goods and luxury shoes, and in Sicily pigs, ox-hides, cheese, and corn—always corn. If she did not succeed in conquering the coveted island, she at least secured a new source of food. All through the IVth century the arrivals from Sicily, not so much as those from the Euxine, but more than those from Egypt, filled the Corn Hall of the Peiræeus and more than once brought down the demands of the speculators.

Beyond the countries which it served direct, Athenian trade reached by means of intermediaries a large barbarian *clientèle*. The part played by Sinope, Ephesos, and Phaselis with regard to Persia, and by Tyre and Sidon with regard to

Ethiopia, was taken on by many other ports, to the greater profit of the Peiræeus. At the head of the Mæotic Gulf Tanais supplied Greek goods to the nomads of Europe and Asia. Cyrene owed her wealth less to the export of silphium and hides than to the import of goods destined for the caravans. By Taras and Adria the pottery of Attica reached the interior of Italy and the barbarous regions of the north. Massalia, too, the Queen of the Far West, received vases which she sent away among the Celts and the Iberians.

So, one after another, all countries in communication with the Mediterranean became tributary to the Peiræeus. Athens arrogated to herself alone the mission which was shared in past centuries by several cities. Through her merchants or her brokers she concentrated the trade of the whole world.

Let us try to picture this double flow of exchanges. Athens imports, first and foremost, food-stuffs, over a million medimni of cereals, dried fish, salt meat, wine, cheese, and fruit; then raw materials, iron, copper, timber (for building, joinery, and cabinet-making), pitch, wax, ivory, hides, wools, flax, and papyrus fibre; manufactured goods, tiles from Corinth, beds from Chios and Miletos, carpets from Carthage and Persia, common clothing from Megara, fine textiles from Egypt, boots and bronzes from Etruria, and perfumes from Arabia. To cover her purchases, Athens has the products of agriculture and stock-breeding—oil, wine, figs, honey, and fine wools; the products of the mines and quarries—lead, silver, and marble; the products of industry and art—common crockery and precious vases, arms, and terra-cotta statuettes; and, lastly, books.

Of this volume of business it is not impossible to obtain an approximate valuation. At the beginning of the IVth century, when exchanges suffered from war abroad and at home, the farming of the fiftieth on goods entering and leaving the Peiræeus brought the State between 30 and 36 talents. But the gross proceeds of the customs were one quarter and perhaps one third greater than the net proceeds, that is to say it varied between $37\frac{1}{2}$ and 48 talents. The total value of imports and exports in Attica came therefore, in a period of depression, to a sum varying between 1,875 and 2,400 talents (between £440,000 and £560,000). How was this figure made up ? All that can be said is that imports exceeded exports, and that the great part of the duty was paid by corn, either on import or on transit; for the grain brought into Attica in one year represented at that time a value between three and four million drachmas. But, to obtain a truer notion of Athenian trade, we must add that of the empire to that of the capital. When in 413 Athens replaced the federal tribute by a duty of one twentieth on goods entering or leaving the federate cities, she counted on taking 1,200 talents, and therefore on gross proceeds amounting to 1,500 or 1,600 talents; this gives for imports and exports a total of 30,000 to 32,000 talents (£7,200,000 to £7,600,000). For a better appreciation of these figures it must be remembered that they belong to a time when the price of corn, by which the value of money must be governed, was about 1s. 9d. the bushel. Moreover, at the time of her greatest prosperity Athens must have had a much more intense business activity.

And the Athenians were never tired of talking about the part played by their city in the economics of the world. The man in the street marvelled at all the " good things " which the ships brought, from Paphlagonian chestnuts to embroidered cushions of Carthage. Thinking men explained the concentration effected by Athenian trade as Isocrates did. " There is no country sufficient to itself, but in all there is a shortage of one product and a surplus of another, so that all are hard put to it to find outlets and to import what is lacking. Athens has dealt with this problem; she has established an emporium in the centre of Greece, and has made of the Peiræeus a store where everything abounds."

The politicians, too, regarded with a complacent eye these piles of riches; and they saw the first condition of commercial prosperity in sea empire. " Every delectable thing in Sicily, Italy, Cyprus, Egypt, Lydia, the Euxine, the Peloponnese, and every other country, flows to one spot, thanks to the dominion of the sea. . . . Alone among Greeks and barbarians, the Athenians are capable of making themselves rich. One city may abound in timber for ship-building, another in iron, another yet in copper or flax, but where can they sell these goods without the consent of the mistress of the seas ? It is with all this that I have ships; one supplies me with wood, another with iron, yet another with copper, flax, wax. . . . I get nothing from the earth but obtain everything by sea." This was truly the object for which the creators of the Athenian empire had striven with marvellously clear conceptions and obstinate energy. It was right and inevitable that the big merchants of the Peiræeus should one day come to the head of the Government. Imperialism was their affair. Athens must have an empire, through this empire she must exercise hegemony in Greece, and Greece must rule over the barbarians, in order that all, barbarians and Greeks, might without any possibility of resistance be the suppliers and customers of the Athenians. Pericles is the mouthpiece of the national conscience when, on a solemn occasion, he utters these words: " The greatness of our city attracts, one after the other, the products of the whole world." It is a profound utterance, for it implies a whole commercial policy; it suggests that Athens must give the law to the world market and, buying where she wishes, and selling where she pleases, must conduct the international division of labour in the way that suits her.

This magnificent dream almost became a reality. There was a moment when no exchange took place without the permission of Athens. She passed a decree, and Megara was condemned "to die of hunger." Her agents decided the destination of every ship leaving the Euxine; her diplomats limited the tonnage of the Peloponnesian ships allowed to sail during an armistice. The sailors of Aphytis owed to her friendship the right to carry corn; the citizens of Methone in a year of dearth humbly asked her for leave to import a little.

Even when she fell from political hegemony Athens did not lose her commercial supremacy. Means changed, but the end remained the same. What could no longer be enforced by "tyranny" was obtained by persuasion; by treaties the Athenians secured privileges and exemptions by which they continued to be masters of the market. Refined taste, the regular, honest issue of money, the wealth already acquired, the powerful organization of banking, and the fleet which was still the best in the world, did the rest. The business men, who had once formed the war party, now formed the peace party. They suggested all kinds of schemes to restore the financial situation and to give new facilities to trade;

they proposed that the State should hire transport vessels to them, and should build bazaars, warehouses, and hostelries. " Who, in peace time, could do without us ? Not the shipowners and merchants—the wholesale dealers in corn, in common or fine wine, in oil, or in cattle; nor yet those who grow rich by their brains or their money. If any man wants to sell or buy quickly, where should he go rather than to Athens ?" The claim was justified. To appreciate the skill and daring which the business of the Peiræeus displayed in its operations on every market, attracting every ship and interesting itself in every dealing, we have only to consult the files of the legal pleadings spoken in cases of bottomry. Here we have the Athenian Demon advancing to a foreigner enough to load at the Peiræeus a Massaliot ship which is going to Syracuse for corn. Here is the Athenian Androcles, in partnership with a Carystian, lending money to a Phaselis man in order that he may take on wine at Mende in Chalcidice, sell it at Panticapæon, and bring his return cargo back to the Peiræeus. In truth Athens in her defeat could console herself when she looked at the Peiræeus.

In spite of the intercrossing of commercial relations and the unity of civilization, the establishment of a world market still met with difficulties. The excessive cost and bad organization of transport made any kind of proportion in the current prices of goods impossible. But above all there was still far too much uncertainty in international law. Athens did much for the security of navigation, but it took time. In 470 the Teians were still obliged to protect themselves against the sea raiders by a curse. Where the authority of the Athenian name did not make itself felt, in Locris or in Crete, the cities had to make special treaties to prohibit or restrict privateering. When the fleet of Athens relaxed its supervision or lost its power, at once the practice of reprisals and the taste for piracy broke out again; Alexander of Pheræ attacked all ships, and the Illyrians made their waters impassable. The policing of the seas was still merely a matter of power. But what could be done to abolish the survivals of the old hatred of foreigners, to conquer the inveterate passion for autonomy, to break down all the barriers which prevented men and goods from going about freely ?

The means already tried were improved. The regulations of the great religious gatherings served as patterns for less important fairs. The privileges which raised the condition of the non-citizen were multiplied and made more definite. From the rank of Metic you might, through *ateleia* and through *isoteleia*, rise to quite a good position. The *proxenos*, the accredited patron of a city, gave her citizens all kinds of help as an intermediary or as a surety. Presently relations between men of different states came to be governed by reciprocal agreements, *symbola*. Common principles were established guaranteeing business men the execution of contracts, ensuring for them the benefit of consular jurisdiction, and making the judgements given in one country valid in both. So private international law was born. Eventually the rights granted by name to certain foreigners were enjoyed by all, even in the absence of formal clauses; the *jus commercii* was in common law. Thenceforward the trading cities ceased to conclude agreements, except to grant each other privileges. Provisions of an economic nature appeared in the acts of confederations and in contracts of *sympoliteia ;* they took an ever larger place in treaties of peace and alliance. Finally they were the subject of special treaties, genuine commercial treaties. Amyntas, King of Macedon, and the Chalcidians regulated the export of pitch and timber; Ceos gave the Athenians the exclusive right to export vermilion; the kings of the Cimmerian Bosphorus granted priority in loading and exemption from export duties to the Athenians, and considerable reductions to the Mytilenæans. Already, too, the commercial practices of the city which dominated the market tended to acquire force in the other cities, and to form a body of international law.

But, great as was the progress achieved, trade had not yet succeeded in uniting men in a single economic whole. It did not yet offer to them, even in a purely material form, that conception of " humanity " which was to radiate over the Hellenistic world.

# PART FOUR
# THE HELLENISTIC PERIOD

## CHAPTER I

### POLITICAL AND SOCIAL ORGANIZATION

CITY against city, class against class, Greece was in a state of continual conflict. The extension of commercial relations aggravated the effects of a system which set neighbouring cities in violent antagonism. Many attempts had been made to unite these scattered " snow-flakes " into one compact mass, but the audacity of imperialistic ventures and the prudence of federal unions had been equally unsuccessful. In Athens the struggles between oligarchs and democrats were rendered less savage by the immense wealth accumulated in that city, but almost everywhere else exasperated hatred placed arms in the hands of poor and rich. For this evil, too, remedies had been sought, but theories of patriarchal socialism only proposed an impossible return to a dead past, and the generation of tyrants which sprang up in the IVth century simply gave to the individualism of the time its supreme expression, unscrupulous egoism. How, then, was the old framework of political and social life to be broken ? How would the new societies organize themselves ?

When Alexander broke down the barriers which separated Greece from the barbarian world, by the same act he overthrew all those which stood in Greece itself. From that day the political horizon widened. Instead of suffocating in confined cities, the Greek race saw boundless spaces opening before it; it spread out freely into great states. It had all the eastern basin of the Mediterranean; it had the vast empires of the East. The young hero, whom it had followed willy-nilly, aspired to the kingdom of the world. Checked in his course by death, he bequeathed to his successors, as their model, conquered Persia, Persia where the Great King had ruled over twenty satrapies. Macedonia, which had once crushed Thebes and Athens with its weight, was itself small, with its 35,000 square miles and its three or four million inhabitants, in comparison with the kingdoms which fell to the Ptolemies and the Seleucids. Egypt, in the 47,000 square miles of the valley alone, contained seven million souls, and the kings of Syria were the lords of 1,400,000 square miles and about thirty million subjects.

The distinctions which had so long sundered the Greeks were gone. From every city immigrants came pouring into the newly opened countries, and their descendants no longer knew what was their original home. Even the dislike of the Greek for the barbarian, which a Macedonian like Aristotle believed to be based on a natural fact, was to weaken. As Hellenism spread, the East reacted on the Greeks. Races, which had at first lived side by side, blended. In the heterogeneous mass of mercenaries settled in Egypt we find, by the side of proud Macedonians and haughty Greeks, Thracians, Asiatics, Persians, Libyans. As time went on many of these foreigners married native girls, and we see in a list of " Greek farmers " names like Harphaesis son of Petosiris. Greece proper could not resist the movement of ideas which the new world brought with it. Citizen rights, which had once been granted in recompense for distinguished services, were now lavished on whole classes of foreigners; more, they were sold, and at Ephesos anybody could have them for six minas. Besides, what was the good of them ? The Metics traded freely in every port, and very often they could acquire houses and land. Pagasæ in Thessaly was so full of foreigners that one wondered where the natives of the place were.

We see the most extraordinary exchanges of population going on. A Lucanian bronze-worker establishes himself in Rhodes; a silk manufacturer of Antioch dies in Naples. Look at the population of Delos. First of all, the *proxenoi* of every country meet on the island. The Egyptians open chapels, the merchants and ship-owners of Berytos found a brotherhood, and bankers from Taras, Tenos, and Syracuse fight as rivals or combine as partners. You need not be a citizen to obtain a contract for public works, the farming of the sacred domains, or the *choregia* in a religious festival. Then the Phœnician and Arab traders Hellenize their names. The Roman community on the island, which is connected with that in Alexandria, receives into its bosom any individual of Italian or Sicilian origin, as if to prepare, just when the Greek city is expanding, for the final expansion of the city of Rome. Even at this date documents of general interest are drawn up " in the name of the Athenians, of the Romans, and of the other Greeks established or temporarily residing in Delos." All sorts of things are done which would have seemed impossible in the preceding period. Branches of a family of Cypriot merchants settle in Delos, Athens, and Taras. The president of the Berytian Association at Delos is the brother of an *ephebos* who represents Athens at the festivals of Delphi. The banker Philostratos of Ascalon dedicates monuments at Delos as a citizen of Naples. This mobility of individuals and this pluralism in nationalities show how the facts forced philosophers to preach Hellenistic cosmopolitanism in theory and constitutions to create it in law. The different parts of the Mediterranean world merged one into another, and difference of states made no obstacle to the unity of civilization, which was essential to a world market.

In the big countries, where the Greeks were in contact with barbarians, and there were so many conflicting private interests, the assembly of citizens no longer sufficed as the organ of the common interest. Now antiquity never rose to the conception of representative government. Henceforward the idea of the State had to be embodied in a chief. For a long time the system-builders, Xenophon, Plato, Isocrates, had called in their writings or looked in real life for the good tyrant who should undertake to make justice reign. They were prophets. Monarchy appeared as a necessity, to hold together the opposing classes, to govern the relations between different races, and to define the rights and to mark the place of each. On the king, the son of God, fell the superhuman mission of arbitrating the destinies of men. The State enjoyed omnipotence in order to organize society.

But political and economic relations had become so complex that only a scientific organization could maintain them in harmony. Such was the technical progress which had been made everywhere that even the division of social labour was perfected. It no longer seemed true that an understanding of public affairs was compatible with the exercise of a trade, nor that the same man could obey and command in turn. A permanent distinction became necessary. It was not enough that the king, assisted by his ministers, should divide the work of administration; offices, elaborately graded and specialized, must be filled by permanent officials. The defence of the country became less and less a duty of the citizen; it was the business of the mercenary. But the State had no bigger or harder task than the supervision of economic matters with a view to ensuring a fair division of wealth and labour.

For this purpose it made the fullest use of its sovereign power. The collective ownership of the soil, described in the romance of Euhemeros, was simply the law of Ptolemaic Egypt. Foreign trade constituted a public service, not only in the ancient land of the Pharaohs, where it was treated in the same way as agriculture and industry, but in a small colony on the Adriatic, Apollonia. Nearchos was sent on a mission to the Persian Gulf, Patrocles to the Caspian, Megasthenes to India, Euthymenes and Pytheas to the Atlantic. Everywhere attention was turned to great works of public utility. Demetrios Polyorcetes dreamed, like Cypselos long before, of cutting the Isthmus of Corinth, Pyrrhos proposed to build a bridge between Dyrrhachion and Brindisi, Antiochos I planned a canal from the Euxine to the Caspian, and the Ptolemies fulfilled the project of Necho and Darius by connecting Alexandria with the Red Sea by water. The kings of Pergamon issued town regulations which would one day serve as models to the Roman emperors. The *Agoranomoi* no longer confined themselves to inspecting weights and measures; they fixed compulsory units for each class of goods, they enforced the use of Government weighing-machines, and they decreed tariffs of prices. Many cities had official registries for private contracts, and public banks. The king had his threshing-floor, his granary, and his bank in almost every village in Egypt.

Since, in a well regulated society, each should have his occupation and be completely adapted to it, would it not have been best to imitate the close castes which travellers studied with such interest in India ? This ideal was not, however, reached, except in the dreams of over-logical philosophers. But the successors of the Pharaohs found in the eternal tradition of the country laws which were sufficiently strict to keep soldiering or farming for ever in the same family. Even in places where a profession might be chosen with complete liberty, the growing need of technical knowledge and skill worked steadily towards the development of apprenticeship and the hereditary transmission of acquired experience. One might quote a dozen Athenian families in which, from the IIIrd to the Ist century, the statuary's art was handed from father to son. The accounts of works carried out at Delos justify the statement that this practice was general. The son succeeded his father in every profession, and at every turn we meet obscure lines of farmers, masons, carpenters, blacksmiths, wood-merchants, and contractors.

This heredity in callings was clearly the result of the division of labour. The Hellenistic period carried specialization very far. At Delos the joiner who fits a door does not set up the post which is to hold it. Before the carpenter lays upon the top course of a wall the elm plank which is to support the cross-beams of the ceiling, the mason is called in to level that course. The stone-masons attached to the temple do not sharpen their own tools. At Miletos the workmen who do the fine cutting of the marble squares of the facing are not the men who rough-hew the stone blocks of the inner core. It has been possible to draw up from the papyri an endless list of the trades practised in Egypt. A man may make his living as bee-keeper, pig-breeder, goose-breeder, onion-seller, fruit-grower, corn-measurer, or mat-maker. The sack-carrier and the milk-carrier are quite different from the baggage-porter. There is a special baker for fancy bread. Among the medical specialists Monsieur Purgon would rejoice to see the clysterizer. The forges and pot-banks have their oven-men and stokers. The quarry-man, the man who cuts the stone, refuses to sweep away the sand or to remove a layer of gravel; it is not his job. The men who sell beer, oil, and clothes are not the manufacturers; in the oil-mills there are grain-crushers, and special workmen for castor oil; garments of common cloth and fine *othonia* are neither made nor sold by the same people; and the textile trade includes a wool-waste-gatherer. Everyone to his trade.

Between the two ends of the social ladder there was a vast distance; but, however highly placed or humble they might be, all the king's subjects worked under the common protection and for the common good of the State. Therefore ideas on labour in the Hellenistic period present a singular mixture of lofty disgust and human sympathy for the craftsman. Now that the differentiation which the philosophers had desired, between the occupations which required leisure and those which left none, had been in great part realized, the officials and warriors, the writers and artists, and even the big merchants and wealthy manufacturers felt for manual labour some of the contempt which was once bestowed on it by doctrinaires and oligarchs. But there is no creature so low that he is not raised by his contribution to a work which is far above him; there is no condition so vile but it is ennobled by a universal solidarity. In these temperate, composite beliefs Greek and Oriental were in communion; one brought the pride of individual thought, and the other a vague feeling of social pantheism. From Judæa, the land where prophets used to leave their work-bench to lecture kings, comes the voice which gives the most striking expression to the new opinions. Listen to Jesus son of Sirach. "The wisdom of the man read in the Scriptures is acquired thanks to leisure. How can a man become wise when he drives the plough? And so it is with the workman and the master mason, and the blacksmith whose skin is cracked by the smoke, and the potter, bowed over his work and thinking only how many pieces he must deliver. These men do not come forward in the Assembly, they do not know the code of the laws, they never sit in the seats of the judges. But without them no city is built. They maintain everlasting production, those whose prayers are about the practice of a trade." A man must belong to that age if he thinks thus of the necessity and the advantages of the division of labour, and extols the work of the head while proclaiming respect for the work of the hand.

The steady development of the division of labour and of the classes gradually led to the formation of new groups. Aristotle had known only associations "formed to offer sacrifices and to give their members opportunities for meeting." The most solid and active of these had been brotherhoods of a religious nature, in which men of the same profession honoured a patron deity. At the very most some of them had a vague purpose of mutual assistance. At bottom they were all very much the same, in consequence of the absence of any economic idea. It could not be otherwise at a time when the city satisfied the material and moral needs of individuals and, as Aristotle says again, the political community left to the associations nothing but "the pretext for agreeable recreation."

But when the cities were reduced to the condition of mere administrative centres they left a terrible void. From the moral point of view there was no longer anything between the individual and mankind, and the State worships, with their cold, distant ceremonies, hardly warmed the heart. Then, more and more, community of national and religious sentiment was reinforced by professional solidarity. Just as before, it was in the commercial towns, where men of every country, every religion, and every trade mingled, that the need for association was most keenly felt. It appears in Delos in every form. For a whole century a family of wood-merchants absorbed all its competitors by marriages, and formed a kind of family corporation. The goldsmiths, the importers of oil, or the importers of wine acted in concert. Foreigners formed associations the name of which indicated their profession, their nationality, and their god. The " Merchants and Ship-Owners of Heracles of Tyre " and the " Merchants, Ship-Owners, and Forwarding Agents of Poseidon of Berytos " did not only employ themselves in holding sumptuous festivals, like the Association of Sarapis and the Syrians, or in praying, like the Jews. The Italians of Hermes or Mercury owned enormous premises for doing business. At Rhodes the foreigners, both merchants and soldiers, forgathered in innumerable clubs in which, in the intervals of banqueting, they drafted rhetorical decrees or pompous epitaphs in the honour of generous patrons. In Egypt the Ptolemies kept up the Pharaonic tradition of groups according to trade; it was so convenient for the Government to give orders to the farmers of a village as a body, and to settle the service of the donkey-men through their Secretary. But the men of various professions took advantage of these arrangements to organize real trade unions. The millers, with their Managing Committee of elders, the pastry-cooks, or the ditchers were evidently out for the defence of their professional interests. The country teemed with associations of farmers, craftsmen, and merchants.

The trade unions even began to form federations. There were some in Egypt which covered a whole nome. The forwarding agents of Alexandria were incorporated in a *synodos*, a union of different societies with a branch at Delos. Outside Egypt we find remarkable examples of federations among the Dionysiac artists. At this time, when a refined civilization gave an important place to the theatre, all those who lived by it, authors, managers, flute-players, comedians, tragedians, and costumiers formed a trade union. But, since the companies frequently went on tour, the unions were obliged to expand, and combined in a federation covering a certain district. The artists of Athens formed the earliest group of this kind. They soon encountered the competition of the Isthmic-Nemeian society, which transferred its headquarters from Corinth to Thebes and there gave birth to a multitude of affiliated groups. In the East these big societies placed themselves under the patronage of princes. The Artists of Ionia and the Hellespont at first had Tenos as their centre, and then they formed the company of the Theatre Royal at Pergamon. In the West similar institutions operated at Rhegion and Syracuse.

Let us take a general view of the constitution of the Hellenistic societies. The downfall of the cities causes cosmopolitan doctrines to prevail. But political necessities range individuals in big states, administrative necessities and the division of social labour divide them by provinces and subject them to a graded organization of officials, and the division of economic labour groups them by trades and drives corporative associations to organize themselves by districts.

## CHAPTER II

## THE SPREAD OF THE MONETARY SYSTEM

As a result of the conquests of Alexander enormous quantities of precious metal were thrown on the Greek market, and in addition this market was extended to vast countries in which natural economy had hitherto prevailed. In consequence a circulation of money of unprecedented intensity quickly affected the economy of countries which had hitherto not felt the need of money. After a sudden upset of the equilibrium in the price of commodities the abundance of specie was corrected by a vaster output of goods coming on to the market, and at length a new equilibrium was established.

Even in the course of the IVth century masses of gold had been put into circulation all over Greece. But what were the 10,000 talents seized from Delphi, and the 1,000 talents which King Philip took annually from Mount Pangæos, in comparison with the treasures which Alexander found in the palaces of Persepolis, Susa, Ecbatana, and Babylon? There, in bullion piled up for two centuries, lay enough to stagger the imagination; it was reckoned at a value of 170,000 talents (£40,000,000). All this was put into circulation with incredible speed. The extravagances of a young and luxury-loving king, his gifts to members of his family, his rewards to common soldiers and generals alike, the offerings which he sent to the temples, and the sums which he expended on buying political help would very soon have dispersed the reserves of the Achæmenids.

The monetary system which Athens had given to Greece was transformed. For some time the abundance of gold had reduced the ratio of the yellow to the white metal to 1 : 10. The gold "Philips," weighing the same as darics, had for subsidiary money silver currencies which conformed to this ratio and were able to compete with the owls of Laureion; Darius's bi-metallism had been modernized. Alexander made the system agree with the Attic standard. He thus refrained from damaging the Athenian tetradrachm, which continued to be accepted on the market and was even given a pan-Hellenic value at the beginning of the Ist century by an Amphictionic decree. But the gold " Alexandrines " none the less had a universal success, surpassing that of the Philips. Their name was preserved for a long time. They were imitated as far as Gaul, and cities of the Euxine which had

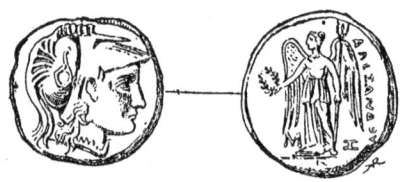

Fig. 48.  Gold stater of Alexander.  (*D.A.*, Fig. 215.)

never belonged to the Macedonian were striking silver coins with the head of Alexander a hundred and fifty years after his death. On the other hand, the Æginetan silver standard, issued by Rhodes, took its revenge on the Attic standard and spread to Egypt, Sicily, and even Carthage.

At first the greatest sums went to Europe. The Greek allies, dismissed after the conquest, took with them, in addition to what they had saved on their high pay, 2,000 talents

Fig. 49.  Didrachm of Rhodes.  (*D.A.*, Fig. 2569.)

in bonuses. When Harpalos came to bribe the Athenians he had 700 talents in his cash-box. The governor Menes had 3,000 talents at his disposal with which to fight Agis. Queen Olympias sent darics to Delphi, and the *naopoioi* there often did their accounts in darics. Indirectly, the Oriental magnificence of the court enriched the artists, merchants, and manufacturers of the more refined towns. A flood of gold poured over Greece.

# SPREAD OF THE MONETARY SYSTEM

But the countries of production on a large scale were soon to have their share. Being obliged to obtain its farm produce and raw materials abroad, Greece could not go on indefinitely draining the treasures put into circulation, nor even keep all the wealth which it had attracted thanks to exceptional circumstances. The Greek peoples were now mixing with other peoples whose material life had been very different. Among these latter some were to remain faithful to their tradition of natural economy, while the others, being ready to give the surplus of their enormous production, and having nothing to demand in exchange but money, moved steadily towards money economy.

To the former class most of the provinces ruled by the Seleucids seem to have belonged. Despite the proximity of the Phœnician coast, despite the obstinate efforts of the ruling house to extend the city system, the countrysides of Asia did not cease to pay their taxes in corn, and, except in the big towns, the royal treasuries were storehouses. Epeiros presented a more curious spectacle. Right in the IIIrd century, when Pyrrhos set forth to conquer the world, this mountain land was still at the most primitive stage of natural economy, the pastoral. Large and small cattle, such was the chief wealth of the king and nobles. The general supervision of the royal flocks and herds was one of the highest dignities in the State; the Herdsman-in-chief was one of the officials of the Court; to reward the zeal of a subject, the king would give him a yoke of oxen. Countries which exported little lived on their home-grown resources and hardly used the instrument of universal exchange.

Very different was the situation which gradually arose in Ptolemaic Egypt. The ancient valley of the Nile, where men seemed petrified in the institutions of centuries, like the statues in their hieratic attitudes, and so many generations had lived on the year's harvest without their thoughts going further, stirred and woke to a new life. The kings of Persia had taught Egypt the value of money when they demanded of her as tribute, in addition to the 120,000 measures of corn which cost her almost nothing, a sum of 700 talents. But, if she then converted corn into precious metal, she only procured just the amount which she must send to Susa. When the Macedonians and Greeks became masters of the land, they saw all that was to be got from the inexhaustible fertility of the soil and the admirable position of the coasts. In making themselves rich they enriched the conquered people. Even before Alexander had completed the subjection of Asia, the governor whom he had left in Memphis profited by a general famine in a masterly way. He bought up all the corn in Egypt, and, having the market in his hand, diverted to himself some of the stream of gold which was flowing from Persia into Greece. The Ptolemies exploited their kingdom systematically, in their own interest and that of the country. For the first time the need of a national currency in precious metal was felt; hitherto a few clumsy copper pieces had sufficed. After the Attic and Rhodian systems had been tried, the preference was given to the Phœnician system, because it best permitted the harmonizing of the Greek standards with the copper weights hitherto current. The ratio of silver to copper was fixed at 1 : 120. It is true that copper was always most widely used. Considerable sums in copper were handled. Silver was at a premium. In the IIIrd century the official documents allowed, for payments owed in silver and effected in copper, an exchange fee of 10%. In the IInd century silver became still scarcer; debts and even fines were paid almost entirely in copper. The result was a depreciation of copper, which grew worse until the end of the dynasty. The ratio of the two metals rose to 1 : 240, then to 1 : 375, and even to 1 : 500. It is none the less true that the Ptolemies greatly furthered money economy in Egypt.

And indeed we see, in every manifestation of public and private life, natural economy steadily ebbing. This does not mean that, even in three centuries, Egypt recovered all the advantage which Greece had over her. Egypt always did far more exchange in kind than Greece. Sometimes, it is true, in the cities of Asia Minor or in the isles, land-rent was still paid to the temples partly in grain, wood, or cattle, and the sacred administration of Delos supplied two workmen with corn and clothing for two years, and paid only their *opsonion* in coin, but these were survivals or exceptional cases, which cannot be taken as typical of the economic system. In Egypt, on the other hand, native society was still everywhere wrapped up in ancient custom. In almost every village we

## SPREAD OF THE MONETARY SYSTEM 329

find, opposite each other, the public bank, into which the money went, and the public granary, into which the harvest went. In both establishments the same operations were carried on. One accepted the deposits and effected the payments of craftsmen and traders, and the other was the centre of business for the farmers. The economic development of Egypt is expressed by the fact that the business of the granary declined in favour of the bank.

The State did not wish the peasant to be placed at the mercy of the retailer and the usurer by the need for procuring coin. It accepted the payment of the land-tax in kind, when the tax-payer brought commodities which were easily preserved and were used by the State, corn and oleaginous seeds. With the wheat and barley it maintained the soldiers and officials, selling the surplus and thus reducing the proportion of wealth in kind in its receipts. Croton and sesame served as raw materials in the royal oil-mills. But all other taxes, even the duty on vineyards, palm-groves, and olive orchards, were paid in money. Of all its revenues the treasury collected only one thirtieth in kind. For the royal domain, as for the temple lands, the leases stated the rent in natural values. The tenant owed so much corn per *aroura*. The relative value of products was fixed by a scale, just as that of minted metal was fixed by the monetary system. Wheat was equal to lentils; it was to barley as 5 to 3, and to durra as 5 to 2. But provision was also made for conversion into money; it must be done according to the rate. And the priesthood encouraged this more and more, for it was always wanting more capital for its commercial dealings.

As receipts in kind diminished, the expenses which they covered necessarily became more limited. The State paid officials from its granaries or from its banks. The minor staff received food-stuffs. The high dignitaries were allotted mixed emoluments; the scholars of the Museum were boarded and lodged, and drew a salary. Sometimes even salaries which were fixed in money were paid in kind. But the history of army pay well shows the economic development. From the IIIrd century onward the original pay, called *sitarchia* because it once consisted of corn, was issued in coin; to designate the supplement issued in kind a new word was needed, *sitometria*, in distinction from the old. In its turn the *sitometria* tended to undergo the same change. In the IIIrd century a soldier got 150 drachmas of copper and 3 *artabai* (3¼ bushels) of corn; in the IInd century only one of these three *artabai* was supplied in kind, and the conversion of the rest into coin brought the amount of money paid to 350 drachmas, representing three quarters of the total pay. The foot-soldier who was entitled to wine and the cavalryman who was entitled to his horses's forage drew an allowance. The purveyors to the State were paid in coin alone.

In the private life of the Egyptian villagers natural economy survived in part. They continually borrowed corn or wine. But if a debtor did not pay up when the debt fell due it was converted into its money value at the rate of the day. This conversion, which was at first favourable to the creditor and was enforced by a penal clause, was soon to have a beneficent influence; for it was admitted that in the case of obligations in money the compound interest could not make the debt exceed double the principal. In workmen's wages, as in army pay, the part paid in kind decreased. We find a carter who receives, for himself and his men, daily rations of bread, wine, and oil, with a small pig on holidays, without counting the hay for his beasts. But we also find a gang of quarrymen who get, in addition to an *artabe* of corn and a small measure of oil, 12 drachmas in money; the proportion of the cash is 83%. The priests, who used, in their byssos-works, to leave a part of the output to the workmen, came gradually to adopt a more modern method of payment. Soon labour was not paid in foodstuffs at all. Navvies got one tetradrachm per cube of sixty *naubia*. By now, in Egypt as elsewhere, the name *opsonion* given to wages had no longer any reference to reality. In short, money became necessary everywhere. Every fellah needed it. The papyri show us housekeeping accounts in which the expenses of the very humblest houses are noted down day by day. Everything is bought; those who have their corn pay the baker in drachmas; even the beggar gets his coin. Money, or rather copper, was not only the most convenient standard of value, but the instrument of exchange used in the most remote villages.

The changes brought about by the progress of money economy in the distribution of the precious metals and of

## SPREAD OF THE MONETARY SYSTEM

commodities led to marked variations in prices. When, after Alexander's conquest, Greece received the rain of gold which the east wind brought, it was not much the richer, nor did it remain so for long. The total amount of products was not increased; indeed a succession of bad harvests diminished it. A rise in prices was inevitable, and its rapidity was fantastic. But, thanks to the expansion of the market, the amount of commodities put into circulation soon began to counterbalance that of the precious metals. It weighed heavily on prices. From the end of the IVth century to the middle of the IIIrd, a strong and steady fall almost corrected the enormous rise of the years 330-320, and restored the balance of values on a greatly enlarged market. Once the countries of high production and those which held the precious metal had made the necessary exchanges, and monetary economy had thus come into force everywhere, about the middle of the IIIrd century, the fall, being no longer needed to unify and clear the market, ceased spontaneously. Things resumed their natural course. Until the Roman conquest, prices once again were steady or rose by slow, healthy movements.

## CHAPTER III
## THE TOWNS

THE decisive encounters between Greece and the East had as an inevitable consequence the displacement of the centre of gravity of the economic world. Once the conquest of Ionia by the Persians had prepared for the greatness of Athens; the conquest of Asia by Alexander diverted big production and big business towards the East.

It had the same effect on the cities of ancient Greece as the discovery of America on the countries of modern Europe. An enormous crowd of emigrants made for the new world. Mercenaries greedy for high pay or good land, traders confident of making their fortune in a new country, artists, writers, and scholars summoned by enlightened and generous princes, physicians and tutors required by the immigrants and, soon after, by the natives, parasites, adventurers, and courtesans dazzled by the example of the illustrious Thais, they spread in their thousands as far as the Cataracts of Syene and the banks of the Indus. The spontaneous exodus was followed by systematic colonization, organized by the kings. Their object was military and political as much as economic and social. By settling the soldiers on *kleroi* and attracting business men, they hoped to defend the frontier and to form a body-guard for themselves, and also to extend agriculture, to enlarge the cities, to mix the populations, and to increase the general wealth. At the call of the Ptolemies the Greeks came in haste; they filled the newly built metropolis, occupied the fields of the Delta, and rescued from the desert and fertilized the whole province of the Fayum. At a beck from the Seleucids another swarm distributed themselves over the centres of administration and civilization assigned to them. Greece was being emptied. To compensate these losses it could not count on a rise in the birthrate. People were too fond of comfort to burden themselves

## THE TOWNS

with a big family; they practised systematic celibacy and the exposure of new-born infants. Greece suffered from that deep-seated, incurable evil which Polybius called " the lack of children " and " dearth of men."

Resources diminished with the population. Greece grew poor. Its mediocre land could not support the competition of the most fertile plains in the world; it had not enough raw materials to develop its industry; it was too far from the great routes which were now opening to trade. Gradually it lost the habit of work. The rich shut themselves off from the world in their selfishness. In their greed they thought only of quietly rounding off their estates; in their extravagance they indulged in unbridled luxury or sought out the vilest pleasures. The picture which we have of Bœotia, with its banquets and its drinking-bouts, is simply appalling. Beside this class, which could no longer make productive use of its wealth, was a wretched proletariat whose hatred grew daily greater. The more manly of the poor had gone to the East; those who remained had too often no other resource than to wait for the bounty of *euergetai*, or to evade difficulties by debts, and debts by demands backed with violence. Plots and riots followed each other without interruption. The fewer men there were, the more fiercely they contested the land. They fought over ruins. The land remained untilled. The deserted cities fell into the condition of overgrown villages. Grass grew on the squares, and the cattle came and browsed there. Ancient Greece was at the point of death.

A few cities only, in Europe, retained some remnants of their lost splendour. Corinth still enjoyed the advantages afforded by her Isthmus. Syracuse did not cease to attract the agricultural riches of Sicily, and even to take a part in the exchanges between Greece and the West. Athens continued to be queen of the universe, but her sovereignty changed in character. Political power was out of the question for her now. Demetrios of Phaleron undertook to inculcate resignation upon her and to bend her pride to fate; he made himself the organizer of Athens at her smallest. He abolished the democratic fiscal system with its " liturgies " and its *misthoi*, and he reduced the fleet; he was the trustee of an immense bankruptcy. The poor left in crowds, the miners for

Thrace and the rest for Cyrene. The population decreased in the city, and still more in the agricultural Mesogæa. On the coast at least it remained stationary. For the commercial decline was slow, thanks to the force of habit; the Attic tetradrachm was still legal tender all over Greece, and ships deserted the Peiræeus only gradually. In any case it was no longer there that the emporium of the world must be sought. Athens was henceforward a city of art and science, of luxury and pleasure. Foreigners came because life there was more pleasant than anywhere else. Over the squares, with their population of lovely statues, brilliant processions passed. In the theatre the Dionysiac artists organized excellent performances. The courtesans set the fashion in dress as in other things. The sculptors received orders from kings, and the architects and contractors were invited in every direction by cities which vied with each other in magnificence. A crowd of students came to sit under rhetoricians and philosophers, whose schools constituted a veritable university. Athens remained the intellectual metropolis. She distributed glory; she was " the beacon which alone sheds forth the renown of men to the confines of the earth."

While economic life withdrew imperceptibly from the centre towards the extremities, it flowed towards the historic towns of Asia Minor. It was they which profited by the increasing relations with the interior of the continent. Ephesos and Smyrna prospered once more; Miletos again had a hundred thousand inhabitants; Pergamon had, as a capital, a short life but a brilliant one; Lampsacos, Cyzicos, Heracleia, and Sinope grew rich. An extraordinary development of city life appeared in every form. The towns competed in aggrandizement. By grants of *isopoliteia* and citizenship they snatched single individuals from one another; by *sympoliteia* burghs were amalgamated; by synœcism big towns absorbed small. For municipal administration, once so neglected, the golden age began. The authorities regulated the width of the streets and the upkeep of the public fountains, and ordered the removal of refuse. Quite a second-class town, Priene, was remarkable for its clean appearance and its air of daintiness and gaiety. The townsfolk were proud of the fine architecture of their covered markets. Miletos boasted three; the Corn Hall was 535 feet long, the

## THE TOWNS

North Agora, at the foot of stairs 459 feet broad, was surrounded by marble galleries in two storeys, lined with stalls, and the South Agora was on a colossal scale, with its porticoes one over the other, its hundreds of columns, and its endless rows of shops and workshops.

But it was not these cities of ancient Greece which profited most by the extension of the Greek market; for new connexions new centres were needed. In the countries recently opened to the activity of the Hellenic race the need for urban concentration was met in an original and grandiose manner. Never in the history of the world, except in America in the XIXth century, did so many cities rise from the ground at once. At a nod from a king they appeared out of nothing. The conquerors must not scatter and lose themselves in the conquered peoples. They were kept together. Thus strategic positions were occupied, stations were placed along the trade-routes, points of attraction were created for the nomad tribes, and centres were established from which civilization would radiate. It was a vast policy of military, administrative, economic, and moral dominion, a great foundation for the future. The rules of the system were laid down at the very outset by the powerful intuition of Alexander. From Egypt to Sogdiana, from the Caucasus to India, he founded over seventy cities, and the names of Alexandria, Alexandretta, Herat, and Kandahar are sufficient evidence of his wide view and his foresight. The Ptolemies had merely to carry out the programme which he had drawn up. The internal government of the Seleucids lay entirely in the distinction between the military administration of the countryside and the civil administration of the towns and their outskirts; but these towns, which were intended for Greek settlers, had almost everywhere to be created lock, stock, and barrel, after which their territory was extended in proportion to the influence which they exercised over the surrounding peoples. In the seventy-two satrapies Seleucos I founded nine Seleuceias, six Antiochs, five Laodiceias, three Apameias, and one Stratonice. From Latakia to Merv every city in his empire recalled to him family memories and his glory as the founder. In one century Antioch on the Orontes increased fourfold. The kings of Pergamon followed the example of the Seleucids. Even the kings of Thrace and Macedonia had their Lysimacheia, or Cassandreia, or Demetrias. These towns could not all be equal successes; some were still-born, many did modest service, some were destined to an illustrious future, and one was to become the true capital of the Hellenistic world.

Never had the genius of Alexander revealed itself with more force than on the day when he declared that he would make Rhacotis, a fishing village, the future capital of Egypt. Between the island of Pharos and Lake Mareotis, sheltered from the silt which a regular current carried eastwards, the place was marked out for a huge city and for excellent harbours, to which the Mediterranean, the Nile, and the Red Sea could bring the merchandise of the whole world. The great king's idea was realized by Ptolemy I, the plans drawn by Deinocrates of Rhodes were carried out by Sostratos of Cnidos, and Alexandria was the result. Two great avenues crossed at right angles in the centre of the town and ran to its four ends. They thus bounded four quarters, in which all the streets crossed at right angles. Everywhere there were drains, a novelty, and there was drinking-water in abundance. A few years were enough for Alexandria to show, against the monuments of the most famous cities, the tomb of Alexander, the king's palace, the Sarapeion, and that unequalled Museum with its Library, which offered students a catalogue of two hundred thousand volumes. When the city was completely built, over five hundred thousand inhabitants crowded inside it, a turbulent medley of Macedonians, Greeks, Persians, Jews, Egyptians, Arabs, and negroes. Scholars were attracted by the pensions which ensured them a respected existence in a studious shade, rich men rushed to the centre of luxury, fashion, and pleasure, and the innumerable plebs, the true plebs of a great city, filled the lower quarters. Active manufactures produced textiles, metal goods of all kinds, chariots, furniture, vases, terra-cottas, glass ware, and papyrus. But the great resource and pride of Alexandria were her ports, full of ships. The roadstead, sheltered by Pharos, was divided in two by the Heptastadion mole, which ran from the shore to the island. On the east was the War Harbour, and on the west the Merchant Harbour, the Eunostos. Both were magnificently lit up at night by the first of lighthouses. A canal connected the sea harbours with

## THE TOWNS

the inner harbour on Lake Mareotis. Other canals allowed ships to reach the Nile valley and, very soon, the Red Sea. The great routes of the south and south-east thus met those of the north and west. There were vast warehouses for goods intended for export, for masses of corn and manufactured articles, and for the Eastern goods which went through in transit. Alexandria, worthy to give her name to the new civilization, took for many centuries the place of the Peiræeus as the emporium of world trade.

But there was still a good position to be had in the Ægean, where two currents of trade met, one from south to north and the other from east to west. It was taken by Rhodes. Her situation gave her great advantages. All ships from Egypt had to rest there before scattering in every direction; all goods from the Euxine, Asia Minor, Cyprus, and Phœnicia must concentrate there before sailing for Sicily and Italy. The fall of Tyre and the foundation of Alexandria opened vast prospects to Rhodes; the skill and energy of her sailors and the practical sense of her ship-owners and merchants conquered all markets for her. Her realist policy was one of peaceful commercialism, based on a powerful fleet and a jealous love of independence. The Rhodians, ready to go to any length to safeguard their liberties, victoriously stood up to Demetrios the Town-Taker, compelled the Byzantines to abolish the toll which they used to levy on passing ships, fought Eumenes when he wanted to close the Euxine to them, and waged energetic war on the Cretan pirates. They spread their monetary system at the expense of Athens, and promulgated a code which was to govern Mediterranean navigation for centuries. This republic of merchants enjoyed sufficient prestige to be able to seek the friendship of kings without abasement; she had such means of information and such astute diplomatists that she foresaw the greatness of Rome, and as early as 306 she made with that city a commercial treaty which was a veritable draft on the future. She treated others as she expected them to treat her, conferring on foreigners established in the island more extensive rights than Athens ever granted to her Metics, and permitting them to form associations without even grouping by nationalities. On the whole, no city did so much to win and make use of the favours of fortune. The results were splendid. The vases with the Rhodian stamp were almost the only ones received at Pergamon and Alexandria, and even the competing cities of Delos and Athens had to accept them. A big transit business passed through the port of Rhodes. The customs duties, which were 2%, brought in a million drachmas net; this must have represented a movement of goods, inwards and outwards, worth considerably over fifty millions. But the Rhodians, who sailed everywhere, made still more money as international brokers. They were celebrated in antiquity for their great wealth, and they displayed it with the grandiloquent pomp and love of colossal size affected by parvenu peoples. For a century and a half the Rhodians had no competition to fear. They were as sure of their customers as of themselves. When an earthquake destroyed their city in 225 they were able to rebuild it speedily, thanks to the liberality of every state. This remarkable zeal shows both the importance of Rhodes as a commercial centre and the solidarity of interests which united all the markets.

Then, all of a sudden, this prosperity dried up, cut off at the very source. For a long time Delos, the Holy Island, had striven to become a centre of trade. She had entered into relations with Egypt, and had then turned to Macedonia. As early as 179 her dealings with the West had been sufficiently continuous for Massinissa to send her a royal gift. She had thus become an *entrepôt* for corn. The Agora, surrounded by porticoes, was very fine; the Trade Exchange was imposing, with its pillared front facing the sea and the four aisles of its hypostyle hall. The growth of the foreign population caused a rapid rise in rents. Already the Phœnicians were coming to sell their ivory, the Egyptians were building themselves shrines, and the Italians were beginning to appear on the scene. Then the Roman merchants, tired of paying double duties at Rhodes on goods in transit, persuaded the Senate to quarrel with their old ally. In 166 the Athenians were placed once more in possession of Delos, on condition that they established a free port there. The result was immediate. In two or three years the proceeds of the Rhodian customs fell from a million drachmas to 150,000. Delos was going to take the place of Rhodes.

Delos offered every security to shipping and every convenience to trade. The anchorage was protected against the north wind by a strong breakwater. A mole divided it into two parts. On one side was the Sacred Harbour, intended for the caiques which carried the pilgrims; the landing-stage with which it was provided adjoined a big meeting-place of streets and an agora. On the other side was the Merchant Harbour, where the heavy cargo-boats came in. It was divided into portions, bounded by stones, and was fringed with wharves on to which warehouses and stores opened. Behind were the Deigma and the market, divided into sections in which each class of commodity was sold by sample or in bulk. All around stretched the commercial quarter, with shops, workshops, bazaars, and hostelries all heaped together. There the craftsmen were established, marble-workers, potters, blacksmiths, dyers.

But it was not local industry which maintained a business activity which was at least equal to that lost by Rhodes. Delos, now become " the common emporium of the Greeks," collected all the products of Oriental Greece, from Egypt to the Euxine, in order to forward them to Italy, either to Taras or to Puteoli, the " Little Delos." She organized the uninterrupted passage of slaves, grain, spices, etc. This almost barren islet served as a meeting-place for men of every country and every race; only the Rhodians stood aloof. Many of these foreigners disappeared as soon as they had settled their business. Almost all belonged to brotherhoods in which nationalities or related professions were grouped; the Merchants and Ship-Owners of Heracles of Tyre formed a society of mutual assistance, the Merchants, Ship-Owners, and Warehousemen of Poseidon of Berytos founded a club with its own shrine, and exchange, the Egyptians forgathered in dining-halls and the Jews in the Synagogue, and the merchants and ship-owners trading in Bithynia, the Hermes-makers, and the oil-merchants discussed their common interests together. As men came together, families were founded by mixed marriages. A certain Dionysios was the son of one Sostratos of Athens and a Rhoumatha of Antioch. The only association which stood aside and took a political attitude was that of Mercury, in which the Romans placed themselves at the head of the other Italians. For, though Delos might be officially a dependency of Athens, she was much more the trading station of Rome in Eastern waters.

The finest monument on the island was the Agora of the Italians. The great bankers were P. Æmulius, Marius Gerillanus, and Lucius Aufidius. The vases which took the place of those of Rhodes in Sicily bore the Delian stamp of Trebius Luisus. All these foreigners gave the economic life of Delos extraordinary breadth and intensity. Land and houses acquired an enormous value; the smallest corners were taken up by buildings all entangled one in another; the population steadily moved further towards the higher quarters. Who would recognize the Holy Island now? Even on the days when the festival attracted, as of old, the boats of the neighbouring islands, in the midst of the hymns and the processions, the merchants lingered to beat down the price of slaves under the colonnades of the market.

CHAPTER IV

LANDED PROPERTY AND AGRICULTURE

IN the Hellenistic period the distribution of the soil underwent profound transformations. In the great monarchies the omnipotence of the State enabled the king to effect a wholesale distribution of land favourable to the reigning house and the immigrants alike. In the cities of Greece the diminution of the population, the conflicts of the classes, and the decay of agriculture, and perhaps, too, the vague influence of the examples set in the East, gave rise to serious disturbances in landed property.

Even before the conquest of Asia, a system existed in Macedonia of which the Greeks had no idea. Patriarchal kings, at once feudal and absolute, owned a domain which comprised a vast extent of arable land, forests, and mines. They made lavish use of this in favour of the great lords. Philip and Alexander had many a time granted concessions, with reserve of the royal confirmation in case of transfer. Thus there was formed in Macedonia, above the free peasants, a class of great land-owners. The eight hundred Companions (*Hetairoi*) of Philip owned, it was said, as much land as ten thousand Greeks.

When the son of Lagos became master of Egypt, he must all the same have been a little bewildered by the principle which the Pharaohs had bequeathed to him. Here the king had an eminent right over all the land of which he was the chief and the god. He was the sole landlord. His word governed absolutely the relations of men with the soil.

The Crown especially reserved to itself a vast domain, the *Royal Land*. The king, who never renounced the mines and quarries, also possessed in every nome vines, palm-groves, orchards, and, above all, fields in which he harvested cereals, oil-seeds, and textile fibres. The lands of the domain were very scattered, and comprised quite small parcels or great stretches containing whole series of villages. They were not worked direct by the Government; the "king's farmers" were tenant-farmers. But the leases, although they were of long duration in practice, were not for a fixed period. The fellah submitted a tender in writing, but there was no formal contract; the Government accepted an offer, declared the proposed undertaking binding, and bound itself to nothing. The "understanding" was an agreement by which one side had all the profit and the other all the obligations. For a long time, however, the position of the farmer was not bad. When he had paid his rent the rest of the harvest was his. There was a certain amount of bidding for farms. Moreover, the farmers of a village were responsible to the State as one body. They formed an association managed by the "elders," with a scribe to keep its accounts. Being bound by mutual guarantees, they formed one civil personality, under the supervision of the royal administration. But gradually the fiscal authorities became more exacting, the position of the farmer grew worse, and even his liberty was compromised. The officials saw how they could profit by the bond by which they held the king's farmers. When a farmer asked for an advance of seed-corn, he had to undertake to work the land until he had paid his rent; he was attached to the soil at least for one farming season. This was the origin of *colonatus* in Egypt. Towards the end of the IInd century work on the royal land left so little profit to the farmers that they fled as soon as they could. To maintain the returns at the old rate was now out of the question; the authorities resigned themselves to farming out land "on an estimate," with a reduction on the official price. But, if no one appeared to make a tender, then the king remembered that he was absolute lord of men and of lands. Recourse was had to the system of "constraint without agreement," of "designation"; tenures were distributed and rents were fixed by administrative decree; the tenant had not the right to leave his village, and could be evicted in the course of the lease. The king's farmers were indispensable; in the sweat of their brow they kept the court and the officials alive, fed the monopoly factories, and supplied commodities for export which could be converted into coin. They certainly deserved to be able to live on their labour. Subjected to taxation and forced labour, driven by blows of the stick,

# LAND AND AGRICULTURE

they were the victims of the system of which they were the backbone.

But, distinct from the Royal Land, there was the *Concession Land*. This comprised the property of the clergy, and also considerable portions of the royal domain which had been conceded to private individuals. The Crown jealously kept the land which was reached by the floods, but on other ground it readily entrusted reclamation to chosen concessionnaires, and realized the rights of the State in the double form of administrative control and annual rent.

The *Sacred Land* was left to the god to enjoy. But the god could not be represented by the priests, who were merely servants, especially with regard to the king, who was supreme god. The king remained lord of the land which he left to the temples. It was managed by the Government, and worked by farmers on the same terms as the land of the royal domain, the rent being paid into the same treasuries.

Very occasionally, in reward of exceptional services, the king presented his high officers with great properties known as *Gift Land*. These estates embraced whole villages with fields in full bearing; they could be leased in parcels to tenants; they were even exempt from burdens, so far as this supreme favour did not infringe the sovereign rights of the State.

The *Cleruchic Land* was important in another way. The new dynasty wanted to settle in Egypt as many loyal soldiers and officials as possible, while giving a strong impetus to agrarian policy. For all schemes of internal colonization the first condition was the distribution of *kleroi*. In this way the Lagids gained a whole province at a stroke; the Fayum was won for agriculture. The Cleruchs, who were soldiers of the regular army liable to be called up when required, were free most of the time to work their land. The improvements which they made were bound to strengthen their right of ownership. At the beginning the State not only declared the concession inalienable; it regarded it as essentially revocable, and occasionally it actually revoked it, on the death of the Cleruch. It maintained such strict control over all these men that sometimes it even compelled them to reside on the spot and forbade them to take tenants. About 218 the State still had the right to take a lot back on death; it sequestrated the vacant property and did not recognize the heir's claim unless the transfer under his name had been recorded within a prescribed time and the " Crown gold " had been paid. In the IInd century hereditary transmission became customary, without being recognized as a right, and the families of Cleruchs, by an unconscious return to the national tradition, tended to form a class which grew closer with time. But it was not until the Ist century before Christ, when the Cleruch was allowed to make a will in favour of any paternal relation, that the Cleruchic Land became true private property.

In these circumstances, how was it that Ptolemaic Egypt always had land known as *Private Possession?* About this we know practically nothing. We can only surmise that individuals succeeded, either by usucaption or by agreement with the authorities, in making for themselves on parcels of the domain a position similar to that of the other concessionnaires. Greek colonists obtained waste land near Alexandria for planting; perhaps they kept it by means of an emphyteusis. In villages in which the State did not find willing tenants, sons occasionally put in a claim to inherit their father's farm; the State could only encourage such inclinations. Thus there were formed in Egypt small farms which the holder had the right to sell, cede, pledge, or leave to his heirs. But they were few, and the king always counted them among the Concession Lands.

We see how strictly the Græco-Egyptian monarchy treated the question of property. So long as the kings were conscious of their duties as well as their rights, the country was sufficiently prosperous to enrich the treasury and to give the fellahs a decent existence. The hydraulic machine invented by Archimedes lifted and distributed the water of the river. The desert receded. Crops improved. Exact rules of rotation were laid down by the administration of the royal domain, and were generally practised on the lands of the Cleruchs and private individuals; the farm was divided into three breaks, each of which was sown two years running, and in the third year was not left fallow, but was rested by a light crop. The State organized the keeping and sale of farm produce, and public services of transport and export kept prices up to a remunerative level. In spite of the extension of cultivated land, stock-raising seems to have advanced; horned

# LAND AND AGRICULTURE

cattle, horses, and asses were very numerous, geese were exported, and camels began to appear. But the regulations were already excessive. Everybody's harvest was threshed on the royal floor, gauged by the measurers, registered by the scribes, and taken to the royal granary. Vine-growers were subject to inspection and had to pay one tenth or one sixth of the vintage. About the middle of the IInd century the effects of a system which took no account of individual welfare were fully felt. The peasant now worked for the treasury alone, and the treasury, by overburdening the producer, dried up the sources which it would tap. The Cleruchs no longer found tenants; they were forced to farm their own allotments, but could not cope with the work. The Government then tried to encourage highly productive crops, and granted privileges to vine-growers and market-gardeners. All these efforts were in vain. In fifty years half of the domain lands situated in the district of Cerceosiris fell out of cultivation. The desert reconquered the ground which had been taken from it.

Just as the Lagids carried on the Pharaonic tradition in the Macedonian manner, so the Seleucids were in their own way the heirs of the "Royal Administration" and the "Satrapic Administration." They too owned an immense domain. There they established studs and a forestry service, while for agriculture they depended on tenants, who paid their rent in kind. All that was not comprised in the domain constituted the free land, managed by the "City Administration" or "Private Administration," and subject to taxes in money. The king's tenants were serfs. They owned their house, ploughing implements, and cattle; when they had paid their rent they kept what remained. But they were attached to the soil, and passed with it to those to whom the king presented it. Cities, temples, and private individuals had their serfs, like the king. Other methods of exploitation were also known, the ordinary lease and emphyteusis. This organization was developed in a remarkable way by the urban policy of the Seleucids. They constantly detached parcels of land from the domain and built on them new cities in the Greek manner, or else absorbed them in the territory of existing cities. At the same time they waged energetic war on the feudal lords and annexed their fiefs. With one thing and another, the royal domain remained more or less the same in size, and became unified, while private property developed by the side of it, and the serfs supplied every class of land with the requisite labour. Great progress was made; the vine was acclimatized in Susiana.

What, meanwhile, was happening to landed property, in the old Greece? It had ceased to split up, and, on the contrary, was rapidly moving in the opposite direction. Many emigrants sold their property; families died out, and their patrimony went to swell that of the collateral branches. The "dearth of men" inevitably led to a reconcentration of the soil, which had been broken up into minute portions. At the end of the IVth century the comic poets could speak without improbability of estates measuring ten thousand cubits across (about 5,000 acres). The 700,000 acres of Laconia belonged to about a hundred proprietors. But the reconstitution of the big property, combined with the growing competition of foreign countries, produced disastrous results on the agrarian situation, and particularly on what remained of the small land-owners. There were not enough hands for agriculture; besides, what was the use of working land which no longer fed a man? The countrysides were deserted. In Thessaly several cities bought land, divided it into allotments, and distributed it to the poor. But it was all in vain; the territory of Larissa remained uncultivated. Two thirds of fertile Euboea were allowed to run wild, and the towns sent officials to buy corn abroad. In Attica the rural population of the Mesogæa dwindled rapidly.

This general decay of agriculture made the question of food-supplies extremely important, and one might say chronically acute. In the Hellenistic period, far more even than in the Vth and IVth centuries, Greece proper was obliged to ask foreign markets for its food. The reason why the situation of Athens, between the Northern kingdoms and Egypt, was so difficult, and sometimes so desperate, was that she must know whether she would have enough corn, and whence it was to come, from the Chersoneses or from Alexandria. Every island and every city of Asia Minor had the same anxieties. Therefore the State included among its duties the *sitonia* or corn-supply. It was no longer sufficient, as it once had been, to encourage free trade and to protect

# LAND AND AGRICULTURE

the consumer against the excesses of the merchant; the State must itself turn corn-merchant in order to ensure cheap bread for the citizens. Its first duty was to provide for the public feeding without realizing a profit. Formerly Athens had appointed *Sitophylakes* to supervise dealings between individuals on the spot; now she elected *Sitonai* whom she sent, provided with the necessary funds, to the chief corn-markets. There was no city, however small, which had not, from the IIIrd century, its "corn-buyers" or its "importers." At Samos the State provided for the food-supply out of the interest on a fund formed by an extraordinary tax; two elected citizens bought the wheat grown on the sacred domain, at the fixed price of 5 dr. 2 ob.; if this harvest was not sufficient, a *Sitones* went to seek the balance abroad. At Tauromenion in Sicily we find the institution fully developed, with three bodies of officials, namely buyers, receivers, and wardens entrusted with the sale.

The position of the farmer grew more and more alarming. The least unfortunate were those who, by renouncing their right of ownership, obtained that of living on their land as tenants. Some sold their property to a god on terms of a perpetual lease; this was equivalent to a mortgage loan in which the capital had been sunk and the interest was disguised as rent. Others rented the farms for which the temples invited tenders. We can see the results which they obtained at Delos. When the lease expired the farmer could renew it by paying one tenth more rent, but he seldom made use of this faculty. Rents rose slightly for about fifteen years, then they dropped sharply, and this fall lasted almost uninterrupted for more than a century. The finest of these farms, containing several dwellings, a two-storeyed granary, a cow-byre, a sheep-fold, an oven, a mill, 72 fig-trees, and 560 vines, all in good condition and enclosed, was leased for 3,111 dr. in 297 and only fetched 799 dr. rent in 179. For the sacred domain as a whole the total of rents dropped in the same period from 16,356 dr. to 6,980 dr. Many tenants could not pay their way. They were most of them men of good family and good reputation, but agriculture did not pay. When Delos became the *entrepôt* for foreign corn they turned their attention to vines and figs, but it was no use; they were constantly being evicted as insolvent, and the administration seized their harvest and wrote them down on the list of debtors for one and a half times the sum which they owed. From this example it is clear that, while the development of leasehold farming was a sign of the times, it only partially remedied the distress of the rural class.

And how many there were who envied the lot of these tenant-farmers! The small proprietors often had nothing left with which to sow their field. They sought work elsewhere; or else they contracted debts, and then their downfall began. Those who had no land of their own lived wretchedly from hand to mouth. There were thousands like Menander's rustic, who goes into service that his mother may not die of hunger, thousands who were obliged to pledge themselves with wife and children to their creditors. Agrarian pauperism was the cancer of Greece in Hellenistic times. More than any other factor, it precipitated a decline which was first economic and then became political. On one side we have the wealth of a satrap, seeking articles of luxury from all over the world, and vast estates and capital which continue to attract land and money to themselves. On the other there is a mass of men without resources and often without work. Such a violent contrast could not but excite terrible envy. There was nothing theoretical about agrarian socialism now. The question of property arose everywhere in Greece, and was everywhere complicated by the question of debt. The evicted men and debtors formed one class, driven by the like destitution to attack wealth. From the Peloponnese to Ætolia the land echoed with cries of hatred, followed by massacres, banishments, and spoliations. Patriotism of the city and even that of the confederacy, already shaken by monarchic and cosmopolitan ideas, could not stand against the international solidarity of parties. Greece went down in a whirlwind, and her last defenders fell with promises of sharing land and abolishing debts on their lips.

CHAPTER V

INDUSTRY

1. THE SITUATION OF INDUSTRY

THE entrance of populous countries into the sphere of Greek civilization increased the total of wants to be satisfied; the extension of money economy furnished the indispensable capital; the development of town life kept pace with the general progress of the division of labour, and collected sufficiently plentiful and skilful workers in groups. For industry, then, conditions were eminently favourable, but only if it abandoned the cities of Greece proper and settled in the Eastern monarchies, where the population was dense and government strongly organized. Vigorous interference of the State with a view to intense production—that was the essential feature of industry in the Hellenistic period. Nowhere was it more clearly marked than in Egypt and the kingdom of Pergamon.

In Egypt the king, who was the chief land-owner, was also the chief manufacturer. To feed his treasury he counted on his workshops almost as much as on his fields. The priesthood, too, made money by trades of every kind. The Egyptian temple, like the mediæval convent, was an important centre of economic enterprise. With its lands and its flocks and herds, its mills and its bakery, it sold its surplus of grain, flour, bread, vegetables, and salted goods; the *Klosterbrau* made beer, and paid for a licence for the public houses in which it established tenants. The priests had also their workshops, for luxury manufactures; they produced the fine oil and the beautiful byssos fabrics demanded by the gods. In the country they were almost the only stonemasons, sculptors, and painters. To make the best use of their wealth, they did banking. In a word, their accounts of receipts give a good place to "income from trade and crafts." But, in spite of this double competition, individuals erected thousands of workshops in the big towns, and managed to make a living as craftsmen in the very smallest villages.

There was no lack of labour. With its seven million inhabitants, Egypt contained an enormous mass of small farmers who, between seed-time and harvest, in summer and in winter, left the sun and the river to do their work. At home they were weavers, smiths, brick-makers, masons; one had his little workshop, another took work with a neighbour. Some left the village; Alexandria, the first of " octopus " cities, attracted hundreds of thousands of workers. They congregated by trades in quarters and streets, even in a second-class town like Arsinoe. They formed corporate associations which, from the country town or the great city, extended their action out into the nome. These men, abstemious, trained to obedience, and delighted to draw a wage in money, were easy to please. It is true that the discipline in the royal factories was not always to their liking, and they fought shy of the excessively hard labour of earth-works, quarries, and mines. But when the State wanted their labour it could impress them. Free labour (if one can speak of freedom under such a system) was therefore sufficient for almost all tasks.

Indeed it is surprising how small a part slave labour played in Ptolemaic Egypt. The land needed none; there were quite enough fellahs. In the country a few wealthy Greek houses owned slaves, but only in small numbers, never more than four. They were chiefly women, either domestic servants or, very often, the master's concubines. The crafts did not employ slaves except in the Greek cities. Alexandria perhaps contained two hundred thousand; but many of them served only for luxury and pleasure, and those engaged in a trade generally led an independent life, apart from settling their accounts with their master. Thus in Egypt there was practically no reason for slavery to exist, and where it did exist, having been introduced by the Greeks, it appeared in a remarkably mild form.

For even in Greece slavery was no longer what it had become exceptionally in certain industrial cities. Alexander's expeditions, which might have been expected to throw multitudes of prisoners on to the market, on the contrary reduced very few to slavery; and the reason was that this circumspect policy did not conflict with economic interests. The field for recruiting opened to dealers in human flesh might be larger, but the slaves were not more numerous. At Delos, where a big market was held, the customers came chiefly from Italy. From Greece, where free labour was almost sufficient for work which had become much less, one must go to Asia to find fairly large gangs of slaves employed in the trades. The kings of Pergamon maintained a slave staff, male and female, in their workshops; Miletos employed public slaves of both sexes on stock-breeding and weaving, while Didyma used sacred slaves for the extraction of marble and building; in a small Carian town a well sinker had five superior workmen and thirty other labourers at his disposal. But at Delos, the very centre of the trade, the temple owned not more than half a dozen, and it is very rarely that one finds in the accounts of works a carpenter or a mason accompanied by his slave. While the economic decline reduced the number of slaves, moral progress improved their condition. The coming together of races, the spread of Athenian philanthropy and of Stoicism, the idea, ever more definite, of the brotherhood of man, all helped to transform slavery. The number of freedmen increased as that of the slaves went down. We can reckon the servants to whom Aristotle and his three successors at the Lyceum granted freedom in their wills. At first we find five freed out of thirteen, then, in succession, five out of nine, four out of six, and eleven out of twelve. From 200 onwards the inscribed walls at Delphi are covered with deeds of manumission placed under the guarantee of the god. No doubt the masters lost nothing by the act; they got the ransom and, very often, they obliged the freedman to continue to serve them. But even that was a remarkable phenomenon; slavery was gradually superseded by free or partially free labour.

The division of labour required more and more intense training in the craftsman. Trades were not only learned in the family. In the papyri apprentices' indentures appear fairly often; we find slaves bound to a wool-carder, to a fuller, to a stenographer, to a flute-woman. The master received an allowance for feeding and clothing the apprentice, and had a right to his services. Precautions were taken in the interest of discipline and good morals; the apprentice could not go out without leave. In other cases, where the family could pay nothing, the apprentice was attached to his master as a domestic servant.

It seems as if technical processes were on the point of being transformed by the wholesale application to industry of the great discoveries of science. The screw of Archimedes made it possible to build engines, with drums or wheels, driven by human motors, for raising water. Ctesibios invented the pump and opened the path of fertility which Heron of Alexandria would follow. Egypt, the land of surveys, canals, and shadoofs, was the right place for the use of geometry for the most delicate land-measuring, levelling, and hydraulic operations. The *groma*, which was fairly difficult to regulate, was superseded by the *dioptra*, a portable water-level with a leg, which could be fitted easily on any plane. The engineer solved problems hitherto insoluble; he could determine the difference in level between two given points, measure the distance and altitude of an inaccessible point, or reckon the volume of water supplied by a fountain. A new machine for hoisting and traction, the *baroulkos*, usefully supplemented the old windlass and sheers. The water-mill replaced the hand-mill, many years before Antipatros of Thessalonica exclaimed " Mill-girls, touch the quern no more! Sleep in peace, and let the cock announce the dawn with his song. Demeter has bidden the Nymphs do your work. They rush on to the top of a wheel and make its axle turn, which, by moving spokes, sets in motion the heavy mass of four hollow-faced millstones."

In spite of these timid experiments, ancient industry was never governed by machines, in Alexandria, or earlier in Athens, or later in Rome. There was no inducement to adopt them, for human labour was not scarce or expensive. But, at least in the artistic industries, technical methods and the division of labour had made great strides. To meet the fashion for rich garments, which revived like a vengeance of Asia on Europe and of aristocratic ideas on democracy, Cos wove bombyx fibre into muslins like those of Babylon, Alexandria made brocades on looms with many heddles, and the royal factory of Pergamon produced fabrics worked with gold wire. Moulders sold the bronze-workers and gold-smiths matrices with which they could

# INDUSTRY

reproduce decorative motives taken from the masterpieces of chased-work.

The participation of the State in industry manifested itself in the Hellenistic period in the systematic exploitation of Crown rights, especially of the right to the subsoil. In Attica the State had left soft materials to the owner of the surface, and reserved for itself the mines and quarries of hard stone; it confined itself to putting concessions up to auction and collecting rents. In the new Greece the city extended its rights and sometimes realized them direct. At Rhodes, Cnidos, Smyrna, Paros, Thasos, Olbia, an official stamp was punched on the vases, because they were made of clay from clay-pits of which some were worked direct by the State and others were leased. In the former case the stamp mentioned the director of the manufacture, in the second it named the concessionnaire and certified that a tax had been paid. We need not ask whether, in the great monarchies, the eminent right of the king over the whole land extended underground. The Seleucids included among their revenues " the riches contained in the soil." The Ptolemies left only the commonest materials to private individuals. The mines, with which the quarries of precious stones and precious materials like alabaster were classed, were worked direct; agents of the Government supervised the work of impressed men and convicts. But as a rule the quarries were farmed out in the same way as the land of the domain and the taxes. Since the materials extracted went to the State, the contractor did no more than hire out labour. He undertook to furnish and maintain the number of workmen needed for a given output; in many cases even tools were placed at his disposal. The administration exercised a permanent control over his management; he was told what cuttings to undertake, and he was obliged to send periodical reports to the " architect " or engineer of the Government. In return for this he received allowances at fixed intervals.

Moreover, the working of the mines and quarries in Egypt was part of a great system. There were countless monopolies, of production, of manufacture, and of sale. The organization in question was not a developed form of household economy; nor was its object to furnish models to private industry, nor to educate the public taste. It was a purely fiscal institution, with no object except profits. The methods of exploitation varied greatly; certain monopolies were farmed out under control, others were worked direct by the officials, while leaving room for free competition, some did not touch manufacture but reserved sole rights of sale, and others were absolute.

Of all these monopolies we best know the monopoly of oil. We have the decree by which it was organized. It provides for everything. The king's manager and the nomarchs (governors of provinces) include among their duties the cultivation of oleaginous plants. They decide the surface of land to be sown, they fix the quantities of each kind to be grown—sesame, croton, safflower, colocynth, linseed, etc.— and they supervise the harvest. The whole produce must be sold to the king's agents, at the king's price, less tax. Manufacture is concentrated in the royal factories. When the monopoly was created, individuals who owned presses and mortars were obliged to hand them over to the nearest factory, and minute precautions were taken against clandestine pressing. The priests alone have a privilege, and it is limited. They can make sesame oil, the finest kind, but only for the use of the temple, during two months, under the eye of the inspectors. They are forbidden to sell what they do not consume to any but the king. Thus sale to the public is most severely monopolized. It is effected in shops licensed by the State. Each village has its oil-merchant, who receives the goods at the legal wholesale price, and sells them at the legal retail price, which leaves him a profit of one eighth. To prevent foreign competition, the State forbids all importation of the kinds which it produces. Olive oil, which it does not produce, can come in, but only on payment of a duty of 25% on the price of the best home-grown quality. Thus the oil monopoly makes a profit of one third. To protect itself against any miscalculation, the treasury completes the system by an insurance; every two years it forms a guaranteeing syndicate which, in return for a premium on every metretes manufactured, takes upon itself the risks of a bad harvest.

We may imagine similar arrangements for the growing, manufacture, and sale of papyrus, and no doubt also for the textile monopoly. Wool, tow, and cotton were converted in the royal mills into fabrics and garments of every kind. Here again the temples had a privilege; they made the finest materials, those of byssos; but they sold to the king all that was not required to clothe the priestly personnel and the statues of the gods. Licences were granted to individuals; but they could only work in the workshops, and perhaps with the looms, of the king, and they took their output to the authorities, who paid them the tariff price. All the subsidiary industries, such as fulling and dyeing, were attached to the textile monopoly.

Foreign precious articles, the frankincense of Arabia and the myrrh of the Troglodytes, were distributed in Egypt and abroad through the king. In addition to this monopoly of sale, the king, or perhaps the queen, had the exclusive right of manufacturing pomades, ointments, and balsams.

These are only examples. To obtain a complete notion of the part played by the royal administration in the industry of Egypt and in its economic life in general, it would be necessary to know more exactly to what control the breweries of the temples and of private individuals were subjected, by the side of the royal breweries (the *Hofbrau*), to have more information regarding the king's rights over wine, bees and honey, wood, rope-making, the building and hiring of boats, tanning, brick-making, luxury glass-ware, the working of precious stones, artistic bronze-work, and goldsmith's work. All these trades were monopolies. The king even reserved to himself elephant-hunting and the sale of ivory.

In the kingdom of the Seleucids and in that of the Attalids the same principles of policy led to the same economic results. The balm of Gilead was sold for the profit of a dynastic monopoly. The kings of Pergamon, who had their own stores of corn and wine, also possessed tile-works and brick-fields, their parchment competed with the Ptolemies' papyrus, and they placed their beautiful gold-worked fabrics on the market. At the head of the industrial service a director of the royal workshops was placed. What the king did on a large scale the independent cities of the Asiatic states did on a small scale. The authorities at Miletos sold wool from the public sheep-runs or transformed it into cloth, garments, and carpets in the municipal factories; they authorized the temple of Didyma to maintain its own quarrymen, stone-cutters, and masons.

The services done by this strong organization of industry may be gauged by the poverty of the means at the disposal of private individuals, not only in countries with a State monopoly but also—and especially—in cities which remained true to the system of freedom in industry and trade. The individuals themselves were compelled to form a group, to combine their capital, if their business was of any size. In Egypt small contractors could offer tenders for the exploitation of a quarry, because such concessions were given out in small lots; but work on the dams and canals was given out to companies (sometimes comprising a whole village), the director of which, chosen from among the lenders of money or the high officials, was alone competent to make a contract with the State. At Delos, where private initiative was not hampered by any restriction, it is amazing to see how little money and how few men the citizens, even with the help of foreigners, could give to building work. The concessionnaires received part payment beforehand in instalments, the first of which was almost always equal to half the total; and even then, if an undertaking was of any size at all, they combined in twos, threes, or fours. Theophantos of Carystos does minor repairs by himself, he combines with Xenophanes of Syros for a job valued at 40 dr., and both of them have to bring in Democrates in order to get, at the auction, an order worth 1,300 dr. Associations like these, made for one operation only and never comprising the same partners for two years running, give the impression of a paltry, unenterprising industry.

## 2. Workers and Wages

The position of the workers varied with the country and with the trade. The condition of the convicts and their families in the mines on the Nubian border was ghastly. The underground workers were buried in dark, narrow, winding galleries. Day and night they hacked at the rock with plain iron picks, lamp on forehead, naked, bent in every position, loaded with chains, under the whip of the overman. Behind them the children picked up the ore which had been dug and carried it away. The surface workers were divided

# INDUSTRY

into gangs of crushers, washers, and smelters. The men over thirty years old broke up the ore in mortars, while the women and old men worked at the hand-mill in twos and threes to reduce it to powder. The washing in running water required continuous attention. The smelting was done in vessels which stood on the fire five days and five nights. All these unfortunates were supervised by foreign soldiers. They never obtained more than the scantiest nourishment and they soon succumbed to their hard work. Only the impressed men who were added to them in case of need were entitled to wages.

Even the free workers were subject to harsh discipline under the Græco-Egyptian regulations. In the king's workshops and on the farmed-out building-yards there was a large body of supervisors. Cleon, the chief engineer on the reclamation of the Fayum, had a whole staff of inspectors under him to supervise the contractors, and the contractors had foremen and overseers to help them to manage an army of navvies, grouped in gangs of ten, one of whom was the gang-leader. There was a holiday (without pay) one day in ten. Abstention from work was forbidden under the most severe penalties.

Workers by the day were generally fed, but for their *opsonion* they received a money allowance, which soon became a regular wage. The land-worker got one obol a day under this head. We find quarrymen getting 2 ob. in coin, one chœnix of corn (nearly 2 pts.), and a *kyathos* of oil ($12\frac{1}{2}$ drams), which brings the daily wage to rather over $2\frac{1}{3}$ ob. When Ptolemy Euergetes sent 100 masons and 350 labourers to the Rhodians he set aside a sum of 14 talents for their yearly salary; that is to say, he probably allowed $2\frac{1}{2}$ ob. a day to the labourer, 4 ob. to the skilled worker, and 1 dr. to the gang-leader. The rate of these salaries was a quarter of that which obtained in Attica in the IVth century.

Work by the job underwent exactly the same transformation. Brick-laying, which had cost between 12 and 17 dr. the thousand in Attica, now came to 4 dr. Since it took a gang of three men about two and a half days to lay a thousand bricks, we again get the average salary of 3 ob. a day. Navvies were paid at one tetradrachm for a cube varying between 40 and 75 *aoilia*, the difference in the rate being due to the nature of the ground and the season. In any case, the navvy's pay was only one obol a day on the average; but we must regard this as an allowance for impressed labour, and not a true wage.

In the king's oil-mills the crushers, although paid by the job, had to dispose of a minimum amount in a day, for example at least one *artabe* (1 bushel) of safflower. Their pay was low. But from the profits of the sale they got a share of $2\frac{1}{2}$ dr. per metretes of oil, which was brought down by costs to 1 dr. 4 ob. Since 8 *artabai* of seed gave one metretes of oil, they thus made an extra $1\frac{1}{4}$ ob. or $1\frac{1}{2}$ ob. a day. It should be noted that their share was higher than that of the contractor, who was entitled to only 1 dr. per metretes.

All the information which the papyri give about wages comes from the country towns. In Alexandria pay was better in appearance; hence the exodus of workers to the great city. But the high cost of living there cut down savings and made it impossible to rear a large family. We have the letter of a workman to his wife, who has remained in the country. He promises to send her the pay which he is going to receive, and advises her, when the child which she is expecting is born, to expose it if it is a girl. In the country wages were lower, but on the whole they ensured a supportable standard of living, because prices were not high. They averaged 10 or 15 drachmas a month. Now the financial authorities gave the recorder 10 drachmas a month and the beadle 20 dr.; the army authorities allowed the elephant-hunters 4 ob. a day. A woman who lived by the work of her hands in a small town earned enough to be able to go and have a hot bath regularly.

The position of the worker in Ptolemaic Egypt would therefore not have been too bad, if his chiefs had always carried out their undertakings. Unfortunately the managers of the royal factories and the contractors committed all kinds of abuses. Euergetes II had to pass an edict forbidding work below the tariff in the textile mills. The correspondence of the engineer Cleon tells us of the continual complaints of the quarrymen and the difficulties resulting from their discontentment. One gang complains of the foreman, who always puts it to work on hard stone; they have to wait for assistants to clear away the small stones and sand; the Government does

# INDUSTRY

not supply the proper wedges, the iron is of bad quality; food is short, the money does not come; the contractor cannot use his vouchers because they are not in order; the Departments do not answer, but put the responsibility off on one another. What with all this, the men are fed up; they throw down their tools or pawn them; they have struck. And then they get worked up; things are beginning to look ugly; for, as he says in a letter to another engineer, " you know what goes on in the gangs when they stop work."

In Greece proper and the islands emigration and the general decline of industry led to a serious shortage of labour. Employers had great difficulty in keeping their men for the whole duration of a contract job. Provision was made for this difficulty in the contracts. At Delos, for a building order of 300 drachmas, it was stipulated that the contractor must keep permanently on the yard at least four workers with their assistants, failing which the sacred administration would replace the missing men and require a fine of one drachma per man per day. Voluntary relinquishing of work was therefore feared more than shortage of hands.

But, even without competition, the remuneration of labour inevitably diminished from the IVth century to the IIIrd. The general fall in prices caused a greater fall in wages. At Delos skilled workers now made only 2 dr. a day instead of $2\frac{1}{2}$ dr. (masons, carpenters), and $1\frac{1}{2}$ dr. instead of 2 dr. (plasterers); unskilled labourers returned to the one drachma of the Vth century; assistants had to be content with even less. It is true that the cost of living was no longer what it had been; a grown man could just manage on 2 dr. a day, and with one drachma he could provide a wife and one or two children with absolute necessaries. But lack of employment prevented him from always being sure of this minimum, and certainly from raising himself to a perceptibly higher standard of living. Then engagements by the month and by the year were introduced; this system gave every advantage to the administration, which was sure of its labour, and to the worker, who was sure of his pay. Thus stonemasons form part of the personnel attached to the temple. But their position is hardly as good as that which the public slaves once enjoyed in Athens. For the first two years they receive their *sitos*—a chœnix and a half of wheat (2·8 pts.)

or three chœnices of barley (5·7 pts.) a day—, clothing, and an *opsonion* of 120 dr. in coin. Then, for fourteen years, their *sitos* is paid, like the *opsonion*, in money, 240 dr. in all, plus clothing, which is worth 20 or 22 dr. So these men, who might have worked by the day at 2 dr., preferred a regular salary on an average of 4⅓ ob. The reason probably was that they would not have earned the 2 dr. on more than one day out of three. Even the architect's salary was much reduced. For about fifty years it remains at the normal rate of 720 dr. a year or 2 dr. a day; for artists of repute it may be 3 or 4 dr. These figures are already 30% lower than those given in the accounts of Delphi about 345. From 250 onwards a further fall brings the salary down to the rate of 1½ dr., which was paid by Epidauros more than a century before.

What kept pay by the day low was the combination of work by the piece and the measure with the system of auctioning contracts. If the mason at Delos got 20% less per day than the mason in Athens once received, it was because he accepted 25% less per square yard (6 dr. for ashlar foundations, instead of 8 dr.). And the mason could better resist the fall than other men, in an island where much building was done and brick-laying remained unalterably at 8 ob. the hundred. But, by skilful alternation of contracts by the whole job and contracts by the piece, the administration succeeded in bringing the blacksmith, who got an obol for every tool he sharpened in 281, down to accepting half an obol seven years later. The varnisher, who in 296 was paid 3 dr. 4 ob. for every metretes of pitch employed, received only 1 dr. 4 ob. in 250—55% less. The stone-engraver's pay fell even more. Already in the second half of the IVth century, at Delphi and Epidauros, the price for a hundred letters had been reduced from one Æginetan drachma to one Attic drachma. At Delos the rate of one drachma the hundred soon gave place to that of one drachma the three hundred. This rate became permanent, at Delos and also at Lebadeia. In general, the price of labour fell quicker and further than that of commodities in the last quarter of the IVth century and the first half of the IIIrd; then, when the price of commodities showed a slight tendency to rise, that of labour remained at the lowest level for good.

These wretched wages were not even certain. The contractors, being responsible for bad work, shifted the onus on to their workers. For a serious fault the employer deducted part of a man's pay; or even forfeited it all. If he was rapacious or dishonest, he found a way of dismissing the workman without pay, on the pretext that his work was worth nothing. Once Laomedon had driven Apollo away like this, and threatened to cut off his ears; so, too, in a comedy a cook is obliged to pack off empty-handed. Athens in her great days settled such disputes through the ordinary channels. The *Nautodikai* of the Peiræeus dealt justice rapidly to the workers of the port, and craftsmen and labourers could benefit by the same proceedings as enabled a sophist to claim his fee. In the Hellenistic period disputes regarding the payment of wages were bound to multiply. They grew more bitter. Strikes ensued. But the new theories of the rights of the State authorized its representatives to intervene between employers and employees without waiting for a formal complaint to be submitted. According to contracts from Lebadeia and Tegea, commissioners of supervision were empowered to fine or to expel from the yards inefficient or disobedient workmen. There is a decree from Paros in honour of an *Agoranomos* who had successfully " prevented wage-earners and employers from wronging each other, for, in accordance with the laws and agreements, he compelled the men to abstain from striking and to carry out their task, and the employers to pay the workers their wages without legal proceedings."

So the working classes had much to endure, but far more in the districts of Greece proper, which had no raw materials, than in the eastern countries, where the building of great cities and the riches of the soil favoured industry. We can understand why public office and the liberal arts exercised an ever stronger attraction on the townsman. We can understand why so many workers left their country and exchanged their tools for arms, at the prospect of the fine pay offered by the kings. The brilliance of Hellenistic civilization covers more misery than can be reckoned.

CHAPTER VI

TRADE

1. THE ORGANIZATION OF TRADE

THE conquest of the East widened the field of expansion hitherto open to Greek trade. It had never strayed away from the Mediterranean. Now it annexed vast continental tracts; it penetrated to the Ister, the Indus, and the Cataracts of the Nile; it assumed a universal character. Over the political frontiers unity of civilization and of economic life was created and firmly established. Already Hellenism radiated over the whole of Italy and over Carthage, over the Celts of La Tène and over the kingdom of Sandracotta, from the Atlantic to the Indian Ocean.

All conditions combined to give this market intensity as well as breadth. The circulation of money increased the power to purchase in every land. The specialization of agricultural production gave rise to countless exchanges between corn countries and oil or wine countries. Industry clamoured for raw materials and drove men to create new outlets. The progress of comfort and luxury developed the use of perfumes, spices, rare fabrics, and precious woods, which must be obtained from the most distant regions. The Governments systematically pursued a commercial policy. Not only did they build cities, dig harbours and canals, maintain roads, and send explorers in every direction; they placed their diplomats and armies at the service of commercial interests. Philadelphos opened relations with Rome and with the kings of India; the Seleucids and the Lagids disputed the great roads which ran from Syria; kings paid court to the merchants of Rhodes.

Everywhere local trade displayed increasing activity. Between the importer and the retailer, the *emporos* and the *kapelos*, the number and the importance of the middlemen became greater. Let us visit Delos. The streets are lined

# TRADE

with shops, most of them quite small; on their fronts are the signs and symbols which advertise their wares; inside, the walls are full of niches. From the objects found on the spot we identify pottery-merchants, ironmongers, sellers of household articles, the ivory-turner, and the sculptor. Near the harbour the shops are grouped according to their special line, and their double-bayed fronts call to the public. Let us go on to Priene. The nearer we come to the markets, the more shops and little windowless workshops there are. Here is a meeting-place of streets—the Small Market. On all sides we see the bakers' shops. The marble tables with the water-channels along them are the butchers' and fishmongers' stalls. Further on is the square of the Great Market; there is a large altar in the middle, and the four sides are lined with spacious arcades, with rows of shops inside.

It is in such settings that we must place all the small folk whom Alexandrian literature and art made into the glorious figures of their favourite inventions—the sheepskin-clad shepherd lost in the town, the old peasant woman with a lamp under her arm, fishermen stinking of fish, persuasive shopmen and hawkers bawling their lungs out, slaves and slave-dealers, rowdy porters and affected middle-class females. Who could ever puff his goods better than the shoemaker of Herondas, when he enumerates to his pretty customer all the shoes on his shelves ? Not for nothing is his name Cerdon, Moneymaker. The retail trade was, moreover, accustomed to large profits. At Delos tiles cost 4 ob. the pair on the wharf, and 5 from the retailer; the importer delivered lime at 3 dr. the medimnus, the retailer at 4 dr.; if you bought 2,000 bricks they cost 4 dr. the hundred, if you bought 1,450 they cost 5 dr., if 290, $6\frac{1}{2}$ dr., if 100, 7 dr., and if 60, nearly 8 dr. Advertisement was done shamelessly by some and skilfully by others. Pharmaceutical specialities were sold in pots of clay or lead which bore the name of the chemist with the arms of the city or with the name of the doctor who recommended them. By his stamp the potter advertised his make wherever the exporters of oil and wine took his goods.

The commercial association was very frequent. At Delos contractors combined to undertake public orders, and merchants to do business which required a big outlay. A Delian document mentions, for example, the banks of Nymphodoros and Heracleides, of Philon and Selenos, of Hellen and Mantineus, of Philophon and Pactyes. In Egypt we know of Archidamos and Metrophanes, Ship-Owners, and the bank of Prœtos, Conon and Co.; these were companies which generally farmed public works and taxes. There were even companies which ran small concerns; at Magdola three wine-retailers in partnership had suppliers who were also in partnership. The State did not allow any civil personality to the association, but dealt with a single individual, who represented all the others, and could be a woman. When the partners submitted a complaint to the legal authorities, the Strategos replied to " So-and-so and Associates."

New combinations of interests arose on all sides. In 324 the Rhodian Antimenes invented the first system of insurance mentioned in history. He guaranteed owners against the flight of their slaves for an annual premium of 8%. Understandings were formed, cartels were created. The boatmen of Smyrna combined to abolish the disadvantages of competition and to raise prices, until the city came down on them with a crushing decree. Speculators had the inspiration of limiting production in order to impose their own prices. There was even talk of an attempt to restrict corn-growing by artificial means. But of all the manœuvres of which we hear in the Hellenistic age the most characteristic was that which so brilliantly inaugurated it, the wheat corner planned and brought off about 330 by Cleomenes, the governor of Memphis. There was general famine in Greece; the harvest in Egypt had been good. Cleomenes stopped exportation. Sudden fall in Egypt, a further rise abroad; while the fellah had his barns full, the Athenian was paying 32 dr. the medimnus (17s. 6d. the bushel). Then Cleomenes bought up the whole Egyptian harvest, but he took good care not to be tempted by the slump into offering too little; he gave a very remunerative price, so as to secure an absolute monopoly of purchase. Then, too, he organized exportation on a large scale. In every port he had his agents for information and sales, who corresponded with him and among themselves by a private mail. Being kept informed of all demands and all fluctuations, he was able to send the goods without hesitation to the markets where prices were best. The results were glorious.

In times when the activity of industry, and above all of trade, was intense, and the amount of money increased less than that of commodities, credit, which had made a brilliant appearance in Athens, naturally made progress on the entire market. The bank became the essential organ of economic life. Productive circulation increased, and borrowing was easier. The mortgage, once dreaded as a first step to dispossession, was regarded as a convenient means of procuring money at a comparatively moderate rate. The working classes had no longer so much difficulty in obtaining capital. No doubt commerce still made only rare use of long-term credit, and the bottomry loan continued to be the favourite transaction. It is not certain that the Hellenistic age was ever acquainted with the true bill of exchange, the paper draft requiring some one abroad to pay a sum to a third party and conferring the right to sue the issuer. But the use of the cheque expanded in an astonishing way. The system of transfers offered business facilities which Greek ingenuity multiplied and elaborated. Through the diffusion of credit the total amount of profits increased to enormous dimensions; but interest went down as risks diminished. The normal rate fell from 12% to 10% even in the IIIrd century, and to 7% about the middle of the IInd; and it did not rise until the Roman conquest turned the provinces into a happy hunting-ground for the usurer.

The concentration of capital in the banks henceforward offered the State great advantages. Before that, public credit had not existed. It had been impossible for citizens to have any confidence, in the presence of a sovereign power which legalized forced loans, and foreign creditors had had no recourse against their all-powerful debtor but risky reprisals. So borrowing by the State had never been more than a political deal. Now, however, the credit establishments were able to render purely economic services to embarrassed treasuries. Every State gave letters of credit on foreign bankers to its ambassadors and the agents whom it sent to buy corn. Certain Rhodians at Delos facilitated the victualling of Histiæa and Ios in this way. But State borrowing was very different according as the money came from home or from abroad. In the former case the State appealed to the generosity of wealthy patriots, who gave subscriptions, free loans. In the latter case it had to accept very severe terms; as a rule it agreed to the interest being doubled in case of protest; Olbia pledged the sacred vases, a Naxian obtained from Arcesine a right of execution on all properties, public and private, on the island and outside, and a creditor distrained on the porticoes of Cyme when payment fell due. We can understand what an attraction good interest, on such securities as these, must have had for the Roman *negotiatores*.

Private banks might be able to risk every kind of enterprise, but the administrations of the sacred treasures had to be cautious, and therefore to demand more substantial guarantees. Accordingly, they did not address themselves direct to the public. At Ilion the temples entrusted the greater part of their funds to the commonwealth, which undertook to make use of them and paid 10%. The *hieropoioi* of Delos lent to bankers and to cities. For State loans they required endorsement by the city, as collectively responsible, that is, first by the Council, secretary, and treasurers, and in the next line by the sureties, considered personally as debtors, and underneath by the sureties of the sureties. It needed only one step further to turn this kind of establishment into a State bank; and the step was taken.

The public bank was an institution which expanded over a great part of the Hellenistic world, especially around Byzantion. An establishment was not granted an absolute monopoly, but it was allowed certain privileges in the interest of the State. It generally obtained the sole right of exchanging money, and sometimes that of minting. At Ilion and Delos the public bank had at its disposal funds borrowed by the city from the temples, and it was managed for the Government by officials. As a rule these banks were farmed out to the man who offered the highest rent.

Nowhere was the organization of credit brought to a higher pitch of perfection than in Egypt, although natural economy still survived there in the midst of money economy. Nothing shows better how careful one should be with theories which treat natural economy, money economy, and credit economy as three successive stages in the history of communities. Under the Ptolemies every little town in the poor nomes, and every village in the fertile nomes, had its public granary (*thesauros*), managed by a *sitologos*. The smallest village had its public bank (*trapeza*), which the State farmed out to the highest bidder. With the help of these two types of establishment it was possible to effect transfer operations of every form in goods, in money, or in paper.

The public granaries received, over and above the taxes and rents of the domain which were levied in kind, all the produce deposited by the cultivators. They were genuine banks, with a capital consisting of natural wealth. Each kind of corn had its fixed price each year. The current accounts of deposits made it possible to effect payments without displacing the goods, by a mere transfer in the books. The system lent itself to the most complex transactions. With the receipts of the *sitologos* the tax-payer or debtor could pay an amount anywhere, and it was eventually carried to the debit of his account in his village. Each depositor could issue cheques in proportion to his balance. In the capitals, where the accounts of the *sitologoi* were audited, there were regular clearing-houses.

The public banks played the same part as the granaries, with money for their means of action. They were, first and foremost, tax-offices under the central administration, but they took the metal deposits of individuals, opened current accounts for them, and placed money-orders and cheques at their disposal.

Finally, a way was found for making every certificate of title negotiable, even without a deposit. Notarial instruments were kept in the temples, after the Egyptian fashion, or in the archives of the *Syngraphophylax*, in the Greek way; they were put into circulation by means of transfer-notes. A special establishment, the *bibliotheke enkteseon*, or Titles Registry, guaranteed to all comers a credit value represented either by movable or by real property. It may be said that never, in any country in the world, was credit more universally practised than in Ptolemaic Egypt.

To complete the organization of commerce, means of communication became comparatively quick and convenient.

Navigation by sea enjoyed facilities hitherto unknown. When the lighthouse of Alexandria was provided with a fire which could be seen thirty-eight miles off, this useful invention spread rapidly. There were good *Sailing Directions* for the ship's captains; the Egyptian admiral Timosthenes of Rhodes wrote a work on harbours, giving distances. The absolute speed of ships had not changed much, but their commercial speed had increased greatly, since they crossed the open sea and sailed at night. Instead of doing 65 to 80 nautical miles in the twenty-four hours, they did 80 to 135, maintaining a rate between 4 and 6 knots on end. From Alexandria to Rhodes the crossing took four days; with a good wind it took six or seven days to go from Alexandria to Sicily. Ship-building made such progress that the tonnage exceeded requirements. In the war navy the triremes were superseded by quinqueremes, and the *Lioness* of Heracleia had perhaps eight banks of a hundred rowers. The *Syracuse*, which Hieron II ordered from the yards of Archias the Corinthian, held 3,900 tons of cargo and offered passengers every comfort imaginable, numerous cabins and luxurious saloons. She was manned by 600 seamen and 300 marines. For protection against pirates she carried turrets and armouries. This mammoth must therefore have had a burden of 5,000 tons. She was intended to run from Syracuse to Alexandria and to Greece; but when she was tried her dimensions appeared to be too great, and Hieron, to get rid of her, gave her to Ptolemy as a present.

That anyone should have thought of launching a merchant vessel of this size shows that sea-borne trade was concentrated in big ports with a highly developed equipment. The pattern of these ports was Alexandria, where the marine docks were provided with warehouses for imported cargoes and the huge stores on Lake Mareotis received goods for export. Everywhere services of transport by sea were organized. Sometimes they were private enterprises, but these had difficulty in holding their own. The boatmen of Smyrna made a vain attempt to limit competition; the city made short work of their schemes. As a rule the State made transport a monopoly, which it farmed out. Delos included the proceeds of the *porthmeia* among her revenues, and at Myra the concessionnaire had to add 25% to the fare, for the benefit of the treasury. But Hieron evidently meant the gigantic *Syracuse* to be managed by the Government itself.

Thanks to these various organizations, navigation by sea formed into big currents. The Euxine remained rather

## TRADE

outside; under stress of Scythian inroads and the Galatian invasion it could not resist the competition of Egyptian corn, and kept its old importance only for salted goods. The greatest volume of exchanges was carried on by Alexandria and Rhodes with Corinth, Taras, Syracuse, and Carthage, and later by Alexandria and Delos with Puteoli. Transactions were sufficiently numerous to bring the distinction between *emporoi* (merchants), *naukleroi* (ship-owners), and *ekdocheis* (forwarding agents) into general application. But they all combined in associations which extended their activities to several ports. The marine code of Rhodes was gradually adopted by all mariners in the Mediterranean; many of the rules which it laid down were even to be handed down to modern times by Roman and Byzantine law.

The new conditions of navigation did not cause freights for short voyages to fall. From Paros or Naxos to Delos the carriage of marble costs 11-15 ob. the cubic foot (11$d$.-1$s$. 3$d$. per cwt., for a distance of twenty nautical miles); from Syros to Delos tiles pay 1$\frac{1}{8}$ or 1$\frac{1}{4}$ ob. the pair (1$\frac{3}{4}d$. or 2$d$.), and bricks 3 dr. 4$\frac{1}{2}$ ob. the hundred (2$s$. 10$\frac{1}{2}d$.). But for long voyages the greater speed, higher tonnage, and better organization must have worked for a reduction of expenses in general and therefore of the freightage. In any case, the diminution of risks affected marine loans; where the interest was once 30%, lenders now accept 24%.

Now that the Greeks had established themselves in countries with big rivers, they turned their attention to river craft for the first time. Alexander organized navigation on the lower Tigris. By the Thracian waterways Greek goods were sent towards the Carpathians. Alexandria served as port to an innumerable fleet which went up the Nile as far as the Cataracts, carrying passengers, but chiefly intended for bringing down agricultural and manufactured products. Feluccas bearing a few dozen sacks passed imposing dahabiahs with a burden, sometimes, of 10,000 *artabai* (over 300 tons). Some of these boats belonged to the king or the queen, others to private individuals. We know of one Papiris who owned a total tonnage of 80,000 *artabai* (at least 2,500 tons) on the river. The owner (called in Egypt the *misthotes*) did not concern himself with the cargo; he hired his boat to the *naukleros*, who in Egypt was the transport agent. The chief customer was the State, and the chief business was the handling of grain. All the surplus of the country had to be sent to the royal granary in Alexandria. The *naukleros* went to the port of embarkation indicated to him. He took delivery of the cargo brought to the wharf by order of the *sitologoi*, and presented his mandate in exchange for a detailed bill of lading. For the carriage of bulky articles, for example obelisks destined for the adornment of Alexandria, the device invented by the engineer Satyros was used; the object was laid across a canal from one bank to the other, and a boat full of stones was slipped underneath; then the boat was emptied, and as it rose it lifted the object which it was to carry.

Land transport also developed in Macedonia and the East on a scale which it had never attained in Greece. From Pydna to the Adriatic, separate stretches of road ran along the line of the future Via Egnatia. In Egypt grain from distant granaries was carried to the port of embarkation on donkey-back. The owners brought their beasts to be requisitioned, and obtained compensation in corn. They formed a corporation under the auspices of the State, not in order to protect their interests against it, but to organize the procedure of requisitions. Stones were conveyed along slide-ways which were kept wet; at Syene the granite went by a great causeway from the quarry to the wharf; the porphyry of Gebel Dukhan went down by a network of ways which grew broader as they descended and were set with posts at regular intervals and paved on the steep gradients. Caravan routes multiplied; some served the Libyan oases and took the profits of this intercourse away from Cyrene, now in her decline, while others, marked in places, even to this day, by huge watering tanks, connected Cænepolis and Coptos with the topaz and emerald mines and the new ports on the Red Sea. The Seleucids gave their attention to land routes far more than the Ptolemies. The missions of Megasthenes in India, the exploration of the Caspian Sea by Patrocles of Rhodes, and of the Sea of Aral by Demodamas of Miletos, the military expeditions into Arachosia, and the pursuit of the Arab pirates could only give practical results if the royal roads were properly maintained. The great north road ended at Trapezus and in Asia Minor. The roads to the Far

East converged on the Tigris, at Seleuceia; from there they went on either to Damascus and the port of Berytos or to Antioch and the port of Seleuceia. At Damascus the caravans from Egypt to Arabia arrived; from Antioch the great road started which ran to Ephesos and Pergamon. In forty days one went from the Indus to the Tigris, in fifteen days from the Tigris to the Mediterranean. The immediate object of this magnificent scheme was to provide for the requirements of the royal mail and of military transport, but trade could not but benefit by it. The Government drew up a list of the *stathmoi* or stages, which was the model of the Roman itineraries. Movement became active, and the taste for travel spread. On the roads soldiers and traders met tourists on their way to visit the Seven Wonders of the World. Hotels of every kind were set up in the big towns, and there was no village so small but the stranger would find an inn.

The post, which had been an indispensable instrument of government in the empire of the Achæmenids, the direct bond between the satrapies and the king, continued to be a State service under the Seleucids, and was organized by the Ptolemies in Egypt. Since it was reserved for official correspondence, we should not need to speak of it, were it not that the king was the biggest merchant, the biggest manufacturer, and the biggest banker, so that it was used in the interest of commerce as in that of the treasury. The Egyptian post took the name of *angareia* from Persia and handed it down to Rome. For express mails, reserved for the correspondence of the king and the central power, mounted messengers were employed. At Hibeh, the name of which perhaps recalls a stage (*hipponon*), a register has been found, on which the postmaster entered, day by day and hour by hour, the rolls which he received, with the addresses, and the names of the postmen who brought them and took them away. The ordinary slow mail carried the correspondence of local officials within the borders of each nome, and the postmen went on foot.

## 2. THE EXPANSION OF TRADE

To estimate the volume of foreign trade it would be enough to look at Alexandria, Rhodes, and Delos, among so many cities which became great. But we have a figure which enables us to appreciate the amount of business done in the big ports. At Rhodes, about 170, the customs yielded 166 talents, five times more than at the Peiræeus towards the beginning of the IVth century. It is true that in two centuries the value of money had diminished; it is none the less true that in foreign trade Rhodes outdid Athens by far. What, then, must we think of Alexandria?

It was in the Mediterranean that the great movements of business took place, namely those which carried the products of Greek and Græcized countries to the depths of the European continent. But we should dwell upon relations with the more distant countries of the earth, for, though their importance is historical rather than economic, they are the great novelty of the Hellenistic period, and did much to turn the great highways of world trade towards Egypt and Syria.

Following the example of the great Pharaohs, the Lagids did much to encourage Egyptian trade with Ethiopia and the countries of the Indian Ocean. Ptolemy Philadelphos sent explorers in every direction, Dalion to the other side of Meroe, Ariston to the shores of Arabia, and Dionysios to India. Although Alexander had already revealed to his master Aristotle the sources of the Nile, the Sudan was rarely entered by the upper river; the Red Sea route was preferred. Originally drawn to this region by the hunting of warelephants, the Ptolemies attached themselves to it for commercial reasons. They found there many harbours, periodic winds, and markets frequented by civilized populations. They could obtain there ivory and gold from the interior of Africa, myrrh and frankincense from Arabia, cinnamon, spices, drugs, and cotton from India, and even silk from China. In exchange, they could offer the articles which the Egyptian workshops manufactured for export, in particular " clothing for savage wear." From Berenice, Leucos Limen, and Myos Hormos the precious consignments from the Far East were borne by caravans to the banks of the Nile, or else they took the sea-to-sea canal right to the wharves of

Alexandria. High officials supervised the unloading of these exotic goods and convoyed them to Coptos. A series of forts and watering-stations ensured the dominion of the Græco-Egyptians over the Troglodyte Coast and the Spice Coast. With the Nabatæans, the Meinæans, the Sabæans, and the Homeritæ there was regular intercourse. From Guardafui, the South Horn, mariners ventured forth into the Ocean, even before Hippalos had familiarized them with the monsoon. From time to time an emissary of the king made his way as far as India; the Indians, too, reached Egypt, and left a trace of their visit in their dedications.

Hitherto the Persian Empire had been an insurmountable obstacle to relations between the Mediterranean and the Indus. The Macedonian conquest brought the Indians face to face with those whom, in Persian fashion, they called the Yavanas or Yonas. Alexander's expedition against King Poros was not a mere thunderbolt, alarming but unproductive. At once a vast campaign of exploration began. Literary men took picturesque notes on countries and inhabitants, the king's secretary, Eumenes of Cardia, collected detailed observations for the official *Ephemerides*, the *Bematistai*, officers of the Topographical Section of the General Staff, drew up a systematic report on the Gandhara and the Punjab, the admiral Nearchos, cruising in the Indian Ocean, kept his log, a first-class document for the seas and coasts, and specialists were sent on missions to study scientific and economic questions, like the man who wrote an account of the mines of salt, gold, and silver in the kingdom of Sopeythes. After the evacuation of India, Seleucos Nicator carried on a policy of peaceful penetration in that country; Megasthenes visited it and brought back from his travels a narrative which had a great success. About the same time Dionysios, sent out by Ptolemy Philadelphos, was collecting information about the people. Thus was amassed a store of knowledge which scholars disseminated among the general public. By the overland road which the Seleucids guarded, by the Red Sea route held by the Ptolemies, the Yavanas secured a new field of expansion for their civilization and their trade.

Soldiers, artists, philosophers, traders, the Westerners poured into these fairy countries. They knew that princes with fabulous wealth and a passion for luxury heaped gold on men who organized feasts and women who played the flute, on coin-engravers who presented the master's features, haloed with his name, to the admiration of his subjects, on architects who built temples with columns rolling into volutes or blossoming into acanthus, and on sculptors who turned stone into gods with supple gestures and gentle smiles. Others would have feared to approach a people who pitilessly kept out every stranger from their rigid framework; but these devils of Greeks soon managed to insinuate themselves among the seven recognized castes and to have new castes formed for themselves. How should the wise men, the Brahmins, have been strict with them ? They brought a new writing, they taught the laws of astronomy and astrology, they measured space and time. How should the warriors, the Kshatriyas, have remained untouched by the glory of the stout fellows who set up a throne in a day ? The husbandmen and shepherds were delighted to see the labour of the Sudras developed by men who caused canals, wells, and tanks to be built at their own cost. But, more than any other caste, the craftsmen and traders were dumbfounded at the daring of the merchants who sprang up by land and by sea, full of heroism and wiles. The miraculous rice-harvests, the gifts of the cotton-plant and the sugar-cane, the enormous profit to be made on spices and rare woods, the mines of gold, silver, and precious stones, the abundance of ivory, the opportunity of getting elephants for the armies, all excited the appetite of the Yavanas. To make themselves welcome, they would dedicate a casket, a crypt, or a pediment in some hallowed sanctuary, or a refectory in a monastery; their generosity would be recorded in an inscription—an incomparable advertisement. After that they could go everywhere, offer their goods, and collect native produce. They brought the wheat of Alexandria (*âlisandaga*), flowered fabrics (*yavanikâ*), Arabian frankincense (*yavâna*), and liquid storax (*yavanadesaja*), and they presented the kings with slaves skilled in dancing and singing for their zenanas. In exchange, they asked especially for Chinese silk—" Seric stuff "—and for pepper, their " passion " (*yavanapriya*). When the precious loads, for which they paid in silver *drammas*, reached the Mediterranean, by the Oxus or the Indus, they were worth golden staters.

Later the Greeks obtained silk in more direct ways. The kingdom of Bactriana, an advanced post of Hellenism, was so situated as to communicate with the Chinese as soon as circumstances should be favourable. Until the end of the IIIrd century the Mongol incursions cut China off from the West. The silk reached even India only after passing through the hands of several intermediaries in the course of petty dealings. But once the Great Wall was complete, about 126, the Han Dynasty occupied the Tarim Basin and the passes of the Pamirs. From 114 contact was established with the Greeks. Exchanges developed with incredible rapidity. Every year a dozen caravans arrived at the Iaxartes and the Oxus. About 105 the Emperor Wu-ti authorized foreign merchants to travel freely in his dominions. When the Greeks succumbed beneath the blows of the Parthians they had knit relations which their fellow-countrymen in Syria inherited.

In all periods of history the advances or withdrawals of Hellenism in the East were accompanied by similar movements in the West. Alexander's campaigns were followed by great voyages of discovery, in the course of which the Phocæans of Massalia broke down the barriers raised against them by the Phœnicians of Carthage; and for the *periplus* of the Persian Gulf there was a corresponding *periplus* of the Atlantic. Ever since she had existed, Massalia had found the Pillars of Heracles well guarded. In the end she went through. Euthymenes was the first to venture in the footsteps of Hanno and to visit the coast of Africa. Then, about 325-320, Pytheas set out on the trail of Himilco, northwards. He was a cross between a sea-wolf and a scholar, full of curiosity and daring; he resolved to penetrate the secrets of the Northern lands and to look for the tin and amber in the countries which produced them. The merchants and shipowners of Massalia had to provide the funds of the expedition. From Cadiz he made the Isle of Ushant, sailed right round Britain, entered the mouth of the Elbe, explored Norway almost to the Arctic Circle, and only stopped when the fog and ice prevented him from going further. He brought back a plentiful harvest of new knowledge. In the narrative of this voyage he calculated distances and gave many details on the manners of the inhabitants, the products, and the markets. The practical results of this remarkable exploration were destined to be nil. The peninsula which produced the tin and the island on which the amber trade concentrated were too far away. But such attempts show, no less than the multitude of ships riding in the harbours or the long caravans strung over the roads, the spirit of enterprise which animated Greek trade and carried it to the confines of the world.

# CONCLUSION

HAVING come to the end of our study, let us stop for a moment, to cast a glance over the road traversed.

We have seen, in the course of about a thousand years, the historical framework of Greece growing continually. At the beginning the Hellenic race, infinitely split up into families, into clans, groups its energies into autonomous cities. One of these cities exercises over the others a hegemony which is marvellously fruitful, and might, if it lasted, lead to unity. The attempt fails, but at least the Greeks are soon distributed in great monarchies which prepare the ground for the unity of Rome.

With these political changes goes a corresponding economic and social development.

The Homeric period starts from a half pastoral, half agricultural way of life, in which the big family works in common on a collective property and tries to be self-sufficient with the aid of a few slaves. But soon private property is formed by encroachments on the pasture-land of the community, reclamation of waste, and the planting of trees. About the markets, where the families exchange their produce, towns grow up. Professional craftsmen work for the public and go to their customers' houses to work wood, metal, leather, and clay. Labourers hire themselves out wherever they find employment. Movable goods increase in value; so metal, in the form of bullion or utensils, becomes an instrument of exchange. Articles which cannot be procured on the home market are sought far away, and pirates open the road for traders; so the ports grow rich. Before the Greeks have abandoned household institutions, when they are only beginning to be acquainted with city institutions, they are already visiting Thrace, the Troad, and Egypt.

While the cities in which an agrarian aristocracy predominates adhere to natural and family economy, the others, to satisfy the growing needs of trade, set their stamp on the pieces of precious metal which serve for exchanges, and the use of money spreads from the Asiatic cities to those of

Europe. *Chrematistike* appears and transforms everything. Social inequalities become greater; the rich find more opportunities for increasing their wealth and the luxury which is a sign of it, while the impoverished peasants escape serfdom only by revolution. Sparta vainly strives to maintain an obsolete order of things, to maintain a caste of warriors on the work of Helots attached to the soil and Periœci bearing the stigma of labour. Sparta remains a unique case. Elsewhere, all want new land and new trading stations; colonization gives these, and attaches to little Greece almost the whole Mediterranean sea-board. Far behind the merchant, the craftsman completes his education; technical methods are increased by useful inventions, the stock of human tools by the development of slavery; crafts become further specialized, and the workshops attain a level of medium-sized industry. As resources grow, so do desires and jealousies. The competition of the trading cities provokes terrible wars. Corinth seizes the supremacy from Miletos, until she loses it to Athens.

The economic development of the Greek city is brought to the pitch of perfection by Athens, for Athens gives to individualism, of which that development is the product, all the rights reconcilable with the power of a sovereign democracy, and Athens concentrates on her market all the goods hitherto dispersed or only partially brought together. Labour is esteemed in a city which owes her prosperity to it. The citizens live by the land, public office, and the liberal professions, and in a much less degree by trade and industry; they leave to the Metics the chief place in the shops and workshops, in banking and the higher forms of business; they consider slavery necessary for the manual occupations and for the city itself. The division of labour attracts the attention of the philosophers, who lay down the principles of a truly "political" economy. The circulation of coin becomes very active; the Athenian gives up hoarding and invests his money. Agriculture becomes commercial and more intensive; the very splitting up of landed property facilitates the reconcentration of land and speculation; agricultural science teaches the vine-grower, fruit-grower, and market-gardener intelligent methods. Industry makes some progress, but does not succeed in triumphing over the adverse conditions which continue to hamper it; it has no machinery,

## CONCLUSION 379

only slaves. The persistent survival of family labour, the dispersion of workers in small establishments, the small amount of money invested, all point to a middling industry which hardly ever produces in advance. The craftsman, working at his leisure, gives his work a finish which brings industry close to art. So the competition of slave labour does not weigh too heavily on free labour; wages, which are uniform in the Vth century, vary in the IVth century, when all prices rise. But in Athens it is trade which assumes the greatest importance and breadth. By its technical and legal organization it makes itself capable of every kind of transaction. *Emporia* offers the most varied combinations to shipowners, forwarding agents, and lenders of money, the mining and metal-working companies combine large amounts of capital, and banking lends itself to speculation of all kinds. Without other protection than the prestige of undisputed dominion of the seas, Athens makes her port the emporium where all products are brought together and sent far afield. Having become the economic centre of the Greek world, she aims at the formation of a world-wide market.

To realize such a dream was beyond the power of one city. The city system collapses; on the ruins great states are established, which include the barbarians in the Greek world. Races mingle, and cosmopolitanism makes for the unity of civilization. Absolute monarchy assumes the protection of all interests and the regulation of all activities. All through society the division of labour becomes more strongly marked. The crafts are organized, and professional associations form into regional trade unions. Vast countries, confined to natural economy since their beginnings, are opened to money economy, and prices undergo violent fluctuations until equilibrium is restored. New cities arise at the word of the rulers. The centre of gravity shifts eastwards. Alexandria, Rhodes, Delos, these are henceforward the great ports. In Egypt the distribution of the land is of a kind to astonish Hellenic individualism; the king, the sole proprietor, distributes the lots as he pleases, and supervises agriculture. Unable to struggle against the production of the great corn countries, the peasant in Greece resigns himself to holding the land from another, or emigrates. In industry the number of slaves is not great, but technical processes are all the more improved in consequence. The monopolies of production bring a whole army of workers into the royal workshops, but this partial concentration of labour is accompanied by a fall in wages, and the sufferings of the working classes lead to strikes. The brightest spectacle is still presented by trade. The covered markets are splendid edifices; the shops open wide on to the streets. Trading companies multiply. State banks appear on all sides. Never, in any country, was credit organized on so vast a plan as in Egypt, where the king's granaries and banks make it possible for the meanest villager to convert all he possesses into wealth. The shipping companies serve the sea-routes which connect East and West. By land and by sea the Greek traders penetrate into India, and Massalia sends explorers on the Atlantic routes by which the tin comes.

If we reflect for a moment over these successive pictures, we shall see the weakness of hastily formed theories on the economy of the Greeks. Not one can stand against the turbulent stream of history. The more dogmatic they are, the more disastrous they are, and they are unsound in proportion as they are uncompromising.

According to Rodbertus and Buecher, the economy of antiquity never ceased to be properly " economic "; it always lay in the household, and the *autarkeia* of the family never needed to supplement its resources from outside with more than a negligible quantity of articles. But what was this strictly " household " economy, which drove the Greeks to obtain their daily bread from Scythia or Egypt, and to force their goods into the furthest regions of savagery? Obviously, Greece must have been transformed by a powerful process of evolution, and that at an early date. But in that case do we find that the periods which the economists have scientifically determined are clearly distinguished in Greece? German theorists would divide the economic development of man into three big periods, which they name, according as they consider the extension or the intensive nature of phenomena, either *Hauswirtschaft, Stadtwirtschaft,* and *Weltwirtschaft,* or *Naturalwirtschaft, Geldwirtschaft,* and *Creditwirtschaft.* No doubt we may find in Greece a number of facts which support such systems, but the distinctions which they establish cannot for a moment be regarded as definite, and

## CONCLUSION

intercrossings of the so-called different kinds of economy are so frequent and so considerable that hardly anything remains of these majestic constructions but empty truisms. Thus, even in the Homeric age, when household and natural economy prevailed, and city economy was barely beginning, the mariners were already tending to constitute a Mediterranean market. Thus, in the Vth and IVth centuries, when the city system was at its height, the Metics of the trading cities formed an international class. Thus, too, Ptolemaic Egypt, racing ahead, allowed anybody to issue a bill of credit on the smallest sum of money, on a sack of corn, on any article whatever, at a time when she was still only learning the use of money.

For the same reason it is impossible to follow the historians who maintain, like Eduard Meyer and Poehlmann, that, after passing the stage of household economy, the Greeks quickly reached an economy which was not merely of the city, but of the world, and that for this reason they heard the proletariat pressing its socialistic claims with insistent clamour. It is quite true that when we look at Hellenic commerce we are dazzled by the progress accomplished; it goes forward swiftly and steadily, stopping only at the ever receding bounds of the known world. But among the Greeks, whose country is the whole Mediterranean, the trader is far ahead of the craftsman. In Athens, the centre of world trade, industry always has a mean appearance. The absence of machinery prevents the workshop from becoming a big factory, labour from concentrating in great numbers, and wholesale production from killing the work of the family. For machinery is irreconcilable with slavery, and slavery was regarded as necessary. The institution of slavery, inherent in the very conception of the city—that is what creates an essential difference between ancient economy and modern. In Greece, even socialist theories, even when they come down into the people, preserve a character which in certain respects is aristocratic and reactionary, since even they would base the equal welfare of the citizens on the labour of the slaves.

# BIBLIOGRAPHY

## GENERAL

BELOCH (Julius), *Griechische Geschichte*, Strasburg, 1st ed., 3 vols. in 4, 1893-1897-1904; 2nd ed., 1912-20.

ROSCHER (W. H.), *Ueber das Verhaeltniss der Nationaloekonomie zum klassischen Alterthume, in Ansichten der Volkswirtschaft aus dem geschichtlichen Standpunkte*, Berlin and Heidelberg, 1861.

BUECHER, *Die Entstehung der Volkswirtschaft*, Tuebingen, 1st ed., 1893; 2nd ed., 1898.

—— *Die Wirtschaft der Naturvoelker*, Dresden, 1898.

MEYER (Eduard), *Die wirtschaftliche Entwickelung des Altertums.* (Jahrbuch fuer Nationaloekonomie und Statistik, 3rd series, vol. ix, 1895, pp. 696 ff. Republished by the author in his Kleine Schriften zur Geschichtstheorie und zur wirtschaftlichen und politischen Geschichte des Altertums, Halle, 1910.)

GUIRAUD (Paul), *Études économiques sur l'antiquité*, Paris, 1905.

NEURATH (O.), *Antike Wirtschaftsgeschichte*, Leipzig, 1909.

SPECK (E.), *Handelsgeschichte des Altertums*, vol. ii: *Die Griechen*, Leipzig, 1901.

HUVELIN, art. *Mercatura*. (SAGLIO and POTTIER, Dic. des Antiq.)

BUECHSENSCHUETZ, *Besitz und Erwerb im griechischen Alterthum*, Halle, 1869.

—— *Die Haupstaetten des Gewerbefleisses im klassischen Alterthume*, Leipzig, 1869.

BLUEMNER (H.), *Technologie und Terminologie der Gewerbe und Kuenste bei Griechen und Roemern*, 4 vols., Leipzig and Berlin, 1874-85; 2nd ed., vol. i, 1912.

GUIRAUD (Paul), *La Main-d'œuvre industrielle dans l'ancienne Grèce* (Bibliothèque de la Faculté des Lettres de l'Université de Paris, fasc. xii), Paris, 1900.

BILLETER (G.), *Geschichte des Zinsfusses im griechisch-roemischen Altertum*, Leipzig, 1898.

GARDNER (Percy), *A History of Ancient Coinage, 700-300 B.C.*, Oxford, 1918.

GUIRAUD (Paul), *La Propriété foncière en Grèce jusqu'à la conquête romaine*, Paris, 1893.

SORLIN-DORIGNY, art. *Rustica res*. (SAGLIO and POTTIER, Dic. des Ant.)

HEITLAND (W. E.), *Agricola : a study of agriculture and rustic life in the Græco-Roman world from the point of view of labour*, Cambridge, 1921.

WALLON (H.), *Histoire de l'esclavage dans l'antiquité*, 1st ed., 1847; 2nd ed., 3 vols., Paris, 1879.

MEYER (Eduard), *Die Sklaverei im Altertum*, Dresden, 1898. (Republished in the author's Kleine Schriften, quoted above.)

CALDERINI (A.), *La Manomissione e la condizione dei liberti in Grecia*, Milan, 1908.

CICCOTTI (Ettore), *Il Tramonto della schiavitù nel mondo antico*, Turin, 1899. French translation by G. PLATON as *Le Déclin de l'esclavage antique*, Paris, 1910.

PHILLIPSON (C.), *The International Law and Custom of Ancient Greece and Rome*, 2 vols., London, 1911.

POEHLMANN (Robert von), *Geschichte des antiken Kommunismus und Sozialismus*, 2 vols., Munich, 1893-1901; 2nd ed. under the title *Geschichte der sozialen Frage und des Sozialismus in der antiken Welt*, 1912.

HERFST (P.), *Le Travail de la femme dans la Grèce ancienne*, Utrecht, 1922.

## HOMERIC PERIOD

BÉRARD (Victor), *Les Phéniciens et l'Odysée*, 2 vols., Paris, 1902-3.
BUCHHOLZ (E.), *Homerische Realien*, vol. ii, 1: *Das œffentliche Leben der Griechen im heroischen Zeitalter*, Leipzig, 1881.
HELBIG (W.), *Das homerische Epos*, 2nd ed., Leipzig, 1887. French translation by TRAWINSKI, Paris, 1894.
HOGARTH (D. G.), *Ionia and the East*, Oxford, 1909.
LANG (Andrew), *The World of Homer*, London, 1910.
LEAF (Walter), *Troy : a study in Homeric geography*, London, 1912.
—— *Homer and History*, London, 1915.
MURRAY (Gilbert), *The Rise of the Greek Epic*, Oxford, 1st ed., 1907; 2nd ed., 1911.
PERROT (G.) and CHIPIEZ (C.), *Histoire de l'art*, vol. vi: *La Grèce primitive, l'art mycénien ;* vol. vii: *La Grèce de l'épopée*, Paris, 1894-98.

## ARCHAIC PERIOD

BABELON, *Traité des monnaies grecques et romaines*, pt. 1: *La Théorie et la doctrine ;* pt. 2: *Description historique*, vols. i, ii, iii, Paris, 1901-07-10-14.
FUSTEL DE COULANGES, *Étude sur la propriété à Sparte* (Compte rendu de l'Académie des Sciences morales et politiques, 1880).
GILLIARD (Charles), *Quelques réformes de Solon*, Lausanne, 1907.
PERROT and CHIPIEZ, *Histoire de l'art*, vol. ix: *La Grèce archaïque (la glyptique, la numismatique, la peinture, la céramique)*, 1911; vol. x: *La Grèce archaïque (la céramique d'Athènes)*, 1914.
PRINZ (H.), *Funde aus Naukratis : Beitrœge zur Archœologie und Wirtschaftsgeschichte des vii. und vi. Jahrhunderts* (Klio, Beiheft vii), Leipzig, 1908.
RADET (G.), *La Lydie et le monde grec au temps des Mermnades (687-566)*, Paris, 1892.

## ATHENIAN PERIOD

ARDAILLON (E.), *Les Mines du Laurion dans l'antiquité*, Paris, 1897.
BOECKH (August), *Die Staatshaushaltung der Athener*, Berlin, 1st ed., 1817; 3rd ed., revised by FRAENKEL, 2 vols., 1886. English translation by G. C. LEWIS as *The Public Economy of Athens ; to which is added, A Dissertation on the Silver Mines of Laurion*, 2nd ed., London, 1842.
CLERC (Michel), *Les Métèques athéniens*, Paris, 1893.
DEFOURNY, *Aristote, théorie économique et politique sociale*, Louvain, 1914.
GERNET (L.), *L'Approvisionnement d'Athènes en blé au Ve et au IVe siècles* (Bibliothèque de la Faculté des Lettres de l'Université de Paris, fasc. xxv), Paris, 1909.

# BIBLIOGRAPHY 385

PERROT (G.), *Le Commerce des céréales en Attique*. (Revue Historique, vol. iv, 1877, pp. 51 ff.)
—— *Le Commerce de l'argent et le crédit à Athènes*. (Mélanges d'archéologie, d'épigraphie, et d'histoire, 1875, pp. 337 ff.)
SOUCHON (A.), *Les Théories économiques dans la Grèce antique*, Paris, 1906.
TREVER (A. A.), *A History of Greek Economic Thought*, Chicago, 1916.
ZIMMERN (A. E.), *The Greek Commonwealth : politics and economics in fifth-century Athens*, Oxford, 1st ed., 1911; 4th ed., 1924.

## HELLENISTIC PERIOD

*Revenue Laws of Ptolemy Philadelphus*, edited by B. P GRENFELL, Oxford, 1896.
BOUCHÉ-LECLERCQ (A.), *Histoire des Lagides*, 4 vols., Paris, 1903-7. (See especially vol. iii: *Les Institutions de l'Egypte ptolémaïque*, pt. 1.)
—— *Histoire des Séleucides*, 2 vols., Paris, 1913-14.
BURY (J. B.), *The Hellenistic Age*, by J. B. BURY, E. A. BARBER, E. W. BEVAN, and W. TARN, Cambridge, 1922.
GLOTZ (Gustave), *Les Prix des denrées à Délos*. (Journal des Savants, 1913, pp. 16 ff.)
—— *Les Salaires à Délos*. (Ibid., pp. 206 ff., 251 ff.)
KHVOSTOV (Michael), *Enquiries into the History of Commercial Relations under the Hellenistic Monarchies and the Roman Empire*, vol. i: *History of Trade with the East in Græco-Roman Egypt* (in Russian), Kazan, 1907.
LUMBROSO (G.), *Recherches sur l'économie politique de l'Égypte sous les Lagides*, Turin, 1870.
MASPERO (Henri), *Les Finances de l'Égypte sous les Lagides*, Paris, 1905.
POLAND (Friedrich), *Geschichte des griechischen Vereinswesens*, Leipzig, 1909.
PREISIGKE (Friedrich), *Girowesen im griechischen Ægypten, enthaltend Korngiro, Geldgiro, Girobanknotariat mit Einschluss des Archivwesens*, Strasburg, 1910.
RIEZLER (K.), *Ueber Finanzen und Monopole im alten Griechenland*, Berlin, 1907.
ROBIOU, *Mémoire sur l'économie politique, l'administration, et la législation de l'Égypte au temps des Lagides*, Paris, 1875.
WILCKEN (U.), *Griechische Ostraka aus Ægypten und Nubien*, 2 vols., Leipzig and Berlin, 1899.
—— *Grundzuege und Chrestomathie der Papyruskunde*, vol. i, Leipzig and Berlin, 1912.

# INDEX

(*Names from inscriptions which occur only once in the text are not indexed except where confusion might otherwise arise.*)

Ath. = Athens, Cor. = Corinth, Hom. = Homer, Mac. = Macedonia, Ptol. = Ptolemaic

Abdera, 105
Abydos (Egypt), 106
Acarnania, 62, 108
Achæans: Akaiwasha, 17; western colonies, 102, 107-08
Acharnæ, 171-72, 227, 253, 259
Acragas, 108, 122
Acropolis (Ath.), treasures of, 231-32, 304
ADONIS, Ath. Metic, 182, 184
Adria, 124, 312
Ægina: trade, 75, 107, 114, 117, 122, 139, 143, 307; metalwork, 128, 132-33; pottery, 134; slaves, 198; war with Cor., 143; Æginetan standard (see under Money)
Ænos, 105
Æolis, epic in, 58
ÆSCHINES, philosopher, 241, 273
ÆSCHYLIDES, mines, 303
Ætolia, 62, 108, 193
Africa. See Libya
Agathe, 110
AGATHON, two architects at Delphi, 266
AGATHON, stone (Eleusis), 266
AGIS III, K. of Sparta, 326
AGIS IV, 153
Agora (see Market); of Ath., 194, 208, 278, 289-90
AGORACRITOS, sculptor, 187
Agriculture: Hom., 14, 20, 31-32, 38-41; later, 63-65, 202-04, 245-62, 282; Sparta, 89; Attica, 129, 288; Hellenistic, 344-46
Akaiwasha. See Achæans
Alalia, 110
ALCÆOS, 101; on wealth, 77
ALCIBIADES, cook of, 200
ALCIDAMAS, on slavery, 219
ALCINOOS, house of, 12-13, 20
ALEXANDER, K. of Mac.: conquests and discoveries, 316, 332,

372-73; Persian treasures, 233, 325; coinage, 325-26; cities, 335; Tigris navigation, 369
ALEXANDER of Pheræ, 237, 315
Alexandreia. See Alexandria
Alexandretta, Alexandria, 335
Alexandria, various cities, 335
ALEXANDRIA (Egypt): town, port, 336-37, 368-69; trade, 369-70, 372-73; industry, 350, 352; associations, 324; wages, prices, 358; Museum, 329, 336
ALEXIS, comic writer, 190
ALYATTES, K. of Lydia, 101
Alybe, 45, 60
AMASIS, Pharaoh, 106
AMASIS I, II, vase-painters, 129, 140-41, 182
Amber, 121, 124-25, 375
Ambracia, 103-04
AMEINOCLES (Cor.), 131
Amisos, 309
AMMON, Oasis of, 120
Amphipolis, 309
Amyclæ, 95, 232
AMYNTAS, K. of Mac., 316
ANAXAGORAS, philosopher, 187
ANAXANDRIDES, comic writer, 190
Andania, 113
ANDOCIDES, orator, 182
ANDOCIDES, potter, 139
ANDROCLES (Ath.), 185, 315
ANTENOR, sculptor, 129-30
ANTIMACHOS (Cephisia), 175, 266
ANTIMENES (Rhodes), 364
Antioch, various cities, 335
Antioch on the Orontes, 335, 371
ANTIOCHOS I, K. of Syria, 320
ANTIPATROS (Ath.), 185
ANTIPATROS (Thessalonica), 352
ANTIPHANES, comic writer, 190
ANTIPHANES, statuettes, 173
Antipolis, 110

387

# 388 INDEX

ANTISTHENES, banker, 303, 305
ANTISTHENES, philosopher, 188
ANYTOS, 228, 266
Apameia, various cities, 335
Aphytis, 314
APOLLO, 24, 232. See also Delphi
APOLLODOROS, son of Pasion (Acharnæ), 167, 251, 267, 305
APOLLODOROS, nail-maker, 182
APOLLODOROS, ship-owner (Phaselis), 185
Apollonia, 230, 320
APRIES, Pharaoh, 101
Arabia: trade, exploration, 119, 312, 371-73; pirates, 370
Arabs in Attica, 179
Arachosia, 370
Aral, Sea of, 370
Arcadians, 232
ARCESILAS, K. of Cyrene, 121
Arcesine, 366
ARCHERMOS, sculptor, 128
ARCHESTRATOS, banker, 303, 305
ARCHIAS (Cor.), 368
ARCHILOCHOS, poet, 99
ARCHIMEDES, 344, 352
ARCHITELES (Cor.), 231-32, 238
ARCHYTAS, engineer, 269
ARETHUSIOS, slave-hirer, 204
Argos, Argolis, 99, 114, 128, 134, 143, 229, 271
ARISTARCHOS, friend of Socrates, 161, 164
ARISTEAS, explorer, 121
ARISTEIDES, 171, 230; son of, 248
Aristocracy. See under Land
ARISTON, explorer, 372
ARISTOPHANES, 189-90; on agriculture, country, rustics, 165, 171, 252-54, 260; craftsmen, 165, 222, 225, 227-28, 263, 270, 272, 278; Euripides, 165; food, 285; Heliasts, 148; Metics, 178; retailers, 289; slaves, 200-01; socialism, 157-58
ARISTOTLE, 372; *Economics* attributed to, quoted, 300; on aristocracy, magnificence, luxury, 78, 170; associations, 322-23; "Athenian economy," 207-08, 252; barbarians, 318; democracy and men of sea, 308; democracy and slavery, 196; economics, 69-70; financiers, 306; labour, 162-63;

landed property, 248; offices, division of, 220; poverty, 148; servants, 202; Sparta, 96; trade, 117, 288, 295-97
Armenia, 133
Arsinoe, 350
Art: low esteem of, 160-61; Metics in, 187; in industry, 274-75
ARTEMIS: Orthia, 94; of Ephesos, 114
Artemision, C. (Spain), 110
ARTEMON, Metic, 185
Asclepiadæ, 27
Asclepieia, 293
Ascra, 99
Asia: relations with Greece before Mac. conquest, 310-11; roads, 370-71; Seleucid kingdom (see under Syria)
Asia, Central, 121, 312, 375
Asia Minor: wood from, 259; Greek cities in (see Ionia)
Associations, commercial companies, trade unions, 85, 243, 300-03, 318-19, 322-24, 339, 350, 363-64, 369
Assyria, 106, 132
*Astynomoi*, 276
ATHENE: and crafts, 15, 25, 44; Chalciœcos, 94; Promachos, 294
ATHENIS, sculptor, 128
ATHENOGENES, orator, 167, 210, 266, 281
Athens, Attica: for Athens during the Athenian Period, see under the different subjects; arts, 128-29, 321; corn-supply, 64, 125, 346-47; Cretans visit, 50; Dionysiac artists, 324; farming, 64, 129, 346; forests, 63; Harpalos, 326; metal-work, 128; money, 69, 325-26, 328, 334; natural economy, 63; pottery, 117, 124-25, 129-30, 134-35, 138-43; property, classes, 62-63, 76-78, 79, 81-82, 84, 317; quarries, 127; roads, 114; Rome, Delos, 338-39; no serfs, 82; trade, 66, 122; Hellenistic decline, 333-34
Athos, Mt., canal, 116
Atlantic Ocean, explored, 320 375-76

## INDEX

Attalids. See Pergamon
Attica. See Athens
*Autarkeia.* See Labour, family

Babylon, 101, 119
Bacchiadæ of Cor., 75
BACCHIOS, potter, 277-78
Bactriana, 375
Banking, 185, 217, 241, 300, 303-06, 314, 349, 363-67
Barbarians, feeling about, 318
Bards, 24-25, 27
Barter. See Trade
BATTOS, K. of Cyrene, 102
Bebryces, 104
Beer, 348, 355
Bees, honey, 260-61, 312
Beggars, 29-30
Berenice, 372
Berezan, 121
Berytos, 371; association at Delos, 318-19, 323, 339
Bithynia, 104, 339
BLEPÆOS (Ath.), 305
Bœotia: industry, 127-28, 130, 132, 134-35, 160; oxen, transport, 259, 292; road, 291; slaves, 203; Hellenistic decline, 333. See also Thebes
Books, trade, 312
Bosphorus, 99, 106, 125
Bosphorus, Cimmerian. See under Cimmerians
Bottomry, marine loans, 69, 117, 185, 241-43, 298, 300-02, 315, 365
Box-Merchants, St. of, 227, 264
Britain, 124, 375
Bronze: payments in, 55-56; work in (see Metal work); Bronze Age civilization, 7
Building: Hom., 14, 27, 44; Ath. industry, 129; rate of work, 282; slaves, 204-05; wages, 282-85. See also Contracts, public works, and refs. under that head
BUPALOS, sculptor, 128
Byzantion, 104, 106, 193, 300, 337

CACHRYLION, potter, 140
Cænepolis, 370
CALLIAS, inventor of dye process, 270
CALLIAS LACCOPLUTOS, 274
Campania, 123, 311

Canals: proposed, 320; Greece, 116; Egypt, 119, 320, 336-37, 372
Capital: capitalist system, 69; use of, 74-75, 231, 238 ff., 365-66; in industry, 268-69; held by Metics, 186
Capua, 128
Caria, 18, 58, 101, 310
Carthage: opposition to Greeks, 104, 109-10, 124, 375; Greek trade and influence, 126, 135, 312, 326, 362, 369
Cart-wright, 26-27, 44
Caspian Sea, 320, 370
Cassandreia, 336
Catane, 107
Celts. See Gaul, Galatians
Ceos, 295, 300, 316
Cephallenia, 59
CEPHALOS, 163, 166, 182, 185, 205-06, 266-67
CEPHISODOROS, Metic, 186
Cephissos R. (Attica), plain of, 253
Cerameicos, 138, 140-41, 263
Cerceosiris, 345
Ceryces (Eleusis), 27
CHÆREPHILOS and Sons, 184-85
Chæroneia, 199
Chalcedon, 106, 211
Chalcidice, 69, 102, 105, 291, 309
Chalcis. See under Eubœa
Chalybes, 125
CHARAXOS (Lesbos), 75
CHARTRODES, agronomist, 256
CHERSIPHRON, architect, 269
Chersonese (Thrace), 125, 309
China, 372, 374-75
Chios, 59, 85, 105, 122, 126, 193, 248, 266, 312
Cholcis, 310
CHRYSIPPOS, corn-dealer, 184-85, 187, 210
CHRYSIPPOS, philosopher, 201
Cillicyrians, 104
Cimmerians, 60, 103; Cimm. Bosphorus, 309, 316
CIMON, 171, 192
CIRON, land-owner, 200, 208
Cirrha, 291
Citizens, 168-72; in business, 172-77; sale of citizenship, 318
CITTOS, banker, 217
City: beginnings of city economy, 11-13, 48, 65-66; Hellenistic development, 334-36. See also State
Clarotæ, 83

# 390 INDEX

Clazomenæ, 105, 135, 300
CLEANTHES, philosopher, 181
CLEISTHENES (Ath.), 146
CLEITIAS, potter, 139
CLEOMENES III, K. of Sparta, 153
CLEOMENES, Governor of Memphis, 364
CLEON, engineer (Egypt), 357-59
CLEON, politician (Ath.), 166, 172, 225, 266
CLEOPHON (Ath.), 172, 227
Cleruchies, 99, 149-50, 152, 169, 172, 309; Hellenistic, 332, 343-44
Clothing. See Textiles
Cnidos, 101, 353
COLÆOS (Samos), 109, 125, 133
Colonization, 65, 98-111, 332
Colonos, deme, 170
Colonos on Agora, 278
Colophon, 106
Comedy: by Metics, 189-90; on Metics, 186; slaves, 198; Tettix, 181; work, 164
Competition: Hom., 43-44; archaic, 71; local and international, 142-43
CONON, banker (Egypt), 364
CONON, bonnet-maker (Ath.), 225, 228, 269
Contracts: no contractors in Hom., 43; private, 300-01; public works, 181, 226-28, 268, 270-72, 299. See also under Delos, Delphi, Eleusis, Epidauros, Erechtheion
Cooks, 201, 223
Copais, L., 290
Copper: sources, 45, 125, 127, 312; in payments, 55-56, 328; prices, 238
Coptos, 370, 373
Corcyra, 59, 108, 122
Corinth: actors' association, 324; colonies, 99, 102, 105, 108; society, 75, 86, 88-89, 108, 160; metal, 125, 128, 132-33; money, 69, 122; pottery, 117, 124-5, 129-30, 134-40, 142-43; shipping, 114, 116, 129, 131; slaves, 198; textiles, 229, 266; trade, 121-22, 182-83, 299, 307, 311-12; wars, 143; Hellenistic prosperity, 333, 369
Corn: supply, sources, 64, 111, 121, 124-25, 184, 257-58, 297-98, 306-07, 309-13, 346-47, 364-65, 368-70; prices, 237-38; doles, 150, 168, 172; public granaries, 366-67
Corsica, Cyrnos, 110
Cos, 215, 266, 352
Craftsmen. See Industry
CRATES, philosopher, 188
CRATES, poet, on crafts, 26
Credit. See Loans, Banking
CRESILAS, sculptor, 187
Crete: Minoan, 7, 49, 64, 116; Hom., 12; crafts, 128, 132-34; Gela, 108; mercenaries, 101; payments, 67; pirates, 50-51, 315, 337; property, 62; serfs, 83-84; *syssitiai*, 89-90
Crissa, 116
CRITON, land-owner, 252
CRŒSUS, K. of Lydia, 76, 94, 118, 143, 232
Croton, 102, 108, 143, 156
CTESIBIOS, 352
Cumæ, Cyme (Italy), 107, 110, 123, 128
Customs. See Taxes, etc.
Cyclades: raids on, 49; coins at Taras, 122; iron, 127; mints, 236
Cyclopes, 34, 38
Cyllene, 114
Cyme (Æolis), 65-66, 85, 119, 366
Cyme (Italy). See Cumæ
Cynics, social theories of, 159, 188, 219
Cynosarges, 188
Cyprus: Greek influence, 118; metal, 45-46, 49, 53, 56, 58, 125, 128; Phœnicians, 106; pottery, 129, 134; textiles, 266; timber, 63, 259; trade with Ath., 139, 310
Cypselidæ of Cor., 102
CYREBOS, banker, 205, 264
Cyrene, Cyrenaica: founded, 101-03, 107; land-owners, 37; money, 69; pottery, 94, 120, 122, 125, 131, 135; trade, 120-22, 135, 312; Aths. migrate to, 334; decline, 370
Cyrnos, Corsica, 110
Cythera, 127
Cyzicos, 232, 236, 334

Dædalids, 95
DALION, explorer, 372
Damascus, 371

## INDEX

Daphnæ, 106
DAREIOS, Metic (Ath.), 185
DARIUS I, K. of Persia, 232
Debt, 73-74, 80, 82, 146, 153, 193, 243, 249, 333, 347-48
Deceleia, 206, 281, 291
DEINARCHOS, orator, 189
DEINOCRATES, architect, 336
Delos: associations, 318-19, 323-24, 339, 356; banks, 363-64; Confederacy of, 230, 236, 304, 309, 313; farming, 347-48; festival, 113, 118, 299; loans, 154, 304, 366; population, 318-19; pottery, 134; prices, 363; public works accounts, 321, 328, 356, 359-60, 363; slaves, 351; trade, prosperity, 338-40, 362-63, 369; trade regulations, 297; transport, 368; wages, 359-60
Delphi, Oracle of Apollo: art, dedications, etc., 128, 142, 151, 231; building works, 227-28, 266, 271, 283-85, 291-92, 296, 302-03, 311, 326; and colonies, 103; Cor. pottery, 143; exchange rates, 233, 237, 304; festival, 50, 113; hostelries, 293; looted, 203, 232; manumissions, 192, 195, 199, 203, 217, 351; pilgrims, 116; roads, 114; subscription, 230; Sybaris, 123; treasures, 231-32, 304, 325
DEMEAS, chiton-maker, 205, 225
DEMETER Thesmophoros, 38
Demetrias, 336
DEMETRIOS, Metic, 182
DEMETRIOS of Phaleron, 200, 333
DEMETRIOS POLYORCETES, 320, 337
Demiurges: Hom. (craftsmen) (see Industry); later (industrials and merchants), 71, 76, 79, 82
DEMODAMAS (Miletos), 370
DEMON (Ath.), 315
DEMOPHILOS (smelter), 303
DEMOSTHENES: clients, 165-66, 176; factories, 167, 205-06, 217, 225, 228, 239, 267-68, 272-73, 281; bottomry cases, 185, 315; on bankers, 185, 306; coinage, 233; credit, 242; Meidias, 202; Phaselis, 310; wealth of State, 248
Diacria, 253; Diacrians, 64
DICÆOCRATES, sons of, mines, 303
Didyma, 351, 356
DIEITREPHES, house-breaker, 175
DIITREPHES, basket-maker, 227
*Diobelia*, 150
DIO CHRYSOSTOM, on ownership, 153
DIOCLEIDES, 208-09
DIODOTOS, 238
DIOGENES, philosopher, 188, 201
DIOGENES LAERTIOS, quoted, 200
DION, merchant, 217
Dionysiac artists, 324
DIONYSIOS, explorer, 372-73
DIONYSODOROS, painter, 180
DIONYSODOROS, ship-owner, 185
DIONYSOS, introduced, 64
DIOPHANTOS, 211
DIPHILOS, mines, 274
Dipylon vases, 112, 134, 139
Doctors. See Medicine
Dodone, 124
DORYCLEIDAS, sculptor, 95
DRACON, 63, 145
DURIS, potter, 182, 226, 267
DUTAS, sculptor, 95
Duties. See Taxes, etc.

Ebro, R., 124
Echinos, 293
Egesta, 311
Egypt, before Ptolemies: Ath. expedition, 297; Egyptians in Attica, 179; corn, 111, 258, 309-11; gold, jewels, 45-46, 125; Greek mercenaries, 100-01; metal-work, 132; Persian conquest, 110, 327; plants from, 261; raids on, 17, 53; textiles, 125, 312; trade and relations with Greeks, 49, 58-59, 75, 106, 120, 126, 139, 310-11
Egypt, Ptolemaic: size, 318; associations, 323-24; banks, 329; canals, 320; Egyptians at Delos, 338-39; finance, 366-67; Greeks in, 318, 332; industry, 321, 349-59; landownership, 320, 329 341-45; mines, quarries, 353-54, 356-59; money, kind, 326-30; monopolies, 353-55; officials, 329-30; public granaries, 329; river navi-

gation, 369-70; State and economic life, 320, 328-29; trade, 362, 371-73
Ekecheiria, 113
Elbe, R., 124, 375
Electron, 46; coins, 68-69, 232-33
Eleusis: agriculture, 247, 253; Ceryces, 27; leases, 230, 254-55; road, 114, 291; public works accounts, 174-76, 180-84, 211-12, 226-27, 266, 271-72, 280-85, 291-92, 295, 302
Elis, 62, 88
Emporia, 117, 288, 295
Emporion, 110, 124
Epeiros, 108, 327
Ephesos: citizenship sold, 318; duties, 116; port, 113-14; slave-trade, 193; trade, industry, 76, 119, 128, 134, 310-11, 334, 371
EPICRATES, mines, 274, 303
EPICTETOS, vase-painter, 141-42
Epidauros: building contracts, 226-28, 271, 283-84, 292, 302; public slaves, 160
Eranos, 240
Erechtheion, accounts, 172-74, 179-80, 183, 187, 204-05, 209-10, 226-27, 271, 280, 282-84
Erembi, 53, 58
Eretria. See under Eubœa
ERGOTELES, potter, 129
ERGOTIMOS, potter, 129, 139
Erythræ, 289, 297
Eschatie, 9, 34-35, 63
Eteocretans. See Crete
Ethiopia, 49, 58, 312, 372
Etruscans, 101, 104, 108-10, 119, 123-24, 126, 128, 135, 138-39, 311
EUANGELOS, steward, 252
Eubœa, Chalcis, Eretria: agreement with Amyntas, 316; alphabet (Ch.), 117, 123; Ath. ships to Ch., 175; building contract (Er.), 302; colonies, 102, 105, 107, 123, 311; communications, 59, 291; expropriation (Er.), 153; farming, 261, 346; Hippobotæ (Ch.), 75; metalwork, 66, 125, 127-28, 130, 133, 229; pottery, 124, 134-35; wars of cities, 143
Euboic standard. See Money

EUCHEIROS, potter, 129
EUCRATES, politician, 172
EUCTEMON, 208
EUDEMOS (Platæa), 292
EUENOR, doctor, 187
EUHEMEROS, 320
EUMARES, painter, 129-30
EUMATHES, banker, 217
EUMENES, Alexander's sec., 337, 373
Eupatrids, 64, 73, 81
EUPHRANIOS, potter, 143
EUPHRONIOS, potter, 142, 164
EURIPIDES: mother, 165, 176; quoted, 197, 252
Europe, Central, 121, 124, 312, 369, 372
EUTHEROS, friend of Socrates, 161-62, 201
EUTHYCARTIDES, sculptor, 132
EUTHYMENES, explorer, 320, 375
EUTHYMIDES, builder, 226
EUTHYMIDES, potter, 143
Euxine, Scythia: coinage, 326; colonies, 101, 103-06; corn from, 111, 125, 257, 298, 309, 311, 314, 368-69; exploration, 60; exports, trade, 117, 121, 125, 138-39, 143, 309-10, 368-69; Græco-Scythian art, 128; Persians, 110; Scythian inroads, 369; slaves from, 125, 212
EXECIAS, potter, 139, 141
EZEKIEL, 118

Family, genos, 7-9, 61-62, 145-46. See also under Industry, Land, Labour
Fayum, 332, 343
Festivals and trade, 113, 290, 316
Fish, fishing, 26, 37-38, 63, 121, 125, 184, 290, 309-10, 312
Foreigners, hospitality, 48 ff., 54-55, 169, 178-79, 183-84, 191, 315-16; at Rhodes, 337. See also Metics, Barbarians
Forests. See Wood
France. See Gaul
Freedmen, manumission, 23, 195, 199, 203, 214-19, 306, 351
Fruit-growing, 40-41, 64-65, 260-61

Galatians, 179, 369
Gaul, France, Celts: Greek trade and influence, 124, 133, 312, 326, 362. See also Ligu

## INDEX

Gaza, 311
Gebel Dukhan, 370
Gela, 108
GELLIAS of Acragas, 246
*Genos.* See Family
Geomori, 73, 102
Germany. See Europe, Central
GITIADAS, metal-worker, 94, 133
GLAUCIAS, statuary, 132
Gold: sources, 45, 68, 121, 125, 231, 309; immobilized in temples, 68; value, 232-34; payments in, 55-56, and see under Money. See also Metal-work
GORGIAS, 161, 187-88
Grave-reliefs, Attic, 164
Great Greece. See Italy
Guardafui, C., 373
GYGES, K. of Lydia, 101
GYPTIS, 103

Halicarnassos, 248
Hallstatt culture, 124
Harbours, 51, 58, 107-08, 113-14, 116, 119, 146, 227, 307-08, 321, 336-40, 362, 368, 370, 372
HARPALOS, 326
Hectemors, *hektemoroi*, 81-82, 84
HEGYLOS, 95
Hellenes, invasion, 7
Hellespont, 50, 298, 309, 324
Helots, 90-93, 96, 202
Hemeroscopion, 110
HEPHÆSTOS, 26-27, 42, 45, 140, 182
HERA, Lacinian, 122-23
Heracleia (Euxine), 104, 334
Heracleia (Italy), 230
HERACLEIDES, banker, 303
HERACLEIDES, banker (Delos), 364
HERACLEIDES, Metic (Ath.), 184
HERACLES of Tyre, association, 323, 339
Heralds, 24-25, 27
Herat, Alexandria, 335
HERMES, 24, 112-13; association of Mercury, 323, 339
Herm-sellers, St. of, 264
HERODOTOS, 309; quoted, 160, 238
HERON (Alexandria), 342
HERONDAS, quoted, 195, 267, 363
HESIOD: father, 99; on family industries, 24; Iron Age, 70-71, 81; navigation, 52, 114-15, 117; peasant, 41, 64; plutocracy, 77; vehicles, 57

Hesperia, 109
Hibeh, 371
HIERON I, tyr. of Syracuse, 232
HIERON II, 368
Himera, 108; battle, 110
HIPPALOS, 373
*Hippeis.* See Knights
HIPPIAS, philosopher, 188, 201, 220, 233
Hippobotæ, 37, 73, 75, 102
HIPPOCRATES, doctor, 187
HIPPODAMOS (Miletos), 156, 187, 308
HIPPONICOS (Ath.), 206, 208, 274
Hired men. See under Labour
HISCHYLOS, potter, 141-43
Histiæa, 365
Homeridæ, 27
Homeritæ, 373
Horses, 36-37, 74
Hospitality. See Foreigners
Hostelries, 292-93, 371
Household economy. See Labour, family
Houses, 11, 22, 285; leases, 239-40. See also Building
House-work, 14 ff., 19-20, 32, 84, 200-02; and see under Slaves
Hunting, 37-38
HYPERBOLOS, politician, 172
Hyperboreians, 121, 125
HYPEREIDES, mines, 303

Iasos, 248
Iberia, Spain, 60, 109, 110, 125, 139, 312
Ida, Mt. (Asia), 127
Ilion, 366
Illyria, 108, 315
India, 320, 362, 370, 372-74
Industry, craftsmen: Hom., Demiurges, 24-29, 31, 42-47, 60; later, 65, 71, 76-77, 119, 126-43, 146, 194-95, 263-87; Ptol. Egypt, 336, 349 ff.; family, 14-16, 19, 24, 26, 61, 85, 127, 132, 200, 223-25, 264-66; social distinctions, 166-67; citizens in, 172-76; aristocrats, 75; Metics, 178-83, 191; freedmen, 216-17; slaves, no machinery, 85, 204-08, 269, 352; scale of, and workshops, 42-43, 130-31, 263-64, 267-70, 278-80; investments, returns, 241,

# 394 INDEX

268-69, 273-74; hereditary crafts, technical education, 128-30, 266-67, 277-78, 321, 351-52; artistic, 129-30, 274-75; and colonization, 100; State participation, 353. See also Labour, Demiurges, Thetes, and under separate branches

Infants, exposure of, 193

Interest, rates of, 241-44, 365-66

Ionia, Asiatic Greeks: actors' association, 324; civilization, 126; costume, 132; epics, 58; industry, 119, 128; land-owners, 37; Lydia, 67, 101, 104, 119, 128; mercenaries, 101; metal-work, 132-33; Neleidæ, 101; Persian conquest, 110; pottery, 124-25, 130, 135; trade, 58, 66, 75-76, 117, 138-39, 307; wine, 260

Ios, 365

IPHICRATES, Strategos, 225

Iron: Hom., 43, 45-46; payments in, 55-56; prices, 238; sources, 125, 127, 310, 312; work in (see under Metal)

ISÆOS, orator, 189

ISOCRATES: father, 250; quoted, 227, 313, 319

Isthmus of Cor., 59, 113, 116, 320; Isthmic-Nemeian association, 324

Italy, Great Greece: colonies, 102, 107-09; money, 69, 233; payments, 67; trade, resources, 59, 121-25, 127, 258-59, 311-12; writing, 117; Italians at Delos, 323, 338-40; Hellenistic influence, 362

Ithaca: town, 12; Cretans visit, 50

Ivory, 125, 355, 372

JASON of Pheræ, mother of, 265

JESUS, son of Sirach, quoted, 322

Jewellery, 46, 125, 370

Jews, association, 323, 339

Kandahar, Alexandria, 335

Kiev, 121

Kind, wealth and payments in. See under Wealth

Kleros, 9-10, 87-88, 91-93, 96. See also Cleruchies

Knights, *Hippeis*, 37, 168-70, 247

*Krypteia*, 93

*Kyanos*, 45

Labour: and democracy, 171-72; division of, 24-27, 117, 129-30, 201, 204, 220-29, 321-22, 351-52, 369-70; international division of (see Trade); esteem of, 70-71, 86, 160-67, 322; family, 8, 14-16, 19-20, 200, 222-23, 264, 380-81; forced, 342, 350, 357; hire of, 29-33, 255, 276, 278; labour laws, 163,176,276-77; workman's life, 279-81, 356-61; decline in Greece, 333; in Ptol. Egypt, 350, 352, 356-59. See also Agriculture, Industry, Slaves, Wages

Lacedæmon. See Sparta

Laciadæ, 299

Laconia. See Sparta

LAERTES, farm and staff, 16, 39, 41, 48

Læstrygons, 60

Lagids. See Egypt, Ptolemaic

LAMPIS, freedman, 217

Lampsacos, 237, 297, 310, 334

Land: family and private ownership, 9-11, 35, 38-39, 61-62, 73, 76, 87-89, 93, 98-99, 146, 246-58; ownership in Ptol. Egypt, 320, 341-45; in Mac., 341; in Seleucid Syria, 345-46; in Hellenistic Greece, 346-48; great landlords, aristocracy, 37, 71, 73-76, 80-82, 146, 160, 165, 170-71, 247-48, 251-52; small proprietors, tenants, 41, 73-74, 79-82, 91, 145-46, 165, 171, 246-55; State restrictions, 87-89, 152-53; Metics excluded, 178, 152; sought by colonists, 98-100; great estates formed, speculation, 239-40, 248-50, 262; value, 247-48, 261-62; leases, 230, 239-40, 254-55, 259, 329. See also Cleruchies, *Kleroi*

Laodiceia, various cities, 335

Laos, 123

Larissa (Æolis), 134

Larissa (Thessaly), 346

Larissa, hostel at Delphi, 293

# INDEX

Latakia, Laodiceia, 335
La Tène culture, 362
Latium, 123
Laureion: new veins discovered, 146; silver from, 229, 234-36; Thracian miners, 178; proposal regarding lead, 300; abandoned, 235. See also Mines
Law, international, 315-16. See also under Trade
Leather-work, 14, 26-27, 47, 95, 181, 225, 272, 311
Lebadeia, 360-61
Lemnos, 49-50, 55
Leontion, 103-04, 311
Lesbos, Mytilene, 59, 75, 105, 135, 150, 236, 316
Leucas, Strait of, 116
Leucos Limen, 372
Libya, Africa: trade, 49, 53, 59, 107, 119-20, 125, 372-73; caravan-routes, 370; exploration, 372, 375
Lighthouses, 336, 367
Liguria, 103, 109-10, 123, 139
Lindos, Chronicle, 133
Lipari Is., 101
"Liturgies," 154, 169-71, 178, 186, 189, 333
Loans, credit, 69, 80, 238 ff., 247-48, 304-05, 365-67; marine (see Bottomry)
Locri, Epizephyrian (Italy), 66, 99, 102, 104, 108, 121, 288-89
Locris (Greece), 62, 88, 203, 315; colonies, 99, 102, 104, 107-08
*Logographoi*, 188
Lycia, 46
LYCON, philosopher, 200
LYCURGOS, lawgiver (Sparta), 88, 157
LYCURGOS, manufacturer (Ath.), 175
Lydia: trade, industry, 58, 76, 118-19, 125, 128; coinage, 67-68; public works, 116, 118; slaves, 18, 125; relations with Greeks, 104, 106, 126; Persian conquest, 110; Lydians in Attica, 179, 182
LYSANDER, 304
LYSIAS, 167, 239, 266, 272; client, 204; on landed property, 254
LYSICLES, politician, 172
Lysimacheia, various cities, 336
LYSIPPOS, sculptor, 277

Macedonia: size, 317-18; coinage, 233; coins at Taras, 122; exports, 184, 259, 270, 309; land-ownership, 341; roads, 291, 370; Strymon mines, 231
Macedonian conquest: and coinage, 237; and slavery, 219; corn question during, 298
Machinery, 269-70, 279, 344, 352; absence of, 204-07, 228-29, 274, 352
Mænace, 110
Magdola, 364
Malea, C., 52, 59
MANTITHEOS, mines, 241, 305
Manumission. See Freedmen
Marathon, battle, 146
Mariandynians, 104
Market, agora, *Agoranomoi*, 12, 48, 113-14, 290, 296-97, 320
Maroneia (Attica), 231
Maroneia (Thrace), 41, 105
Massalia, 103, 110, 124, 312, 375
MASSINISSA, K. of Numidia, 338
Meat, 38, 63
Media, 106
Medicine, doctors, 24-25, 27, 187, 266, 321
Megara (Greece): Ath. boycott, 299, 314; Ath. slaves, 198; colonies, 99, 106, 108; Cor. war, 143; faction, 82, 153; farming, 261, 290; industry, 205, 229, 266, 312; nobles in business, 75
Megara Hyblæa (Sicily), 108
MEGASTHENES, 320, 370, 373
MEIDIAS, Demosthenes' opponent, 202
MEIDIAS, potter, 226
Meinæans, 373
Melampidæ, 27
Melite, 290
Melos, 128, 134-35
Memphis, 106
MENANDER, on agriculture, 254, 348
MENES, governor, 326
MENON, cloak-maker, 205, 225
MENON, locksmith, 182
Mercenaries, 100-01, 232, 318, 332
MERCURY. See under Hermes
Mermnadæ of Lydia, 67, 106
Merv, Antioch, 335
Mesogæa, 253, 257
Messapians, 104, 107

# INDEX

Messenia, 88-89, 202
METAGENES, architect, 269
Metal: sources (see Mines); wealth in, 11, 55-56; circulation of, 231-32; work in, statues, etc., 26-27, 42, 44-47, 94, 120, 128-29, 130-33, 182, 187, 205, 225, 270, 311-12, 352-53; speculation, 306-07
Metapontion, 121
Methone, 314
Metics: condition, 163-64, 178-79, 316; in art, 187; business, 140, 173-77, 179-85, 239, 242, 306, 318; freedmen, 215, 218; intellectual activity, 187-90; excluded from land, 178, 182, 239, 242; wealth, influence, 186, 190-91; at Rhodes, 337
METON, astronomer, 187
MICCIADES, sculptor, 128
MICON, artist, 130
MIDAS, slave, 210, 281
Miletos: *Aeinautai*, 75, 125; alphabet, 117; colonies, 101, 105-06, 123; Egypt, Milesians' Wall, 106-07; Thales' oil-trust, 126; trade, industry, 66, 85, 117, 119, 121-23, 125, 128, 130, 132, 134, 138, 143, 229, 266, 312; Hellenistic business, prosperity, public works, population, 321, 334-35, 351, 355-56; wars, 143
Mines (chiefly Laureion): State rights, concessions, 151-52, 182-83, 231, 303, 341, 353; organization, working, 183, 206, 208-09, 225, 263, 267, 272-73, 282, 356-57; plant, 269-70; capital invested, 194, 268, 273-74; profits, 273-74; labour laws, 276-77; treatment of slaves, 198, 206, 280-81, 356-57. See also Copper, Gold, Iron, Silver, Tin
*Misthoi*, 147-49, 172, 333
MNESIERGOS, letter of, 253
Mnoitæ, 83
Money: circulation of metals, 231-32, 325; economic and social effects, 63, 71, 75-78, 80, 116, 237, 325-31; gold and silver, 68, 232-33, 325-26; electron, 68-69,

232-33; copper, 328; local currencies, 63, 233-34, 236; Æginetan and Euboic systems, 67-69, 237; exchange, 233, 236-37, 297, 304; value in fourth century, 306; Ath., 211, 234-37, 311, 314; Sparta, 95. See also Wealth, Banking, Loans, Capital
Monœcos, 110
Mortgage, 241, 249, 365
Music, 189, 266 (and see Bards); instruments, 227
Mycenæ, 59
Mycenæan civilization, 7, 47, 55, 57, 128
Myconos, 134
MYLIAS, freedman, 217
Myos Hormos, 372
Myra, 368
MYS, bronze-worker, 187
MYS, potter, 182
Mytilene. See Lesbos

Nabatæans, 373
Natural economy. See under Wealth
Naucratis, 104, 106-07, 113, 116-17, 119-20, 124-25, 135, 143
Nanrouze, Col de, 124
NAUSICLES, mines, 303
NAUSICYDES, miller, 205, 228, 264
*Nautodikai* of the Peiræeus, 276, 301
Navigation. See Ship-building
Naxos, 127, 130, 132
NEARCHOS, admiral, 320, 373
NEARCHOS, potter, 129, 141
Neleidæ, 99
Nemea, 113; Isthmic-Nemeian association, 324
NESIOTES, sculptor, 187
Nicæa, Nice, 110
NICIAS, 206, 208, 274, 281
NICOBULOS, merchant, 241
NICOMACHOS, clerk, 217
NICOSTHENES, potter, 139, 141-43, 225-26
Nile: navigation, 369-70; sources, 372
Norway, explored, 375

ODYSSEUS: wealth, 11, 35-36; slaves, 16, 20; as worker, 14-15; as trader and adventurer, 53
Œnoe, name, 64

# INDEX

*Oikistes*, 103, 105
Oil: olive, 41, 64-65, 125, 129, 237, 259-60, 309-10, 312; other plants, 321, 349, 354, 358
Olbia (Liguria), 110
Olbia (Scythia), 106, 119, 124, 128, 236, 259, 297, 309, 353, 360
Olive. See Oil
Olympia, 113-14, 123, 130-31, 133, 230, 232
OLYMPIAS, Queen, 326
Olynthos, 309
ONATAS, statuary, 133
ONESIMOS, dyer, 181
ONESIMOS, painter, 142
Oratory, 188-89
Oreos, 291
Ortygia, 101
Oscans, 123
Oxus R., 374-75

Pagasæ, 318
Painting, 130, 266, 277; vase-painting (see Pottery)
PAMPHÆOS, potter, 141-43
PAMPHAES (Ephesos), 76
PAMPHILOS, Metic, 185
Panathenæa, 170, 260
Pangæos, Mt., 231-33, 309, 325
PANTÆNETOS, mines, 208, 241
Panticapæon, 106
Paphlagonians: in Attica, 179; slaves, 310
*Parastasis*, 117, 295
PARMENISCOS, Metic, 185
Parnes, Mt., 253, 259
Paros, 99, 101, 105, 127, 130, 132, 353, 361
PARRHASIOS, painter, 187
Parthians, 375
PASION, banker, 182, 185-86, 205, 210, 217, 268, 303, 305
PASION, mason, 302
Pastures. See Stock-breeding
Patræ, 266
PATROCLES, 320, 370
Peiræeus: town, harbour, 146, 187, 227, 307-08; roads, 291; business, 184-85, 190, 227, 263, 267, 269, 307-08, 312, 315; corn, customs, 298-99, 303; democracy, 171-72, 190; Metics, 179; 310; theatre, 303
Peisistratids, 257, 291
PEISISTRATOS, 63, 82, 146
Pelasgians, 50
Pellene, 229, 266

Peloponnesian War, 171, 232, 249, 250, 253, 309-10
Penestæ, 83
Pentacosiomedimni, 168-69, 247
Pentelicon, Mt., 130, 132, 291
"Peoples of the Sea," 49
Pergamon, 320, 324, 334, 351-52, 355, 371
PERIANDROS, tyr. of Cor., 86, 116, 122
PERICLES: power, 171-72; policy, 148, 163, 168, 307; public works, 150, 163; on Ath. trade, 314; estate, 166, 201, 230, 252; in Euxine, 309; Anaxagoras, 187
Perioeci, *Perioikis*, 88-89, 93-96
Persia: and Phœnicians, 106; conquers East, Egypt, 110, 327; relations with Greeks, 232, 307, 310-11; Persian Wars, 110, 145-46; Alexander conquers, 233, 317, 373; lucern from, 258; coinage, 68, 232; treasures, 232-3; carpets, 312; Persian Gulf explored, 320
Phæacians, Scheria, 9, 12-13, 57-58, 99, 102-03
PHAEINOS, astronomer, 187
PHÆNIPPOS, land-owner, 250-51
PHALEAS (Chalcedon), social theory, 156, 211
Phaleron, 307
Pharos I., 336
Phaselis, 310-11
Phasis, city, 106, 309-10
PHEIDIAS, doctor (Rhodes), 187
PHEIDIAS, sculptor, 130, 270
Pheiditia, 89-90
Pheræ, 293
PHILEMON, comic writer, 190, 219, 254
PHILIP, K. of Mac., 232-33, 325-26
PHILIPPOS, mines, 303
PHILOMELOS (Phocis), 202
PHILOMENIDES, 208
PHILON, banker (Delos), 364
PHILON, iron-merchant (Ath.), 175, 182
Philosophy: and science, 126; in Ath., 187-88; in West, 109
PHILOXENOS, musician, 189
PHINTIAS, potter, 140, 142
Phocæa, 68, 103, 106, 109-10, 122, 124, 236
Phocis, 62, 134, 199, 202-03, 232, 291

## 398　INDEX

Phœnicia, Tyre, Sidon: early trade, piracy, relations with Greeks, 17-19, 46, 49-50, 53, 58-59; power and decline, 109; industry, 18-19, 46, 49, 128; trade, 49, 106, 117-18, 310-12; writing, 116; Greek influence, 126; influence on Greece, 128; on Cythera, 127; at Delos, 323, 338-39. See also Carthage
PHORMION, Metic, 185, 208, 210, 217, 250, 303, 306
*Phortegia*, 117, 295
Phrygians, 178-79
Picentini, 124
PINDAR, on land-owners, 246
Pirates, 10, 17-18, 48-53, 100-01, 112, 315, 337, 370
PISTOXENOS, potter, 142
Pitchers, Feast of, 212
PITTALACOS, Govt. slave, 212-13
Platæa, 203, 293; battle, 110
Platea I., 101, 103
PLATO, 188, 200, 249; social theory, 148, 156-57, 319; on Cleruchies, 149; colonization, 98; farming, 255, 259; forestry, 227, 256-57; labour, 162, 220-21, 265-66, 276; slaves, 196-97, 202, 211; Sparta, 90; trade, 48, 288, 296, 300
Plough, 40, 256
PLUTARCH, quoted, 95, 160-61
POLEMARCHOS, 266, 272
POLOS, philosopher, 188
POLYBIUS, quoted, 333
POLYCLEITOS, 130
POLYCRATES, tyr. of Samos, 130-31
POLYGNOTOS, 161, 187
POLYIDOS, musician, 189
POLYPHEMOS, dairy, 37
Population: excess, 98; decrease, 332-34, 359, 361; Sparta, 96
POSEIDON of Berytos, association, 323, 339
Posts, 293, 371
Potidæa, 105, 309
Pottery, vase-painting: Hom., 26-27, 47; archaic, 134-35; hereditary, 266; apprentices, 277-78; specialization, 130, 225-26; plant, 270; Metics, 182, 187; State, 353; trade, 117, 121, 124-25, 143, 309-12, 363; Ath., 138-42; Cor., 129,

135-38; Cyrene, 120, 131; Delos, 339; Sparta, 94, 131; Rhodes, 338
Pramnian wine, 41
PRIAM, household, 8
Prices: Hom., 55-56; effect of money on, 80, 237-38, 331, 359; cost of living, 285-87, 358-60. See also under the Commodities
Priene, 334, 363
PRODICOS, philosopher, 188
Property: private, 9-11, 61; movable, 9-11, 69, 71, 74-75, 82, 191; State and, 146-54, 248. See also Wealth, Socialism, and under Land
Propontis, 106, 143, 309-10
PROTAGORAS, 187
PROTOGENES, sculptor, 277
PROTOS, Metic, 185
Proxenos, 316
PSAMMETICHOS, Pharaoh, 101
Ptolemies. See Egypt, Ptolemaic
PTOLEMY I, SOTER, 336
PTOLEMY II, PHILADELPHOS, 362, 372-73
PTOLEMY III, EUERGETES, 357-58
Purple, 127-28, 132
Puteoli, 339, 369
Pydna, 370
Pylos, 50, 59
Pyrene, 110
PYRRHOS, K. of Epeiros, 320, 327
PYTHAGORAS, philosopher, 156
PYTHAGORAS, sculptor, 130
PYTHEAS, explorer, 320, 375-76
PYTHIOS, Lydian, 118, 231, 238
PYTHOCLES, 307
PYTHON, potter, 142
Pyxus, 123

Quarries. See under Stone

Rarian Plain, 257
Red Sea, 370, 372
*Rentiers*, 166-67
Rhacotis, 336
Rhegion, 107, 123, 311, 324
Rhode (Spain), 110, 261
Rhodes: founded, 99; associations, 323; coinage, 326, 328; colonies, 101, 108; Cor. vases, 134; Delos, 339; marine code, 337, 369; mercenaries, 101; metalwork, 142; pottery, 124, 134, 353; Ptolemy III,

# INDEX

357; Rome, 337-38; siege, 195; Hellenistic trade and prosperity, 337-38, 369, 372
RHODOPIS, 142
RHŒCOS, metal-worker, 120, 130, 132
Rhone, R., 124
Roads, land communications: Greece, 57, 114, 291, 370; Asia, 118-19; Africa, 370, 372-73; slaves, 211
Rome: early, 123, 311; and Delos, 318-19, 338-40; and Rhodes, 337-38; usury under, 365

Sabæans, 373
Saïs, 119
Salamis, battle, 110, 146
Salentines, 104
Samos: colonies, 106; corn, tax, 347; industry, 128, 132-33, 143; shipping, 116, 129, 131; trade, 106-07; war, 143
SARAPIS, association, 323
Sardis, 67-68, 118
Sarmatians, 103
SATYROS, banker, 217
SATYROS, engineer, 369
Scambonidæ, 290
Scapte Hyle, 231
Scheria. See Phæacians
Science, 126. See also Machinery
Scopads of Crannon, 246
Sculpture, 44, 95, 128-30, 132, 141, 172, 187, 226-27, 266, 270, 277; bronze statues (see under Metal)
Scythia. See Euxine
Sea-marks, 294
*Seisachtheia*, 82, 84
Seleuceia, various cities, 335
Seleuceia on Tigris, 371
Seleuceia Pieria, 371
Seleucids. See under Syria
SELEUCOS I, NICATOR, 373
Selinus, 108
Serfs, 23, 71, 82-84, 104, 202, 345. See also Helots
Ship-building, navigation, 15, 27, 31-32, 44, 51-52, 57-58, 114-16, 129, 131, 184, 227, 293-96, 315-16; Ath. fleet, control of shipping, 147, 169-70, 178, 268, 314-15, 333; Hellenistic, 367-68, 373, 375-76; Alexandria, 336; Rhodian code, 337, 369; river, 369-70

Siberia, 121
SICELOS, potter, 182
Sicily: early trade, 59, 101, 107; colonies, 102, 104, 107-09; land-owners, 37, 121; money, kind, 63, 67, 69, 109, 233, 326; trade, 107, 121-22, 311; farming, corn, 111, 121, 124, 258; culture, 109; Sicilian expedition, 291, 297, 311
SICON, figurines, 143
SICONIDES, vase-painter, 141
Sicyon, 123, 128
Sidon. See Phœnicia
Sigeion, 125
Sigynnes, 124
Silesia. See Europe, Central
Silphium, 120-21, 312
Silver: Hom., 46; coinage, value, 232-34; sources, scarcity, 45, 60, 125, 231, 312. See also Laureion
Sinope, 106, 309-11, 334
Siphnos, 68, 151, 231
Siris, 123
SISYPHOS, Metic, 180, 182
Slaves: ideas on slavery, 155, 158-59, 188, 191-92, 195, 218-19, 351; sources, trade, 17-19, 62, 84, 121, 125, 192-94, 309-11, 351; prices, 18, 194-95; hire, 204, 207-11, 240, 273; numbers, 199-200, 350-51; legal position, condition, 20-23, 193, 195-98; house and family work, 16, 19-20, 84, 200-02, 350; agriculture, 20, 22, 84, 202-04, 207, 350; industry, 84-86, 140, 204-07, 228, 267-69, 273, 350-51, 381; State slaves, 160, 211-13, 282; insurance against flight, 364. See also Freedmen
Smyrna, 334, 353, 364
Socialism and communism, 148-49, 154-59, 348
SOCLES, banker, 217
SOCRATES, banker, 207
SOCRATES, philosopher, 167, 280, 304; social theory, 156, 163; on farmers, 251; on investments, 209, 240; on labour, 161-62, 164, 263
SOLON: in business, 75; social reforms, 82, 84, 146, 168, 301; economic legislation,

# 400 INDEX

63-64, 129, 166, 257, 296; quoted, 71, 77
Soothsayers, 24-25, 27
Sophists, 187-88, 219
SOPHOCLES: father, 167, 205; quoted, 311
SOSIAS, mines, 183, 186, 206
SOSTRATOS, architect, 336
SOSTRATOS, Metic, 182-83
Spain. See Iberia
Sparta, Laconia, Lacedæmon: reputation in antiquity, 86, 161; organization, 87-97; land-ownership, 87-89, 93, 96, 153, 346; money, wealth, 63, 67, 246; agriculture, 89-92; stock-breeding, 94-95; horses imported, 124; art, industry, trade, 89-90, 94-96, 112, 122, 127, 131, 133-35, 143, 232; army, 89-92; population, 96; Talthybiadæ, 27; road, 59; colonies, 104, 107-08. See also Helots, Pericœci
Speculation, 69, 250, 298, 306-07, 311, 364
Spice Coast, 373
State: domains, 151-52, 254-55, 341-46, 353 (and see Mines); finance, loans, banking, 153-54, 233-37, 305, 365-66 (and see Money); State banks, 366-67; public works fostering trade, 116, 118, 362, 370-71, 373; control of economic life, monopolies, 300, 320, 329, 349-50, 353-56, 368, 370-71; public offices, 319-20, 329-30; State and colonization, 103; and interest, 242; and labour, 163, 176, 276-77; and property, 87-89, 152-54, 159, 248; the large Hellenistic State, 317 ff. See also Sparta, Taxes, and under Contracts, Slaves, Trade
*Stathmoi*, 118-19, 371
STEPHANOS (Ath.), 200
Stock-breeding, pasture: Hom., 8, 11, 20, 26, 30, 34 ff.; prices, 80, 237; archaic, 63-64, 127; Sparta, 94-95; West, 121; Attica, 258-59; import of stock, 309-11; Ptol. Egypt, 345-46

Stoics, 188; theories, 159, 351
Stone, stone-work, quarries, 44, 127, 129-30, 132, 172, 226-27, 281, 310, 312, 321, 349, 358-59, 370; State quarries, 152, 353. See also Sculpture, Building
STRATON, philosopher, 200
Stratonice, 335
Stratoniceia, 134
Strikes, 359, 361
Strymon, R., 231
STYPHAX, sculptor, 187
Sudan, 120, 370
Sunion, 194
Sybaris, 102, 108-09, 122-23, 132, 143
Syene, 370
Syracuse: founded, 99, 101, 103-04, 108; organization, 102, 104, 121; city, coinage, 108; taxes, 230; industry, 266, 281; trade, 333, 369; and Ath., 311; actors' association, 324
Syria (Asia), relations with Greece before Mac. conquest, 125, 138, 179
Syria, Seleucid kingdom: size, 318; associations, 323-24; government, 335; Greek immigrants, 332; industry, 355; land, agriculture, 345-46; natural economy, 327; State domains, 353
Syria I., 50
SYRISCOS, potter, 182
*Syssitiai*, 89-90

Talthybiadæ (Sparta), 27
Tanais, city, 312
Taphians, 17, 45, 49, 55
Taras, 104, 107-08, 122, 266, 312, 339, 369
Tarsos, 118
Tartessos, 60, 109, 110
Tauromenion, 347
Taxes, duties, tolls, 116; in kind, 327, 329; Ath., 153-54, 169, 178, 183, 298-99, 312-13; Byzantion tolls, 337; Olbia tax, 297; Rhodes customs, 338, 372; Samos tax, 347
Tegea, 128, 361
*Tekton*, 25-27, 44, 226-27
Telchines (Rhodes), 142
TELECLES, statuary, 128
TELESTES, musician, 189

# INDEX

*Temenos*, 39
Temples: treasures in, 231, 233, 238, 303-04, 366; leaseholds, 254-55; economic activity in Egypt, 330, 343, 349
Tenos, 324
Teos, 62, 106, 315
Textiles, clothing: home industry, 15, 19, 38, 85, 132, 200, 223-25, 264-65; separate trade, 85, 125, 129, 131-32, 181, 266, 270, 321; imports from East, etc., 48-49, 59, 125, 310, 312, 372; prices, 238; Cos, 352; Miletos, 355; Pergamon, 352; Sparta, 95; Ptol. Egypt, 349, 352, 355, 358
THALES, 126
Thasos, 99, 105, 151, 231, 294, 353
Thebes (Bœotia), 88, 114, 160, 203, 261, 272, 293, 324
Theline, 110
THEMISTOCLES, 171, 307, 311
THEOCLES, sculptor, 95
THEODOROS, Metic, 185
THEODOROS, statuary, 94, 128, 130, 132
THEOGNIS, quoted, 75, 82, 153
THEOPHRASTOS, 188, 200; miser of, 208, 210, 244
THEOPOMPOS, land-owner, 249-50
*Theorika*, 150-51
Thera, 64-65, 102-03, 134
Theseion, 175, 289
*Thesmothetai*, 301
THESON, potter, 129
Thespiæ, 160
Thesprotians, 17
Thessaly: society, 37, 62, 83, 202, 246; pottery, 134; slave-trade, 193; taxes, 230; Cyrene, 102, 107; road, 291; agricultural decline, 346
Thetes: Hom. (hired men), see under Labour; later (small craftsmen, retailers, labourers), 79, 168-70 (and see under Land, small proprietors)
THETTALE, Metic, 181, 184
Thirty Tyrants, put down, 153-54
Thoricos, 281
Thrace: trade (Hom.), 49-50, 58; wealth, colonies, 105; exports, 41, 50, 125, 127, 184, 231, 260, 309; slaves from, 309; miners from, 178; coins at Taras, 122; road, 291; waterways, 369; Aths. migrate to, 333-34
THRASYMEDES (Paros), 275
Thria, Plain of, 247
THUCYDIDES, quoted, 34, 62, 163, 171
Thurii, 311
Tigris R., navigation, 369
TIMARCHOS, shoe-manufr., 205-06, 210, 249, 267-69, 273, 281
TIMODEMOS, banker, 217
TIMOMACHOS, woodman, 167
TIMOSTHENES, admiral, 368
TIMOTHEOS, general, 270, 305
TIMOTHEOS, musician, 189
Tin, 45, 125, 375
Tithorea, 113
TLEPOLEMOS, hero, 99
TLEUPOLEMOS, potter, 141
Tools, Hom., 44
Trade: Mycenæan, 107; Hom., 8, 48-60; later, 65-66, 69-70, 77, 106-07, 112-26, 146, 288 ff.; and colonization, 101-03, 108-10; Mediterranean market, 111-12; law, 112-14, 183, 288-89, 296-301, 315-16; capital in, 241, 243, 302; merchant class, 125-26, 150, 176-77, 183-86, 190-91, 209, 216, 314-15, 362 (and see Demiurges, Thetes); aristocrats in, 75; social and moral effects, 65-66, 70-72, 125-26, 130, 245; Sparta, 95; Ath. supremacy, 307-16; Hellenistic, 334, 337-39; as State service, 320, 355. See also Labour, and under various commodities
Trade unions. See Associations
Tragedy, 189
Transport, 206, 227-28, 291-93, 295-96, 315, 368-71
Trapezus, 106, 370
Troad, 50
Trœzen, 102, 238
Troglodyte Coast, 373
Tyrants, 79, 317
Tyre. See Phœnicia
TYRTÆOS, quoted, 87

Umbrians, 123
Ural Mts., 121
Utensils as currency, 55-56

VARRO, 255
Vegetable-growing, 40, 261, 288
Vehicles, 44, 57, 191-92. See also Cartwright
Venetia, 123-24
Vine, wine, 40-41, 64-65, 125, 129, 247, 259-60, 309, 312, 345-47

Wages, 32, 43; in food, 230; rates and methods, 166, 174, 204-05, 212, 282-87; Hellenistic, 329-30, 357-61
War: and slavery, 17; retailers and armies, 290-91; Ath. army, 147-48, 169-70, 178; Spartan army, 89-92
Wealth, 77-78; in cattle, 11, 38, 55; metal, treasure, 11, 48, 55-56, 231-32; wealth and payments in kind, 63, 69, 230, 327-30, 366-67. See also Property, Capital
Weapons: Hom., 45; right to bear, 74; manufacture (see Metal, work in)
Weights, measures: length, area, 39, 55; capacity, 55; Æginetan and Euboic systems, 66 ff.; *Metronomoi*, 297
Wine. See Vine
Women: Hom., 14-16, 31-32; slave, 18-19, 199; freed, 217; crafts, 263

Wood: forests and supplies, 8, 63, 125, 127, 175, 256-57, 259, 309-12, 341; work in, 14-15, 25-27, 44, 94-95, 172, 175, 226-27
Writing: effect on trade, 116-17; Chalcidian alphabet, 123
WU-TI, Emp. of China, 375

*Xenelasia*, 95
XENOPHANES (Colophon), 84
XENOPHANES (Syros), 356
XENOPHON: proposals about mines, 182, 206, 209, 211, 243, 273; on Ath., 308; division of labour, 221-23; farming, 203, 245, 251-52, 255-56, 259, 262; household staff, 201; industry, 267, 272, 277; monarchy, 319; sailing speeds, 294; troops and trade, 291
XERXES, K. of Persia, 116, 118, 238

ZACYNTHOS, 63, 127
Zancle, 101, 107-08, 123
ZENO, 188
Zeugitæ, 79, 149, 168-71, 247, 251
ZEUS: Idæan, 128; of Olympia, 123; Xenios, 54
ZEUXIS, painter, 187

# THE HISTORY OF CIVILIZATION

## *Titles in the series*

| | | |
|---|---|---|
| Pre History | Language - A Linguistic Introduction to History | *J Vendryes* |
| | A Geographical Introduction to History | *Lucien Febvre* |
| | The Dawn of European Civilization | *V Gordon Childe* |
| | The Aryans | *V Gordon Childe* |
| | From Tribe to Empire | *Moret & Davy* |
| | Death Customs | *Effie Bendann* |
| | The Migration of Symbols | *D Mackenzie* |
| | The History of Witchcraft and Demonology | *Montague Summers* |
| | The History of Medicine | *C G Cumston* |
| | Money and Monetary Policy in Early Times | *A R Burns* |
| | Life and Work in Prehistoric Times | *G Renard* |
| | Social Organization | *Rivers & Perry* |
| Greek Civilization | The Ægean Civilization | *G Glotz* |
| | Ancient Greece at Work | *G Glotz* |
| | The Formation of the Greek People | *A Jardé* |
| | Art in Greece | *de Ridder & Deonna* |
| | Macedonian Imperialism | *Pierre Jouguet* |
| | Greek Thought and the Origins of the Scientific Spirit | *Léon Robin* |
| | The Greek City and its Institutions | *G Glotz* |
| Roman Civilization | Primitive Italy | *Leon Homo* |
| | Rome the Law-Giver | *J Declareuil* |
| | The Roman Spirit | *Albert Grenier* |
| | The Roman World | *V Chapot* |
| | Roman Political Institutions | *Leon Homo* |
| | The Economic Life of the Ancient World | *J Toutain* |
| Eastern Civilization | The Nile and Egyptian Civilization | *A Moret* |
| | The Peoples of Asia | *L H Dudley Buxton* |
| | Mesopotamia | *L Delaporte* |
| | A Thousand Years of the Tartars | *E H Parker* |
| | Ancient Persia and Iranian Civilization | *Clement Huart* |
| | Chinese Civilization | *Marcel Granet* |
| | The Life of Buddha | *Edward J Thomas* |
| | The History of Buddhist Thought | *Edward J Thomas* |
| | Ancient India and Indian Civilization | *Masson-Oursel et al* |
| | The Heroic Age of India | *N K Sidhanta* |
| Judaeo Christian Civilization | | |
| | Israel | *Adolphe Lods* |
| | The Prophets and the Rise of Judaism | *Adolphe Lods* |
| | The Jewish World in the Time of Jesus | *Charles Guignebert* |
| | The History and Literature of Christianity | *Pierre de Labriolle* |
| European Civilization | The End of the Ancient World | *Ferdinand Lot* |
| | The Rise of the Celts | *Henri Hubert* |
| | The Greatness and Decline of the Celts | *Henri Hubert* |
| | Life and Work in Medieval Europe | *P Boissonnade* |
| | The Feudal Monarchy in France and England | *C Petit-Dutaillis* |
| | Travel and Travellers of the Middle Ages | *Arthur Newton* |
| | Chivalry | *Edgar Prestage* |
| | The Court of Burgundy | *Otto Cartellieri* |
| | Life and Work in Modern Europe | *Renard & Weulersse* |
| | China and Europe | *Adolf Reichwein* |
| | The American Indian Frontier | *W Christie Macleod* |

For Product Safety Concerns and Information please contact our EU representative GPSR@taylorandfrancis.com
Taylor & Francis Verlag GmbH, Kaufingerstraße 24, 80331 München, Germany

www.ingramcontent.com/pod-product-compliance
Lightning Source LLC
Chambersburg PA
CBHW071141300426
44113CB00009B/1041